The Lion
and the Star

The Lion
and the Star

Gentile-Jewish Relations
in Three Hessian Communities,
1919-1945

Jonathan C. Friedman

THE UNIVERSITY PRESS OF KENTUCKY

Publication of this volume was made possible in part
by grants from the Lucius N. Littauer Foundation and the
National Endowment for the Humanities.

Editorial and Sales Offices: The University Press of Kentucky
663 South Limestone Street, Lexington, Kentucky 40508-4008

02 01 00 99 98   5 4 3 2 1

DS
135
.G4
F664
1998

Library of Congress Cataloging-in-Publication Data

Friedman, Jonathan C., 1966-
   The lion and the star : gentile-Jewish relations in three Hessian
communities, 1919-1945 / Jonathan C. Friedman.
      p. cm.
   Includes bibliographical references and index.
   ISBN 0-8131-2043-8 (cloth : alk. paper)
   1. Jews—Germany—Frankfurt am Main—History—20th century.
2. Jews—Germany—Giessen (Hesse)—History—20th century. 3. Jews
—Germany—Geisenheim—History—20th century. 4. Jews—Germany
—History—1933-1945. 5. Holocaust, Jewish (1939-1945)—Germany.
6. Germany—Ethnic relations. I. Title.
DS135.G4F664   1998
943'.4164—dc21   97-33201

This book is printed on acid-free recycled paper meeting
the requirements of the American National Standard
for Permanence of Paper for Printed Library Materials.

Manufactured in the United States of America

To my parents
Saul and Nancy
and to my siblings
Molly and Jason

Contents

List of Tables   iv

List of Maps   vii

Preface   x

Introduction   1

1. Jewish Emancipation to 1919   15

2. Demography and Socioeconomic Structure   25

3. The Liberal-Jewish Model: Under Attack from Within   47

4. *Gesellschaft* vs. *Gemeinschaft:* Gentile-Jewish Relations before 1933   63

5. Jew-Hatred or "*Arbeit und Brot!*" Antisemitism and the Electoral Rise of the Nazis   103

6. Close to the Edge: Relations during the Early Years of the Third Reich   125

7. Relations during the "Final Solution"   153

Epilogue   181

Conclusion   185

Notes   187

Bibliography   271

Index   285

Tables

1. Religious Affiliation in Germany in 1925   27
2. German Jewish Population, 1910-1933   28
3. Jewish Population in Frankfurt, Giessen, and Geisenheim, 1910-1933   29
4. Foreign-Born Jews in Germany, 1890-1935   31
5. Gentile and Jewish Population in Germany by Size of Community in 1933   33
6. Gentile and Jewish Population in Hessen-Nassau by Size of Community in 1933   33
7. Gentile and Jewish Population in Hessen by Size of Community in 1933   34
8. Jewish Residence in Selected German Cities in 1933   34
9. Occupational Structure of Jews and the General Population in Germany in 1907 and 1933   39
10. Occupational Structure of Jews and the General Population of Hessen and Hessen-Nassau during the Weimar Republic   39
11. Occupational Structure of Jews in Frankfurt, Giessen, and Geisenheim During the Weimar Republic   40
12. Comparison of Jewish and Gentile Social Status in Germany and Frankfurt During the Weimar Republic   41
13. Jewish Associations in Frankfurt in the 1920s   55
14. Attendance by Religion in Frankfurt City High Schools for Boys in 1928   73
15. Attendance by Religion in Frankfurt City High Schools for Girls in 1928   74
16. Attendance by Religion in Frankfurt City Middle and Elementary Schools and Schools for Children with Disabilities in 1928   74
17. Attendance by Religion in Private Schools in Frankfurt in 1928   75
18. Attendance by Religion at Giessen Schools   79
19. Attendance at Giessen's *Oberrealschule*, 1914-1937, by Confession   80
20. Intermarriage Rates for Jews in Frankfurt, Giessen, Geisenheim, Darmstadt, and Mainz During the Weimar Period   92
21. Entries to and Withdrawals from the Jewish Community (IG) of Frankfurt, 1919 to 1932-33   96
22. Entries to and Withdrawals from the Evangelical Churches in the Frankfurt Metropolitan Area, 1919-1928   97

23. Entries to and Withdrawals from the Evangelical Church in Giessen, 1919-1932   98
24. National Elections in Germany in 1919, 1920, and 1924   109
25. Results of the National Elections of 1928, 1930, 1932, and 1933   118
26. Jews Deported from Frankfurt from 1941 to 1944   174

Maps

1. Hessen in Relation to All of Germany   3
2. Hessen, 1918-1945   4
3. Distribution of Jews in Frankfurt in 1925 by Percentage of Jewish Population   35
4. Location of Jewish Households in Giessen by Percentage of Jewish Population According to 1932, 1933, and 1935 Tax Lists   36
5. Location of Jewish Households in Geisenheim by Percentage of Jewish Population During the Weimar Period   37

Preface

The history of German Jewry, as well-known as it is, continues to evoke emotions of profound distress. Hitler's Third Reich and the Holocaust forever altered the perception of Germany before 1933 as the model of Jewish integration into Gentile society on the European continent. To many Jews, the Holocaust constituted proof that German Jewry had never successfully integrated into Germany's Gentile world. In recent years, historians, anthropologists, and sociologists who have studied the pattern of German Jewish integration have reached more complex conclusions. Some have even suggested that German Jews found greater acceptance from non-Jews than had been traditionally assumed and that the events of the 1930s and 1940s were not necessarily the ill-fated consequences of dysfunctional integration.

It is with this historiographical background that I have chosen to investigate everyday relations between Jews and Gentiles at the local level from 1919 to 1945. My choice to study three Hessian towns, Frankfurt am Main, Giessen, and Geisenheim, was complicated, but all three were diverse communities as yet unexplored on the issue of Gentile-Jewish relations. My hope was to contribute to the above historical debate and to the fields of both Jewish and German history by merging the focus on integration among Jewish historians with theories of antisemitism held by German historians.

I wish to thank numerous individuals and institutions for their help over the course of my research: the University of Maryland, the Friedrich Ebert Foundation, and the Leo Baeck Institute for funding portions of my research; Helga and Walter Pretzel and Wilhelm and Elisabeth Will for their gracious hospitality during my stay in Geisenheim in the fall of 1993; Martin Berger from Youngstown State University for editing an early draft of the manuscript; Marsha Rozenblit, Richard Wetzell, George Kent, and Hasia Diner from the University of Maryland for their comments and criticisms during the defense process; Saul Friedman, also from Youngstown State University, for being a constant source of inspiration; and James F. Harris for all of his guidance during my years at the University of Maryland.

Introduction

Until the 1960s, most historians viewed the Third Reich (1933-45) as an aberration in Germany's otherwise "normal" historical development, placing blame for the Terror, the war, and the extermination of Jews squarely on the shoulders of Hitler and his henchmen. As more documentary evidence surfaced, scholars came to see the Nazi dictatorship as a labyrinth of competing satrapies that possessed broad ideological antecedents in German history. In so doing, they began to implicate a broader spectrum of German society in the daily activities of the Reich and, specifically, in antisemitic persecution.[1] In the 1970s, surveys of German public opinion during the Nazi period appeared, investigating popular compliance with anti-Jewish legislation.[2] This book widens the focus of that historical pursuit and follows in the path of German historians of everyday life (*Alltagshistoriker*) by examining relations between German Jews and Gentiles, a theme that encompasses a diverse set of human experiences.[3]

Despite the vast literature on German public opinion, surprisingly little is known about the interaction between Jews and non-Jews at the local, everyday level during the Nazi period and before. Several examinations of the so-called Gentile-Jewish symbiosis during the democratic Weimar Republic (1919-33) merit particular revision. In this study, I intend to recast the Jewish integration experience before 1933 in a more complex light—as tenuous but not inevitably doomed. A focus on relations may also help clarify the extent to which persistent antisemitism in German society attracted or simply inured Gentiles to the more radical Jew-hatred of Nazi campaign rhetoric in the depression years, between 1929 and 1932. Moreover, such an investigation may enhance our understanding of popular reactions to antisemitic persecution under National Socialism.[4]

This book centers on three Hessian municipalities, Frankfurt am Main, Giessen, and Geisenheim, from 1919 to 1945. Hessen is useful for comparative purposes as a cross section of German society—heavily rural yet home to urban metropoleis, mostly Protestant, but possessing a sizable Catholic minority. These three communities attest to the diversity of the area. Frankfurt am Main is Germany's banking and commercial center. Giessen is a Protestant university city in rural Oberhessen, and Geisenheim is a small Catholic town on the eastern banks of the Rhine River. The Jewish communities in each municipality were once equally diverse, running the gamut from secular to Orthodox. During the Weimar period, Frankfurt was home to the second largest Jewish community in Germany, and Giessen and Geisenheim had a cross section of mercantile and professional Jews. I have selected these towns, loosely symbolized by Hessen's heraldic lion, to compare the texture of Gentile-Jewish relations in three different environments and, from a microcosmic perspective, to offer some clues as to how German Gentiles and Jews related in the course of their daily lives.

Methodologically, I employ a combination of qualitative and quantitative evidence, including the 1925 and 1933 German national censuses, statistical yearbooks, interviews, memoirs, diaries, letters, newspapers, and church records dealing with marriages, births, and conversions. Augmenting this material, to discern popular reactions to Nazi legislation, are the reports from the Nazi Party's Security Service (the Sicherheitsdienst or SD), the Secret State Police (Gestapo), and the Social Democratic resistance (the Sopade).[5] Repositories consulted for this book include the Leo Baeck Institute in New York, the City Archives of Frankfurt, Giessen, and Geisenheim, churches in the three towns, the Hessian Main State Archives and the Hessian State Library in Wiesbaden, the Hessian State Archives of Marburg and Darmstadt, the Central Archives of the Hessian Evangelical Church (also in Darmstadt), the Friedrich Ebert Foundation in Bonn, and the Bundesarchiv in Koblenz.

Half of the area that is now the state of Hessen was under Prussian control until 1945. Hessen first existed as a county (*Grafschaft*) in the twelfth and thirteenth centuries. The Hessen that emerged after the World War II was the result of the fusion of two states, the People's State (*Volksstaat*) of Hessen and the Prussian province of Hessen-Nassau. The Volkstaat Hessen derived from Hessen-Darmstadt, an independent county since 1567, which had been raised to the level of grand duchy (*Grossherzogtum*) twice in the nineteenth century, once in 1803 after Bonaparte's Rhenish conquest, and again in 1815, after the Congress of Vienna. Hessen-Nassau was the brainchild of Prussia. After its victory against Austria in the Seven Weeks' War of 1866, Prussia created its own Hessian province by annexing and unifying the

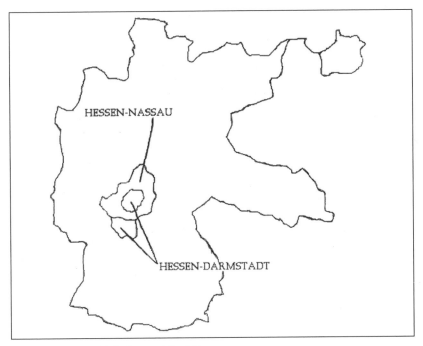

Map 1. Hessen in Relation to All of Germany

electorate (*Kurfürstentum*) of Hessen and the duchy (*Herzogtum*) of Nassau. Like Hessen-Darmstadt, the electorate of Hessen and the duchy of Nassau had been established during the Napoleonic Era. The electorate of Hessen consisted of the territory under the control of the landgraviate (*Landgrafschaft*) Hessen-Kassel, while the duchy of Nassau controlled a small section of east Rhenish country.[6] From 1871 on, Hessen-Nassau was divided into two government districts (*Regierungsbezirke*) defined by their administrative seats—Wiesbaden and Kassel. Frankfurt am Main was a part of the district of Wiesbaden, as was Geisenheim (within the county of the Rheingau). Hessen-Darmstadt, meanwhile, was divided into three provinces, Starkenburg, Oberhessen, and Rheinhessen. Giessen city and county were both regions within Oberhessen (see Maps 1 and 2).[7]

Frankfurt am Main, the city of Goethe, the Rothschilds, and Anne Frank, dates from the year 794, although recent archaeological findings have suggested that a Roman post occupied the site as early as the first century. Charlemagne held his imperial assembly in Frankfurt, and Emperor Louis I chose it as his headquarters in 822. The Golden

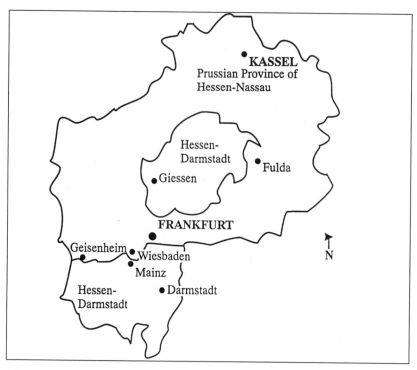

Map 2. Hessen, 1918-1945

Bull of 1356 designated the city as the seat for the election of the Holy Roman emperor, and, beginning in 1562, the official coronation of the emperor took place in Frankfurt's Gothic cathedral. After the Congress of Vienna, Frankfurt became the seat of the German Confederation. During the revolutions of 1848, it hosted the German National Parliament, which met to draft a parliamentary constitution. After siding with Austria in its war with Prussia in 1866, Frankfurt was occupied by the victorious Prussian army and subsequently incorporated into the province of Hessen-Nassau, ending its status as a free city. Situated at a convenient crossroads between north and south, the Main metropolis developed into Germany's financial and transportation hub, and by 1925 its population numbered nearly 470,000.[8]

Located about thirty miles north of Frankfurt in the heart of rural Hessen, Giessen was an almost exclusively Protestant enclave of 33,600 people in 1925.[9] The "town by the Lahn" was officially incorporated in 1248. In the sixteenth century, Count Philip the Magnanimous built it into a major fortress. Since 1604, Giessen has belonged to Hessen-Darmstadt as the seat of the province of Oberhessen. It is a center of industry, pharmaceuticals, rubber goods, optics, and foodstuffs but is most well-known for its university, the Ludwigs Universität, founded in 1607 and renamed the Justus-Liebig Universität in 1950. The current county (*Landkreis*) of Giessen includes the city proper and an adjacent rural area known as the Giessen Basin. The administrative district (*Regierungsbezirk*) of Giessen encompasses the entire county and city of Giessen, the counties of Lahn-Dill and Vogelsberg, and the regions of Limburg-Weisburg and Marburg-Biedenkopf. In this book I concentrate on the city of Giessen, extending my reach into the countryside only when applicable.

Geisenheim lies on the eastern shore of the Rhein in the Rheingau-Taunus Kreis, between the cities of Rüdesheim to the west and Östrich-Winkel to the east. Predominantly Catholic, the town is one of the oldest mentioned places in the Rheingau, dating back to 772. Geisenheim developed a small industrial base and became a major seat of botanical research and viticulture. A printing press and a factory specializing in machine parts provided contrasts to the bucolic life of Geisenheimer vintners in the nineteenth century.[10]

Although an analysis of Gentile-Jewish interaction at the everyday level during the Third Reich can enhance our understanding of the depth of popular support for or opposition to Nazi policy toward Jews, tracing the roots of that behavior is more problematic. One might argue that such an endeavor results in an undue, if not determinist, focus on Germany to the neglect of other European nations where the fascist right took hold. Such was the pitfall of German academicians of the 1960s, who embraced the Sonderweg theory, which held that Germany had experienced a uniquely flawed development of economic modernization and political authoritarianism following unification in 1871.[11] But Germany presents us with the troubling case of a nation deemed more "civilized" and friendlier to Jews than Poland, for example, initiating and implementing the unparalleled barbarism of the Holocaust.

Indeed, a patriotic German Jew in 1890 mused that Jews and Germans had blended together so successfully that the Jewish diaspora had finally been brought to an end.[12] Having been granted political and civil rights in the process of emancipation during the nineteenth century, Jews in Germany, so the patriot believed, no longer had to wander in search of a home. In return for equal protection under the law, enfranchisement, the right to hold public office, and the removal of economic restrictions, Jews had become German citizens of the "Mosaic" faith, jettisoning the notion that they belonged to a separate Jewish nation, relegating their Jewish identity to the realm of religion, and immersing themselves in German culture and values. Jews spoke German, dressed like Germans, and embraced German heroes. They championed both the humanistic values stemming from the eighteenth century German Enlightenment (*Aufklärung*) and liberalism, the ideology of their emancipation which had brought market capitalism and parliamentarianism to Europe. And they went on to fight for the Fatherland in World War I. The renowned Jewish sociologist Franz Oppenheimer captured the essence of German Jewry's patriotism when he wrote: "I have been fortunate to have been born and educated in the land of Kant and Goethe, to have their culture, their art, their language, and their knowledge as my own. My Germanism is as sacred to me as my Jewish forefathers."[13]

Some may argue that the search for preconditions could lead one to propose unwarranted connections between disparate eras in German history, but a focus on Weimar is crucial. The Nazi rise to power was firmly linked to the unraveling of popular support for democracy in the depression years (1929-32). For Jews, opportunities for advancement under democratic rule gave way to a reaction that threatened the very premise of emancipation. Scholars such as H.G. Adler once regarded German Jewish integration in the 1920s as a success, arguing that unprecedented numbers of Jews entered public service, intermarried, and contributed to German culture.[14] According to Gershom Scholem, Enzo Traverso, and S.M. Bolkosky, however, German Jewry remained socially insular and politically marginal during the Weimar era, clinging to an illusory perception of Germany as the guardian of the *Aufklärung*.[15] In their eyes, the electoral pluralities achieved by Nazis during the depression, aided partially by the calumny that Weimar was a "Jewish" republic, confirmed that the republican years had done little to alter Gentile attitudes toward Jews. While agreeing that Jewish integration into Weimar politics and society had its limits, historians such as Donald Niewyk and Monika Richarz have criticized Bolkosky's and Scholem's teleological approach.[16]

Research into the postemancipation transformation, or modernization, of the Jews has accompanied this debate, suggesting that the problem of Jewish integration may have been rooted in the internal development of German Jewry. Economically and demographically, Jews became concentrated in urban commerce and trade after emancipation. Jewish retail merchants who benefited from the shift to a market-based economy therefore incurred the wrath of peasants and artisans. Politically, as standard-bearers of liberalism, Jews came under attack as that ideology failed to deal with political chaos and harsh fluctuations in the economic cycle.[17] Social psychologists of the nineteenth century, like the Austrian Jewish Social Democrat Hermann Bahr, suggested that under stress, Gentiles often abandoned reason and blamed their troubles on the Jews.[18] Some academicians, including Hannah Arendt and the German Jewish theologian Hans Joachim Schoeps, however, have indirectly blamed Jews for incurring the wrath of Gentiles. Arendt has insisted that Jews were economically overprivileged and hence objects of universal hatred, while Schoeps has argued that Hebrew religious tradition encouraged narcissism and a tendency to ignore Gentile sensibilities.[19]

More accurately, Jacob Katz, Peter Pulzer, and Uriel Tal believe that the problem lay not with Jews but with non-Jews. Instead of converting to Christianity and disappearing altogether in the wake of emancipation, Jews remained Jewish, the overriding point of irritation.[20] Although there was no absence of antisemitism in Germany's western neighbors, these countries witnessed the fairly painless disappearance of the debate on Jewish rights from the constitutional agenda, the so-called Jewish Question or Jewish Problem. In Germany, according to Pulzer, the question as to whether Jews, either as non-Christians or non-Germans, could ever qualify as full citizens, never disappeared. Neither the Basic Rights of the German People, as adopted by the Frankfurt Assembly in 1848, nor the Law on the Equality of All Confessions, passed by the Parliament of the North German Confederation in 1869, resolved the issue.[21] Citizenship continued to reflect an ethnocultural understanding of nation-state membership, and German naturalization laws remained based on descent, keeping eastern European Jewish immigrants—the *Ostjuden*—legally outside of, and native-born Jews culturally ostracized from, the community of citizens.[22]

To understand the "Jewish Question" completely, it is necessary to define the issue it addressed, namely assimilation. In *Assimilation in American Life: The Role of Race, Religion, and National Origins*, Milton Gordon separated assimilation into two categories: acculturation, or cultural integration, and structural integration.[23] He defined acculturation as the absorption by one group, typically a minority or an outgroup, of the cultural attributes of another group, a majority or in-group. Structural integration referred to broader, social intermingling of that minority with the majority through friendships, sexual relationships, and marriage. When the German government spoke of assimilation in the nineteenth century, it assumed a process by which Jews, after their emancipation, would ultimately fuse with the majority by converting to Christianity.[24] Uriel Tal and David Sorkin have argued that assimilation for Jews did not mean disappearance as a group. Rather, assimilation signified acculturation, that is, assimilating German culture into a Jewish framework, some structural integration, and, more important, the retention of Jewish identity.[25]

Culturally, German Jews in the postemancipation era maintained both a sense of Jewishness and an attachment to their *Aufklärung*-inspired values. Even many of those who had become totally secular and detached from Judaism as a religion by the 1920s occasionally came to hear lectures or took courses on subjects ranging from the Hebrew language and Yiddish literature to Jewish ethnology and history.[26] The existence of a sizable Orthodox German Jewish population, coupled with the immigration of traditional Jews from the East and the emergence of Zionism in the late 1800s, acted as additional bulwarks against Jewish cultural breakdown. In terms of structural integration, Jews concentrated in commercial and mercantile pursuits following emancipation, but they made inroads into fields from which they had been traditionally excluded, such as public service, especially during the republican period. Although Jews accounted for less than 1 percent of the population in 1925, they were often represented in the national parliament (the Reichstag), sometimes as high as 3 percent.[27] And Frankfurt am Main had a Jewish mayor, Ludwig Landmann, between 1924 and 1933. An increasing number of Jews befriended and married Gentiles as well over the course of the Kaiserreich and Weimar periods. Total structural integration remained elusive, however, mostly because the surrounding Gentile environment was never fully tolerant of Jews qua Jews. German Jews interacted primarily among themselves and retained a pattern of endogamous (in-group) marriage into the Weimar era.[28]

In a study of a small German village, Frances Henry pointed to a gap between language and reality when describing three German Jewish perceptions of "assimilation" in the 1920s. A Prussian woman, whose father had been an army officer, remembered experiencing discrimination simply because she was Jewish, even though she had lost all ties to Judaism: "We were a very assimilated Jewish family. . . . I studied

Hebrew, the Old Testament, and the history of the Jews. But I had no strong feeling for it. My awareness of being Jewish came when the tennis club was restricted. I joined a Jewish club because there was no other way I could get to play. . . ." A Frankfurt man recalled less overt hostility: "Growing up in Frankfurt, if you were a Jew, you were bound to have strong feelings of identity because your whole world was Jewish. . . . This was the Germany of the Weimar Republic, and we were free to come and go before Hitler took over, but we definitely lived in a Jewish world." Finally, a Jewish survivor from Berlin offered a slightly different view: "I grew up without knowing I was Jewish, with no Jewish religion, no Jewish instruction, no Jewish cultural interests . . . [but] many, if not most, of our friends were Jewish . . . [however] separations between people depended on economics rather than religion."[29]

My own research has uncovered much the same sentiment. In her unpublished memoirs, Heide Hermanns Holde mused, "My family was German. Or so we always considered ourselves. Germany was the homeland, and we loved it. My father came from a family that had lived in Cologne since the twelfth century. We were Jews, of course, and associated with the Reform synagogue, but our culture, our way of life was German."[30] Clearly, the German Jewish assimilation experience was not uniform, some Jews holding to a measure of Jewishness, others astonished that they were regarded as Jews despite the lack of a Jewish upbringing. But all of these memories convey a sense of Jewish separateness within German society, both in consciousness and in everyday practice.

Because the literature on Jewish integration in nineteenth-century German society is extensive, I will explore German Jewish assimilation in the 1920s through an analysis of Gentile-Jewish and intracommunal Jewish interaction. A study of relations within the various Jewish communities shows how Jewish identity was maintained, while an examination of interethnic relations reveals the limits to Jewish integration. According to Helen Fein, explanations of individual differences in attitudes to Jews stem largely from Theodor Adorno's *Authoritarian Personality* (1950), which focused on the genesis of prejudice during early childhood. The most prevalent alternative explanation to Adorno is that of cognitive theorists who relate prejudice to broader patterns of faulty generalization and learning. Both schools presume that contemporary prejudice is a function of individual vulnerability. Another body of research on antisemitism explains the retention of ethnic stereotypes as a product of intergroup relations and conflict rather than of individuals and dispositions.[31] I employ the latter model, although I do not believe that any of these theories are mutually exclusive.

For the relations under scrutiny here, Gordon Allport's *Nature of Prejudice* provides an excellent starting point. Qualitatively, there are many levels of human interaction—casual contact, acquaintances, friendships, sexual relationships, and marriages. Relations can also be between individuals, groups, or both. In a quantitative sense, the frequency of contact, the duration of contact, and the number and variety of contacts at once influence and are influenced by the qualitative side of relations. Qualitative and quantitative aspects of interaction cut across various areas of contact, which, according to Allport, include residential, occupational, recreational, religious, political, educational, goodwill, and familial.[32]

Chapter 1 describes the history and social makeup of the Jewish communities in Frankfurt am Main, Giessen, and Geisenheim before 1918, and Chapter 2 points to the specific socioeconomic challenges facing Jews during the Weimar years. Chapter 3 provides a basis for our understanding of the Jewish position on Gentile-Jewish relations by focusing on Jewish approaches to their own interaction. Chapter 4 studies relations between Jews and Gentiles on an everyday basis, centering on a variety of contact areas, progressing from the most public relationships (political and economic) to the most private (social and familial). The following questions are posed in this chapter: What were the intermarriage rates for the three Hessian towns before 1933? How did both Jews and non-Jews regard intermarriage? Did Jews, whether secular, Orthodox, or Reform, or of German or eastern European descent sustain intimate personal friendships with Gentiles? Were relations improving or worsening during the republic? How did German Jews and non-Jews perceive their relationship? Was there in fact a mutual perception?

A study of interaction between Jews and Gentiles in Weimar Germany is complicated because neither group was individually or collectively homogeneous. Not all German Jews or non-Jews held to similar religious or ethnic convictions or came from similar social and economic classes. Especially vexing has been the trend of historians of European Jewry to concentrate on German Jews as Jews whereas modern German historians generally regard them as Germans.[33] There is also the problem of classifying Jews racially, either by birth or ancestry, and thus employing a restrictive, Orthodox Jewish, or worse, Nazi, categorization. For this study, I consider as Jews those who belonged to Jewish community institutions (*Glaubensjuden*) together with those who did not belong but still defined themselves as Jews and were so regarded by Gentiles. Conversely, I employ the term "Gentile" rather than "Christian" to cover the mass of German non-Jews. In addition, I make every effort to trace the fate of Jewish converts to Christianity and the Christian children of marriages between Jews and non-Jews (the so-called *Mischlinge*). The challenge is to acknowledge the complexity of Jewish and non-Jewish identity and to recreate the Gentile-Jewish relationship without degenerating into reductionism or elevating marginal experiences to the typical.

One would be venturing into similarly dangerous territory by conflating social and state-sponsored discrimination into a monolithic theory of antisemitism or by imparting to Jew-hatred a one-dimensional quality shared with equal intensity by all Gentiles. Michael Marrus has argued that prejudice against Jews at the everyday level in Weimar society came in a variety of forms—religious, economic, political, social, and racial—and ranged from unspoken discomfort, avoidance, and antilocution (or prejudicial discussion of Jews) to legal discrimination, physical attack, and (rarely) a desire for extermination.[34] At the same time, one cannot discount the role played by benign forms of antisemitism in numbing ordinary people to increasingly vicious invectives against Jews. During the Weimar period, Jew-hatred surfaced in antipathy toward eastern European Jewish refugees (*Ostjuden*), the exclusion of Jews from in-group rituals, incidents of name-calling at school, the frequent labeling of Jews and Jewish houses,[35] the preservation of spurious notions of Jewish physical attributes, and the association of Jews with the feckless republican order. Particularly ominous in hindsight was the German government's incarceration and deportation of *Ostjuden* at the end of World War I. The endurance of antisemitism in everyday Weimar society confirms a cultural and structural limit to Jewish integration and may help historians fashion a better understanding of the lack of moral indignation against Jew-hatred in the years of economic and political chaos from 1929 to 1932.

The role of ordinary Germans in the so-called *Judenpolitik* of the Third Reich was conspicuously absent from scholarly literature until the 1970s and 1980s. One of the reasons for this lack was the contention of historians such as Karl Dietrich Bracher, Eberhard Jäckel, Jacob Talmon, Hannah Arendt, and Eva Reichmann that research on the independent characteristic of social attitudes under totalitarianism was a priori irrelevant.[36] This "intentionalist" school perceived the Nazi state as a streamlined, hierarchical structure at the center of which was the Führer and the driving force of National Socialist ideology. The emergence of the "functionalist" school in the late 1960s led to a major conceptual shift in the historiography of the Third Reich. No longer attracted to political science but to social history, such scholars as Martin Broszat and Hans Mommsen believed that the ruling Nazi elite had to make use of an extremely complex, bureaucratic network that involved industry, banks, and different branches of the police, army, and civil administration.[37] The declassification of archival material on popular opinion from Nazi Party institutions aided the functionalist cause. Reports compiled by the Sicherheitsdienst (the SD or security service of the Schützstaffel or SS) and the Gestapo (the secret state police) made it clear that the Nazi regime was anxious to have reliable sources of information on public reactions to every aspect of its policies.[38]

In a 1973 essay, Lawrence Stokes concluded that "much, although not all, of the terror and destruction inflicted upon the Jews of Europe by the Nazis was generally known among the German people." Covering the broader ground of German public opinion during World War II, Marlis Steinert maintained that "only a few people knew about the monstrous scope of the crimes." Both based their studies almost exclusively on national SD reports for the war years. Subsequent works by Aron Rodrigue, Ian Kershaw, Sarah Gordon, and David Bankier drew on a combination of material, including eyewitness accounts, memoirs, SD and Gestapo reports, and dispatches from the SPD press in exile (the Sopade).[39]

According to Kershaw, Gordon, and Bankier, the "muddled mass" of Germans, neither full-hearted Nazis nor outright opponents, were largely indifferent to Jews and antisemitism. Jeremy Noakes observed that in Lower Saxony Jew-hatred had limited appeal among a population that was far more interested in economic matters. William Sheridan Allen also concluded that Germans "were drawn to antisemitism because they were drawn to Nazism, not the other way around." Historians like Kershaw and Allen have been taken to task for underplaying spontaneous expressions of antisemitism by ordinary Germans during the Third Reich. Otto Dov Kulka, Daniel Goldhagen, and John Weiss, in particular, have contended that there was substantial popular initiative for action against the Jews and that there was a widespread popular conviction that "something, one way or another, had to be done to solve the 'Jewish Question.'" [40]

Chapters 5, 6, and 7 assess the impact of everyday German antisemitism on the electoral rise of National Socialism and the enforcement of antisemitic legislation during the Nazi period. In what relational context did Gentiles vote for Nazis and then either ignore, resist, support, or actively help implement Nazi policy toward Jews? There may be no simple answer to this question. If, however, historians have supplanted the monolithic approach to the Third Reich with a polycratic interpretation, then the role of ordinary Gentiles in the functioning of Hitler's regime assumes greater significance. Following this line of argument, it seems reasonable to suggest that the persecution of Jews could not have been facilitated without at the very least the indifference or passivity of ordinary Gentiles. Michael Marrus argues that a subtle, "genteel" form of Jew-hatred made Gentiles insensitive to Nazi antisemitism during the economic and political crises of the late 1920s and helped pave the way for massacre during the Third Reich. [41] In this book, I seek to understand these developments in greater depth by concentrating on relations in three Hessian localities between Gentiles and Jews—the lion and the star.

1

Jewish Emancipation to 1919

The historian Jakob Katz described Jewish emancipation as the event that brought western and central European Jews "out of the ghetto" in the eighteenth and nineteenth centuries.[1] Though more a "tortuous path" than a single occurrence, emancipation nevertheless ushered in a process of Jewish integration into Gentile society by granting Jews civil rights and political privileges such as citizenship, suffrage, and eligibility for public office.[2] In return for the acquisition of rights, Jews were obliged to abandon their separate communal status and become "useful" citizens. Most Jews welcomed the chance both to play a role in a larger polity and to find new ways of sustaining aspects of their singularity. Sadly, the reality of life after emancipation was not nearly as bright as the future its supporters had envisioned because many Christians remained intolerant of Jews for traditional religious and economic reasons, and some invented more vicious charges against them. This chapter sets the scene for my analysis of Gentile-Jewish relations in Frankfurt am Main, Giessen, and Geisenheim during the Weimar era by focusing on the consequences of Jewish emancipation in those towns before 1919.

Before emancipation, the Jews of western and central Europe lived in communities that were segregated from Gentile society. In the German states, the Jewish community (*Gemeinde*) was a legal entity, a "corporation" that exercised certain decentralized functions of self-government within its precincts and acted as the official representative of Jews to the Gentile world.[3] The community paid taxes to non-Jewish authorities and administered synagogues, cemeteries, schools, and various cultural institutions. After emancipation, the Jewish community did much the same, although it was no longer a corporation representing segregated Jews but a religious congregation made up of Jewish citizens. Despite the lack of a centralized organization such as existed in England and France and the eventual appearance of diverse forms of religious beliefs within their midst, Germany's Jewish communities assumed a measure of unity by referring to themselves as Israelitische

Gemeinden (IG).[4] By 1933, there were 1,611 Jewish communities in Germany, and most of them were rural.[5]

Jewish communities had existed in Frankfurt since 1150, in Giessen since the mid-fourteenth century, and in Geisenheim since at least 1300.[6] According to Ulrich Friedrich Kopp, an eighteenth-century lawyer who addressed the "Jewish Question" in Hessen, "The history of Hessen's Jews was no different than Germany overall; Jews were also persecuted here."[7] As elsewhere in continental Europe, Jews in Hessen were ghettoized, forbidden to own land, denied guild membership, taxed heavily (for instance, through the *Leibzoll*, a duty imposed on traveling Jews that taxed them literally as cattle), and frequently harassed by antisemites. The only occupations open to them were certain forms of commerce, namely, cattle trading, peddling, hawking, and moneylending. Before Jews could engage in any of these vocations, they needed special, aristocratic dispensations of protection that were sold arbitrarily and limited in number. In this restrictive environment, only a few Jews succeeded in becoming well-to-do by the end of the eighteenth century. The vast majority of Jews in Hessen (and in Europe) remained mired in poverty.[7]

The situation changed with the advent of rationalism and the development of European nation-states in the 1700s. Intellectuals and political leaders began to support the removal of economic and political restrictions on Jews. Eagerly seeking to free up Jewish capital for national purposes, kings and nobles in central Europe curried favor from wealthy Jewish merchants, appointing some to court positions (*Hofjuden*). At the same time, rationalist philosophers wanted to emancipate Jews both out of a commitment to individual freedom and a desire to transform them into educated, productive members of European society as adherents of the Jewish or "Mosaic" faith. Ultimately, Jews were to be granted civil and political rights in return for their loyalty to the surrounding nation and their "moral and civic betterment" (*sittliche und bürgerliche Verbesserung*). France emancipated its Jews in the 1790s, and Bonaparte's armies brought an end to ghettoization in central Europe at the beginning of the nineteenth century.

After Napoleon's defeat, restrictions on Jews resurfaced in many German cities and states. In the 1820s, officials denied marriage licenses and residence permits to Jews in Geisenheim.[8] An 1833 law from Hessen-Kassel excluded poorer Jews in its bestowal of legal equality.[9] In the county of Giessen, an 1844 ordinance decreed that Jewish ritual baths were to be filled with dirt.[10] Following the revolutions of

1848, in which liberals briefly held power in central Europe, Jews regained and then quickly lost various freedoms. After 1848 in the duchy of Nassau, only Jews possessing letters of protection could become citizens and obtain voting privileges. On 27 September 1851, Duke Adolf rescinded those rights. In Frankfurt, the city senate voted on 5 October 1852 to extend Jews neither active nor passive suffrage. Yet nine years later, Adolf voided a law that preserved the second-class status of Jews, and in 1864, the Frankfurt Assembly agreed to end restrictions against "citizens of the Mosaic faith." Meanwhile, an 1848 edict from the elector of Hessen-Kassel, which had emancipated the Jews of Kurhessen, was nullified in 1852. The electorate's Jews received lasting civil and political rights after Prussia's annexation of Hessen-Kassel in the late 1860s.[11] These rights were extended to all Jews following the unification of Germany under Prussian auspices in 1871.

The fleeting nature of emancipatory laws in nineteenth-century central Europe fostered Jewish emigration but also an intensified effort among Jews to blend into Gentile society within a framework that safeguarded Jewish identity.[12] Jews adopted German as their mother tongue, took German names,[13] conformed to German fashion trends, attended German schools, moved to cities, voted for Germans who supported their emancipation (mainly liberals), and engaged in economic pursuits such as retail trade that were "respectable," although still highly problematic. The economic transformation of the Jews was particularly striking. By 1870, nearly 80 percent of all Jews belonged to the middle class, and nearly 60 percent were in upper-income brackets. No longer at the extremes of the economic scale, as they had been a century before, Jews were firmly bourgeois by 1900.[14]

Accompanying this socioeconomic change over the course of the nineteenth century was the emergence of a Jewish subculture that fused Enlightenment philosophy, cosmopolitanism, and cultivation (*Bildung*) with secular appreciations of Jewish history and new approaches to Jewish theology, two elements that often competed for the soul of the modern Jew.[15] In the late 1700s, Jewish intellectuals led a movement that proposed the incorporation of *Aufklärung* philosophies into Judaism. The Jewish Enlightenment or *Haskalah* desired the reconstruction of community based on the principles of ethical rationalism and humanitarianism. The *Haskalah*'s espousal of integration and use of Enlightenment discourse, along with the continued presence of Jew-hatred, however, produced an upswing in Jewish conversions to Christianity.[16] In subsequent generations, intellectuals like David

Frankel and Leopold Zunz and religious movements such as Reform, Neo-Orthodoxy, and Conservatism sought different ways out of this dead end.

Proponents of Reform saw Judaism as an evolving religion that needed to be updated so as to convey effectively its message of ethical monotheism. Reformers therefore jettisoned aspects of the religion deemed vestigial, the observance of dietary laws for one, and emulated many aspects of Christian worship through the introduction of decorum and sermons. Frankfurt am Main proved to be a focal point of Reform.[17] It hosted the second synod of Reform rabbis in 1845 and was home to two of the most important figures in the Reform movement, Isaac Marcus Jost and Abraham Geiger. Progressive Rabbinism, a moderate branch of Reform led by Leopold Stein, found a home in Frankfurt as well. The main synagogue in Frankfurt's Jewish quarter on Bornestrasse, in the Judengasse, embraced Reform ritual, and so did the main synagogue in Giessen on the Sudanlage.[18]

Frankfurt and Giessen also had a number of Jewish followers of Neo-Orthodoxy, a mid-nineteenth-century phenomenon which began in the Main metropolis and spread throughout Germany as a reaction to Reform. Led by Samson Raphael Hirsch, the Neo-Orthodox opposed Reform religious doctrine and held to strict observance of Jewish law without rejecting German citizenship. In 1850, an Orthodox conference in Frankfurt dubbed its movement the Israelitische Religionsgesellschaft (IRG—Jewish Religious Society), and four years later, the IRG opened a synagogue on Schutzenstrasse. The IRG officially parted from the Frankfurt Gemeinde in 1876.[19] The Neo-Orthodox went so far as to declare themselves members of a religion apart from Reform; hence they became known as secessionist Orthodox or *Austrittsorthodoxen*.[20] In Giessen, the Neo-Orthodox established a synagogue of their own on Steinstrasse in 1900.[21] According to Gershom Scholem, the proportion of Orthodox Jews in Germany at the beginning of the twentieth century hovered around 20 percent.[22]

While Germany's large urban areas proved fertile ground for Reform Judaism, its presence in Hessen's smaller villages during the nineteenth century was limited.[23] By the same token, not all traditional, rural Jews supported Hirsch's separatists. Some became advocates of Positive-historical or Conservative Judaism, a compromise between Reform and Orthodox, some chose to stay within the general Jewish community as adherents to Orthodoxy, the so-called *Gemeindeorthodox*, and others adopted an amorphous mixture of the two.[24] The Jews of Rüdesheim,

Geisenheim, and Winkel attended Gemeinde services in Rudesheim that were relatively traditional, and Geisenheim's Jewish community also maintained a small Orthodox chapel.[25] Further affecting the German Jewish religious landscape was the urban influx of eastern European Jews (*Ostjuden*) fleeing persecution in the late 1800s. Both Frankfurt and Giessen had sizable foreign Jewish contingents: by 1910, 3,541 out of 26,228 Jews in Frankfurt were foreign-born, in Giessen, 57 out of 913.[26]

One of the major dilemmas facing Germany's "citizens of the Mosaic faith" was a decline in religious observance over the course of the nineteenth and early twentieth centuries, which was mitigated slightly by the infusion of *Ostjuden* and a religious revival sparked by rising antisemitism after World War I. Leo Baeck, Berlin's Reform rabbi during the Weimar period, feared that Jews would allow themselves to be seduced by the unrestrained individualism of modern culture. Only the Jewish religion, he argued, could save them from "anarchism of the soul."[27] The shift away from religion notwithstanding, most German Jews in the postemancipation era continued to identify themselves as Jews at some level while remaining loyal to *Deutschtum* as an overarching national and cultural identity.[28]

What endangered this tentative symbiosis far more than secularization, nonreligious approaches to Jewish identity, or the seductive lure of assimilation was the endurance of well-rooted religious animosities toward Jews and the growth of new manifestations of antisemitism, some actually spawned by failed expectations of Jewish conversion to Christianity following emancipation.[29] In the ongoing debate over German identity, itself fueled by the unsettling results of unification by Prussia in 1871, some believed that Germany was a Christian state and that to become a German, one had first to become a Christian.[30] Tensions within the very premise of Jewish emancipation as well as resentment against the acquisition of civil and political rights on the part of Jews sparked a host of new accusations that, for the first time, constituted fodder for party politics and mass politicization.

From a religious standpoint, Jews were still targets for their rejection of Jesus and for the crime of deicide. But Jews became linked to modernity, and specifically to liberalism, the ideology of their liberation which had championed parliamentarianism, capitalism, and industrialization. Jewish financiers were blamed for the banking crashes of 1873 in Vienna and Berlin which ushered in a depression and a period of liberal retreat. Peasants, moreover, protested Jewish cattle trading and moneylending practices, and artisans complained about Jewish retail salesmen, both groups ignoring the vast Gentile presence in commerce. Eleanore Sterling has postulated the essential continuity of medieval and modern antisemitism by finding in the latter a secularized variation of the former. The Jews remained devils to powerless and exploited people of unsophisticated social and political awareness.[31]

Political antisemitism found spokesmen in individuals like Wilhelm Marr, who coined the term "antisemitism," Adolf Stöcker, who founded one of the first antisemitic parties in Germany in the Christian Social Workers' Party, Georg von Schönerer, a pan-German nationalist, Heinrich von Treitschke, an antisemitic Prussian historian whose dictum "the Jews are our misfortune" later became a Nazi rallying cry, and Karl Lueger, Vienna's mayor in the fin de siècle who ran on an antisemitic platform.[32]

Accompanying the rise of political and economic antisemitism was the far more radical emergence of racial antisemitism. Whereas traditional and political antisemites viewed conversion to Christianity as the ticket to societal acceptance, racial antisemites like Houston Stewart Chamberlain and Theodor Fritsch argued that Jewish integration was not only undesirable but biologically impossible.[33] As polar opposites on the race spectrum, "Semites" and "Aryans" could never mix.[34] A direct result of the rise of *völkisch* ideologies, Social Darwinism, and eugenic science, racial antisemitism found a vulgar spokesman in Adolf Hitler.[35]

Hessen was a particulary notorious hotbed of Jew-hatred in the late nineteenth century. In 1887, Otto Böckel, a former Marburg university student and librarian, led an antisemitic peasant movement in rural Hessen to become the first political antisemite ever to hold a seat in the lower house of the German parliament.[36] In Marburg and Giessen, Gentile students eased insecurities over their own futures by bemoaning the rise in university attendance among Jews, while many farmers out in the countryside resented Jewish cattle traders who sold on credit. In Frankfurt, antisemitism was largely the preserve of student groups, academic organizations (the Verein akademisch gebildeter Lehrer), marginal nationalist associations (the Deutscher Verein), writers (Johann Baptist von Schweitzer), and political cartoonists (notably those from the *Frankfurter Latern*).[37] Jew-hatred in Geisenheim, by contrast, was less pronounced. Catholics constituted a majority there and in the Rheingau, while they were a minority throughout Hessen as a whole. It is most likely that their existence as a once persecuted minority as well as their close association with political parties that opposed the radical right made Catholics more critical of antisemitism.[38]

But Gentile resentment against Jews as merchants or cattle traders was also absent from daily life in Geisenheim. The antisemitic political parties of the late imperial period in Germany suffered major defeats in the 1912 national elections when an economic recovery and voter dissatisfaction with their single-issue nature set in. In hindsight, the demise of political antisemitism proved ephemeral.[39]

German Jews responded to the rise of new forms of prejudice in a variety of ways.[40] Some chose to increase the pace of their integration by converting to Christianity or by simply affirming their German identity. Others came to the defense of their Jewishness and continued to hope for the realization of *Aufklärung* ideals. In 1893, the Berlin Jewish community established the Central Association of German Citizens of the Jewish Faith (the Centralverein deutscher Staatsbürger jüdischen Glaubens or CV), which not only engaged in a defensive campaign against antisemitism but also reasserted Jewish loyalty to Germany and liberalism. A federation of student fraternities, called the Convention of Fraternities of German Students of the Jewish Faith (Kartell-Convent), emerged in 1896 with a similar approach. In 1891, before the founding of either organization, Jews and Gentiles had established the Association to Resist Antisemitism (Verein zur Abwehr des Antisemitismus), a small but active organization that carried its uphill battle against Jew-hatred into the Weimar years.

By the 1920s, membership in the CV numbered more than sixty thousand. Following the reorganization of the CV into regional groups (*Ortsgruppe*), Jewish leaders in Frankfurt set up their own chapter of the CV in 1907. Leaders in Frankfurt's Reform community, including Ernst Auerbach, Hugo Apolant, Rudolf Geiger, and Salo Adler, joined with Neo-Orthodox separatists such as Elias Fink to combat Jew-hatred through antidefamation and the cultivation of Jewish self-esteem. The CV embarked on a vigorous campaign of enlightenment by publishing books, newspapers, and brochures, the most significant of which was its "Anti-Anti" handbook on the myths of antisemitism. Despite selling over thirty thousand copies of the pamphlet in Germany by 1932, the CV was ultimately unsuccessful in its efforts. The Frankfurter *Ortsgruppe* even encountered difficulties trying to convince Jews in the city not to subscribe to the antisemitic *Frankfurter Beobachter*.[41]

Many Jews saw the recrudescence of antisemitism as a sign that emancipation had failed, and they turned to Jewish nationalism.[42] In 1897, ten years before the establishment of the Frankfurt CV, a group of Zionists formed the Zionist Association of Germany (Zionistische

Vereinigung für Deutschland, ZVfD). Unlike their eastern European counterparts, German Zionists were a small group before 1918, numbering 8,964 at most.[43] Although they too promoted the idea that Jews constituted a "nation" that needed a homeland to defend against antisemitism, German Zionists initially focused more on bettering the lives of *Ostjuden* than on settlement in Palestine.

Support for the Zionist movement in Frankfurt early on came from poverty-stricken "eastern Jews" who bore the brunt of fin-de-siecle German antisemitism. However, the leaders of the Frankfurt Zionist *Ortsgruppe*, which had a total membership of 153 in 1905, were *Gemeindeorthodox* and included Fritz Sondheimer, Jakob Goitein, Sali Geis, and Salomon Hirsch Goldmann—the father of the future president of the German Zionist movement, Nahum Goldmann. Many Orthodox Jews heeded the Zionist call out of a desire both to help their eastern European counterparts and to curb waning interest in the religious aspects of Judaism by focusing on Jewish communal pride. But most, like Markus Horovitz, head of the IG's Orthodox faction in the late nineteenth century, opposed Zionism because of its secular, nationalist orientation.[44] In the Hessian countryside, in Giessen and in Geisenheim, the Zionist presence was even weaker, if not nonexistent.

At no time were Jews better able to prove their commitment to the Fatherland than during World War I. On 1 August 1914, the CV lent its support to the German cause and called on all Jews to do the same. Frankfurt, Giessen, and the Rheingau all supplied Jewish foot soldiers for the war effort. A Jewish soldier from Frankfurt remembered that a rabbi beseeched God for a German victory during services held behind the front lines.[45] Yet as prospects for success in the war eroded, German Jewish loyalty to the kaiser was called into question. Although they refrained from siding with the Allied powers (Great Britain, France, the United States, and Russia), Zionists became targets of antisemitic invective after England issued the Balfour Declaration in 1917, which championed a Jewish homeland in Palestine.[46] A year earlier, the German government had conducted a *Judenzählung* or "Jew census" of Jewish soldiers in response to charges that German Jewry was shirking its patriotic duty.[47] Later studies by Franz Oppenheimer and Jakob Segall actually revealed that the Jewish contribution to the war effort, in the number of Jews killed or wounded, was disproportionately high.[48] Although its findings were never published, the Jew census constituted the most spectacular symptom of the increase in antisemitism during the last years of the war.[49]

The experience of German Jews in World War I demonstrated how Jewish perceptions of their integration were at odds with reality; 12,000 Jews, including 467 from Frankfurt, 18 from Giessen, and 3 from the Rheingau, had died for their country.[50] Jewish veterans even formed the Imperial Union of Jewish Front Soldiers (Reichsbund jüdischer Frontsoldaten), which emphasized Jewish wartime patriotism. For all of their flag-waving, Jews still met widespread antipathy and disregard from Gentiles.

With Germany's defeat in the war and the subsequent establishment of the Weimar Republic in 1919, the future of Jewish integration into German society appeared brighter. The imperial political system, dominated largely by Prussia's conservative landowning class, the Junkers, gave way to a democratic constitution. Germany's Jewish communities were accorded legal and fiscal equality with the established Christian churches. Berlin became an unparalleled center for Jewish culture in Europe, intermarriage rates rose, and more Jews held public office than ever before.[51] Five of the nine Nobel prizes won by German citizens during the Weimar years went to Jewish scientists, two for medicine and three for physics, including one to Albert Einstein. Weimar's literary world was also replete with Jewish names. Books by Jakob Wassermann, Stefan Zweig, and Lion Feuchtwanger made bestseller lists, and a 1926 poll of the readers of the prestigious magazine *Literarische Welt* revealed that Franz Werfel stood second only to Thomas Mann in their affections.[52]

These contributions, however, only served to link Jews with a democratic order that fell into disfavor because of its association with the unpopular Treaty of Versailles, political instability, cultural modernity, and economic chaos (hyperinflation, harsh stabilization, and then depression).[53] At the heart of the critique of the radical right, in particular, stood "the Jew," the embodiment of all the forces allegedly "stabbing Germany in the back" and undermining German economics, politics, and culture. Justified or not, most German Jews clung to liberalism and *Aufklärung* as the bases for German Jewish identity during the Weimar period, hoping that through education and antidefamation they could transform German society into the amicable home envisioned by their emancipators. Only in hindsight did this optimism seem misplaced.

2

Demography and Socioeconomic Structure

An examination of Gentile-Jewish relations in Frankfurt am Main, Giessen, and Geisenheim during the Weimar era would be incomplete without an assessment of the social and economic makeup of their Jewish communities from 1919 to 1933. Clearly, differences or similarities in occupational structure, class status, and residency patterns affected the form and extent of Jewish-Gentile interaction, as well as the overall shape of Jewish integration. More important, though the republic's democratic structure provided opportunities for Jews to integrate further into German state and society, persistent antisemitism and economic uncertainty saddled Germany's Jewish communities with a deep anxiety and accelerated their ongoing demographic decline.

Overall, population change in the Weimar Republic was characterized by a rise in life expectancy, a falling birth rate, and an "aging problem" brought about by the loss of young and middle-aged men in World War I. The latter phenomenon actually reinforced the perception that Germany was undergoing terminal decline or *Volkstod.* Yet though the population of the German Reich dropped from nearly sixty-five million in 1910 to sixty-two million in 1925, it climbed back to sixty-five million by 1933, largely because death rates fell more sharply than birth rates.[1]

A striking feature of Jewish demography in the 1920s was a downturn in population figures. Census records indicate that Germany's Jewish communities hit record numbers in 1910 but began to shrink thereafter. In 1910, there were 615,021 Jews in Germany (0.95 percent of the overall population),[2] but only 564,379 (0.9 percent) in 1925, and 503,000 (0.76 percent) in 1933. The 1910 numerical total, though a record high, camouflaged a declining percentage. In 1871, Jews had made up 1.25 percent of Germany's total population.[3]

Demographic changes in the Jewish communities in Frankfurt, Giessen, and Geisenheim paralleled those at the national and provincial levels. In Frankfurt and Giessen, the percentage of Jews exceeded their national proportion. Whereas in 1871 Frankfurt's 10,009 Jews accounted for nearly 11 percent of the city's inhabitants, in 1910, their number of 26,228 was only 6.23 percent of the total population. Again, a large proportional decrease accompanied a numerical increase as the growth of the Jewish community fell behind the city's leap from 91,040 (in 1871) to 414,576 (in 1910). As elsewhere, the Jewish population of Frankfurt declined between 1910 and 1933, but only slightly. In fact, the 1925 census displayed a momentary increase of nearly 3,000 before falling to 26,158 in 1933. The number of members of the Israelitische Gemeinde and Israelitische Religionsgesellschaft increased as well between 1910 and 1925. In 1910 there were approximately 9,000 dues-paying members of the Reform IG but over 18,000 in 1925. The IRG experienced a less dramatic growth, rising from 1,056 in 1910 to 1,446 in 1925.[4] Meanwhile, Frankfurt's total population continued a steady, if unspectacular, rise to 468,000 in 1925 and 555,857 in 1933.

The Jewish communities of Giessen and Geisenheim declined between 1910 and 1933. Although remaining above the national average, the percentage of Jews in Giessen fell from 3.32 percent in 1910, to 3.02 percent in 1925, and 2.38 percent in 1933. Meanwhile, Giessen's total population grew from 31,158 in 1910, to 33,600 in 1925, and 35,913 in 1933.[5] Geisenheim witnessed a drop both in the number and proportion of its Jews even before Giessen, counting 39 Jews in 1871 (1.5 percent of village inhabitants), 31 in 1905 (0.8 percent), 25 in 1925 (0.6 percent), and 21 in 1933 (0.5 percent). The total population of Geisenheim rose from 2,662 in 1871 to 4,252 in 1925.[6] (See Tables 1, 2, and 3)

Monika Richarz suggests that lower birth rates among Jews, the failure of birth rates to stay above mortality rates, and rising numbers of elderly Jewish communities prevented their numbers from keeping pace with the general population.[7] Most historians reject a monocausal explanation for these developments. Smaller Jewish families, and hence smaller Jewish communities, were the combined result of emancipation, urbanization, industrialization, emigration, the "rise of bourgeois values," and insecurities brought by antisemitism.[8]

During the early years of the republic, the average number of births in Germany came close to 850,000 per year (13.5 per 1,000, or 1.35 percent), deaths to around 580,000 (9.2 per 1,000, or 0.92 percent).[9] The growth rate was therefore a robust 0.43 percent per year. Within Germany's Jewish communities, however, annual deaths outnumbered births by about five hundred, producing a death rate of 1.03 percent and a birth rate of 0.949 percent (a negative growth rate of 0.081 percent).[10]

Table 1. Religious Affiliation in Germany in 1925[a] (percentages in parentheses)

Region	Evangelical	Catholic	Jewish	Other
Germany	40,014,677 (64%)	20,193,334 (32%)	564,379 (0.9%)	1,638,229 (3%)[b]
Prussia	24,804,018 (65%)	11,943,264 (31%)	404,446 (1%)	1,024,261 (3%)
Hessen-Nassau	1,683,807 (69%)	676,461 (28%)	53,234 (2%)	39,185 (1%)
Hessen	891,867 (66%)	415,685 (31%)	20,401 (1.5%)	19,326 (1%)
Frankfurt	272,567 (58%)	145,570 (31%)	29,385 (6%)	19,998 (4%)
Giessen (city)	30,982 (86%)	3,534 (10%)	855 (2.4%)	542 (1.5%)
Geisenheim	561 (13%)	3,601 (85%)	25 (0.5%)	65 (1.5%)[a]

Sources: Paul Troschke, *Evangelisches Kirchenstatistik Deutschlands: Kirchenstatistik* Issues 2 and 3 (Berlin, 1929), 6-8; *Statistisches Jahrbuch für das deutsche Reich: Zweiundfünfzigster Jahrgang 1933* (Berlin, 1933), 18; *Statistisches Handbuch der Stadt Frankfurt a. M.: Zweite Ausgabe Enthaltend die Statistik der Jahre 1906/07 bis 1926/27* (Frankfurt, 1928), 70; *Statistik des deutsches Reiches : Die Bevölkerung des deutschen Reiches nach den Ergebnissen der Volkszählung 1933. Die Bevölkerung des deutschen Reiches nach der Religionszugehörigkeit*, Vol. 451, Issue 3 (Berlin, 1936), 64; Paul Arnsberg, *Die Geschichte der Frankfurter Juden seit der Französischer Revolution* (Darmstadt, 1983), 2:481; "Aufstellung der am 30. 1. 1933 wohnhaften Juden in Giessen," "Verzeichnis der zur Israelitischen Religionsgemeinde Giessen steuerpflichtigen Personen: Stand Januar 1932," and "Verzeichnis der Mitglieder der Israelitischen Religionsgesellschaft, Giessen, Stand vom 13. 3. 1935," in Erwin Knauss, *Die jüdischen Bevölkerung Giessens, 1933-1945: Eine Dokumentation* (Wiesbaden, 1976), 54-118; "Verzeichnis der abgemeldeten Personen Mai 1928 bis April 1942," Stadtarchiv Geisenheim, 123-03, and the city's "Einwohnerliste," Stadtarchiv Geisenheim, 123-03; and *75 Jahre Rheingaukreis: Rheingaukreis vom Landrat Leopold Bausinger im Auftrag des Kreistages und des Kreisausschusses* (Rüdesheim, 1962), 199.

a These figures refer to the year 1925, with the exception of Giessen, whose figures come from 1933. The tallies include both official members of the various religious communities and those who may not have belonged (i.e., paid taxes) to a specific community but who identified themselves as adherents of a particular faith.

b This category includes other Christians and those who might not have belonged to any religious community (miscellanous-[*sonstige*], general faithful [*gottgläubige*], or without confession [*glaubenslos*]). Those in the *sonstige* category increased dramatically after 1910 when they counted for 0.36% of the population. In 1925, they made up nearly 2.6% of the total population, and many of them were Jews who chose not to belong to any religious community.

Table 2. German Jewish Population, 1910-1933

Year	Jewish population in number (then, percentage of Jews in relation to overall population)		Jews in Hessen-Darmstadt number (%)		Jews in the Prussian Province of Hessen-Nassau number (%)	
1910	615, 021	(0.95%)	24, 603	(1.88%)	51, 781	(2.33%)
1925	564, 379	(0.90%)	20, 401	(1.51%)	53, 234	(2.16%)
1933	503, 000	(0.76%)	17, 888	(1.25%)	46, 923	(1.82%)

Sources: Statistisches Jahrbuch für das deutsche Reich: Zweiundfünfzigster Jahrgang 1933 (Berlin, 1933), 8, 18; *Statistik des deutschen Reiches: Die Bevölkerung des deutschen Reiches nach den Ergebnissen der Volkszählung 1933. Die Glaubensjuden im Deutschen Reich*, Vol. 451, Issue 5 (Berlin, 1936), 7, 9, 35, 36, 41; *Statistisches Handbuch der Stadt Frankfurt a. M.: Zweite Ausgabe , Enthaltend die Statistik der Jahre 1906/07 bis 1926-27* (Frankfurt, 1928), 70; Monika Richarz, *Jüdisches Leben in Deutschland: Selbstzeugnisse zur Sozialgeschichte, 1918-1945* (New York, 1982),14, 67; Bruno Blau, *Die Entwicklung der jüdischen Bevölkerung in Deutschland* (New York, 1950), 276; and Salomon Adler-Rudel, *Ostjuden in Deutschland, 1880-1940* (Tübingen, 1959), 164-65.

German Jewry was aging as well. By 1925, one-third of all German Jews were over forty-five, as compared to one-fourth of all Gentiles. The number of Jewish children in Germany under the age of fifteen sank by half from 1871 to 1933. The 1933 census reported that 9 percent of all Gentiles in Germany were not yet of school age, compared to only 5 percent of its Jewish population.[11]

Mixed marriages and secessions from the various Jewish communities also affected demographic totals. The concentration of Jews in cities had led to greater social contact with Gentiles and a gradual weakening of opposition to intimate relations. In 1875, marriage between Jews and Gentiles in Germany was legalized. From 1900 to 1930, the percent of German Jews marrying non-Jews nearly tripled, from 8 to 22 percent. In 1928, 27 percent of Jewish marriages in Berlin and 33 percent in Hamburg were mixed.[12] However, intermarriage rates during the Weimar period benefited more from a decline in marriages among Jews than a meteoric rise in the number of unions between Jews and Gentiles. In 1924, for instance, the number of intermarriages was 1,535, and the number of endogamous Jewish marriages was 3,310, for a 31 percent intermarriage rate. In 1930, the number of intermarriages was 1,642 and the number of endogamous Jewish marriages 2,851, for

Table 3. Jewish Population in Frankfurt, Giessen, and Geisenheim 1910-1933[a]

Year	Jews in Frankfurt number (then % of overall population)		Jews in Giessen number (%)		Jews in Geisenheim number (%)	
1910	26, 228	(6.23%)	1035	(3.32%)	31	(0.776%, a1905 number)
1925	29, 385	(6.28%)	1017	(3.02%)	25	(0.49%)
1933	26, 158	(4.71%)	855	(2.38%)	21	(0.476%)[b]

Sources: Statistik des deutschen Reiches: Die Bevölkerung des deutschen Reiches nach den Ergebnissen der Volkszählung 1933. Die Glaubensjuden im Deutschen Reich, Vol. 451, Issue 5 (Berlin, 1936), 7, 9, 35, 36, 41; Statistisches Handbuch der Stadt Frankfurt a. M.: Zweite Ausgabe Enthaltend die Statistik der Jahre 1906/07 bis 1926-27 (Frankfurt, 1928), 70; Paul Arnsberg, Die Geschichte der Frankfurter Juden seit der Französischer Revolution (Darmstadt, 1983), 2:481; Erwin Knauss, Die jüdische Bevölkerung Giessens, 1933-1945: Eine Dokumentation (Wiesbaden, 1976), 17; 75 Jahre Rhein-gaukreis: Herausgegeben vom Landrat Leopold Bausinger im Auftrag des Kreistages und des Kreisausschusses (Rüdesheim, 1962), 199.
a During the republic, Jewish women outnumbered men in Frankfurt and Giessen while the reverse was true for Geisenheim. In 1933, the gender distribution of the Jews in these communities was 12, 449 men, 13, 709 women in Frankfurt (26,158 total), 408 men, 447 women in the city of Giessen (855 total, 726 men and 821 women in the entire county for a total of 1, 547), and 12 men, 9 women in Geisenheim (21 total).
b Since no census records of Geisenheim's Jewish community were available to me for this particular year, I based this number on a count of residents from Geisenheim's "Verzeichnis der abgemeldeten Personen, Mai 1928 bis April 1942," Stadtarchiv Geisenheim, 123-03, and the city's "Einwohnerliste," Stadtarchiv Geisenheim, 123-03.

an intermarriage rate of nearly 37 percent.[13] More important, the number of intermarriages declined between 1930 and 1932 during an era of economic depression and rising antisemitism.[14] As for conversion, approximately 15,000 German Jews adopted Christianity in the first three decades of the twentieth century, but between 1911 and 1925, the average number of Jews who converted to Christianity declined from 415 to 302 as more Jews chose "nondenominationalism" over baptism.[15]

Several aspects of Jewish demography in Frankfurt from 1910 to 1925 reflected the national pattern as 130 more Jews died than were born.[16] The number of Jewish school-age children also plummeted.[17]

At the same time, the proportion of marriages between Jews and non-Jews in the city between 1919 and 1931 grew from over 10 percent to 35 percent. In 1932, during the height of the depression and rising anti-semitism, mixed marriages fell back to 30 percent. As at the national level, the rise in intermarriage before 1932 was attributable to a decline in endogamous Jewish marriages. In Frankfurt in 1920, there were 425 marriages between Jews and 109 intermarriages. In 1932, city records showed only 137 endogamous and 61 exogamous Jewish marriages.[18] Meanwhile, between 1919 and 1926, an average of 28 Frankfurt Jews converted to Christianity while 14 Evangelicals and 6 Catholics entered the IG per year, offsetting a potentially severe drain from Jewish conversion.[19] During the depression, when antisemitism was high, the number of Jews seceding from the Jewish community increased, although most did not convert to Christianity. When the Nazis came to power, more Frankfurt Jews chose conversion over communal secession.[20]

Unlike the national pattern, Frankfurt's Jewish communities, the main Israelitische Gemeinde and the separatist Orthodox Israelitische Religionsgesellschaft, experienced growth between 1910 and 1925. In 1925, the IG had 18,469 members, nearly twice the number in 1919. The IRG increased its membership modestly from 1,350 in 1919 to 1,449 in 1925. The total Jewish population in the city was up from over 26,000 in 1910 to 29,000 in 1925. Much of this growth can be traced to in-migration, specifically that of *Ostjuden*, whose entrance into the established IG rather than the separatist IRG constituted a major coup for the Gemeinde.[21]

Table 4 shows that the number of foreign-born Jews in Germany nearly quintupled between 1890 and 1925. By the mid-1920s, immigrants constituted nearly a fifth of all German Jewry. Almost 80 percent of these immigrant Jews had come from either Poland or Russia seeking asylum from antisemitic persecution.[22] As traders, small merchants, craftsmen, peddlers, hawkers, and beggars with large, religious families, *Ostjuden* came to be concentrated in Germany's main urban areas. In 1910, 78 percent of them resided in cities of over 100,000 people, and by 1925, approximately 20 percent of all Jews in Frankfurt were foreign-born.[23]

The drop in Frankfurt's Jewish population to 26,125 in 1933 was due to a combination of factors—mortality surpluses, withdrawals from the Jewish community, and emigration out of the city and country. Fewer births and more deaths did not necessarily indicate that German Jewry's distress was solely the result of the economic crisis of the late

Table 4. Foreign-Born Jews in Germany

Year	Jewish population (% of overall population)		Foreign-born Jews (% of Jewish population)	
1890	567,884	(1.15%)	22,000	(3.9%)
1910	615,021	(0.95%)	78,746	(12.8%)
1925	564,000	(0.90%)	107,747	(19.2%)
1935	499,682	(0.76%)	98,747	(19.8%)

Sources: Monika Richarz,*Jüdisches Leben in Deutschland: Selbstzeugnisse zur Sozial-geschichte, 1918-1945* (New York, 1982), 14; Trude Maurer, *Ostjuden in Deutsch-land, 1918-1933* (Hamburg, 1986), 72.

1920s or the rise of Nazism. The death rate for Jews had been on the rise since the first decade of the twentieth century. Frankfurt's Jewish community may have simply become more elderly and less able to reproduce itself. But it is true that smaller families, migration, communal secession, and conversion were options for survival in times of high antisemitism and economic and political uncertainty. From 1926 to 1933, Jewish deaths outnumbered births in Frankfurt by 749, and there was a mortality surplus of Jews during each of those years. In 1929, the city's Jewish birth rate stood at 1.04 percent compared to 1.24 percent for the general population. Likewise, the Jewish mortality rate was higher than that of the overall population, 1.48 percent versus 1.14 percent.[24] Between 1929 and 1932, 381 more Jews officially left the Gemeinde than entered (although the number of converts to Christianity was lower), and 1,596 more Jews left Frankfurt than took up residence there.[25]

Giessen's Jewish population peaked at 1,035 (3.3 percent of the town's population) in 1910 but dropped to 1,017 in 1925, 943 in 1927, and 855 in 1933.[26] This decline was largely the result of Jewish out-migration and a mortality surplus. In the last three years of the republic (1930-32), Jewish deaths outnumbered births by a total of 46.[27] *Ostjuden* who settled in Giessen did little to replace losses. In the nineteenth century, migration from the countryside, and later from outside Germany, had helped fuel the tripling of Giessen's Jewish population from 288 in 1852 to 895 in 1900. By 1905, 57 of the city's 913 Jews were foreigners hailing mostly from the eastern regions of Austria-Hungary.[28] That number held steady until 1933.[29] Interestingly, conversion was not a major factor in the demographic freefall of Giessen Jewry, and intermarriage fluctuated yearly. In 1928 one of the four marriages involving Jews in Giessen was an intermarriage, in 1930 three of seven, in 1931 three of four, and in 1932 zero of six. From 1919 to 1933, only six Jews converted to Protestantism, although three did in 1932, and they may have been spouses from the three intermarriages that had occurred in the previous year.[30] In the final analysis, data on Giessen Jews only loosely confirm the pattern of declining intermarriage and rising conversion during the later years of the republic. The information more accurately establishes that Jews married proportionately less in Giessen than in Frankfurt.[31]

Before 1918, Geisenheim had already lost the bulk of its Jewish population. Falling from thirty-nine in 1871 to twenty-five in 1925, Geisenheim's small community became even smaller thereafter, losing four individuals to out-migration from 1928 to 1933.[32] The available records do not show any Jewish marriages, births, or deaths in this period.[33] Nor were there any mixed marriages or conversions to or from Christianity.[34] Perhaps the most interesting characteristic of Geisenheim Jewry was its kinship; thirteen Jews in the village were members of the extended Strauss family.[35] The older generation of Strausses, those in their forties and fifties during the Weimar period, included Liebmann, his wife, Karolina, Max and Auguste, Moritz and Henriette, and Georg and Emma. Max and Auguste Strauss had three children, Alex, Enna, and Kurt. Georg and Emma had one son, Alfredo. These children would have reached marrying age by the late 1920s and early 1930s, just as the Nazis rose to power. But Geisenheim Jewry in the 1920s may not have been able to reproduce itself even without the latter development. Only in-marriage to Jews from other communities or out-marriage leading to an influx of converts into Judaism plus a desire to settle in Geisenheim would have staved off demographic collapse.

Accompanying the demographic downturn of German Jewry during the years of the republic was the continued movement of Jews to large cities.[36] In 1871, 20 percent of all German Jews resided in metropolitan areas, in 1910, 58 percent.[37] By 1933 more than 70 percent of Germany's Jews lived in cities whose populations exceeded 100,000, in comparison to only 30 percent of the general populace. The majority (50.6 percent) of Germans still lived in villages of under 10,000, while only 15.5 percent of Jews did (see Tables 5, 6, 7, and 8).[38]

Jewish residence patterns during the republic also mirrored earlier forms of settlement and developed along class and cultural lines. In Frankfurt after emancipation, Jews stayed concentrated in what had been the city's ghetto, the Judengasse, located in the eastern part of town. But many chose to leave the East End. Those who left moved north and west or further east, setting in place the residential pattern

Table 5. Gentile and Jewish Population in Germany by Size of Community in 1933

Size of community by population	General population		Jewish population	
Under 10,000 residents	33,039,082	(50.7%)	77,168	(15.5%)
10,000 to 20,000 residents	3,930,115	(6.0%)	17,172	(3.4%)
20,001 to 50,000 residents	5,028,133	(7.7%)	25,714	(5.1%)
50,001 to 100,000 residents	3,418,495	(5.3%)	25,508	(5.1%)
Above 100,000 (including Berlin)	19,802,336	(30.4%)	353,580	(70.9%)
Total	65,210,461	(100%)	499,682	(100%)

Source: Statistik des deutschen Reiches: Die Bevölkerung des deutschen Reiches nach den Ergebnissen der Volkszählung 1933. Die Glaubensjuden im deutschen Reich, Vol. 451, Issue 5 (Berlin, 1936), 9.

Table 6. Gentile and Jewish Population in Hessen-Nassau by Size of Community in 1933

Size of community by population	Hessen-Nassau population		Jewish population	
Under 10,000 residents	1,478,375	(57.2%)	12,404	(26.4%)
10,000 to 100,000 residents	195,546	(7.6%)	3,347	(7.2%)
Above 100,000	910,907	(35.2%)	31,172	(66.4%)
Total	2,584,828	(100%)	46,923	(100%)

Sources: Statistik des deutschen Reiches: Die Bevölkerung des deutschen Reiches nach den Ergebnissen der Volkszählung 1933. Die Glaubensjuden im deutschen Reich, Vol. 451, Issue 5 (Berlin, 1936), 14; Statistik des deutschen Reiches: Die Bevölkerung des deutschen Reiches nach den Ergebnissen der Volkszählung 1939. Stand,- Entwicklung-, und Siedlungsweise der Bevölkerung des deutschen Reiches, Vol. 552, Issue 1 (Berlin, 1943), 26, 27.

for Frankfurt Jewry that endured into the 1930s (see Map 3).[39] Jews who settled in the west-northwest were, by and large, economically better off and more liberal in matters of religion than Jews in the East End. In 1910, Jews from the nordwestliche Aussenstadt area built a Reform temple on Königstrasse that became known as the West End Synagogue. The school of the Reform Gemeinde, the Philanthropin, was relocated to the nördliche Aussenstadt in 1908. In the meantime, almost all of Frankfurt's *Ostjuden* and many Neo-Orthodox Jews settled in its eastern districts, creating a subculture that was not only

Table 7. Gentile and Jewish Population in Hessen by Size of Community in 1933

Size of community by population	Hessen population		Jewish population	
Under 10,000 residents	874,578	(61.2%)	9,282	(51.9%)
10,000 to 100,000 residents	292,932	(20.5%)	5,997	(33.5%)
Above 100,000	261,538	(18.3%)	2,609	(14.6%)
Total	1,429,048	(100%)	17,888	(100%)

Sources: Statistik des deutschen Reiches: Die Bevölkerung des deutschen Reiches nach den Ergebnissen der Volkszählung 1933. Die Glaubensjuden im deutschen Reich, Vol. 451, Issue 5 (Berlin, 1936), 14; Statistik des deutschen Reiches: Die Bevölkerung des deutschen Reiches nach den Ergebnissen der Volkszählung 1939. Stand,- Entwicklung-, und Siedlungsweise der Bevölkerung des deutschen Reiches, Vol. 552, Issue 1 (Berlin, 1943), 34-35.

Table 8. Jewish Residence in Selected German Cities in 1933

City	Total population	Jewish population	% of city's residents	% of Germany's Jews
Berlin	4,242,501	160,564	3.78%	32.1%)
Frankfurt a.M.	555,857	26,158	4.71%	5.2%)
Breslau	625,198	20,202	3.23%	4.1%)
Hamburg	1,129,307	16,885	1.5%	3.4%)
Cologne	756,605	14,816	1.96%	3.0%)
Leipzig	713,470	11,564	1.62%	2.3%)
Munich	735,388	9,005	1.22%	1.8%)
Essen	654,461	4,506	.69%	0.9%)
Dresden	642,143	4,397	.68%	0.9%)
Dortmund	540,875	4,108	.76%	0.8%)
Total	10,595,805	272,205	.57%	54.5%)

Source: Statistik des deutschen Reiches: Die Bevölkerung des deutschen Reiches nach den Ergebnissen der Volkszählung 1933. Die Glaubensjuden im deutschen Reich, Vol. 451, Issue 5 (Berlin, 1936), 9.

separate from Gentile society but from West End Jewish life as well. The synagogue, hospital, and high school of the Orthodox stood in the Ostend, as did the synagogue of the Gemeindeorthodox.[40]

In Giessen, the highest concentration of Jews was on Walltorstrasse, in the city center, and Bahnhofstrasse, the central thoroughfare from the train station into town. But Jews resided throughout Giessen,

Map 3. Distribution of Jews in Frankfurt in 1925 by Percentage of Jewish Population

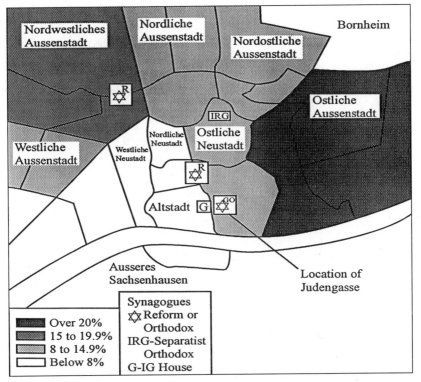

Map 3. Statistically recreated from information in *Statistisches Handbuch der Stadt Frankfurt a. M.: Zweite Ausgabe Enthaltend die Statistik der Jahre 1906/07 bis 1926-27* (Frankfurt, 1928), 69.

settling mainly south of the Altstadt, on Alicenstrasse, Liebigstrasse, Süd- and Westanlage, and in the old city itself, Landgrafenstrasse, Seltersweg, Neustadt, and Marktstrasse. With two exceptions, the Nordanlage (or Werner Wall), which had a sizable number of Orthodox Jews, and Steinstrasse, the site of the IRG synagogue, there was no clear residential segregation of Orthodox and Reform, unlike Frankfurt. It also does not appear that the town's small number of foreign Jews gravitated toward a visible enclave (see Map 4).[41] In Geisenheim, most of the Strauss family lived in the village center on Marktstrasse. The rest of Geisenheim's Jews resided on Kirchstrasse, Landstrasse (in the 1930s, Adolf Hitlerstrasse, today, Winkelerstrasse), and Taunusstrasse (see

Map 4. Location of Jewish Households in Giessen by Percentage of Jewish Population According to 1932, 1933, and 1935 Tax Lists

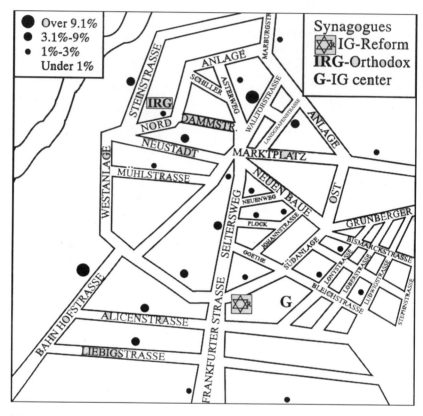

Map 4. *Sources:* "Aufstellung der am 30. 1. 1933 und später in Giessen und Giessen-Wieseck wohnhaft gewesenen jüdischen Personen,""Verzeichnis der zur Israelitischen Religionsgemeinde Giessen steuerpflichtigen Personen: Stand Januar 1932," and "Verzeichnis der Mitglieder der Israelitischen Religionsgesellschaft, Giessen, Stand vom 13. 3. 1935," in Erwin Knauss, *Die jüdische Bevölkerung Giessens, 1933-1945: Eine Dokumentation* (Wiesbaden, 1976), 54-118.

Map 5).[42] Although not as clustered among themselves as their Frankfurt counterparts, Jews in Giessen and Geisenheim were relatively noticeable because of their commercial orientation.

The urban attraction endured for German Jewry primarily because of its unique commercial character.[43] By 1933, over 60 percent of German Jews, as compared to only 18 percent of Gentiles, engaged in

Map 5. Location of Jewish Households in Geisenheim by Percentage of Jewish Population During the Weimar Period

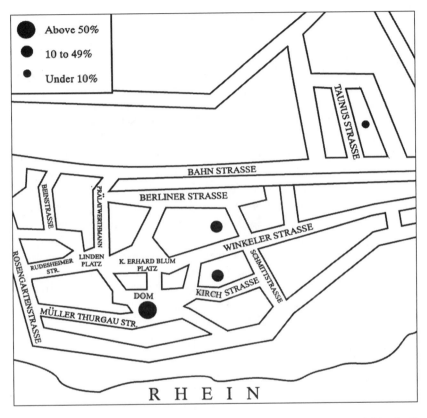

Map 5. *Sources:* "Verzeichnis der abgemeldeten Personen Mai 1928 bis April 1942," Stadtarchiv Geisenheim, 123-03, and the city's "Einwohnerliste," Stadtarchiv Geisenheim, 123-03.

commercial pursuits.[44] Orthodox Jews in Germany were almost exclusively mercantile, devoting their lives to finance and the textile, metal, and cattle trades.[45] The number of Jews with careers in the free professions also stood well above the national rate.[46] At the same time, a mere 1.7 percent of Jews were farmers, in contrast to 28.9 percent of the general population.[47] And one and a half times fewer Jews than Gentiles worked in industry throughout all of Germany.

In the 1920s, roughly half of all Jews in Frankfurt, Giessen, and Geisenheim were merchants. By contrast, about one-third of the general population in Frankfurt and Giessen and only 15.2 percent in Geisenheim dealt in trade. Almost no Jews engaged in agriculture in any of the three communities, although the same could be said for Gentiles in Frankfurt and Giessen, where farming occupied only 1.7 and 2.5 percent of the total population.[48] The percentage of Jews in craft and factory work was one and a half times less than the overall rate in Giessen, twice less than in Frankfurt, and four times less than in Geisenheim. This lower rate was attributable to the inability of Jews to own land or belong to guilds before emancipation, which prevented them from becoming peasants or artisans, the two groups that provided the bulk of Germany's industrial labor force.[49] Antisemites who accused Jews of "avoiding honest and hard labor" conveniently overlooked this fact.

Despite making more money and paying more taxes than Protestants and Catholics in the early 1900s,[50] German Jews experienced a major socioeconomic decline during the Weimar period. Jews who lived on fixed incomes from savings and investments were ruined during the inflation of 1922-23, and small Jewish merchants in Frankfurt, Giessen, and Geisenheim were as likely as their Gentile competitors to be threatened by big, occasionally Jewish-owned, department stores.[51] During the depression, fifty thousand German Jews were out of work, and the percentage of unemployed Jewish men under the age of twenty-five in Frankfurt was higher than the rate for non-Jews (36 versus 30 percent).[52] In 1931, the banker Gustav Brenario estimated that Jews in Frankfurt generated only one-third as much local tax revenue as they had before World War I.[53]

In merchant trade, German Jews mainly sold ready-made wear in small parlors and large department stores. Frankfurt's central shopping promenade, the Zeil, was replete with Jewish clothing stores (Führlander, Oberländer, and Cohn), shoe stores (Joseph, Speier, and Herz), and department stores (Wronker, Schmöller, and Tietz, today Hertie).[54] Most Jewish merchants in Frankfurt, however, had small shops tucked away on side streets, especially in the poorer, eastern part of town where the majority of Orthodox and eastern European Jews lived.[55] Thirty percent of Jewish women in the work force in Frankfurt were merchants, and their contingent of 1,474 amounted to 18 percent of all Jewish merchants in the city by 1925.[56]

Giessen's commercial Jews ranged from tobacco sellers, art dealers, vintners, liquor vendors, furniture salesmen, and watchmakers, to common clothiers and cattle dealers.[57] Jewish stores were located mostly in the center of "old" Giessen, that is, the area of the former wall, on Bahnhofstrasse, Westanlage (in the 1930s, Horst Wessel Wall), Markt-

Table 9. Occupational Structure of Jews and the General Population in Germany in 1907 and 1933 (by percent)

Occupation	1907 Jews	1907 General	1933 Jews	1933 General
Farming or agriculture	1.6	36.8	1.7	28.9
Industry and crafts	27.1	42.0	23.1	40.4
Commerce and trade	62.6	13.0	61.3	18.4
Public service, free professions	8.1	6.5	12.5	8.4
Other	.6	1.7	1.4	3.9
Total	100	100	100	100

Sources: Monika Richarz, *Jüdisches Leben in Deutschland: Selbstzeugnisse zur Sozialgeschichte, 1918-1945* (New York, 1982), 19; *Statistisches Jahrbuch für das deutsche Reich: Zweiundfünfzigster Jahrgang 1933* (Berlin, 1933), 19.

Table 10. Occupational Structure of Jews and the General Population of Hessen and Hessen-Nassau During the Weimar Republic (by percent)

Region	Occupation	Jews	General
Hessen	Farming/agriculture	2.3%	34.5%
	Industry and crafts	17.7%	40.6%
	Commerce and trade	55.2%	14.5%
	Other (independents, public service, free professions)	24.8%	10.4%
	Total	100%	100%
Hessen-Nassau	Farming/agriculture	2.4%	31.7%
	Industry and crafts	16.4%	38.2%
	Commerce and trade	51.9%	17.6%
	Other (independents, public service, free professions	29.3%	12.5%
	Total	100%	100%

Sources: Statistik des deutschen Reiches: Die Bevölkerung des deutschen Reiches nach den Ergebnissen der Volkszählung 1933. Die Glaubensjuden im deutschen Reich, Vol. 451, Issue 5 (Berlin, 1936), 69, 71; *Statistisches Jahrbuch für das deutsche Reich: Zweiundfunfzigster Jahrgang 1933* (Berlin, 1933), 21.

Table 11. Occupational Structure of Jews in Frankfurt, Giessen, and Geisenheim During the Weimar Republic [a](by percent)

Place	Occupation	Jews	General
Frankfurt			
	Farming/agriculture	0.1	1.7
	Industry and crafts	17.9	. 37.8
	Commerce and trade	51.5	32.2
	Public service and free professions	5.1	5.5
	Health care	4.0	3.3
	Domestic and other	5.2	9.5
	No profession (retired, self-supporting, welfare recipients, students)	16.2	10.0
	Total	100	100
Giessen			
	Farming/agriculture	0.7	2.5
	Industry and crafts	17.8	27.5
	Commerce and trade	51.9	31.0
	Public service and free professions	7.3	28.8
	Health care	4.3	(included above)
	Domestic, other, and no profession	18.0	10.2
	Total	100	100
Geisenheim			
	Farming/agriculture	0.0	34.8
	Industry and crafts	9.1	39.9[b]
	Commerce and trade	54.5	15.2
	Public service, health care, free professions	9.1	10.1
	Domestic, other, and no profession	27.3	(included above)
	Total	100	100

Sources: Statistische Jahresübersichten der Stadt Frankfurt a.M. Ausgabe für das Jahr 1927/28, Erstes Ergänzungsheft zum Statistischen Handbuch der Stadt Frankfurt a.M. Zweite Ausgabe (Frankfurt, 1929), 19-22; Heinrich Silbergleit, "Die jüdische Wohnbevölkerung am 16. Juni 1925 nach Wirtschaftsabteilungen, -gruppen, und -zweigen sowie nach der Stellung im Beruf," in *Die Bevölkerungs -und Berufsverhält-nisse der Juden im Deutschen Reich : Freistaat Preussen* (Berlin, 1930),231-33;"Aufstel-
a The figures for Frankfurt come from statistics published between 1925 and 1928, those for Giessen and Geisenheim refer to the years 1932 and 1933.
b In Geisenheim, many workers were also farmers, supplementing their income with two jobs.

Table 12. Comparison of Jewish and Gentile Social Status in Germany and Frankfurt During the Weimar Republic (by percent)

Region	Standing	Jews[a]	Gentiles
Germany	Independents	46.1	17.3
	Salaried employees	34.3	16.5
	Wage laborers	8.7	45.1
	Domestic servants	1.2	4.1
	Working family dependents	9.7	17.0
	Total	100	100
Frankfurt	Independents	58.16	19.12
	Salaried employees	33.13	33.84
	Wage laborers	7.34	45.75
	Domestic servants and working family dependents	1.37	1.29
	Total	100	100

Sources: Statistisches Jahrbuch für das deutsche Reich: Zweiundfünfzigster Jahrgang 1933 (Berlin, 1933), 19; *Statistisches Jahrbuch für das deutsche Reich* (Berlin, 1938), 22; *Statistische Jahresübersichten der Stadt Frankfurt a.m. Ausgabe für das Jahr 1927/28, Erstes Ergänzungsheft zum Statistischen Handbuch der Stadt Frankfurt a.m. Zweite Ausgabe* (Frankfurt, 1929), 19-22; Heinrich Silbergleit, "Die jüdische Wohnbevölkerung am 16. Juni 1925 nach Wirtschaftsabteilungen, -gruppen, und -zweigen sowie nach der Stellung im Beruf," in *Die Bevölkerungs -und Berufsverhältnisse der Juden im Deutschen Reich: Freistaat Preussen* (Berlin, 1930), 231-33; Heuberger, *Hinaus aus dem Ghetto*, 168.
a The figures for Jews in Germany come from 1933 statistics, whereas the other percentages, although reported in later yearbooks (1927, 1928, 1933) refer to the census of 1925.

Table 11 *(cont'd.)*
lungder am 30.1.1933 und später in Giessen und Giessen-Wieseck wohnhaft gewesenen jüdischen Personen," 54-111, in Knauss, *Die jüdische Bevölkerung Giessens, 1933-1945: Eine Dokumentation* (Wiesbaden, 1976), 112-18; *Statistik des deutschen Reiches: Die berufliche- und soziale Gliederung der Bevölkerung des deutschen Reiches. Süddeutschland und Hessen*, Vol. 456, Issue 33 (Berlin, 1935), 36; Wolf-Heino Struck, *Die Geschichte der Stadt Geisenheims* (Frankfurt, 1972), 266; "Verzeichnis der abgemeldeten Personen Mai 1928 bis April 1942," Stadtarchiv Geisenheim, 123-03, and the city's "Einwohnerliste," Stadtarchiv Geisenheim, 123-03. The Giessen record lists 1,266 Jews, but there were only 855 Jews in the city as of 1933. The Statistical Office of the Giessen City Archives completed the list between 1961 and 1962, not only including Jews from the surrounding northern suburb of Wieseck but also those individuals labeled as Jewish (*Volljuden*) by the 1935 Nuremberg Laws. This accounts for the increase in number.

strasse, Steinstrasse, Nordanlage (Wernerwall), and Walltorstrasse (see Map 5).[58] Nearly 73 percent of the town's taxpaying Orthodox Jews were merchants compared to only 41.5 percent of its Reform Jews. And like their Frankfurt counterparts, Orthodox Jewish merchants in Giessen tended to run smaller operations. Many Jewish women who worked in town also did so as merchants, either as independent store owners or partners in business with their spouses.[59] In Geisenheim, the most interesting aspect of Jewish merchants there was their genetic relationship: five out of six were members of the extended Strauss family. Max and Liebmann Strauss owned a furniture shop, Georg Strauss a feed store. Jewish businesses in Geisenheim were located primarily in the center of the village near the cathedral.[60]

German Jews also worked in finance, but not to the extent that antisemites often alleged. Although Jews directed 45 percent of Germany's private banks during the Weimar period, they controlled less than 1 percent of its more powerful joint-stock banks and credit institutions.[61] Likewise, though Jews were particularly active in Frankfurt's financial scene in the early and middle decades of the nineteenth century, their involvement in banking steadily declined as the twentieth century approached. In 1812, 37 percent of all Frankfurt Jews were active in banking; by 1875, that ratio had fallen to 17.9 percent. During the Weimar period, only 5 percent of the city's Jews were in banking. In Giessen as of 1932, 7 of 289 bankers were Jews, and 4 of those were bank directors.[62]

Not surprisingly, in industry and crafts, German Jews were concentrated in textiles. During the republic, twenty-two thousand Jews worked in the clothing industry. Almost one-third of them were women and *Ostjuden* who labored as spinners, weavers, milliners, and shoemakers.[63] Like their counterparts in banking, German Jewish industrialists overall became fewer in number over the course of the nineteenth and early twentieth centuries. In Frankfurt, however, the proportion of Jews who took part in industry increased from 13 percent in 1876 to 18 percent in 1925, and only 20 percent of those Jews were day laborers (*Arbeiter*).[64] Areas of Jewish specialization in Frankfurt industry included textiles, luxury goods, food production, metalwork, tailoring, cookery, and leatherwork. One of the city's prominent Jewish industries was Cassella and Company, a chemical and dye manufactory that merged with I.G. Farben in 1925. In Giessen, according to a 1932 tax list and a 1933 residence list, there were ten Jewish industrialists (one of whom owned a soap factory, another a varnish and dye plant), twenty-three factory workers, twelve butchers, sixteen tailors, six bakers, three shoemakers, and numerous other craftsmen.[65] The 1933 list of Giessen's Jews also revealed fifty-six female domestic servants, the largest occupational concentration of Jewish women in the town, many of whom were also housewives, widows, and merchants.[66] Geisenheim's lone Jewish artisan, Felix Neufeld, was a butcher, and the only woman listed with a profession was Marir Heitlinger, a domestic servant.[67]

The entry of Jews into the free professions was a further hallmark of their postemancipation metamorphosis (as well as an added grievance among antisemites). By 1933, 16.2 percent of Germany's lawyers, 10.8 percent of its doctors, 8.6 percent of its dentists, 5 percent of its writers, 2.6 percent of its university professors, and 4 percent of its university students were Jews.[68] In Frankfurt, a 1913 figure put the number of Jewish doctors at 147 (out of 405 citywide, or 36 percent), the number of Jewish dentists at 17 (out of 67, 25 percent), and the number of Jewish lawyers at 133 (out of 218, 62 percent).[69] Many Jews also held positions at Frankfurt's Johann Wolfgang von Goethe Universität, among them law school dean Berthold Freudenthal, scientist Karl Herxheimer, art historian Georg Swarzenski, sociologists Franz Oppenheimer and Karl Mannheim, historian Ernst Kantorowicz, mathematician Paul Epstein, Orientalist Josef Horovitz, the father of Gestalt psychology, Max Werthheimer, founder of the Frankfurt Institute for Psychoanalysis, Erich Fromm, and the renowned philosopher Martin Buber. After 1933, the Nazis discharged over 30 percent of the university's professors because of their Jewish origins.[70] In addition, the proportion of Jewish students attending the university was disproportionately high at 10 percent.[71] Finally, the Marxist-oriented Institut für Sozialforschung, founded by Felix Weil and led by Carl Grünberg, constituted a major force in sociological research although it often prompted the association of Jews with left-wing causes.

Jews were prominent in Frankfurt politics in the 1920s but as adherents of a variety of political affiliations, from Democrats and Liberals to Socialists and a few Conservatives. Democrat Ludwig Landmann was lord mayor of the city from 1924 to 1933, Social Democrat Bruno Asch served as *Bürgermeister* in the Frankfurt suburb of Höchst, and Bertha Pappenheim, Henriette Fürth, and Jenny Apolant were active in welfare organizations. In cultural affairs, Jewish activity was diverse as well, and not, as antisemites claimed, uniformly modernist. The Jewish-funded Neues Theater (New Theater) was a forum of experimentalism, but it also staged plays dealing with traditional Jewish life;

more important, it was popular among Gentile theatergoers. Other Jews who were involved in the cultural life of the city in the 1920s included the stage actress Mathilde Einzig.[72] Prolific, too, were Jewish artists, including Jakob Nussbaum, Hans Nathan Feibusch, Samson Schames, and Benno Elkan, writers such as Ludwig Fulda, publishers like Heinrich Simon, and journalists like Siegfried Kracauer (none especially modernist).[73] Fulda in particular typified the tragedy of Jews in German culture. In 1926, he was inducted into the Berlin Academy of Poets, and seven years later, the Vienna Civic Theater awarded him its prestigious "Ring." He had written in defiance of antisemites, but in 1939, his view of Germany long since shattered, he committed suicide at the age of seventy-two.[74]

In Giessen in 1933, there were seven lawyers, eighteen doctors, four dentists, and nine teachers in the Jewish community.[75] Although most working Jewish women in the city were either domestic servants or merchants, four were doctors and four were kindergarten teachers.[76] Hedwig Burgheim, the director of an institute for the training of elementary and preschool teachers, was an important Jewish pedagogue in Giessen in the 1920s.[77] Margarete Bieber was an archaeologist and art historian at the Universität before her emigration to England in the early 1930s. Other Jewish personalities at the university in the Weimar era included historian Richard Laqueur, Orientalist Julius Levy, economist Paul Mombert, and psychologists Erich Stern and Kurt Koffka.[78] Literature, too, had its Jewish contingent. Alfred Bock, listed without a profession in the 1932 tax list, wrote novels; his son Werner was a poet and a member of the German Academy for Language and Poetry.[79] Geisenheim's lone Jewish professional was a physician, Dr. Siegfried Nathan, after whom a street in the village is now named.[80]

In Germany as a whole and in the Hessian lands, the Jewish population increased numerically but not proportionately before 1910. Between 1910 and 1933, Jews declined both numerically and proportionately in Germany, Hessen-Darmstadt, and Hessen-Nassau. A relative drop in percentage intersected with a numerical increase in the size of Frankfurt's Jewish community by 1910. The city's Jewish population grew until 1925 but shrank in the later years of the republic. Giessen's Jewish population reached a high point numerically in 1910 but dwindled over the next twenty years. In Geisenheim, the Jewish community had begun to decline before 1910 and continued to do so during the Weimar period.

Jews preserved a pattern of urban migration into the republican era. When they settled in places like Frankfurt, Giessen, and Geisenheim, they chose areas based on economics, social class, and culture. Poorer, more traditional Jews clustered together in Frankfurt's East End, while the more affluent and secular settled in the city's north and west districts. In Giessen, Orthodox and Reform Jews exhibited a more integrated living pattern among themselves, but they were still heavily bunched around the area of the old city. Almost all of Geisenheim's Jews lived on three streets in the town center. During the Weimar years, Jews in all three towns remained concentrated in trade, but in Frankfurt and Giessen they achieved prominence in politics and culture as well.

In the end, the economic and political uncertainty of the Weimar era perpetuated, and then, during the Great Depression (1929-32), hastened German Jewry's demographic decline. As Jews faced the dual burden of financial hardship and rising antisemitism in the later years of the republic, Jewish emigration, communal secession, and conversion rose while intermarriage decreased. Ultimately more threatening to the survival of Germany's Jewish communities than their demographic cascade, however, was the collapse of democracy and the establishment of Hitler's National Socialist regime.

The Liberal-Jewish Model: Under Attack from Within

No single Jewish voice addressed the challenges facing German Jewry in the Weimar period. In fact, in order to understand the texture of Gentile-Jewish interaction, it is necessary first to describe the complex ways in which Jews themselves tackled questions of identity during the republican years. An analysis of intracommunal Jewish relations in the Hessian towns of Frankfurt am Main, Giessen, and Geisenheim provides an appreciation not only of the heterogeneity of Germany's Jewish communities but also of the role communal institutions continued to play in shaping German Jewish identity in the context of rising antisemitism and demographic contraction.

During the Weimar era, the liberal Jewish model of *Bildung*, progressive theology, and cosmopolitanism came under increasing attack from Orthodox Jews, who feared its secular implications; from Zionists, who bemoaned the persistence of Jew-hatred and the loss of Jewish national identity;[1] from right-wing German Jewish patriots, who sought to cancel the equation of Jew and liberal;[2] and from radical left-wing Jewish intellectuals, who rejected liberalism's patriotic elements.[3] Growing numbers of Jewish voters were also turning away from the liberal German Democratic Party (DDP) and embracing both the Catholic Center Party (Zentrum) and the more left-wing Social Democratic Party (SPD). The effects of this multifaceted, anti-liberal offensive on Jewish assimilation and Gentile-Jewish relations were admittedly modest. The liberal paradigm endured as the defining element of German Jewish identity throughout the republican period, while most non-Jews remained uninterested in Jewish integration.[4]

Holding its meetings in a former Rothschilds bank house, the main Jewish community in Frankfurt (the Israelitische Gemeinde) administered synagogues, an Orthodox Yeshiva, a ritual bath, a cemetery, a library, and a museum of Jewish antiquities.[5] The Gemeinde also published a news journal (the *Frankfurt Israelitisches Gemeindeblatt*) and created several commissions to deal with culture, welfare, the maintenance of the Jewish hospital, and the functioning of the community's primary and secondary school, the Philanthropin.[6] Of the four IG synagogues, two were liberal or Reform (the West End synagogue on Königsstrasse and the main synagogue in the Börnestrasse), and two were Orthodox (the Börneplatz and Böckenheim synagogues).[7]

As of 1925, five rabbis were on the Gemeinde payroll—three Reform (Caesar Seligmann, Arnold Lazarus, and Georg Salzberger) and two Orthodox (Jakob Horovitz and Jakob Hoffmann, who succeeded Nehemiah Anton Nobel after his death in 1922). Seligmann, the rabbi of the West End synagogue, became one of the major figures in the Reform movement over the course of the 1920s, founding the German Association of Liberal Judaism and the Association of Liberal Rabbis in Germany. Salzberger was cofounder of the Society for Jewish Education, an institution of Jewish culture. From 1910 to 1922, the leader of the Gemeindeorthodox was Nehemiah Nobel. Of Hungarian descent like his predecessor Markus Horovitz, Nobel studied under the Neo-Kantian philosopher Hermann Cohen seeking a synthesis of Orthodox tradition and modern Zionism. Reform Jews repeatedly protested references to the Land of Israel in Nobel's sermons, and he eventually purged them of their more nationalist elements.[8] His successor, Jakob Hoffmann, was also a committed Zionist. Jakob Horovitz presided over the Orthodox religious school on Unterlindau.

Article 137 of Germany's Constitution of 2 August 1919 officially proclaimed the separation of church and state and accorded legal and fiscal equality to the various Jewish religious communities within the Reich. This meant that the Gemeinden were, for the first time, on equal footing with their Christian counterparts. In Frankfurt, this constitutional change prompted a wholesale restructuring of the main Jewish community. On 31 May 1920, the leadership of the Frankfurt IG approved a new charter which created a fifteen-member executive council and a representative board of twenty-seven individuals. Seventeen Reform (or Liberal) and ten Orthodox constituted the first representative delegation after the war.[9] The Orthodox group included two Zionists and two representatives of the city's *Ostjuden*. Of the fifteen executive council members, nine were Reform, six Conservative. The chair of the council during the years of the Weimar Republic was Julius Blau, a lawyer and Reform member of the IG since 1894.[10]

In 1919, German women won the right to vote in all elections, and Germany's Jewish communities reacted accordingly, extending suffrage to members of both sexes as long as they paid communal dues and were twenty years of age or older. The Frankfurt IG was the first

Jewish institution in Germany to allow women to vote and to hold community office. By 1924, four women held seats on the representative assembly, and one was a member of the executive council.[11] Surprisingly, it was not Reform activism that made female suffrage within the IG possible but its gradual acceptance by the *Gemeinde-orthodox* and their spiritual leader Nehemiah Nobel, who turned to the Talmud to justify his supportive position.[12] Jewish women were already making contributions to numerous IG organizations. Among them were the Jewish Women's Association, founded in 1847 with the purpose of caring for orphans; the Jewish Women's Union, concerned with the welfare of poor women and children; the Orthodox Stronghold for Jewish Girls, founded in 1913; the Daniel Doctor Foundation, founded in 1769 to help young Jewish women; the Women's Association of the Frankfurt Lodge; and the Jewish Vacation Home for Women and Girls, founded in 1914 with administrative offices in Frankfurt.[13] The opening up of community institutions to Jewish women widened their spheres of contribution to Jewish life, from private, domestic work to political and welfare activity.

The first legislative period of the IG council, which lasted until 1923, was plagued by internal discord and financial insolvency. The inflation of 1923 nearly brought the community to the brink of bankruptcy as expenses far exceeded income. During the fiscal year 1922-23, the IG spent over eighteen million marks (two million more than it took in) to maintain the Philanthropin, the community hospital, the local branch of the CV, and the library, among other organizations. In December 1922, the *Frankfurt Israelitisches Gemeindeblatt* warned of impending fiscal doom, and six months later, the IG council increased the fee for renting out rooms and halls in the synagogues by four hundred times the 1918 rate.[14] In 1926, the IG continued to raise the ire of members by hiking its "culture fee" from 15 percent of individual income tax to 18 percent.[15]

Political developments within the IG during the 1920s were equally troublesome, characterized by conflict between its Reform and Orthodox factions and a gradual yielding to Orthodox and Zionist demands on the part of the Reform wing.[16] According to Reform rabbi Caesar Seligmann, "all efforts to find common ground with liberal ritual failed because of the conservatives [i.e. Orthodox] within the community, the hefty opposition of the separatist Orthodox, and the Zionists."[17] Disputes between observant and more liberal Jews had been commonplace in the imperial period, and they intensified after the publication of the Reform Code of Conduct (*Richtlinien für das liberale Judentum*) by a general assembly of Germany's liberal rabbis in 1912.[18] In the 1920s, Orthodox members of the IG and their mouthpiece, the Central Association of Jewish Community Members, continued their attack on liberal Judaism, demanding a return to religious tradition.[19] Orthodox Jews were able to exert more influence on the curriculum of the Philanthropin, and they received increased funding for their religious school and Yeshiva, as well as support for the construction of a new synagogue (which was never built).

Adding to the divisions within the community was the Jewish People's Party (Jüdische Volkspartei, JVP), which received seven seats on the communal diet in March 1926.[20] Under the leadership of Julius Simon, a lawyer, the JVP assimilated much of the Zionist and Orthodox agenda, defending religious tradition and assailing Reform Jews for rejecting Jewish nationalism. The JVP, the Zionists, and most Orthodox Jews also favored cooperation with the Jewish Agency, an organization founded in 1929 with the purpose of fostering Jewish emigration to Palestine. Blau and most Reform Jews initially opposed collaborating with the Agency because it entailed patronage of a nationalist cause. After much debate, Blau took a seat on the Jewish Agency Council, but not as an official representative of the Frankfurt Jewish Community.[21]

A cultural forum that bridged the gap between Zionists, Orthodox, and Reform Jews was the Free Jewish House of Learning (Das Freie Jüdische Lehrhaus).[22] In late 1919, Rabbi Salzberger and community representative Eugen Mayer, among others, founded the Society for Jewish Education. It became the Free Jewish House of Learning after Franz Rosenzweig, a Kassel-born philosopher and historian who had criticized the Society's secular orientation, became its director in 1920. A model of adult Jewish education, the Lehrhaus offered lectures and courses in scripture, the Hebrew language, Jewish law, Jewish history, mysticism, and philosophy. It was, in many respects, Rosenzweig's personal gift to secular Jews like himself who had lost ties to Judaism. Growing up in an assimilated environment and nearly opting for baptism in 1913, Rosenzweig returned to the Jewish community after a "transcendent" experience in a local shul. His major work, *Star of Redemption*, written while he was a soldier in World War I, detailed his transformation of conscience.[23]

According to Jehuda Reinharz, Rosenzweig advocated the study of classical sources and a renewed practice of Jewish law to reorient German Jews toward their religion. He believed that no inflexible guidelines could be set for a new educational movement except for sincere and honest attempts to learn and understand. Learning would turn ritual observance and ceremony into an informed and valid manifestation of religious truth. In this way, Rosenzweig rejected the Orthodox dogma that emphasized legal and mechanistic observances of Jewish law.[24]

In its first semester, the Lehrhaus had five hundred students in attendance. Classes were held in rented halls, synagogues, and private homes, from six to ten in the evening, Monday through Thursday.[25] Among its many lecturers were Nobel, Salzberger, and Seligmann, along with Zionist Richard Lichtheim and chemist Eduard Strauss. Because of his commanding oratorical skills, Nobel's offering on Halacha (Jewish law) was the most popular course during the Lehrhaus's first semester. Others who participated in the school's lecture series were Nachum Glatzer, Ernst Simon, Leo Strauss, Gershom Scholem, Erich Fromm, Margarete Sussmann, and Samuel Joseph Agnon. The most well-known member of the Lehrhaus was Martin Buber, philosopher, mystic, Zionist, and professor at Frankfurt University. A deep friendship developed between Rosenzweig and Buber, and the two collaborated on a German translation of the Torah until Rosenzweig succumbed to lateral sclerosis in 1929.[26] Perhaps more significant for this study was that the House of Learning never attracted more than 4 percent of Frankfurt's Jewish population, and regular lectures ceased after 1926.[27] So while communal relations may have benefited at an elite, intellectual level from the activities of the Lehrhaus, efforts to sustain the interest of ordinary Jews were less successful.

Accompanying recurring frays within the Gemeinde was the task of dealing with the separatist Orthodox Israelitische Religionsgesellschaft. From 1890 to 1926, Salomon Breuer, the son-in-law of Samson Raphael Hirsch, held the IRG's rabbinical post. Breuer, like Nehemiah Nobel, came from Hungary and held to a thoroughly Orthodox perspective. Under his direction, the IRG opened a new synagogue on Friedberger Anlage in 1907, established a Yeshiva, and financed a host of institutions: the Samson Raphael Hirsch School, which was open even to Orthodox members of the IG, a rabbinical seminary, a newspaper (Der Israelit), a ritual bath, a hospital, a cemetery, and several kosher eateries.[28] Yet the search for a successor to Breuer, who died in 1926, split the IRG into two camps. One group supported the appointment of Breuer's son Raphael, then rabbi in Aschaffenburg. The other, led by Jakob Rosenheim, argued that the Hirsch-Breuer dynasty had actually weakened Orthodox cohesiveness. A compromise candidate, Rabbi Josef Jona Horovitz from Hundsdorf, took office in the summer of 1929 after a year of tumultuous infighting. In the midst of this internal power struggle, on 16 April 1928, the IRG attained legal equality with the established Gemeinde.[29]

From existing sources it is difficult to measure the full extent of improvement in relations between the two communities during the later years of the republic. We do know that in the Hirsch-Breuer era, the relationship between the Orthodox Religious Society and the main Jewish community had been turbulent. Breuer was an outspoken opponent of the religious leaders of the IG, even Orthodox rabbis Markus Horovitz and Nehemiah Nobel. According to one memoir, Breuer refused to attend Horovitz's funeral in 1910.[30] He was less fond of Nobel, an Orthodox (Mizrachi) Zionist. As a way of countering the Mizrachi, the IRG established a local affiliate of the Polish Orthodox organization Agudas Israel. Following in the path of the Free Association for the Interests of Orthodox Jewry, a group formed by Samson Raphael Hirsch in 1885 as an alternative to the liberal, German-Jewish Community Association, the Frankfurt office of Agudas Israel promoted Orthodox Jewish religious interests. The eventual leader of Agudas's international body, Jakob Rosenheim, had been the editor of the Orthodox newspaper, *Der Israelit*, in 1906. He had also co-founded the Association for Protection Against the Dismissal of Employees Who Observe the Sabbath, a group that served as both employment agency and insurance company for Frankfurt's Orthodox Jews.[31]

The *Ostjuden* problem exacerbated the fragmentation of Frankfurt Jewry. Fleeing persecution in the late nineteenth and early twentieth centuries, Polish and Russian Jewish refugees settled in large German towns as small merchants and traders. They brought with them a different language, Yiddish, a deeper commitment to religious tradition, and a more "national" sense of identity. By 1925, nearly 20 percent of German Jewry hailed from eastern Europe.[32] In Frankfurt, *Ostjuden* clustered in the cheapest part of the city's eastern district, the Ostend, where they established their own house of worship (the Stibl) and several small chapels.[33] Residentially, economically, and culturally set apart from their German Jewish counterparts, eastern European Jews received an ambivalent welcome from Frankfurt's two Jewish communities. Bruno Ostrovsky, a Zionist doctor who lived in the city until 1919 and who later married an *Ostjudin*, described the relationship as one between the "Jewish People" or *jüdisches Volk*—his term for the *Ostjuden,*—and "Jewish cosmopolitans" or *jüdische Weltbürger*—native-born secular, Reform, and Orthodox Jews of the middle and upper middle classes.[34] Liberal Jewish leaders greeted the new immigrants with a mixture of private disdain and public activism. Simultaneously aware of the need for relief work and of the potential fuel *Ostjuden* provided for antisemites, Reform Jews distanced themselves from their eastern European coreligionists while seeking to "Germanize" them as best they could through education and welfare. In the end, the majority of *Ostjuden* became members of the established Gemeinde (IG), mainly because they received a cooler reception from the separatist Religious Society and had little desire to endure the process of communal secession.[35]

A network of Gemeinde welfare institutions provided an additional impetus for eastern European Jews to remain within the IG fold. In 1919, the community created the Consular Department for Eastern European Jewish Refugees which managed assistance to the city's *Ostjuden.* One year later, welfare efforts on behalf of the Gemeinde were brought under the rubric of the Center for Jewish Welfare Work. During the 1920s, a Jewish Loan Account made loans available to a host of Jewish artisans and merchants, and two pre-Weimar organizations, the Association of Independent Jewish Craftsmen and Merchants and the Association for the Promotion of Craftsmen of Jewish Faith, continued to act as charitable and educational foundations. The Jewish Women's Union concerned itself with female *Ostjüdinnen,* as did noted Frankfurt philanthropist Bertha Pappenheim's Home for Orphans and Unwed Mothers, established in 1907.[36] Further centralization of Jewish welfare efforts came in 1929 with the founding of the Frankfurt am Main Public Jewish Welfare Work, or the OJW (Offene Jüdische Wohlfahrtspflege FfM), which had under its aegis the Center for Jewish Welfare Work, the Charity Fund of the Jewish Community, the local office of the Jewish Relief Association, and the Working Community for the Fight Against Tuberculosis Among Jews.[37] On the council of the OJW sat three IG members and two representatives from the Religious Society.

Zionism provided an additional challenge to Jewish communal unity. First, Zionists rejected the belief that a Jew could be nationally German and confessionally Jewish, especially in light of persistent antisemitism and increasing religious nonobservance. Second, by engaging in welfare work for *Ostjuden* and providing them with a political discourse to which they could relate, Zionists undercut efforts by the IG to provide relief and concurrently transform eastern European Jews into respectable German citizens. Third, Zionists angered IG leadership by drawing support from several *Gemeindeorthodox* who agreed with Zionism's philanthropic activism and its focus on national regeneration.[38] Most Reform and many Orthodox Jews feared that antisemites would wrongly seize upon Zionist nationalist rhetoric to portray Zionism as the defining ideology for German Jewry and thereby arouse support for their program of de-emancipation. Ultra-Orthodox Jews of the IRG also objected to Zionism on spiritual grounds. In their eyes, only divine intervention, not a secular movement, could legitimate the creation of a Jewish homeland.

In 1897, the Zionists established an office of the Zionist Association for Germany (Zionistische Vereinigung für Deutschland, ZVfD) in Frankfurt to promote Jewish nationalism, social work for poor Jews, and Jewish settlement in Palestine. During the 1920s, membership in the Frankfurt ZVfD grew from 153 to 600, and membership in the organization nationwide peaked in 1923 at 33,339.[39] Zionist sport clubs from the pre-1914 era, like Association Bar Kochba and the Blue-White hiking union, also remained popular in the city during the republic.[40] But the Zionists were no more unified than their Reform and Orthodox counterparts. The Cartel of Jewish Associations (Kartell Jüdischer Verbindungen, KJV), the main Zionist student group in Frankfurt, was divided on a variety of issues, such as the necessity to participate in university activities.[41] The Association of Jewish Students (Saronia) emerged within the KJV as a *Stammtisch*, a specially reserved section or table in a meeting place, and it too suffered a split.[42]

All disunity aside, the list in Table 13 reveals the emergence of several Zionist organizations in Frankfurt in the early 1920s and early 1930s (before 1933). This is important for our consideration of Jewish integration, particularly if the 1920s are to be seen as a period of heightened Jewish assimilation on both the established liberal model, with its emphasis on *Bildung* and its tendency to foster a cultural appreciation of Jewishness, and the Orthodox paradigm, *Torah im derekh Eretz* (Torah with the way of the land). One of the reasons for the rise of Zionist associations during the early years of the republic was the perception that Zionism had become a viable political option in the wake of the Balfour Declaration of 1917. Chronic antisemitism in the political and social realms also led many to conclude that the solutions offered by the main Reform and Orthodox communities no longer

Table 13. Jewish Associations in Frankfurt in the 1920s

Name	Founding year	Ideology
Frankfurt Lodge	1888	Liberal
Association of German Students of the Jewish Faith Nassovia	1896	Liberal
Jewish Literary Society	1902	Orthodox
Mizrachi	1903	Religious Zionism
Association of Jewish Academics	1906	Orthodox
Agudat Israel	1912	Orthodox
Jewish Hiking Union (Blue-White)	1912	Zionist
Sport Association Bar Kochba	1913	Zionist/nationalist
Association of Jewish Students Saronia	1917	Zionist
Zeire Mizrachi	1918	Religious Zionism
Jewish Youth Union (Esra)	1918	Orthodox
Imperial Union of Jewish Front Soldiers	1919	Patriotic German
Hermann Cohen Lodge	1920	Liberal
Marcus Horovitz Lodge	1920	Liberal
Brith Haolim (Young Jewish Hiking Union)	1920	Socialist Zionist
Zionist Association Hasmonea	1920	Zionist
Union of Zionist Revisionists	1924	Revisionist Zionist
Jewish Liberal Youth Association	1925	Liberal
Youth Group of the Jewish Women's Union	1925	Neutral
"Kadimah" Union of Jewish Youth	1925	Zionist
Gymnastics and Sport Association "Schild"	1925	Patriotic German
Union of Jewish Boy Scouts	1926	Neutral
Jewish Gymnastics Union	1926	Orthodox
Conservative Jewish Youth Association FfM	1927	Orthodox
Jewish Youth Union OF	1928	Neutral
Zionist-Revisionist Youth Group Herzliah	1929	Revisionist Zionist
Jewish Workers Sport Club	1930	
Brith Trumpeldor	1930	Revisionist Zionist
Zionist Student Group	1930	Zionist
"Black Flag"	1932	Patriotic German

Source: Arnsberg, Die Geschichte der Frankfurter Juden, 2:48-55.

worked. Although Zionist organizations continued to surface in Frankfurt, membership in the national Zionist Association actually declined after 1923, as hopes for the realization of Balfour's promise dwindled and the situation for German Jews seemed to normalize.[43]

Despite their small numbers, Zionists put Reform Jews and mainstream community organizations like the Centralverein on the defensive. The CV formally dissociated itself from Zionism in 1912, following a session in Posen, and established an Antizionist Committee one year later to combat Zionism through newspaper advertisements.[44] In 1927, the Association of Liberal Rabbis issued another statement on Zionism: "The basic character of Judaism is and must remain religious. We reject any attempt to cultivate a purely nationalistic Jewish identity. We do grant each individual the right to take his own personal stance on Zionism. We only hope that the settling of Palestine will follow in a spirit which cultivates Jewish religiosity." Nonsectarian members of Reform Judaism's communal apparatus and the liberal Jewish press responded angrily to the rabbis' moderate resolution, which created an additional division within the German Jewish community.[45]

Ultimately, neither the Zionists nor the CV (with its "Anti-Anti" pamphlet campaign) achieved the shared goal of eliminating antisemitic prejudice, but some historians have wrongly minimized the antidefamation and community-building efforts of Frankfurt's non-Zionist Reform and Orthodox Jews.[46] They discount the vast Frankfurt Jewish welfare network and the Free Jewish House of Learning, whose support from ordinary Jews was admittedly modest.[47] A greater success viewed from the perspective of Jewish membership was the Frankfurt Lodge of B'nai Brith, founded in 1888.[48] The popularity of the Frankfurt Lodge prompted the postwar creation of two additional lodges, the Markus Horovitz Lodge and the Hermann Cohen Lodge. Reform and Orthodox members of the IG took part in the activities of the Frankfurt Lodge, but the IRG (under Hirsch) kept its distance and criticized the *Gemeindeorthodox* for cooperating with liberal Jews.[49]

Apostasy, nonobservance, and secularization among Jews constituted added burdens for Reform, Orthodox, and Zionist leaders in Frankfurt over the course of the Weimar period.[50] Only 41 percent of IG members on average attended synagogue on High Holy Days during the late 1920s.[51] Individual examples of this decline in religiosity can be found in the Reform surgeon Albert Ettlinger, the communist activist Emil Carlebach, and Gemeinde council member Selmar Spier. Both Ettlinger and Carlebach rejected their Orthodox roots, and, despite his membership on the IG council, Spier had equally harsh words for

Reform: "Liberal Judaism . . . had lost me. A synagogue with an organ was no synagogue for me. I finally stopped going to services, unless it was out of a social obligation or . . . curiosity as a tourist."[52] Reform leaders of the IG were more accommodating of secular or nondemoninational Jews in the early years of the republic, but they could afford to be. The addition of *Ostjuden* and migrating Jews from elsewhere in Germany between 1910 and 1925 had doubled the community's size from approximately 9,000 to nearly 18,500.

Meanwhile, Orthodox leaders condemned both secularization and nonobservance as instruments of moral decay, while Zionists, advocates of a secular, political ideology, were more critical of Jews who lacked any connection to their Jewishness. Orthodox Jews, Zionists, and a growing number of Reform Jews likewise perceived intermarriage and conversion as threats to communal survival, but Orthodox Jews were the most vocal in their linkage of secularism, mixed marriage, and Jewish communal decline.[53] Some rabbis such as Reform leader Caesar Seligmann viewed the controversy over secularization as much ado about nothing: "The participation in Jewish community life, interest in tradition and history, . . . the growth of Jewish learning centers . . . the emergence of new social institutions, and welfare organizations . . . are all evidence of a growth in Jewish community spirit."[54]

While Jews in Frankfurt felt a growing need to sustain religious, cultural, and political forms of Jewish identity over the course of the 1920s, most never avoided an opportunity to express pride in their German nationality.[55] In 1929, Richard Merzbach, chairman of the Jewish Community Council in Frankfurt, proudly opened a meeting with news of a round-the-world flight by the *Graf Zeppelin*.[56] In the years of the republic, more than ever, the words of Kurt Alexander appeared to ring true: "For us, being German is not a political, but rather a spiritual and emotional concept. For us, being German is an inner experience. In our souls, we can no longer distinguish between what is German and what is Jewish. German and Jewish are fused into oneness in our souls, and never can any power on earth tear the German, the love of our homeland, out of our hearts."[57] Neither wholly delusional nor wholly justified, this view was dependent on the goodwill of a Gentile populace that was, at the very least, inconsistent in its behavior toward Jews—sometimes tolerant, occasionally hostile, and mostly indifferent.

Unlike its Frankfurt counterpart, Giessen's IG suffered only mild internal division. From 1829 to 1896, one rabbi, Benedict Samuel Levi, had held the post as the community's chief spiritual leader. In 1833, he published a treatise titled "The Admissability of German Choir Hymns with Organ Accompaniment," which supported their introduction into Jewish services. However, Levi distanced himself from the more radical movement in town, the Jewish Friends of Reform, because it advocated a harsher break with traditional religious ritual. The lengthy duration of Levi's tenure, coupled with his commitment to a moderate brand of Reform Judaism, provided the community with a sense of stability over the course of the nineteenth century. It was also under Levi's leadership that the IG experienced significant growth. Between 1828 and 1890, the number of Jews in Giessen rose from 200 to 720. Initially, the community held services in a chapel on the old Marktplatz, moving there from a small house in the Judengasse. In 1867, as a consequence of the increase in the town's Jewish population, community leaders built a new synagogue on the Sudanlage. The temple possessed an organ, a choir, and a certain number of seats reserved for men (272) and for women (196).

Thirty years after the construction of the synagogue, two major events occurred. The IG built a community center behind the Südanlage temple on Lonystrasse, and Levi was replaced by David Sander. From 1897 to 1939, Sander presided over a community that witnessed both its numerical peak and its eventual destruction. As the last rabbi hired by the Giessen IG, Sander saw the liberal dream of German Jewish integration shatter in the face of demographic decline and increasing nonobservance in the 1920s and political persecution during the Third Reich.[58]

Since 1887, the IG had had to deal with the existence of a local branch of the separatist Orthodox Religious Society.[59] The IRG financed the construction of a separate synagogue on Steinstrasse in 1898. In strict observance of traditional ritual, the Orthodox made sure that the synagogue practiced divided seating for men and women and conducted its services in Hebrew, without organ or choir accompaniment. The Religious Society also supervised the kosher restaurant of the Central, a local, Jewish-owned hotel.[60] Despite differences in worship, relations between the IG and IRG in Giessen seemed better than in Frankfurt, although information to that effect is fragmentary. Giessen survivor Martin Harth could not recall much overt tension between the leaders of the two communities, Sander and Leo Hirschfeld, the rabbi of the IRG who died in 1933 and was never replaced.[61]

Despite maintaining two separate sections in the town's Jewish cemetery, Reform and Orthodox Jews shared a chapel for memorial services. And the IG preserved several associations that were open to all

Jews: the Jewish Burial Association; the Jewish Relief Association, founded in 1908 with 120 members; the Jewish Casino Society; the Synagogue Choral Association; the Jewish Men and Women's Health Association; the Jewish Women's Association for Social Welfare; the Jewish Charitable Association; the Association for the Promotion of Handicrafts Among the Jews of Hessen; the Association for the Nursing Home; and a local branch of the Centralverein, with 150 members as of 1925.[62] Seven foundations also acted as cultural and financial centers: the Arnstein Foundation, the Dr. Levi Foundation, the Adolf Buch Foundation, the Mortiz Hirsch Foundation, the Dr. Hugo Mayer Foundation, the Heichelheim Foundation, and the Hermann and Louise Katz Foundation.[63] Despite these institutional efforts, relations between the two communities seemed to function more deeply at the level of individual leaders.

Erich Neumann, cantor, teacher, and ritual slaughterer for the IRG after August 1932, remembered how he and his family became close friends of Bernhard Glusman, cantor at the Reform temple, and the liberal Harth family:

> There was also a much bigger congregation in Giessen, maybe double the size of ours. It was a kind of a Reform shul with an organ, although many of the members were very religious people. That's where Bernhard Glusman became cantor. And although he belonged to the other groups, he and his lovely wife and we, in Giessen, became the closest of friends. . . . Martin Harth and I knew each other already in Giessen. In [the 1970s] we collected some money from former Giesseners for the building of the new synagogue in Kiryat Yam near Haifa.[64]

Recollections of a more fractious relationship between the IG and IRG come from Josef Stern's memoir, *Stark wie ein Spiegel*. Stern's father, Julius, was a merchant and a member of the IRG; his mother, Johanna, died at the age of twenty-seven in 1923. From a secondhand account, Stern described a vigorous debate between his liberal grandfather, a baker, and an Orthodox rabbi at the naming ceremony (in German, *Holekraasch*) of his brother Helmut in 1921:

> The baker, who had been chosen as chairman of the Imperial Union of Jewish Front Soldiers, took a medallion of the group "Schild" from his coat pocket, and said triumphantly:

"In hiking, there is no difference between boys and girls; we need a healthy and strong youth, and nevertheless, overtly conscious Jews! Religion alone doesn't do anything!"

The rabbi, who embodied the letter-of-the-law obedient Orthodoxy with zealous ardor and who demanded from his community the maintenance of all 613 commandments and prohibitions with conscientiousness and pedantry, approached the RJF-chair with theatrical stateliness, let a couple of seconds of silence go by, and said with a raised voice:

"Leaf through the book, everything is there. That is what our sages . . . declared. [Jewishness is there] in hiking, sports, everywhere."

"I can't imagine," countered the baker, "that the Talmud knows anything of football or skiing."

"I must make an exception and agree with the rabbi," meddled my liberal Grandfather, "In the bible we have marathon runners, and swimming itself is mentioned."

The rabbi spoke: "You with your profound Jewish knowledge should join the Orthodox, the true Jewish community. You could contribute a word in our Mishnah-course."

"That is certainly one of your basic fallacies," countered the liberal. "Knowledge does not have anything to do with Orthodoxy. You have people in your synagogue, who keep every commandment to your satisfaction, without knowing, what they are doing." . . . "I don't believe myself to be a bad Jew like you and yours consider, even if I conduct business during the Sabbath. One cannot demand of anyone that they work only five days per week, if one must feed and clothe his family for seven days. Think about that!"

An argument over the legitimacy of the use of an organ during services ensued, and finally, [Stern's] mother sought to put an end to the tireless debate:

"Historians, philosophers, politicians, sociologists should get together, writers, pedagogues, artists, and publicists should also be there, scientists, economists, industrialists, financial experts, and rabbis. All of them should discuss and agree upon how our Judaism should be formed in our modern time. It may surely last long, but it must be done."[65]

Of community relations with *Ostjuden* and Zionists in Giessen, we know very little, primarily because they were so few in number. Stern's memoir discusses only the Zionists unification with the community after 1933 and their confrontation and eventual reconciliation with Jewish patriotic groups of the right, namely Black Flag and Comrades.[66] In Giessen, as in Frankfurt, a network of Jewish welfare and cultural organizations was available to eastern European Jews living in poverty. Martin Harth recounted that *Ostjuden* in Giessen did not appear as traditional as they did in Frankfurt or larger cities such as Berlin. He also remembered that his father, Meyer, a tailor and a member of the IG, often invited Polish Jewish friends to dinner.[67] Yet Harth's impression of their appearance and relation to the majority of German Jews may not be entirely representative. Most of the Jews of eastern European descent in Giessen tended to be poorer merchants from Warsaw or Galicia, two strongholds of traditional Jewry. In Frankfurt and elsewhere in Germany, *Ostjuden* were visible newcomers and treated accordingly. In some towns, the label of outsider was not limited to indigent eastern Jews. For instance, a memoir by a Jewish doctor from Friedberg, a small village twenty miles south of Giessen, insisted that any Jew who had not held roots in the town for several hundred years was regarded as alien, even by other Jews:

> In Friedberg, the distinction was always there between the old, settled Jews of our community, and the newcomers, some of whom had established large businesses. They were rich, they had married native girls, but it was never forgotten by some of our conceited local yokels that their place of origin had been somewhere east of Berlin. . . . There were other divisions, more of a local coloration, inside the community. The native Friedberger Jews, whose ancestors had been residents in the Jewish quarter of the city for many generations, considered themselves nobility, and looked down with contempt and derision at the . . . peasant Jews, who only lately had arrived from the surrounding villages.
>
> These old families never fully accepted the newcomers, like ourselves, who had come from Assenheim to Friedberg in 1908 and had not lived there for three hundred years or longer as had some of the older families. They suffered them in their midst, but didn't feel they belonged. The "Landjuden," the country Jews, couldn't care less; they had long since become the majority within the Jewish congregation.[68]

In comparison to Frankfurt and Giessen, an analysis of Jewish communal interaction in Geisenheim is difficult because of its lack of community institutions. Despite maintaining a small chapel, Geisenheim Jewry looked to Rüdesheim, its larger neighbor a few miles to the west, for leadership. It was there that many Jews from Geisenheim attended synagogue services during the High Holy Days. Rüdesheim's Jewish community also provided religious education, although the school had only one teacher, who came in weekly from nearby Schierstein, and two children in attendance as of 1925.[69]

As in other small Hessian towns, Jews in Geisenheim experienced a demographic decline and continued to observe religious traditions more closely than their liberal, urban counterparts during the Weimar period. Geisenheim's Jewish community also was unique because the bulk of its members belonged to the extended Strauss family. Unlike many rural villages and unlike Frankfurt and Giessen, where distinctions between Reform and Orthodox, assimilationist and Zionist, and indigenous and foreign Jews were more noticeable, Geisenheim remained unaffected by community infighting, with the exception of a personality clash between some Jews and the town physician, Dr. Siegfried Nathan, who held little attachment to Judaism.[70]

German Jewry developed a wide variety of mechanisms to maintain Jewish identity during the Weimar years. The emergence of numerous cultural and social organizations in the 1920s, a time of social openness, secularization, demographic decline, and growing antisemitism, demonstrated the extent to which Jews and, more specifically, Jewish communal leaders, felt an increasing need to deal with the fragile synthesis of *Deutschtum* and *Judentum*. In Frankfurt and Giessen, Jewish communal activity during the 1920s was rather vibrant, in Geisenheim almost non-existent, although that did not mean that Jews there were any less interested in issues affecting them. Then, too, one should not conclude that the inward turn taken by many Jewish leaders during the republican period indicated a wholesale rejection of the liberal model of assimilation. Despite the persistence of antisemitism in Weimar society and the vicissitudes of Gentile behavior, most German Jews continued to regard acculturation and limited structural integration as viable. Historians who, like S.M. Bolkosky, lament this development miss the fact that antidefamation and community building remained essential elements of the liberal approach to German Jewish integration to the very end.[71]

4

Gesellschaft vs. *Gemeinschaft:* Gentile-Jewish Relations Before 1933

The sociologist Werner Cahnman has generalized that while relations among Jews were *gemeinschaftlich*, or communal and intimate, Jewish-Gentile contact was *gesellschaftlich*, or societal and more formal.[1] Yet interaction between Jews and non-Jews in the 1920s was more amicable in Germany than in the traditionally hostile environs of eastern Europe and not much worse than in western Europe and the United States.[2] In this chapter I analyze the Gentile-Jewish relationship in Frankfurt am Main, Giessen, and Geisenheim during the years of the Weimar Republic, from 1919 to 1933. I use interethnic contact as a gauge of Gentile acceptance of Jews in an effort to contribute to our understanding of Jewish integration into German life and the continued presence of antisemitism in German society and politics before 1933.

The relationship between Jews and non-Jews was unevenly affected by Weimar's social and political openness, and, in many respects, interethnic relations took a turn for the worse. It was after all the republic's democratic but crisis-laden society that provided a favorable environment for right-wing extremism, National Socialism, and the popular vocalization of antisemitism. Many Jews in the towns under investigation maintain that although they came to enjoy close friendships with non-Jews, most Gentiles did not reciprocate.

Communal relations between Gentiles and Jews in Frankfurt am Main during the Weimar period were skeletal and fraught with ambivalence. But interaction did occur, and examples can be found of political interaction (Jewish foundation activity and involvement in Frankfurt politics), an instance of hostile relations (the city's position on *Ostjuden*), two institutional connections (the IG hospital and the construction of the new IG cemetery), and finally, a case of good intentions (the efforts of Martin Buber and Franz Rosenzweig at Jewish-Christian dialogue).

In the late nineteenth century, Jews in Frankfurt engaged in a variety of philanthropic ventures, among them the Senckenberger Nature

Research Society, the Free German Foundation, the construction of the city opera in 1880, and the Academy for Social and Commercial Science. The latter association, established in 1897 by Wilhelm Merton, a wealthy Jewish merchant who had earlier founded a think tank called the Institute for the Common Good, helped fund the establishment of Frankfurt University between 1912 and 1914. Georg Speyer, a Jewish banker, and his foundation, the Georg and Franziska Speyer Stiftung, contributed to the creation of an institute for romance languages and geography. In 1902, financial assistance from the Ludwig Braunfels Foundation facilitated the building of a library for modern languages, and banker Wilhelm Bonn underwrote a law library. Money for professorships in history, literature, law, political economy, and Semitic philology at the new university came from several Jewish foundations, especially the Dr. Karl Sulzbach and the Jakob H. Schiff foundations. The medical faculty, too, received generous endowments from Jewish philanthropists: Otto Braunfels offered a grant for a children's clinic, Salomon Herxheimer contributed to a dermatological clinic, the widow of jeweler Robert Koch donated money for an institute of biology, and Dr. Ludwig Edinger funded a neurological institute. The Hanna Louise Rothschild clinic, the "Carolium," financed both a dental school and an ear, nose, and throat clinic, and grants from the Georg Speyer Foundation supported a pharmacological institute and research in chemotherapy.[3] In the 1920s, the Henry and Emma Budge Foundation sponsored the building of a nursing home and worked to finance health care for both Gentiles and Jews.[4]

Unfortunately, these financial contributions sparked an antisemitic backlash, most notably from those who cursed the establishment of a "Jewish" university.[5] The problem of discriminatory hiring practices against Jews constituted a further annoyance. While the Centralverein and Jewish notables dealt with the former, the Frankfurt city government, under National Liberal lord mayor Franz Adickes, ended the practice of barring Jews from holding full professorships (*Ordinariat*). Following this change, many Jews went on to make their mark at the new university, including such academic powers as Erich Fromm, Theodor Adorno, Max Horkheimer, Franz Oppenheimer, Herbert Marcuse, and Martin Buber. In 1933, the Nazi decree calling for the dismissal of Jewish academicians from universities affected 30.7 percent of the faculty at Frankfurt University (109 out of 355 professors), the second highest percentage after Berlin.[6]

Jews were also active in the Frankfurt political scene, but less so in Geisenheim and in Giessen.[7] Jews in the three towns and elsewhere in

Germany supported the cause of liberalism primarily because they identified liberals as the authors of emancipation legislation. That meant voting for either the left-leaning Progressives or Democrats (the German Democratic Party, or DDP, in the 1920s) or the more conservative National Liberals (the German People's Party, or DVP, during Weimar). But a growing number of Jews turned to the Social Democratic Party (SPD) and even the Catholic Center Party (Zentrum) in the later years of the republic when both liberal parties lost political viability.

Perhaps the best-known Jewish politician in late nineteenth-century Frankfurt was Leopold Sonnemann, publisher of the *Frankfurter Zeitung*, Democratic delegate to the Frankfurt city assembly, and deputy mayor (*Bürgermeister*) of the city under Lord Mayor (*Oberbürgermeister*) Adickes after 1890. For much of the fin de siècle, Jews served on the city assembly, managed its treasury, and participated on the municipal board. Eduard Lasker, the leader of the Liberals in the imperial parliament, was Frankfurt's representative to the Prussian statehouse until 1879. Lasker pushed through the bill granting secession rights to the followers of Samson Raphael Hirsch.[8]

Although most Jews voted for the DDP until late in the republic, when they won seats in the city assembly it was primarily as representatives of the SPD. Jewish Social Democrats included Wilhelm Epstein, director of the Frankfurt Union for Education, teacher Bertha Jordan, banker and journalist Ernst Kahn, Dr. Julius Neuberger, print-shop owner Benno Schmidt, and bank president Walter Loeb. Jewish members of the DDP were Ludwig Heilbronn, newspaper editor Sally Goldschmidt, lawyer Moritz Philpp Hertz, banker Otto Hirsch, merchant Emil Max Stiebel, and Dr. Wilhelm Hanauer. Architect Richard Lion and merchant Richard Merton, meanwhile, were delegates of the DVP and harsh critics of the more socialist-oriented domestic pursuits of the city administration in the mid-1920s.[9]

Toni Sender, Paul Levi, Leopold Harris, Hugo Sinzheimer, and Hermann Heller also numbered among the notable Jewish political figures in town. Sender worked as a member of the Independent Socialists in the city's worker and soldier councils. She later returned to the majority SPD. Paul Levi, the defense attorney for Rosa Luxemburg at her 1914 trial for sedition, briefly became the leader of the German Communist Party after Luxemburg's assassination in 1919. Like Sender, he rejoined the SPD but died in 1930 after jumping from, or being pushed out of, a window of his Berlin apartment. Harris and Sinzheimer, both Social Democrats, served sequentially as chief of police in Frankfurt in the early years of the republic. The latter, a delegate to the

Reichstag as well, went on to found the Academy of Labor and became professor of labor law at the University of Frankfurt. Heller was another Jewish SPD member who taught law at the university. He belonged to the so-called Hofgeismar Circle, a group of young socialists who sought the integration of working-class activists into the political elite.[10]

Several Jewish politicians rose to even greater prominence in Frankfurt in the mid-1920s, namely Ludwig Landmann, Democratic lord mayor from 1924 to 1933, Bruno Asch, his Social Democratic treasurer, Ernst May, architect of Landmann's affordable housing program, and Max Michel, the mayor's cultural liaison, who transformed Frankfurt into a center of film, theater, music, and art. Early on, Landmann encountered opposition from Social Democrats who regarded him as too centrist and from Catholics who raised concerns about his Jewish heritage. The city assembly nevertheless elected Landmann *Oberbürgermeister*, or lord mayor, and he assumed his post with the blessing of the SPD faction leader: "With no other member of the municipal board have we so often come into conflict than alderman Landmann. When we consider his entire personality, however, when we see the boldly conceived ways he intends to solve future tasks, then in spite of everything, we support Landmann because we want to try to place the most suited personality at the head of the Frankfurt administration."[11] Landmann's administration ushered in an era of growth for the city, instituting worker arbitration and proposing the construction of housing projects, a highway linking Frankfurt, Basel, and Hamburg, a large open-air market, and the Rhein-Main-Donau canal.[12] More significant for this book was that Gentiles from a variety of political affiliations chose a man with a Jewish heritage to be their mayor.

Of major import, too, was the activism of several Jewish women in Frankfurt. Bertha Pappenheim, founder of the Jewish Women's Union in 1904, fought for suffrage rights and engaged in welfare work for orphans and indigent women throughout the Weimar period. Henriette Fürth, a Giessen-born Social Democratic delegate to the city assembly and member of the university's board of trustees, struggled to gain a wider appreciation of domestic work done by women. Finally, Jenny Apolant, born into the Rathenau family of Berlin, moved to Frankfurt, where she became the leader of the General German Women's Association's local office in 1910 and then a DDP delegate to the city council from 1919 to 1924.[13]

In the civil service, Jews were less well represented in Frankfurt, Giessen, and Geisenheim, partly as a result of restrictive hiring practices. Census data for 1925 reveal that only ninety-eight Jews worked in the entire county, district, and city administration of Frankfurt, and we know of only two members of Giessen's main Jewish community who held posts as administrative functionaries.[14] According to the 1928 statistical yearbook for Frankfurt, more than thirteen thousand individuals worked in both the civil service and the free professions. Even if we assume that the civil service number by itself would have been smaller (a distinction not made in the 1928 yearbook), we would still find a noticeably low percentage of Jewish civil servants in the city.[15]

Jews of all political persuasions took a larger part in Germany's sundry *Vereine* (associations). Indeed, Jewish participation in politics at the everyday level ranged from voting to attending political rallies to membership in groups like the Social Democratic Reichsbanner or the patriotic Imperial Union of Jewish Front Soldiers. The Reichsbanner was especially important for several Jews in Frankfurt, Giessen, and Geisenheim. Martin Harth's father, Meyer, was a loyal member of the SPD association in Giessen, as was the father of current Geisenheim resident Margot Freimuth.[16] Georg Salzberger, one of Frankfurt's Reform rabbis, had Gentile friends in an integrated labor union in which he served as the Jewish representative.[17] Numerous Frankfurt memoirs also recounted Jewish attendance at party gatherings, including rallies by the DDP and the Women's League for Peace.[18]

Throughout the Weimar period, antisemitism played an uneven role in Hessian politics. The Nationalists and the parties of the right were often antisemitic, and the communists frequently employed antisemitic rhetoric in their assaults against capitalism. Meanwhile, the parties of the Great Coalition, the SPD, DDP, Center, and DVP, took inconsistent positions on anti-Jewish prejudice. The majority of Social Democrats and Catholics opposed it, but while the former tended to downplay its significance, the latter frequently identified Jews with secularization. Members of the DDP initially rejected antisemitism as incompatible with their ideals of reason, tolerance, and individual freedom, but the image of the DDP as the party of Jews, combined with a move to the right in 1930, resulted in watered-down objections to Jew-hatred and assertions that the party was a-Semitic. The more right-wing German People's Party repudiated antisemitism during the tenure of party leader, foreign minister, and two-time chancellor Gustav Stresemann, who had a Jewish wife. But after his death in 1929, the party increasingly tolerated Judeophobes and passed over the rise of

Nazism in silence.[19] Varying degrees of antisemitic prejudice also pervaded the three major branches of government—the courts, the army, and the police. In Frankfurt during the later years of the republic, the courts did prosecute an increasing number of cases involving Nazi attacks on Jews, although many of these offenses were not so much against Jews per se as they were against Jews as either socialists or communists.[20]

Several Jewish politicians in Frankfurt found it possible to ignore both Jews and their antisemitic detractors. In the Wilhelmine epoch, Leopold Sonnemann was a classic prototype of this phenomenon, but there were others. In the late 1800s, Adolf Sabor, a Social Democrat who had taught at the Philanthropin, left Judaism to become a "dissident," or a member of no particular religious faith.[21] Ludwig Landmann, who had seceded from the Jewish community in Mannheim before coming to Frankfurt, also opted not to join the city's Israelitische Gemeinde.[22] And Hugo Sinzheimer, although a member of the Frankfurt IG, had no ties to or interest in Judaism until after his forced emigration in the 1930s.[23]

In all fairness, several Jewish notables *were* able to balance their involvement in the political affairs of the city with matters affecting Frankfurt's Jewish communities. Jenny Apolant and her husband, for example, took part in IG functions as Reform Jews. Henriette Fürth sought to impart to women the necessity of Jewish education in the home.[24] And city treasurer Bruno Asch served on the board of the Jewish Agency, the Palestine-based Zionist organization, after winning election to it in 1929.[25]

Focusing on non-Jewish issues may have been a way of assimilating, or it may have been a product of genuine concern for the basic problems facing the city. In the end, relations between Frankfurt politicians, whether Jewish or Gentile, and the city's Jewish communities had no meaningful depth during the halcyon period of the mid-1920s. From an entirely political standpoint, Jewish participation in the city administration had distinct disadvantages. Many who held political office during the years of economic crisis (1929-32) became scapegoats for the depression, and the Nazis won support for their portrayal of Frankfurt as a depraved "Jewish" metropolis, degraded by cultural modernism and dominated by the financial needs of "world Jewry."[26]

Although political activity proved a rather inauspicious aspect of Frankfurt Jewish integration in the 1920s, the example of the *Ostjuden* was even less promising, uncovering widespread antisemitism within the Frankfurt city government in the immediate post–World War I period. The deluge of eastern European Jewish refugees between 1880 and 1914 had already created a significant dilemma for Frankfurt's Jewish communities. But the city's poor handling of a new wave of immigration during and after the war, shaped by images of *Ostjuden* as lazy, dirty, devious, and revolutionary, made matters worse. In October 1919, Leopold Harris, Frankfurt's Social Democratic and Jewish provisional chief of police, protested an order to deport refugee Jews and lost his job as a result. To his fiancée, Sonja, he wrote: "I am not the whore of their policy! I'd gladly give up my office, rather than commit such an atrocity."[27]

One month later, Prussian minister of the interior Wolfgang Heine proclaimed a more liberal policy, allowing Ostjuden who posed no security threat to remain in Germany. On 16 February 1920, however, the Frankfurt City Housing Office registered a complaint: "[The dispensation] will suitably nullify all efforts by local authorities to fight illegal profiteering and the housing shortage. . . . Not only will those Ostjuden already in Frankfurt (there may be five to ten thousand of them!) be legitimized, but also innumerable others who have yet to come in."[28] The Housing Office eventually confirmed that most Jewish asylum seekers found accommodations either with relatives or friends.[29] Local and state objections to the government's policy on *Ostjuden* influenced the Prussian Interior Ministry to issue a new order on 1 June 1920 promising to halt any further migration of eastern Jews and to oversee the deportation of refugees who failed to demonstrate a useful occupation.[30]

In the spring of 1921, Prussia established what it called "concentration camps" for eastern deportees in Cottbus and Stargard.[31] The Bavarian government ordered a mass expulsion of eastern European Jews in 1923. That same year witnessed an anti-Jewish riot in the Scheunenviertel of Berlin, a district heavily populated by *Ostjuden*. The *Vossische Zeitung* described the scene on 6 November 1923:

> Howling mobs on all the side streets. Looting is going on under cover of darkness. A shoe shop on the corner of Dragonerstrasse has been ransacked, and the smashed fragments of glass from the shop windows are littered on the street. Suddenly there is a whistle. The police advance in a long cordon, stretching right across the road. "Clear the street" an officer calls. "Everyone indoors!" The crowd moves on slowly. On all sides, the same cry: "Kill the Jews!"

It is inflamed racial hatred, not hunger, that has driven them to looting. If anyone with a Jewish appearance walks past, he is followed by a group of youngsters who pick their moment and then fall on him.[32]

Nearly three years after the first incarceration of eastern Jews, following bitter protests from Jewish leaders and many Social Democrats, the deportation and internment of eastern European Jewish immigrants ended.[33] Ultimately, of the hundred thousand *Ostjuden* who had entered Germany from 1914 to 1921, over 40 percent either voluntarily returned to eastern Europe or were forcibly expelled.[34] Only a few of those who remained ever became citizens.

The examples of the IG hospital and the community's desire to build a new cemetery in the late 1920s point to a less hostile (yet still cursory) relationship between Jewish and Gentile leaders in Frankfurt. The IG hospital, located in Gagernstrasse after 1914, was the city's most modern health facility. Built at an enormous cost to the main Jewish community, the hospital was not opened to Gentiles until 1929. The reasons for this policy are uncertain, and we do not know the exact number of non-Jewish patients who subsequently sought treatment there. An open admission policy may never have been an issue for the hospital administration until, perhaps, demand increased from non-Jews. Opposition to admission of Gentiles was most likely the result of resentment over the long-standing refusal by the city's Senckenberger-Stiftung Hospital to treat Jews. As for the cemetery issue, the Gemeinde experienced difficulties when it attempted to expand its burial site on Rat-Beil Strasse in the late 1920s. The Association of Small Gardeners protested the parceling off of land, and despite extending a generous loan to the IG, the city ruled that the entrance to the new cemetery had to lie "an appropriate distance" away from the portal to the "general," that is, non-Jewish cemetery, which bordered the Jewish burial site to the north.[35] It is entirely conceivable that the city passed this decree out of fear that unsuspecting Gentiles would wander into a Jewish cemetery.

Analyses of Christian publications and reports of Christian-Jewish dialogues have also suggested that apart from the concern demonstrated by Gentiles in the Association to Resist Antisemitism (Verein zur Abwehr des Antisemitismus), non-Jewish interest in Jews and anti-defamation during the Weimar years was low. With the exception of Bavaria, Catholics in Germany tended to be less antisemitic than Protestants, mainly because they had once been a persecuted minority and because political Catholicism served as a force for democracy.[36] Still, German Catholic newspapers were mostly neutral toward Jew-hatred while Protestant Sunday journals were habitually anti-semitic.[37]

Many of the leading members of Frankfurt's Jewish community, including the philosophers Franz Rosenzweig and Martin Buber, lamented the lack of reciprocal activism among Gentiles vis-à-vis Jewish civil rights. Commenting on the state of Jewish integration into German society as early as 1917, Rosenzwieg wrote: "When you [mother and father] wish to feel German, your choice is limited to those Germans who permit you to exist. These are (1) Germans in the same position as yourself, that is, other Jews, (2) some déclassé individuals and bohemians, (3) some liberally inclined and well-off people, (4) *Die Verjudeten*, (5) and your bosom friends."[38] Buber held similar convictions: "To live as a German means nothing other than truly and completely to live as part of the German community, in communion with the Germans of all ages and with Germandom beyond the ages . . .; that, however, is prohibited for [the Jew]."[39]

Despite their skepticism, both Buber and Rosenzweig pursued dialogues with Christian theologians and ordinary Gentiles.[40] In 1924, Rosenzweig longed for the day when "this era of persecution [would] . . . become one of religious discussions."[41] For his part, Buber met with several Christian leaders in Stuttgart from 3 to 5 March 1930 to discuss the rising tide of antisemitism, but the forum produced few long-lasting results. Most of its non-Jewish contingent either engaged in conversion-driven monologues or returned to modes of indifference after the conference ended. In December 1931, for example, the president of Protestant churches in Württemberg, Theophil Wurm, ignored an invitation to attend the centennial celebration of the state's main Jewish communal body.[42] Buber's last attempt at Jewish-Christian dialogue came on 14 January 1933, when he met theologian Karl Ludwig Schmidt in the Frankfurt Lehrhaus, but they made no significant progress, either in theory or practice, in the struggle to bridge the gap between their two very different worlds.[43]

As in Frankfurt, relations between Jewish communal leaders and Gentile authorities in Giessen in the 1920s do not appear to have been overly deep. Only a few documents from the Giessen city archives bear any connection to the theme of Gentile-Jewish relations. A 1930 document detailed the placement of three hundred marks of credit to the IG by the town administration for the use of an elementary school class in the Lonystrasse community center.[44] Years before, reports of the fiftieth anniversary of Benedict Levi's post as rabbi in 1879 revealed that many of the town's political and religious figures attended: "This morning at ten o'clock the delegation of the Jewish Community of the Province Oberhessen, along with leaders of local civic offices, the representative of the county district, the city board of directors, the county school superintendent, and religious delegates from the Protestant and Catholic communities assembled in the festively decorated Synagogue. . . . In recognition of this meritorious occasion, His Majesty Grand Duke Ludwig IV has awarded the honoree the Knightly Cross First Class of Philip the Magnanimous." In his address at the celebration, Levi spoke of positive relations between the two confessional communities and praised Giessen as a place of tolerance.[45] The city also welcomed the philanthropic efforts of Siegmund Heichelheim, banker, Jewish community leader, and commercial adviser, who facilitated the construction of a spa in 1899 and a new theater in 1907. Today, a plaque at the university library bears his name. Despite these examples of intercommunal cooperation, Giessen was a hotbed of political antisemitism, especially at the university. As a small indication of this, representatives from the city's institution of higher learning were conspicuously absent from the Jewish community's two hundredth anniversary celebration of Moses Mendelssohn's birthday in September 1929.[46]

Relations between Jews and Gentiles in the three towns may have been shallow at the level of conscious interaction between community personalities and leaders, but contact between ordinary people was a different matter. Whether as members of different religious affiliations and various social classes or simply as individuals, Jews and Gentiles developed a complex network of crosscutting relationships.

Jewish participation in the German educational system was a basic index of Gentile-Jewish interaction in the public sphere. In Frankfurt, Jews made up approximately 10 percent of the university student body and, according to a problematic Nazi calculation, nearly 31 percent of the faculty.[47] Table 14 shows that in 1928, Jewish attendance at Frankfurt high schools for boys, the college preparatory *Gymnasien* and the more trade-oriented *Realgymnasien*, *Oberrealschulen*, and *Realschulen*, totaled 409, 7 percent of overall attendance. The vast majority of Jewish boys went either to *Gymnasium* or the *Realgymnasium*, and at the Goethe Gymnasium, Jews numbered 138 out of a total student body of 392, nearly 35 percent. At the same time, Jewish girls made up 13 percent of the attendance at Frankfurt's all-girl high schools, almost double

Table 14. Attendance by Religion in Frankfurt City High Schools for Boys in 1928

Institution	Evangelical		Catholic		Jewish		Other	
Gymnasium								
Goethe Gymnasium	168		72		138		14	
Lessing Gymnasium	217		99		24		11	
Selektenschule	–		167		–		–	
Gymnasium und Oberrealschule								
Höchst	304		272		2		8	
Total	689	(47%)	610	(41%)	164	(11%)	14	(1%)
Realgymnasium								
Musterschule	358		90		91		13	
Wohler-								
Realgymnasium	326		84		56		6	
Total	684	(67%)	174	(17%)	147	(14%)	19	(2%)
Oberrealschulen (OR)								
Klinger-								
Oberrealschule	344		78		20		4	
Sachsenhausen-OR	438		116		25		5	
Liebig-OR	429		142		10		12	
Helmholtz-OR	416		131		13		10	
Ziehen-OR	464		116		9		6	
Total	2,091	(75%)	583	(21%)	77	(3%)	37	(1%)
Realschulen								
Adlerflychtschule	284		115		9		3	
Merton-Realschule	53		13		12		2	
Total	337	(69%)	128	(26%)	21	(4%)	5	(1%)
Total	3801	(66%)	1495	(26%)	409	(7%)	75	(1%)
(1933 figures in paren.)	(3,432)	(67%)	(1393)	(27%)	(301)	(6%)	N.A.	

Source: Statistische Jahresübersichten der Stadt Frankfurt am Main 1928 (Frankfurt, 1930), 47, Stadtarchiv Frankfurt.

Table 15. Attendance by Religion in Frankfurt City High Schools for Girls in 1928

Institution	Evangelical	Catholic	Jewish	Other
Elisabethenschule	357	41	113	13
Humboldtschule	278	36	11	6
Viktoriaschule	293	47	153	6
Schillerschule	631	105	47	9
Herderschule	277	64	7	5
Lyzeum Höchst	182	118	4	6
Total	2,018 (71%)	411 (15%)	355 (13%)	45 (1%)

Source: Statistische Jahresübersichten der Stadt Frankfurt am Main 1928 (Frankfurt, 1930), 48, Stadtarchiv Frankfurt.

Table 16. Attendance by Religion in Frankfurt City Middle and Elementary Schools, and Schools for Children with Disabilities in 1928

Institution	Evangelical Boys/Girls	Catholic Boys/Girls	Jewish Boys/Girls	Other Boys/Girls
Mittelschulen (middle schools)	1,328/1,635	625/739	6/16	33/39
Volksschule (elementary schools)	12,937/12,775	7,362/7,252	328/286	552/513
Hilfsschulen (schools for children with disabilities)	252/203	152/120	11/8	8/7
Total	14,517/14,613 (62%)	8,139/8,111 (34%)	345/310 (1%)	593/559 (3%)

Source: Statistische Jahresübersichten der Stadt Frankfurt am Main 1928 (Frankfurt, 1930), 48, 49, Stadtarchiv Frankfurt.

Table 17. Attendance by Religion in Private, Schools in Frankfurt in 1928

Institution	Evangelical Boys/Girls	Catholic Boys/Girls	Jewish Boys/Girls[a]
Kaiser Friedrich Gymnasium	134/0	83/0	11/0
Kaiser Wilhelm Gymnasium	169/0	106/0	9/0
Philanthropin (both high schools)	1/3	0/0	176/208
Samson Raphael Hirsch (both high schools)	1/1	0/0	191/192
Israelitische Religionschule	0/0	0/0	ca. 350
Hassel Realschule	200/0	77/0	21/0
Prof. Brunners Hohe Privatschule	144/0	62/0	18/0
Lyzeum Schmidt	0/119	0/17	0/22
Lyzeum Stermer	0/174	0/12	0/36
Ursulinen Institut	0/5	0/467	0/0
Marienschule	0/0	0/182	0/0
Israelitische Volksschule (Samson Raphael elementary school IRG)	0/0	0/0	322/329
Volksschule beim Philanthropin (elementary school)	0/0	0/0	226/181
Total	649/302	328/678	974/968 (915/910 in Jewish schools) (total with Israelitische Religionschule)
	951 (21.6%)	1,006 (22.9%)	2,292 (55.5%)

Source: Statistische Jahresübersichten der Stadt Frankfurt am Main 1928 (Frankfurt, 1930), 53, Stadtarchiv Frankfurt.
[a]The numbers for the Orthodox Religious School of the IG come from Rachel Heuberger, *Hinaus aus dem Ghetto: Die Juden in Frankfurt am Main 1800-1950* (Frankfurt, 1988), 162.

the percentage of Jewish boys.[48] At the Elisabethenschule, over 20 percent of the student body was Jewish, and at the Viktoriaschule, over 30 percent (see Table 15). A lower number of Protestant and Catholic girls seeking a secondary education in Frankfurt was the main reason for the higher matriculation rate among Jewish girls. In the city's public middle schools (*Mittelschulen*), Jewish attendance was minimal, 22 out of 4,421, or .5 percent (Table 16). Many Jewish students either remained in Jewish schools or avoided this transitional stage of schooling and went directly from primary school to high school. There were far fewer Jewish children in Frankfurt's primary schools as well: 614 out of 42,005 in 1928, or 1.5 percent (see Table 16).

It appears from Table 17 that in 1928 most Jewish children received their primary education from one of the community religious schools, either the IG's Philanthropin, with 407 students, or the IRG's Samson Raphael Hirsch elementary school, with a total of 651. The total number of Jewish students at the various Jewish community schools was approximately one and a half times as great as the number at the city's public schools (2,175 versus 1,419). In fact, parochial and private education in Frankfurt was more evident among Jewish children than Protestant and Catholic youth. The above statistics may suggest that Jewish children were less integrated in the Frankfurt school system during the Weimar era than one might have expected.[49] It is unclear, however, whether the proportionately larger attendance at Jewish schools was prompted more by antisemitism than an internal decision to promote Jewish education.

Donald Niewyk cautions that liberal German Jews generally regarded separate Jewish schools that offered training in secular studies as superfluous, and Frankfurt may have been an exceptional case, perhaps because of its sizable Orthodox communities.[50] The available sources do not indicate the number of Jewish students who obtained an education at a public or private school and had ancillary schooling at one of the community religious schools.[51] In certain Frankfurt school districts, a separate Jewish education was unnecessary because several public schools offered courses in Judaism, for example, the Elisabethenschule as of 1879, the Musterschule as of 1882, and Humboldtschule as of 1885. In 1900, the city introduced Jewish religious training into schools where Jewish students accounted for at least 10 percent of the student body.[52] Leopold Sonnemann had opposed such training on the grounds that it appeared to entail public endorsement of a particular faith.[53] In higher education, Frankfurt fit in more with the prevailing Jewish disdain for separate religious schooling. In 1928, Germany's first public, nonconfessional teachers' academy was established there to provide Jewish student teachers with training in Judaism and Hebrew as well as in traditional academic subjects.[54]

With respect to hiring practices, Jewish teachers seeking employment at public schools in Frankfurt faced an abundance of discrimination before 1918. According to a 1916 statistic, of 287 teachers in Frankfurt's high schools, only 6 (5 men and 1 woman, 2.09 percent) were Jewish.[55] After 1918, the situation improved, although the precise extent is unknown. Heinrich Silbergleit's census of Frankfurt Jewry in 1925 counted 242 Jews in educational and cultural institutions (including the university, libraries, research institutes, and art galleries) but failed to specify the exact number of Jewish teachers in the city's high schools.[56]

Although Jewish teachers in Frankfurt encountered more openness in the realm of secondary education, an undercurrent of antisemitism permeated the university environment, as it had in the late nineteenth century. The political and economic uncertainties of the 1920s and early 1930s pushed university students, already conservative and enamored with racial pseudoscience, even further to the right. In 1924, *völkisch* student groups achieved a major victory when the General Student Council of Frankfurt University, or (AStA) voted to stop admitting foreign Jews.[57] By 1926, AStA was firmly in the hands of Nazi students.[58] Restrictive admissions policies were accompanied by altercations between Jewish and antisemitic student groups. The Jewish fraternity K.C. Nassovia was once threatened when it attempted to march into St. Paul's Church with Gentile student associations. In 1927, members of the fraternity Teutonia harassed four students sitting in a pub, yelling, "Jews are not German," without actually knowing whether their targets were Jewish. Two years later, a student menaced the owner of the pub, Eduard Levy, threatening to "knock his teeth out."[59] A 1929 rally at the university over the war guilt clause of the Versailles Treaty also deteriorated into antisemitic invective.[60]

Despite going after foreign Jewish students with a vengeance, Gentile undergraduates and faculty members rarely focused their energies on Jewish professors, mainly because of their status as "authorities." In fact, Jewish academicians were held in high esteem by many of their non-Jewish colleagues at universities throughout Germany, Frankfurt and Giessen included.[61] The rector of Frankfurt University, Georg Küntzel, even banned the main Nazi student group in 1930.[62] The German professoriate still fell prey to more moderate forms of

Judeophobia and concurred in the linkage of Jews to Marxism and cultural modernity. Racial antisemitism was also no stranger to German universities. During the Third Reich, the Nazis established institutes of race hygiene in seven cities with suitable academic facilities, including Frankfurt am Main and Giessen.[63]

The experiences of several Jewish students at the secondary and primary levels of education in Frankfurt afford additional insight into antisemitism and the Jewish perception of integration. Bertha Katz, in her unpublished autobiography, maintained that her Orthodox parents sent her to a Gentile lyceum to tame her wild "Jewish" spirit and to learn "German" discipline. For her, antisemitism and sexism were less problematic than attending school on the Sabbath and being prohibited, by Jewish law, from writing her classroom exercises. For L. B. (a female student at the Technischen Lehrerinnen Seminar), Hans Salfeld, and Ernst Noam, however, antisemitism constituted a significant issue. L.B., in a collection of reminiscences of one hundred Jewish students in Frankfurt from 1929 to 1931, maintained that "school was O.K., but we always felt like outsiders." Salfeld's father once complained to a teacher at his son's school about the use of a geography text in which doubts were cast on the desirability of Jewish integration into German society. In the end, he received an apology and a promise that the book would eventually be revised. Noam remembered a student who was personable toward him but who evinced a dislike of Jews in general. Finally, Margarete Sallis Freudenthal recalled how an acquaintance who taught at a school in the East End once scolded her students for misbehaving as if they were in a "Judenschule." The father of one of the Jewish students lodged a complaint with the woman, who responded that she used the phrase to chastise the children for disorderliness and not out of antisemitic malice.[64]

The bulk of Jewish students who attended public secondary schools in Giessen received an education at the *Oberrealschule* (45 out of 93 in 1912), but both Jewish and non-Jewish attendance at the school declined after 1920, from 66 in 1919 to 44 in 1929 (see Tables 18 and 19). In the all-girl high school, Jewish students, at 10 percent (46 out of 449), edged out Catholics (38 out of 449). At the primary level, a 1923 count revealed that only 2 percent of all elementary students at Giessen's public schools were Jewish. In Giessen, like Frankfurt, the two Jewish communities maintained separate academies, and attendance at those schools was relatively high. In 1925, 127 students attended the main community school, while 30 were present at the Orthodox religious school.

Table 18. Breakdown of Attendance by Religion at Giessen Schools[a]

School	Total	Protestant		Catholic		Jewish	
Private schools							
Pädagogim	102 (98 boys)	75	(73%)	19	(19%)	8	(8%)
IG school	127	—		—		127	(100%)
IRG school	30	—		—		30	(100%)
Gymnasium							
Landgraf Ludwig							
Gymnasium	257	217	(84%)	23	(9%)	17	(7%)
Vorschule	99	85	(86%)	9	(9%)	5	(5%)
Realgymnasium	286	249	(87%)	19	(7%)	18	(6%)
Realschule							
Oberrealschule	566	489	(86%)	32	(6%)	45	(8%)
Vorschule	132	114	(86%)	10	(8%)	8	(6%)
Höheren							
Mädchenschule	449	365	(81%)	38	(9%)	46	(10%)
Public primary schools (*Volksschulen* and *Mittelschulen*)	11,678	11,158	(95%)	339	(3%)	125	(2%)

aStatistics for the Padagogim and the public primary schools are for 1923, for the IG and IRG schools, 1925. All other school figures are for 1912.
Sources: Verwaltungsbericht des Oberbürgermeisters der provinzial Hauptstadt Giessen für das Rechnungsjahr 1912 (Giessen, 1913), 59-61, Stadtarchiv Giessen; *Statistisches Handbuch für Volkstaat Hessen: Dritte Ausgabe* (Darmstadt, 1924), 95, 96.

Jewish students never amounted to more than 2 percent of the entire student body at the Ludwigs Universität, but by 1933 nearly 20 percent of the *Ordinariat* (full professors) could claim Jewish ancestry.[65] Among them were the archaeologist and art historian Margarete Bieber, historian Fritz Mortiz Heichelheim, physicist Georg Jaffe, mathematician Ludwig Schlesinger, historian Richard Laqueur, law professor Leo Rosenberg, psychiatrist Friedrich Samuel Rothschild, economist Paul Mombert, Orientalist Julius Levy, and medical doctors Julius Geppert, Franz Soetbeer, and Alfred Storch.[66]

As in Frankfurt, antisemitism at Giessen's university was pervasive.[67] Editions of the Nazi *Völkischer Beobachter* from 1932 and 1933 listed thirteen pro–National Socialist professors at the Ludwigs University, many of whom found favor with the attack on *Ostjuden*.[68] In

Table 19. Attendance at Giessen's Oberrealschule, 1914-1937, by Confession

Year	Protestant	Catholic	Jewish
1918-19	734	65	63
1919-20	712	54	66
1920-21	683	60	44
1921-22	665	47	39
1922-23	673	48	38
1923-24	706	60	49
1924-25	683	46	44
1926-27	689	39	26
1928-29	680	40	21
1929-30	625	43	19
1930-31	610	42	15
1931-32	534	40	18
1932-33	473	31	16
1933-34	402	28	7
1934-35	316	20	1
1937	376	22	0

Source: Schülerbestand der Oberrealschule, 1914-1942, 2602/1 Akten 1569, Stadt-archiv Giessen. No figures were available for 1935/36.

addition, several fraternities continued to exclude Jews from membership over the course of the republic. Corps Hassia boasted about its record of not admitting non-Aryans, and paragraph three of the statute for Corps Palatia read, "Whoever seeks membership must prove that he has no Jewish blood as far back as his grandparents."[69] As a result of their exclusion from these German fraternities, Jewish students in Giessen formed their own student group, the Staufia. In turn, students from right-wing brotherhoods boycotted the cafe where Staufia held its meetings and even provoked one of its members into a fistfight. Ludwig Falkenstein was twice jailed and fined for punching students who had harassed him.[70] More threatening to the status of Jewish students at the university were efforts to implement a numerus clausus on the admission of Jews in 1927 and the acquisition by Nazis of an absolute majority on AStA four years later.[71]

The primary and secondary levels of education in Giessen provided a somewhat friendlier environment for Jews. Hedwig Burgheim oversaw the training of kindergarten teachers at the prestigious Fröbelseminar, and Martin Harth remembered schooltime friendships with Catholic and Protestant pupils. Once during catechism, Harth and his friends caused the school to empty out by giving the impression that the *Graf Zeppelin* was flying overhead. Similarly, Alfred Gutsmuth recalled only one negative impression from his school days. A substitute teacher had apparently hit him when he refused to complete an exercise on the Sabbath.[72]

Jewish participation in education in Geisenheim declined over time. In 1880 91 Catholics, 21 Protestants, and 9 Jews were present in village schools; by 1910 there were more Catholics (123) and Protestants (42), but only 4 Jews, reflecting the steady Jewish demographic cascade.[73] According to a local researcher, Elisabeth Will, Geisenheim school records show that a Jewish girl by the name of Wolff attended the all-girl *Ursuline* in 1894.[74] During the Weimar period, the Strauss girls, Enna and Alice, also received their education at the village *Ursuline*.[75] Records for 1928 indicate the attendance of one Strauss child, Alfredo, at Geisenheim's Rheingau Gymnasium. Friedrich Schwank, a classmate and friend of Alfredo's, recalled that the two of them sometimes drove into town to socialize with female friends.[76] Low attendance on the part of Jewish children at both Gentile and Jewish educational institutions in Geisenheim and Rüdesheim did not imply faulty integration but rather that there were very few Jewish children of school age in either town. Antisemitism in Geisenheim schools was essentially limited to the School for Viticulture and Horticulture.[77] Once again, as in Frankfurt and Giessen, an institute of higher learning provided fertile ground for the radical right.

German Jews had a vigorous trading relationship with their Gentile neighbors. The depth and variety of the Jewish contribution to the German economy is evident in the vast banking empire of the Rothschilds, the retail dynasties of Wronker and Tietz, and the thousands of smaller operations like Otto Frank's ventures in Frankfurt banking and commerce, Meyer Harth's tailor shop in Giessen, and Max Strauss's furniture store in Geisenheim. That more Jewish stores were remaining open during the Sabbath was as much a testament to the weakening of traditional religious ties as it was a sign of the importance of Jewish commercial activity to the German economy. When the city of Frankfurt ordered all shops to be closed on Sundays in 1905, numerous Jewish store owners decided to conduct business on Saturday, the traditional day of rest.[78]

Occasionally, intimate friendships between Gentiles and Jews emerged from their economic dealings. Elizabeth Bamberger recalled that some non-Jewish friends patronized her family's men's store in

Frankfurt after Hitler came to power in 1933. Employer-employee relations also resulted in long-lasting friendships. In Geisenheim, Annelise Schnabel's mother worked as a domestic servant in Georg and Emma Strauss's home and in their animal feed store. The friendship that developed between Frau Schnabel and the Strausses in the 1920s has been maintained by subsequent generations to this day. Trudi Berger, in reminiscences of her childhood in Frankfurt, remembered a Gentile nanny named Candy, who taught the young girl English and cared for her when she had scarlet fever. Charlotte Elke Zernik wrote of vacations in the Taunus countryside with her family's non-Jewish maid, Grete. In some instances, a belief in the constancy of Jewish commercial success led to philosemitic prejudice. Otto Frank's landlord welcomed the Frank family as lessee because he believed that, as Jews, they would be reliable in their rent payments.[79]

More often than not, the same economic circumstances that fostered competition between Jews and Gentiles bred a mixture of respect and contempt. Yet it was Jewish involvement in the cattle trade that seemed to typify the way Jews and Gentiles related in the commercial realm. Because of antisemitic political mobilization on the part of farmers in certain regions of Germany, many have assumed that Jewish-Gentile economic relations were generally hostile.

According to Werner Cahnman, however, the relationship between Jew and peasant was not perforce one of victor and vanquished. Contact could not have continued if it had been so. Both Jews and farmers needed each other as buyers and sellers, lenders and borrowers. Moreover, each participant soberly calculated advantage and disadvantage in all transactions. To sell a sick cow as healthy or an old horse as young, for instance, required skill in sales strategy, in which peasant and Jew were every bit the other's equal. In credit operations, too, the risk was mutual. The farmer could lose his farm, and the Jew could lose his money. Besides being traders, Jews and peasants were also frequently neighbors, and neighborly relations tended to carry an element of helpfulness. Josef Stern remembered how family vacations in the Giessen countryside resulted in friendly business ventures with Gentiles: "Sometimes . . . grandfather or an uncle took the two-wheeled one horse wagon to another village, where peasant folk waited in an inn to discuss a cattle transaction. There the Christian village people also used Hebrew expressions."[80]

Jewish merchants commonly put cows in peasants' stables to ensure that they were well fed and ready for sale, a situation from which a farmer could benefit if he availed himself of the cow's service as a draft animal. And peasant girls took the opportunity to work as domestic servants in Jewish homes because it afforded training in home economics. Jewish housewives also provided folk remedies for ill peasants. Even during Easter, a time when church teachings worked against convivial relations, Matzoh and Easter egg exchanges reportedly occurred.[81]

Despite the relative harmony depicted in Stern's and Cahnman's accounts, economic contact did not necessarily produce intimate friendships or diminish prejudice. The emergence of department stores, in which Jews played a role, created resentment among artisans who produced small quantities of goods at comparably high costs. In addition, the spurious perception that Jews possessed a monopoly on deceitful trading practices fueled outbursts of antisemitism that ran the gamut from name-calling ("flour Jew," "dairy Jew," "oil Jew," "egg Jew") to physical assault.[82] Erna Tietz and Annelise Zettler, both Gentiles, told how their parents had befriended Jewish store owners but believed that there was some validity to the claim that Jews were cunning and lazy.[83]

Otto Böckel, the leader of Hessen's right-wing peasant movement in the late nineteenth century, exploited this sentiment and played on popular identification of Jews with Prussianization. According to Rudy Koshar, Böckel linked racial prejudice with appeals to the material interests of local people hurt by Prussian policy, chronic economic difficulties, capitalist penetration, and urbanization. Urging potential supporters to free themselves from "the Jewish middle man," Böckel endorsed an antisemitism oriented toward social and economic issues. This approach differed from the more ideological and racial antisemitism of university students, who paid little attention to the material interests of groups other than their own. Böckel's appeal worked for a while. In the 1887 Reichstag elections, antisemites won 42.1 percent of the vote in the city of Marburg but dropped to 6.6 percent in 1912.[84] The prewar collapse of antisemitic parties in Germany notwithstanding, Hessian farmers continued to demonstrate a propensity for right-wing radicalism during the republic. Peasants from the Giessen countryside marched alongside Nazi storm troopers in Ettingshausen on 17 July 1932, saving their harshest rhetoric for bankers and foreigners.[85] Ultimately, the NSDAP won over farmers by exploiting the widely held notion that Jews "never worked an honest day" and by promising to "liberate the [German] economy . . . from [its] dependence on Jew-banks and Jew-markets."[86]

Overall, economic contact between Jews and Gentiles, like Jewish participation in politics and education, presented a dilemma for German Jewry. If Jews had been absent from any of these spheres, one could argue that antisemites had excluded them or that Jews were incapable of integrating. But a strong Jewish presence in public social, political, and economic realms often led antisemites to accuse Jews of succeeding because of illegal or immoral behavior, cunning, clannishness, and wealth.[87]

Jew-hatred and internal Jewish motivations helped mold an additional characteristic of German Jewish economic activity. Werner Mosse argues that despite intense commercial interaction between Gentiles and Jews, many Jewish merchants maintained contacts primarily with other Jews. There developed something akin to a Jewish sector of the German economy, which, though not a closed society, was a clearly perceptible entity. Jewish merchants often dealt with other Jews at a level beyond the call of pure economic necessity. This economic intimacy persisted because of shared cultural bonds, common networks of acquaintance, apprenticeships, or long-standing trade relations occasionally reinforced by kinship ties. Many Jewish bankers received their training in Jewish banks or under the auspices of fellow Jews, chose only Jewish partners, and kept their businesses in the family, as did the Rothschilds in Frankfurt and the Heichelheims in Giessen.[88]

Contact between Jews and non-Jews in cultural affairs was less turbulent than their economic relationship. In Frankfurt, non-Jews attended performances and art exhibitions of Jewish singers, actors, musicians, and painters without regard to their religious affiliation or ethnicity. The city's illustrious Jewish artists and entertainers included Ernestine Epstein, who sang the lead at the opening performance of Richard Strauss's *Don Juan*; famous Wagnerian vocalists Magda Spiegel and Hermann Schramm; Hans Erl, lead bass vocalist at the opera from 1918 to 1933; Mathilde Einzig, stage actress in productions such as *Wer niemals einen Rausch gehabt*; Max Reimann and Arthur Hellmer, founders of the experimental Neues Theater, or New Theater; Arthur Holde, music director of the Neues Theater and cantor of the main synagogue; Lewis Lewandowski, nineteenth-century composer of synagogue music; Moritz Daniel Oppenheim, nineteenth-century painter, Jakob Nussbaum, Hans Nathan Feibusch, and Samson (Fritz) Schames, renowned painters in the city during the Weimar years; sculptor Benno Elkan; writers Ludwig Börne and Ludwig Fulda; and *Frankfurter Zeitung* publisher Heinrich Simon.[89] In Giessen, Alfred Bock and his son Werner were two of the town's most prolific writers in the early twentieth century.

Many of these cultural figures and institutions dealt solely with non-Jewish themes. Alfred Bock, in short novels *Aus einer kleinen*

Universitätsstadt and *Hessenluft*, wrote primarily about his native Ober-hessen.[90] Other individuals made an effort to combine both German and Jewish worlds. Sculptor Benno Elkan was responsible both for Frank-furt's World War I memorial, *Den Opfern*, and for the menorah that now stands outside the Knesset in Jerusalem. Moritz Oppenheim, although known for his *Portrait of Jewish Family Life*, also did an oil painting of Austrian emperor Joseph II, which currently hangs in the *Kaisersaal* of Frankfurt city hall. Jakob Nussbaum painted scenes of Palestine as well as city vistas, and Samson Schames's works ranged from *Frankfurter Opernplatz* to *Jüdisches Siechenheim*. Some personalities and groups, like Lewis Lewandowski and the "Jewish" Theater in the Löwenhof, a Yiddish theater that attracted mostly *Ostjuden*, concentrated on Jewish life. The Neues Theater, founded in 1911, produced plays with Jewish themes as well, including *Der Fünf Frankfurter*, which satirized the Rothschild family. *The Dybuk*, another Jewish play performed in Frankfurt in the 1920s, dealt with demonic possession.

That these artists and organizations were Jewish did not preclude their popularity among Gentiles. At a summer festival held in 1927, the choirs of Frankfurt's various synagogues performed Lewandowski's music to an enthusiastic and confessionally mixed crowd. And according to the *Frankfurter Nachrichten*, *The Dybuk* was popular among both Jews and non-Jews: "The performance of the Habimah [the Zionist theater group that staged the play *Dybuk*], made a strong impression on both the Jewish and non-Jewish public. Clearly the majority of the people had never seen a play of which they could understand so little [because it was in Hebrew], but it seemed as if never before had a piece sparked so much interest. . . . The performance solved the difficult task of showing non-Jews as well as western Jews the strange and often arcane life of the Jewish East." Eastern European Jewish theater introduced the assimi-lated Jew Rudolf Heilbrunn to a new realm of Jewish culture: "The deepest artistic affect, however, that has remained with me for days, came from a theater, of whose existence western Europe has almost less under-standing than Russian experimentalists—the Hebrew Troupe Habimah. The Hasidic dances opened an unknown world of secret and faith, ardor and ecstasy, in which somber music redeemed and transfigured an op-pressed and degraded existence."[91]

At a more everyday level, an anonymous memoir from the Leo Baeck Institute entitled "Before the Storm: A Portrait of a Way of Life Set Between Two Friday Nights" described a daughter's relationship to her dying mother and in the process revealed several aspects of middle-class Jewish cultural integration in Frankfurt. The matriarch of the family was both an avid reader of Heinrich Heine and Thomas Mann and a defender of Jewish tradition in the home, preserving various *mitzvot* such as the Sabbath.[92] While in the hospital, she took joy in hearing her daughter read aloud from *Faust*, Hermann Hesse's *Demian*, Jakob Wassermann's *World Illusion*, and poems by I.L. Peretz. From the standpoint of discourse, the daughter depicted the Weimar period in a positive light until the death of her mother, which coincided with the rise of Nazism. More interesting were certain family colloquialisms to which the daughter often referred that implicitly mocked Gentile culture. She once remembered a "Happy Homecoming" poster on the front door that looked so amateurish that one might have called it *goyim naches*, slang for kitsch.[93] The reference to *goyim* or Gentiles was undoubtedly common and harmless, but it did reflect at a linguistic level the extent to which sarcasm toward the outside world existed in the homes of even the most acculturated Jews.

Despite the popularity among non-Jews of plays like *The Dybuk*, Jewish participation in Gentile religious and cultural activities was more common than the reverse.[94] Margarete Sallis's home in Frankfurt had a Christmas tree; Otto Frank's daughter Margot took part in her Catholic friend's confirmation; the Strauss family from Geisenheim rarely turned down invitations to Christmas parties; and Martin Harth and his family attended the wedding of their Christian nanny in Giessen.[95] At the same time, none of the above individuals or families appeared to be detached from Jewish culture. Sallis and Frank had traditional spouses, the Strausses were seen by Gentile friends as religiously observant, and the Harths celebrated Hanukkah with their own Santa Claus equivalent. Sallis's husband was also a member of the Centralverein. Naomi Lacqueur's memoir observations on the Jews' dual celebration of Christmas and Hanukkah were especially apt: "Christmans was celebrated in most Jewish middle class homes. . . . It was a feast in which all the maids, cooks, or whoever else was in the house joined in. Everyone had his own table with gifts. . . . We also celebrated Hanukkah. Our Chanukia [menorah] had a history. My brother, Friedrich, was born on the first day of Hanukkah, and his brit milah [circumcision] was on the last day. [The Menorah] was the present of Franz Rosenzweig, one of father's friends and patients."[96]

Not surprisingly, cultural interchanges between German Gentiles and Jews most often resulted from intimate personal ties. In Josef Stern's account of his childhood in Giessen, a Christian friend was present at his brother's *Holekraasch* (infant naming ceremony). Likewise, a Frankfurt memoir reported Gentile attendance at a Jewish funeral. And when Otto Frank took his daughters and their Christian friends to the opera, he did so because they were friends, not because he desired to see his children form a cultural bond with non-Jews. An analogous argument could be made for the various Gentile *Vereine* to which Jews belonged. Margot Freimuth's father was a member of the Östrich Singing Association because he liked to sing, not because he was making a conscious effort at cultural bridge building.[97]

With respect to leisure, Jews held memberships in countless Gentile sporting associations. In Giessen, Eva Steinreich attended an ethnically mixed dance school, although, according to Gershom Scholem, dancing classes were almost exclusively attended by Jewish boys and girls elsewhere in Germany. Martin Scheuer, from nearby Friedberg, told of his membership in the local Gymnastics Association and of his father's membership in the local bowling club. Martin Harth remembered playing soccer with Giessen schoolchildren until Hitler came to power, and, according to his children, Alex Strauss waxed nostalgic about his soccer-playing days in Geisenheim and his parent's sponsorship of the village football association.[98] Finally, Richard Plant lamented leaving behind Catholic and Protestant comrades from his Frankfurt youth group, the Rovers, after emigrating in 1933.[99] Confronting the reality of extensive Jewish membership in non-Jewish recreational associations, the Nazis forced all Gentile sport and gymnastics clubs in Germany to introduce an "Aryans only" paragraph to their charters on 25 April 1933.[100]

The above examples of integration notwithstanding, Jews were barred from many Gentile student groups and even encountered obstacles as tourists. Frankfurt's Hotel Kölner Hof, located next to the main railway station, prohibited Jewish patronage and sold postcards which took pride in that fact. In the 1930s, the Nazis lauded the hotel's proprietor for maintaining a "Jew-free" pension.[101] The exclusion of Jews from certain Gentile clubs in Frankfurt and Giessen helped prompt the establishment of comparable Jewish associations.[102]

According to Frances Henry, a friendlier structure of recreational contact between Jews and Gentiles in Germany was the *Stammtisch*:

> Men gathered [in taverns or cafes] during the evenings primarily to play cards and to drink beer or wine with each other. This custom was so ritualized that each particular group would have its own table—the *Stammtisch*—reserved for it at the cafe or tavern. As men arrived, a place was made for them at their *Stammtisch*, where the main activity was

card playing. These male groups were completely integrated, and Jewish men regularly met and played cards with Gentile friends. Those friends were occasionally work mates or simply people one met at the same *Stammtisch*.[103]

Martin Harth remembered that his father had a group of friends in a Giessen *Stammtisch*, and several Geisenheimers spoke of identical situations. Martin Killian told me how he and one of the Strauss boys frequently cheated in their *Stammtisch* card games. Allusions to *Stammtische* in Frankfurt memoirs were also common. Rudolf Hielbrunn wrote of numerous integrated salons, and Heinrich Simon, editor of the *Frankfurter Zeitung*, remembered the famous Gentile and Jewish denizens of the so-called Friday Table. Meanwhile, *Kaffeeklatsch*, or coffee hour, was a favorite activity of women. According to Henry, "afternoon coffee a couple times a week where conversation and gossip were exchanged was a regular feature of social life." Several interviews confirmed the importance of the coffee social for Jewish and Gentile women, especially those from Giessen and Geisenheim. Participants in *Kaffeeklatsch* and *Stammtische* tended to belong to the same social class, "although the men's tavern pattern was somewhat more egalitarian than the women's get togethers."[104] Indeed, if any of the middle-class Strausses had taken part in a *Stammtisch* in Geisenheim, where a majority were working class, there would have been a visible class mix.

Nowhere is there more disagreement in the sources than on the issue of private relations between Jews and Gentiles, namely, friendships, invitations to house parties, sexual relations, and intermarriage. Some imply that genuine friendships between Jews and Gentiles were unexceptional, while others come to the opposite conclusion. Lily von Schnitzler, the wife of I.G. Farben director Georg von Schnitzler (both Gentiles), asserted that she and her husband had no hesitation about visiting the homes of DVP representative Richard Merton and Arthur Weinberg, a Jewish executive also with I.G. Farben. Alison Owings, however, in her collection of interviews with non-Jewish German women, concluded that most did not know any Jews. Gershom Scholem likewise maintained that his home was visited exclusively by Jews and that his parents paid visits only to other Jews: "I recall my father's 50th birthday, a short time before the outbreak of the First World War. A few members of the directorate of the Berlin Gymnastics Association, to which my father had belonged for thirty years, dropped by to shake hands politely. There came several colleagues with whom he had been sitting from the aforementioned organizations. Two had brought their wives along. Upon my enquiry, my father answered that a social return visit to the families concerned would not be welcome." But he admitted that there were exceptions to this snubbing: "On formal occasions some colleagues of my father's from the typographic profession . . . from the sick fund in which my father held an honorary position, or from a society to which he belonged, came to tender their congratulations, practically always unaccompanied by their spouses." In the end, Scholem declared that the broad Jewish middle class had little social ambition to seek out contacts with non-Jews and ridiculed the upper crust that attached itself to the Gentile world.[105] The situation I found confirms Scholem's depiction on a general level but was less uniform upon closer analysis.

Admittedly, several of my sources which describe intimate Gentile-Jewish relations in the private sphere come from upper-middle and upper-class Jews from West End Frankfurt, but not all of them. Ruth Westheimer, who lived on the city's less affluent north side and whose family was Orthodox, remembered the bond that developed between her family and a Gentile neighbor, Frau Luft, a one-armed women who visited during Sabbath to fire the stove and to switch on all the lights. More liberal upper- and middle-class Jews in Frankfurt provide the following reminiscences: Margarete Sallis Freudenthal often visited the homes of her Christian friends—in particular a priest named Foerster—and Gentiles attended her many soirees. Elizabeth Bamberger took pride in her upper-middle-class Jewish family's history of intermarriage, and Heide Hermanns Holde mentioned the increasing commonness of mixed unions. In Holde's opinion, "Many Christian girls considered Jewish men to be more sensitive husbands and fathers." Finally, Hans Salfeld portrayed the West End as a "metropolis with intimacy" when he spoke of friendships with Gentile families in the neighborhood. Several memoirs of middle-class Jews in Frankfurt pointed less to a chasm between Jew and Gentile than between western Jew and Ostjude. Jenny Apolant once declared that Jewish and Christian "free thinkers" were closer in religious outlook than traditional Jews. Both Salfeld and Holde contended that intimate social contact between West End and East End Jews was limited and that the relationship was characterized by mutual disdain.[106]

Frankfurt reminiscences that intimated less personal social contact between Jews and Gentiles cut across class and cultural lines as well. At first glance, it may seem that only middle- and lower-class Orthodox Jews and *Ostjuden* held perceptions of nonexistent private interaction. From writings of her father and memories of her mother, Florence

Neumann reconstructed a family history of a middle-class Orthodox home that had no personal contact with Gentiles. Joseph Levy, an Orthodox teacher and cantor, discounted the fact that his wife had come from an intermarried family and had a circle of Christian friends, insisting that Jewish friendships with Gentiles seldom occurred:

> The . . . activity of Christians and Jews restricted itself . . . to the areas of science, art, welfare, and commerce. Social, friendly interaction between these two confessions and their members occurred only during large, public social or charitable events. In general, citizens remained separated by religion, and they sought social intercourse in their narrow circles. . . . Personally, my wife and my children now and then had good friends in non-Jewish circles, whom we occasionally met. But there was no general sociable intercourse, something desired from both sides. I observed this segregation mostly in those Orthodox circles which were close to me, while religiously liberal and assimilated Jews found entry in Christian families, an occurrence that frequently led to mixed marriages.

Trude Maurer, in her work on *Ostjuden*, argued that personal interaction between eastern European Jewish immigrants and non-Jews was rare. Even Gustav L., a Gentile, claimed that Jews were different and treated as such: "In the neighborhood, there lived a Jewish family until 1936. The red-haired son in our age group was the *Judenbub*, and when something ever went wrong in our gang, he was always the guilty one."[107]

Yet Bertha Katz, the child of a well-to-do Orthodox family, argued that her parents had no intimate relations with non-Jews even though she maintained a friendship with a Gentile girl that involved Easter egg and Matzoh exchanges and invitations to Christmas parties. Katz's account implies that upper-class German Jews may have interacted more with other Jews of the same economic and social status than historians like Gershom Scholem cared to admit. Her memories also suggest that friendships between Gentile and Jewish children were far more commonplace than close, interethnic relationships between adults. Finally, Ernst Noam and Friedel Rothschild Lichtenberg, two individuals from less traditional backgrounds, befriended mostly Jews and held an affinity for Zionism. Like Katz's family, Lichtenberg's belonged to the upper middle class.[108]

Further intricacies in the texture of private sphere relations between Jews and Gentiles existed in Protestant Giessen and in Catholic Geisenheim. Oddly, though Martin Harth, a tailor and Reform Jew, admitted that home visits from Gentile friends were rare, Julius Stern, whose merchant family was Orthodox, mentioned Christian attendance at his brother's baby-naming ceremony: "Then coffee was drunk and the precarious political situation was discussed. One of those present, however, wanted to know more about Jewish customs; it was a Christian friend of my father. During the war, he saw [my father] wear phyllacteries and obey the dietary laws in the trenches, and that garnered respect and interest. His wartime comrade gladly granted his request to be present at Jewish events."[109] Perhaps this reversal of assumed cicumstances was merely coincidental, but it is surprising that an Orthodox rather than a liberal Jew spoke of such private interethnic contact. For Geisenheim, intimate Jewish-Gentile relationships were even more fascinating given the lack of intermarriages and conversions.[110] Traditional small-town attitudes may have worked against mixed unions between Jews and Gentiles there, but they by no means interfered with the development of meaningful friendships. Georg and Emma Strauss frequently had Frau Schnabel and other Gentile friends as house guests, and their son Alfredo maintained contact with a former classmate until his death in São Paolo in March 1994.[111] Asked to describe Jewish-Christian relations in Geisenheim, Alfredo responded, "The relationship between Jews and non-Jews was very good until the first years of the Hitler era."[112] Alex Strauss, the son of Max and Auguste Strauss, also had a soccer friend by the name of Dillmann, who, during the 1930s, was required to join the Nazi Party as an employee of the post office. Their bond endured in secret until Alex's emigration in 1934.[113] Although rural mores and the religious background of the extended Strauss family acted as obstacles to intermarriage, neither the Strausses nor their Catholic friends saw the latter as a central issue. Of the three towns, Geisenheim may have had the most intimate structure of Jewish-Gentile relations, even without mixed marriages.[114] Still, several Jews and non-Jews from Giessen and Geisenheim shared the perception that most Gentiles had little interest in Jews, let alone contact with them.[115]

Marriages between Jews and non-Jews became legal in Germany in 1875, and the proportion of Jews marrying Gentiles increased from 7.95 percent in 1901 to 22.79 percent in 1929. Throughout the Weimar period, as in the Wilhelminian era, mixed unions occurred largely in

Table 20. Intermarriage Rate for Jews in Frankfurt, Giessen, Geisenheim, Darmstadt, and Mainz During the Weimar Period (by percent)

Cities	Intermarriage rates				
	1923	1925	1928	1931	1932
Frankfurt am Main	26.2	30.1	28.7[a]	35.4	30.8
Giessen	20	40	25	75	0
Geisenheim	0	0	0	0	0
Darmstadt	22.7	25	20	66.7	28.6
Mainz	10	38.9	35.3	45	23.8

Sources: *Statistisches Handbuch der Stadt Frankfurt a. M. Zweite Ausgabe: Enthaltend die Statistik der Jahre 1906/07 bis 1926/27* (Frankfurt, 1928), 79; *Mitteilungen des Hessischen Landestatistischen Amtes* (hereafter, *MdHLA*), Nr. 9, October 1924, 83; *MdHLA*, Nr. 8, August 1926, 99; *MdHLA*, Nr. 9, September 1929, 115; *MdHLA*, Nrs. 9/10, October/December 1931, 147; *MdHLA*, Nr. 4, January 1933, 91; *MdHLA*, Nr. 5, December 1933, 107; Civilstands-Register der Proclamierten und Copulierten in Geisenheim 1918-1933, Katholisches Pfarramt Geisenheim; Verzeichnis der Getrauten, Evangelisches Gemeindehaus Geisenheim.
a This calculation does not include marriages between Jews and those listed as *sonstige* or "miscellaneous." All other tallies deal with marriages between Jews, Protestants, Catholics, those listed as "other Christians," and those listed as "miscellaneous."

metropolitan areas because, according to Frances Henry, the "'ease of social intercourse undermined the traditional authority of religious and social caste lines.'" In Berlin, by the end of the 1920s, 29.21 percent of marrying Jews married non-Jews; 33.83 percent did so in Hamburg. Rural provinces witnessed comparatively less out-marrying: for Bavaria, the rate of intermarriage in 1926-27 was 13.36 percent, for *Volkstaat Hessen*, in 1928, 15.79 percent.[116]

As revealed in Table 20, intermarriage rates for Jews in the three towns studied here differed noticeably. In Frankfurt, the proportion of mixed unions hovered around 26 percent in 1923, increased to over 35 percent in 1931, and then fell back to 30.8 percent in 1932. The figures for Giessen were even more erratic; 20 percent of the marriages involving Jews in 1923 were intermarriages, 25 percent in 1928, 75 percent in 1931, 0 percent in 1932. But the number of intermarriages in Giessen between 1919 and 1933 was much lower than in Frankfurt—between one and three cases annually. In Geisenheim, at no point in the

1920s did civil or religious authorities record an instance of a Christian-Jewish intermarriage or a Jewish conversion to Christianity, suggesting, perhaps, a mutual aversion to mixed marriages and communal secessions in small towns with small Jewish communities.

Information for Frankfurt from 1928 to 1932 reveals a drop in the number of both endogamous Jewish marriages, from 186 to 137, and mixed unions, from 75 to 61. Proportionally, because of the more pronounced drop in marriages between Jews, the percentage of intermarriages increased. To focus solely on mixed marriages as a demographic drain on Frankfurt's Jewish community, however, would miss the point that Jews altogether were marrying less. A specific examination of Jewish nuptiality in 1931 and 1932, during the height of the Great Depression and the rise of Nazism, also shows that the number of endogamous Jewish marriages increased slightly, from 133 to 137, while the number of intermarriages fell from 73 to 61. In Giessen, the number of mixed marriages between 1928 and 1932 declined as well, from 1 to none, but the number of purely Jewish marriages rose from 3 in 1928 to 6 in 1932. From 1931 to 1932, the turnabout was even more striking. In 1931, 3 of the 4 Jewish marriages were mixed unions between Evangelical men and Jewish women, a 75 percent intermarriage rate.[117] (Rates were likewise higher in Darmstadt and Mainz for that year.) Yet none of the 6 marriages involving Jews in Giessen one year later were exogamous.

Statistics show that in Germany, Jewish men were more prone to out-marry and convert than Jewish women.[118] Between 1901 and 1904, 8.5 percent of German Jewish men and 7.4 percent of German Jewish women intermarried; between 1910 and 1913, these figures increased respectively to 13.2 percent and 10.9 percent; the war years, 1914-18, saw them rise to 29.9 percent and 21 percent respectively; finally, in 1929 (late in the republic), mixed marriage among Jewish men was 27.2 percent, among Jewish women, 17.8 percent.[119] In Frankfurt in 1925, nearly 21 percent of all Jewish marriages were between a Jewish male and a Gentile female, while 9 percent were between a Jewish woman and a non-Jewish man.[120]

Jewish intermarrages in Frankfurt were mainly between Jewish men and Evangelical women. Giessen's statistics would have essentially demonstrated a similar situation had the occurrence of three weddings between Evangelical men and Jewish women in 1931 not skewed my sample. Marriage between Catholics and Jews was less common than Jewish unions with Evangelicals, probably because of the larger pool of singles who were Protestant. Again, as with Evangelical-Jewish mixed marriages, it was usually Jewish men who married Catholic women rather than Catholic men marrying Jewish women.

According to Marion Kaplan, among others, German Jewish women intermarried because of economic necessity and an absence of available Jewish partners. One therefore finds that more Jewish males in mixed marriages had middle-class incomes than Jewish females and that in Berlin and Frankfurt, for example, far more Jewish women who entered into mixed marriages had been employed before their marriage than Jewish women who wed Jewish men.[121] Trude Maurer has cautioned, however, that intermarriage was unlikely to occur between a Christian and a female *Ostjudin* of the lower class because of the traditional and insulated lifestyle of eastern European Jewish immigrants. Marsha Rozenblit and Marshall Sklare have also argued that while a desire for economic and social advancement may have provided inducement to intermarry, many Jews wed Gentiles because they happened to fall in love with a particular non-Jewish man or woman.[122] My source material does not afford me the opportunity to confirm or deny this suggestion, although when intermarriage surfaced as a topic during interviews or in memoirs, it was was put more in terms of intermarriage for the sake of marriage rather than for social betterment.[123]

Despite the increasing frequency of mixed marriages, German Jews and Gentiles regarded them with apprehension. Even so ardent a supporter of Jewish assimilation as Gershom Scholem's father opposed mixed marriages within his family:

> When my brother married a Gentile girl, he [my father] never spoke to her after their first short encounter. My mother, on the other hand, in whose parents' house some sort of Jewish milieu of piety had been prevailing, and who accepted her Jewishness without deeper consciousness as a psychological fact rather than as a biological one, was indifferent toward mixed marriages. Neither my brother's marriage nor that of her own sister—who was one of the first female physicians licensed to practice in Berlin—disturbed her in the least. Apart from these, there was in our wider family circle only a single mixed marriage, and the two daughters who issued from it never quite knew where they belonged as long as they lived.[124]

Jews, of course, dated Gentiles, but they were expected to marry within the faith. One woman from Frances Henry's town of Sonderburg recalled her older brother's engagement to a Gentile woman in Frankfurt: "When her brother called home with the news, their father told the rest of the family that 'Arthur is marrying a Gentile, *but* she is a good girl'— the but was always there."[125]

Jews and Gentiles disapproved of intermarriage largely out of fear that it would result in conversion. Spousal conversions and the rearing of Christian children were particular worries of Germany's Jewish communities because of their small size. In the 1800s, conversion to Christianity had been the entrée for Jews into German, if not European, society.[126] By the twentieth century, however, conversion had become less necessary for career or social advancement.

Overall, the number of German Jewish converts to Protestantism dropped from an average of 412 per year between 1880 and 1910 to 302 annually from 1922 to 1925.[127] This decrease in conversions to Protestantism did not mean that secessions from the Jewish community declined. Prussian law permitted a Jew to sever ties with his or her congregation without adopting Christianity. A 1931 supreme court decision applied that right to the rest of Germany. Those who wished to marry Gentiles may have also avoided conversion by agreeing to raise their children as Christians, and Catholic and Protestant authorities issued special dispensations to that effect.[128] As a consequence, the general trend among seceding Jews over the course of the Weimar period was toward non-attachment or so-called nondenominationalism. Donald Niewyk estimates that by the end of the republic, there were nearly sixty thousand Jews in Germany who chose nonattachment or who acknowledged their Jewishness in purely secular terms.[129]

In both Frankfurt and Giessen during the Weimar period, the majority of Jewish converts became Evangelical Protestants, and most of the new entries into the Jewish community had previously been Evangelicals.[130] Table 21 shows that from 1919 to 1932 an average of nearly twenty-eight Jews per year converted to Christianity in Frankfurt, while an annual average of fourteen Evangelicals and six Catholics entered the city's Jewish community. Greater movement out of Judaism might have been expected, but between 1922 and 1925, there were more Christian converts to Judaism than the reverse. The data in Table 22 allows us to draw a further conclusion: from 1919 to 1926, nine Evangelicals left their churches in the Frankfurt metropolitan area to enter Judaism. We do not know if they chose to join the

Table 21. Entries to and Withdrawals from the Jewish Community (Ig) of Frankfurt, 1919 to 1932-1933

Year	Entries to the Jewish community from the		Withdrawals from the Jewish community to both the
	Evangelical Church	Catholic Church	Evangelical and Catholic Churches
1919	16	3	37
1920	25	5	34
1921	8	2	34
1922	8	14	20
1923	16	9	22
1924	7	8	12
1925	19	7	22
1926	14	3	39
1929	18	6	N.A.
1932-33	9	4	N.A.

Sources: Arnsberg, *Die Geschichte der Frankfurter Juden*, 2:494, *Statistische Jahres-übersichten der Stadt Frankfurt a.M. 1928* (Frankfurt, 1930), 168, 175.

Frankfurt IG or the Jewish community of another city. But even if we assume that all of these converts stayed in Frankfurt, they would not come close to accounting for the 113 Evangelical converts to Judaism in the city between 1919 and 1926. Those who converted either did not belong to a specific church or they came from outside the Frankfurt area. In almost every case, Jews who converted to Christianity had previously belonged to the IG.[131] Converts were therefore likely to be middle- to upper-middle-class Reform Jews, whose ties to Judaism may have already been weaker, or lower-class Ostjuden seeking a way out of poverty.[132] Eastern European Jews were more traditional in religious observance, though, and less prone to out-marry or convert as a result.

Table 23 suggests that in Giessen movement in and out of Judaism was almost nonexistent. From 1919 to 1932, there was not one conversion to Judaism by an Evangelical and only six Jewish converts to Protestantism. Jews and Gentiles who intermarried in Giessen may have avoided conversion and simply reared their children, if they had any, as Christians.[133] Whether this lack of conversion was indicative of all small city experiences, I cannot say. Ultimately, to the Nazis, conversion mattered little. Dora Scheuer converted to Catholicism and mar-

Table 22. Entries to and Withdrawals from the Evangelical Churches in Frankfurt Metropolitan Area, 1919-1928

Year	Entries to the Evangelical Church from the		Withdrawals from the Evangelical Church to both the	
	Jewish Community	Catholic Church	Jewish Community	Catholic Church
1919	16	111	1	0
1920	8	124	0	63
1921	8	149	2	5
1922	7	103	0	30
1923	11	130	0	3
1924	9	185	0	7
1925	9	184	2	14
1926	6	274	4	24
1928	6	292	29a	14

Source: Statistische Jahresübersichten der Stadt Frankfurt a.M. 1928 (Frankfurt, 1930), 44-45.
a Twenty-four of these converts came from the Evangelical community in the suburb of Sindlingen/Zeilsheim.

ried a Catholic, but, because of her Jewish parentage, she was classified as a Jew during the Third Reich.[134]

Historians have been unable to reach a consensus on the relationship between conversion and antisemitism. In his 1906 monograph, *Jewish Baptisms in the Nineteenth Century*, Nathan Samter maintained that high antisemitism translated into high rates of Jewish conversion. More recently, Michael Marrus has argued that when Jews were considered a "race," as they were in fin-de-siècle France, they eschewed conversion. Marsha Rozenblit has also found that antisemitism in nineteenth-century Vienna induced older Jews to convert and younger Jews to defend their Jewishness.[135]

In Frankfurt, Jews shedding direct attachments to the Jewish community during the rise of Nazism, between 1929 and 1932, chose the easier and more economical routes of secession and out-migration rather than conversion. In 1929, there were 105 secessions from Frankfurt's Jewish community (68 men, 37 women), but only 1 (male) conversion out of Judaism. In 1933, after the establishment of the Nazi regime, the situation reversed itself: 34 Jews left the community

Table 23. Entries to and Withdrawals from the Evangelical Church in Giessen, 1919-1932

Year	Entries to the Evangelical Church from			Withdrawals from the Evangelical Church to		
	Jewish Com-munity	Catholic Church	Misc.	Jewish Com-munity	Catholic Church	Misc.
1919	0	4	1	0	0	6
1920	0	5	8	0	0	110
1921	1	4	4	0	3	67
1922	2	5	6	0	0	119
1923	0	3	1	0	0	35
1924	0	5	0	0	0	5
1925	0	0	0	0	1	20+
1926	0	7	0	0	0	57
1927	0	3	2	0	0	44
1928	0	7	2	0	0	N.A.
1930	0	4	0	0	0	101
1931	0	4	14	0	0	67
1932	3	4	7	0	0	80

Sources: "Konfessionswechsel: Tabellen uber Austritte und Übertritte zu der evangelischen Landeskirche," Zentralarchiv der evangelischen Kirche Hessen, Darmstadt, 17/470; "Kirchlich-Statistische Haupttabelle: Tabelle II des Kirchenbundesamtes Pfarrerei Giessen—Dekanat Giessen," 1930-32, 9; Zentralarchiv der evangelischen Kirche Hessen, Darmstadt, 17/500.

(19 men and 15 women), but 73 (27 men and 46 women) converted to Christianity. Interestingly, only 8 Jewish "apostates" rejoined the IG in 1929, but 37 did so in 1933, perhaps realizing that conversion did little to exempt them from Nazi persecution.[136] In Giessen, three out of the six Jewish conversions to Protestantism during the Weimar era came in 1932, but they may have had more to do with three intermarriages the previous year than to the rise of Nazism.[137]

Spousal conversion following intermarriage or conversion in Frankfurt and Giessen was a lesser threat to German Jewish demography than out-migration and the decline in endogamous Jewish marriages. Even the rearing of children from intermarriages as Christians had only a slight impact because mixed marriages tended to produce fewer children. Arthur Ruppin calculated that in Prussia in 1929, 611 children were born from mixed and 3,555 from purely Jewish marriages. Reckoning on a statistically derived basis of 10 percent, he estimated that 61 of the offspring of intermarriages were reared as Jews.[138] This number formed 1.46 percent of the total number of Prussian Jewish children born in 1929. The tenuous nature of Ruppin's statistical methodology and conclusions notwithstanding, if we examine births from mixed marriages in Frankfurt and Giessen, we find comparable situations.

In Frankfurt, each purely Jewish union produced 2.2 children on average, whereas Jewish-Gentile mixed marriages resulted in smaller families (0.59 births per union).[139] In 1925, 10.6 percent of "Jewish" births in Frankfurt came from mixed marriages (a total of fifty). Sixty-eight percent of those births involved a union between an Evangelical and a Jew, and the majority in that category were children who had a Jewish father and an Evangelical mother.[140] By contrast, in 1932, there were only thirteen births from Gentile-Jewish mixed marriages (7.1 percent of all Jewish births in the city).[141] If Ruppin's calculation is correct, the number of baptized children from Jewish exogamy in Frankfurt was not only small but becoming dramatically smaller. To focus solely on the issue of baptism also ignores a greater problem plaguing Frankfurt's Jewish communities during the Weimar years, namely the drop in the number of births from marriages between Jews. In 1923, purely Jewish marriages produced 503 births; by 1928, they resulted in 328 births, by 1932, 169 births.[142]

In Giessen, in 1930, government sources recorded six births to Jewish parents, two of which were out of wedlock, while church records cited two births from Evangelical women married to Jewish men.[143] One baptism was also recorded from a such a case.[144] Applying Ruppin's 10 percent formula for Giessen may be pointless, given the small number of births from mixed marriages, but because of the smaller tallies, there may be a clearer correlation between Jewish-Gentile intermarriage and infant baptism. In 1932, one year after three cases of intermarriage between an Evangelical man and a Jewish woman, church sources recorded a baptism from a union matching that description. Generally, however, as in Frankfurt, intermarriage and conversion had only a small effect on Giessen Jewry's demographic decline. Antisemitism, Jewish migration out of the city, a Jewish mortality surplus, and low rates of endogamous Jewish nuptiality presented the community with more acute difficulties.[145]

Gershom Scholem has argued that a negative attitude toward intermarriage on the part of German Jewry was irrational and based on an overblown fear of conversion. But Gentile objections to mixed marriages were no less unreasonable. One could argue that a stance against intermarriage also flew in the face of the liberal Jewish conception of assimilation, that is, the internalization of German culture and limited structural integration within an overarching Jewish framework. Unfortunately, German Jews never had the opportunity to resolve this tension. On the whole, intermarriage was neither the ominous demographic threat to Jews in Frankfurt and Giessen nor the positive index of German Jewish integration that many believed. Most Gentiles and Jews (including all Orthodox and Conservative rabbis and many Reform rabbis) continued to oppose mixed marriages, and antisemitism endured in spite, in some respects because, of their growing frequency.

Viewed broadly, Jewish integration during the Weimar Republic passed through three distinct periods. Between 1919 and 1924, Jews gained ground on the civil rights front as several points of legal discrimination were abolished. At the same time, the economic and political chaos of this period offset many advances by fanning surges in everyday and state-sponsored antisemitism, particularly against *Ostjuden*. From 1924 to 1929, as Weimar appeared to stabilize, relations took a turn for the better, although anxiety persisted among Jews about their future. Finally, between 1929 and 1932, hopes for the realization of a true Gentile-Jewish symbiosis were shattered by the depression and the rise of Nazism.

Overall, relations between the leadership of the Jewish and Gentile communities in Frankfurt, Giessen, and Geisenheim during the Weimar years were not exceptionally deep. In Geisenheim, where no real community structure existed, contact at this level was practically nonexistent. Minimal contact between Jewish community leaders and Gentile political and religious authorities did not necessarily mean that intercommunal relations were bad. Efforts to develop greater interaction failed more out of a lack of interest than outright antisemitism. Meanwhile, the relationship between ordinary Gentiles and Jews in the three towns before 1933 improved in some aspects and worsened or remained unchanged in others. Jews and non-Jews dealt extensively with each other in the public spheres of politics, education, and the economy, and friendships often developed out of such contact. Class status and residential patterns, too, affected interethnic relations, as in Frankfurt, where middle-class Jews from the West End entertained better relations, not with Jews from the poorer East End but with other West End Gentiles. No less important was the effect of age, gender, confessional distribution, and rural-urban dichotomies on the texture of Gentile-Jewish interaction, particularly on the shape of intermarriage.

Despite the friendly nature of many Gentile-Jewish relationships, there were limits to the structure of interethnic contact during the entire republican period. Jews preserved their own cultural institutions and imposed proscriptions on activities perceived as a demographic threat, such as intermarriage, while Gentiles excluded Jews from numerous social organizations and limited their presence in the civil service. Using the increase in intermarriage over the course of the 1920s to measure the success of German Jewish integration is especially problematic, not because Jews were converting to Christianity but because more intermarriages did not necessarily translate into a reduction in Jew-hatred and occasionally fanned antisemitic resentment. Rates of mixed marriage hovered around 30 percent in Frankfurt and Giessen during the Weimar years, but relations between Jews and Gentiles may have actually been more intimate in Geisenheim, where intermarriage was absent.

At issue in subsequent chapters is whether hostile or absent social interaction between Gentiles and Jews affected non-Jewish attitudes and behavior patterns by reinforcing and cultivating varying degrees of antisemitic prejudice. It seems to have done so, but only to a certain extent. Gentile reactions to Jews and antisemitism in the Weimar Period, and later during the Third Reich, were far from homogeneous. It would be untenable to suggest that all non-Jews who lacked intimate relations with Jews were either antisemitic or indifferent to them. Even amicable Gentile-Jewish contact did not always reduce prejudice, overcome personal variables, or prompt action on behalf of Jews.[146] At the same time, more extensive relations may have fostered among Gentiles a greater perception of Jews as human beings and helped generate a mutual concern for the success of German Jewish integration, something which never truly materialized.[147]

Jew-Hatred or *"Arbeit und Brot!"* Antisemitism and the Electoral Rise of the Nazis

Few subjects have prompted as much historical inquiry as the electoral rise of Adolf Hitler's National Socialist German Workers' Party (NSDAP). Thomas Childers and Martin Broszat, among others, have written on the failure of liberal democracy and the ascendance of the Nazi Party at the national level from 1918 to 1933. William Sheridan Allen, Jeremy Noakes, Rudy Koshar, and Peter Fritzsche have offered provincial analyses on the matter.[1] Many have also sought to determine the extent to which antisemitism played a role in the Nazi ascent.[2] Several of these studies have concluded that Jew-bashing was a secondary issue in NSDAP campaign rhetoric and even less of a factor at the polls. Historians have yet to investigate in depth whether the Nazis manipulated antisemitism with much success in Hessen, Hessen-Nassau, Frankfurt am Main, Giessen, and Geisenheim and whether there was any connection between Gentile-Jewish relations and the use of antisemitism in Nazi electoral propaganda. That is the subject of inquiry for this following chapter.

In Hessen and Hessen-Nassau, National Socialists succeeded in mobilizing considerable support after 1928, and by 1930 the NSDAP was politically dominant in ninety-five Hessian communities.[3] Moreover, Jakob Sprenger, the regional Nazi Party head or *Gauleiter* for Hessen, was a radical antisemite, as were Otto Böckel and Ferdinand Werner, the leading figures in Hessen's antisemitic parties before World War I and supporters of the NSDAP during the Weimar period.[4] Yet despite Hessen's long-standing tradition of antisemitism and right-wing radicalism, some researchers have downplayed the importance of Jew-hatred in their evaluations of Nazi campaign strategies.[5] I have found that the Nazis accentuated antisemitic rhetoric in areas of Hessen where anti-Jewish sentiment was strong and to groups in Hessian society that had antisemitic leanings, especially to peasants in the Oberhessen countryside where relations between Jewish traders and farmers had a history of tension, to students and faculty in university settings where the radical right enjoyed broad support, and to middle-class artisans and shopkeepers in homogeneous districts where there were hardly any Jews.[6] More significant, perhaps, than the overt use of or overt support for Nazi antisemitism, was the NSDAP's ability to exploit latent prejudice and the general indifference of diverse cross sections of the Hessian population.

Germany's defeat in World War I was not only a military setback but a catalyst for political restructuring. Revolutions in Kiel and Munich on 4 and 7 November 1918 respectively helped bring down the kaiser and usher in a new era. On 9 November 1918, two days before the signing of the armistice, Kaiser Wilhelm II abdicated, and the leaders of the majority Social Democrats, Germany's largest political party before the war, proclaimed the establishment of a republic. Soon followed the well-known litany of political changes: the establishment of a republic, the granting of universal suffrage to all eligible adult citizens, and the introduction of direct elections through a system of proportional representation. The Weimar Constitution, however, weakened the power of the popularly elected parliament (the Reichstag) by vesting authority in the president to appoint the chancellor and to suspend democratic rule in times of emergency (via Article 48).

As most students of German history are also aware, the initial months and years of the republic were chaotic. In January 1919, the provisional Social Democratic government suppressed an uprising of the communist left (the Spartacists), while disaffected soldiers returning from the war and extremists on the right engaged in paramilitary violence. Nevertheless, on 6 February 1919, following elections, a diet convened in Weimar's national theater, formally bringing the republic into existence. Friedrich Ebert, leader of the SPD, became Germany's president, serving as chief of state until 1925. Hessen-Nassau contributed to Germany's political shakeup in the person of Philip Scheidemann, the son of a craftsmen from Kassel who became Weimar's first chancellor. Needing a majority to govern, the SPD formed what became known as the Weimar Coalition, a pro-republican union of Social Democrats, the Catholic Center Party, and the German Democratic Party.

After the war, Hessen-Nassau remained a Prussian province, but the grand duchy of Hessen, or Hessen-Darmstadt, underwent several changes. In the grand duchy, revolutionary troops deposed Duke Ernst

Ludwig on 9 November 1918, and Social Democrats formed an executive ministry five days later. Hessen-Darmstadt itself became a republic in the coming months, assuming the new name *Volkstaat* (People's State). In the January 1919 national elections, the SPD received pluralities in Hessen-Nassau and Hessen, as well as in Frankfurt and Giessen.[7] In Geisenheim, the Zentrum was the largest party, followed by the SPD. Hessen and Hessen-Nassau also confronted a troublesome provision of the armistice agreement, namely Allied occupation of territory on the left bank of the Rhine. On 6 April 1920, French troops moved into Frankfurt and continued on to Hanau, retreating only after bloody confrontations with angry mobs.[8] Fostering resentment as well was "miscegenation" between black French soldiers and German women. During the Nazi period, the children of such unions, the so-called Rhineland Bastards, were forcibly sterilized.

Discontent over the signing of the Versailles Treaty, the slow pace of social change (labor and land reform), and the government's suppression of the right-wing Kapp Putsch in March 1920 led to a drop in votes for the SPD and DDP and an electoral increase for the center-right German People's Party, the right-wing German National People's Party (DNVP), and the left-wing Independent Socialists (USPD) in the July national elections. After four unstable years that witnessed the assassinations of Versailles signatory Matthias Erzberger and Foreign Minister Walther Rathenau, the failure of the Nazis' November 1923 Beer Hall Putsch, hyperinflation, and harsh currency stabilization, two separate national elections in 1924 revealed a growing polarization of the German electorate.[9] Supporters of the DVP and DDP continued to shift to the DNVP while the left-wing USPD lost votes to the more radical Communist Party (KPD).

More important in hindsight was the modest electoral success of the National Socialist German Workers' Party as part of the German Folkish Freedom Party and the National Socialist Freedom Movement, both of which accused Social Democrats and Jews of stabbing Germany in the back by accepting the Versailles peace accord. Other splinter parties of the right, such as the Economic Party, the Conservative People's Party, the Bavarian Peasant Union, and the Peasant Party, also gained entry into the Reichstag, further signaling the fragmentation and radicalization of traditional conservative constituencies. Prorepublican forces suffered an additional blow with the death of Ebert in 1925 and his electoral replacement by General Paul von Hindenburg, a Prussian Junker and military leader in World War I.

It is interesting, however, that the response to passionate anti-Jewish appeals made by the NSDAP and such organizations as the German *Völkisch* League for Defense and Defiance (Deutsch-Völkischer Schutz und Trutz Bund) was not more enthusiastic. In the May 1924 national elections, antisemites received only 6.6 percent of the vote, in December only 3 percent. Nor was there much violence against ordinary Jews from 1919 to 1923, with the exception of the murder of a Jew by racists in 1920 and the pogrom against *Ostjuden* in Berlin's Scheunenviertel in 1923. Until the Great Depression, antisemitism was the preserve of marginal nationalist associations and political parties that rarely cooperated with each other. Even the DNVP distanced itself from antisemitic radicalism in the wake of the public outcry that followed the June 1922 assassination of Foreign Minister Walther Rathenau, himself a marginal Jew.[10]

Why the republic survived in 1923 and 1924 and not a decade later is a matter of conjecture, but in Weimar's favor during the earlier years was the lack of a viable political alternative. The left had not recovered from the defeats of 1919 and 1920, and the right suffered internal division.[11] A period of relative stability followed the 1923 crisis, and in 1928 supporters of the republic (the Great Coalition of the SPD, DVP, DDP, Center, and Bavarian People's Party, BVP) were able to form a government. By 1930, one year after the beginning of the worldwide economic depression, rule by presidential cabinets replaced the Great Coalition, and National Socialists made their breakthrough in parliament, gaining 107 seats. In Frankfurt and Giessen, where the splintering of the center-right constituency (shopkeepers, artisans, peasants, and civil servants) was more pronounced, the Nazis were able to exploit popular unrest in the Great Depression better than other single-issue parties of the radical right. Exploiting the friendly environment at the universities of Frankfurt and Giessen, the Nazis took their twin messages of Judeophobia and antibolshevism to the streets, winning over more than just the status-anxious middle class.

The city administrations of Frankfurt, Giessen, and Geisenheim confronted many of the same crises in the postwar period—economic weakness, political chaos, and, in some instances, military occupation. In Frankfurt, the workers' movement catapulted Social Democrats into positions of leadership. But as at the national level, the SPD in Frankfurt suffered an intraparty split and was unable to form a majority government on its own. In 1919, the SPD held thirty-six seats in the ninety-six-seat city assembly, receiving 36.2 percent of the popular vote. The second largest party on the city council at the time, with twenty-three seats, was the DDP.[12] The Social Democrats and left-liberal Democrats worked together in coalition until 1924, when both parties suffered defeats in local elections. Voters in Frankfurt were initially disillusioned with the SPD and DDP over the signing of the Versailles Treaty and then irritated by their handling of the 1923 hyperinflation.

At the height of the inflation, the number of unemployed in the city rose to 22,670, and real property and bank savings precipitously lost value.[13] The introduction of the Rentenmark stabilized Frankfurt's financial situation, but fallout from the economic crisis lingered, damaging on the two mainstays of republican democracy, the SPD and DDP. In her recollections of Frankfurt, Nora Rosenthal depicted the situation in 1923 as bleak both for Jews and non-Jews:

> More and more, unemployed, hungry men would ring the back door and beg for bread. In fact, the situation got so bad that eventually vouchers were issued to distribute so that men could get a meal at certain centers. Of course, the beginning of the inflation made things worse, and nobody knew how and when it would end. If B. got paid in the morning, I was sent out to spend the money as it lost part of its value by the evening. . . . My brothers in law were urging us to put money into hides, their business. But I was so against all the family putting their eggs into one basket. It would be the source of endless disagreement. Due to this well-meant advice, we lost every penny and had to start from scratch.

Martin Scheuer, from Friedberg, a village ten miles north of Frankfurt, remembered how antisemites portrayed his family as conspicuous consumers during the time of the hyperinflation:

> My *Bar Mitzvah* was in 1923, the heart of the inflation. I had a large family, and we had a very elaborate dinner for the whole *mishpokhe*. We printed menus with my picture on top. It was natural. We were just very proud to have *Bar Mitzvahs*, just like people here [in the United States]. One of those menus must have fallen into the hands of an antisemite because a few days later it appeared in our local nationalistic

paper. It didn't mention any names, but it said this was to show how some people in our country live. They just wanted to start antisemitic feeling, propaganda.[14]

In May 1924, the SPD received only 24.7 percent of the votes and only nineteen seats in the Frankfurt city assembly. The DDP fell from twenty-three seats to seven, after losing half of its electoral support.[15] After the communal elections of that year, the second largest party on the city council was the nationalist DNVP, which the SPD shunned on ideological grounds. The SPD relied on support from the DDP, Zentrum, other working-class parties such as the Employee Group, and the right-liberal DVP to create a governing majority. This multiparty coalition supported city treasurer Ludwig Landmann's bid to replace Georg Voigt as lord mayor, despite trepidation from several members of the Center Party, who had misgivings over Landmann's Jewish origins, and certain Social Democrats, who believed Voigt to be more left-wing and more personable.[16] As lord mayor, Landmann supervised Frankfurt's geographic expansion, new housing construction, the creation of the Hamburg-Frankfurt-Basel freeway, and the transformation of the Rhein-Main region into a transportation hub. His colleagues, Social Democratic treasurer Bruno Asch and nonpartisan housing director Ernst May, both Jewish, worked to mold Frankfurt into a modern social and cultural center that addressed the needs of everyday Germans. Housing projects, designed in the Bauhaus style and financed through taxes and loans, went up in the suburbs, while theaters, opera houses, and art museums received subsidies from the city assembly at an unparalleled level. However, the economic collapse of 1929, which sent Frankfurt reeling, turned many city residents against Landmann and fueled attacks on Jews in general.[17]

In Giessen, the SPD and DDP predominated during the first year of the republic but lost ground to the center-right DVP and the USPD in 1920, to the DNVP and KPD in 1924, and then to the NSDAP after 1930 (see Table 24). In the mid-1920s, Giessen experienced an economic boom under Lord Mayor Karl Keller, who held his post from 1914 to 1934.[18] With support from the three main factions on the city council, the left-leaning Workers' Community of the Middle, the center-right Economic Union, and the SPD, Keller increased Giessen's geographic boundaries and initiated a plan for citywide beautification.[19] The eastern part of town was a specific center of construction activity; an auditorium and new sporting facilities opened in the city's *Ostviertel* on the occasion of a large gymnastics festival in 1925. Keller also over-

Table 24. National Elections in Germany in 1919, 1920, and 1924 (in percentages)

Year Place	NSDAP	DNVP	DVP	DDP	Z	SPD	USPD[a]	KPD[b]
1919								
Germany	—	10.3	4.4	18.6	19.7	37.9	7.6	—
Hessen-Nassau	—	9.1	6.7	22.0	17.4	41.0	3.8	—
Hessen-Darmstadt	—	6.7	11.4	19.1	17.5	43.5	1.8	—
Frankfurt	—	9.3	4.5	24.3	11.7	45.6	4.5	—
Giessen	—	11.7	16.4	27.5	7.0	32.5	4.9	—
Geisenheim	—	N.A.	4.5	10.4	44.9	39.9	2.8	—
1920								
Germany	—	15.1	14.0	8.4	13.6	21.6	18.0	2.1
Hessen-Nassau	—	15.6	16.1	10.6	17.0	27.3	12.3	1.4
Hessen-Darmstadt	—	14.1	16.1	10.8	16.2	30.5	12.3	N.A.
Frankfurt	—	10.2	15.2	14.9	11.4	29.9	17.9	0.5
Giessen	—	11.7	31.5	14.4	5.0	17.8	19.6	N.A.
Geisenheim	—	1.2	8.8	10.4	39.8	18.3	21.4	0.0
1924c								
Germany	6.6	19.4	9.3	5.6	13.4	20.5	0.8	12.6
Frankfurt	6.4	16.3	9.9	10.2	12.2	27.7	1.4	9.3
Giessen	N.A.	21.0	27.4	11.4	5.6	25.4	N.A.	9.2
Geisenheim	0.0	2.6	9.5	9.9	40.1	35.2	N.A.	2.6

Sources: Statistik des deutschen Reiches: Ergebnisse der Reichstagswahl 6 Juni 1920, 292, Issue 2, (Berlin, 1922), 54; *Statistik des deutschen Reiches: Ergebnisse der Reichstagswahl 4 Mai 1924*, Issue II, (Berlin, 1926), 75; *Statistisches Handbuch der Stadt Frankfurt a.M. 1906/07 bis 1927/28*, 451; Erwin Knauss, "Die politischen Kräfte und das Wählerverhältnis im Landkreis Giessen während der letzten 60 Jahren," *Mitteilungen des Oberhessischen Geschichtsvereins* 5 (1961): 48, 49, 73; Struck, *Geschichte der Stadt Geisenheims*, 249-51; Demandt, *Geschichte des Landes Hessen*, 595; Childers, *Nazi Voter*, 61.

[a] The USPD was dissolved in 1924.

[b] The KPD was not formed and not electorally active until 1920.

[c] Results from the second election that year, held on December 7, are not included because reports from Hessen, Hessen-Nassau, Frankfurt, Giessen, and Geisenheim were either unavailable or fragmentary. Overall, in those elections, the NSDAP vote fell to 3 percent and the DNVP vote rose to 20.5 percent, while the SPD vote rose to 26 percent and the KPD vote fell to 9 percent.

saw hydroelectric projects and authorized the creation of local railway lines to connect neighboring villages.[20] What ultimately hurt the mayor's government was the unemployment deluge generated by the depression and disaffection with the austerity measures implemented by Keller's centrist coalition.

Geisenheim, by contrast, never became an antidemocratic enclave because the SPD and Center held their own in local, state, and national elections during the Weimar years.[21] In elections for the city council held on 26 October 1919, the Center received 678 votes, the SPD 627, the DDP 196, and the DVP 132. A loss of left-wing SPD votes to the Independent Socialists followed the elections on 20 June 1920, but much of this support returned to the SPD when the KPD became the only political alternative remaining on the left.[22] On 13 August 1920, Franz Stahl began the first of many terms as village mayor, defending Catholic interests in matters of religion and education until his death in 1940. Military occupation of the Rhine by French troops and the French-sponsored separatist movement promoting the creation of a Rhenish republic seemed to overshadow all other political issues in the Rheingau during the early 1920s. In late October 1923, separatists stormed the village *Rathaus* in Rüdesheim and extended their influence all the way to Niederwalluf. The Rhenish republican movement lost momentum quickly, and one month later, in Geisenheim, a doll, rather than the green-white-red flag of the separatists, was hoisted over the village center.

In May 1925, less than two years after Hitler's failed putsch and subsequent incarceration and approximately six months after the most recent national elections, the Nazis reemerged in Frankfurt with newfound energy. Thirty to forty brown-shirted storm troopers of the Sturmabteilung (SA), accompanied by other right-wing nationalist groups, marched through the streets of the city in an antigovernment demonstration.[23] Until 1929, the Frankfurt Nazi Party maintained an approach to politics that involved street fighting, staging mass rallies, and the establishment of a propaganda machine. On 3 December 1926, SA men dressed in civilian clothing and bearing arms stormed a meeting of I.G. Farben workers in the suburb of Griesheim. In September 1927, a National Socialist newspaper, the *Frankfurter Beobachter*, went into weekly circulation with the slogan "the only newspaper in Frankfurt which does not serve 'Capital.'"[24]

The anticapitalist message of the Frankfurt NSDAP reflected its left-wing inclination within the Nazi Party. At the first official political demonstration of the NSDAP in the city on 14 November 1927, nearly eleven hundred people came to hear Joseph Goebbels, initially one of leaders of the party's left-wing faction. One month later, five hundred brown shirts staged a rally at the Hessendenkmal. Among the party plenipotentiaries were Nazi "leftists" such as Goebbels, Robert Ley, and Gregor Strasser.[25]

Ultimately more crucial to the success of the NSDAP than rabble-rousing was the decision to achieve goals electorally and to create a party infrastructure. In the suburb of Böckenheim, a long-standing SPD domain, a regional group (*Ortsgruppe*) of the NSDAP held meetings under the leadership of Jakob Sprenger, a postal inspector and, after 1927, *Gauleiter* of Hessen. The Nazis also used Frankfurt University as a base of operations. Agitation by *völkisch* groups on the student council, or AStA, as early as 1924 had resulted in the imposition of quotas on foreign Jews at the university, and a delegate from the National Socialist student group became AStA chairman only a few years later. In 1929, Nazi students organized a rally against the war-guilt clause of the Versailles Treaty and hurled invectives at Jewish students. A *Frankfurter Zeitung* reporter described the scene: "Jewish students were insulted when they appeared. As the chairperson of the assembly began, shouts and whistles interrupted him. Then the situation became violent, as chairs were used as projectiles . . . and a glass pane was shattered." Frankfurt University's rector, Georg Küntzel, responded to the anti-Jewish slurs of Nazi students by banning their organization, an order they quickly defied.[26]

Despite the historical legacy of the radical right in Giessen, membership in the local branch of the Nazi Party before 1929 was small, and there was no National Socialist newspaper in the town before 1931.[27] Initial Nazi rallies in Giessen were also of little consequence. In May 1923, one month after the founding of the Giessen NSDAP *Ortsgruppe*, seventy SA members paraded in a funeral procession to the city's train station.[28] The NSDAP was no more able to win votes than party members in Giessen before 1930. Adam Lotz, leader of the Giessen *Ortsgruppe*, won a seat on the city assembly after the elections of 17 November 1929, and 4.8 percent of all Giesseners chose the Nazi Party in provincial balloting, but it was not until the Great Depression that voters turned to the NSDAP en masse.[29]

As in Frankfurt, though, the NSDAP was popular at Giessen's Ludwigs University well before its overall electoral rise. Even when the Nazi constituency began to grow, Ludwigs University students voted for the NSDAP at a disproportionally high rate. In 1930, 36.9 percent of all students in Giessen voted for the Nazi Party, compared to 19.4 percent of all eligible voters.[30] A tradition of right-wing radicalism, fueled by economic insecurity and status anxiety and buttressed by the respectability of eugenic science and the position of German universities as institutions of a conservative, Christian state had been a part of the Ludwigs University scene since the late 1800s.

It was not surprising that Nazi antisemitism appealed to students as well. Indeed, the situation for Jews at the university worsened during the Weimar years. Nationalist fraternities such as Corps Hassia and Palatia continued to exclude Jews, and in 1927, the Giessen Student Association supported a numerus clausus on Jewish students.[31] Gentile professors held radical antisemitism in low regard, but they frequently disparaged *Ostjuden*. More important, thirteen professors at the university (approximately 16 percent of the faculty) openly expressed their affinity for Nazism by 1933.[32] Efforts on the part of the Hessian government to discuss the dangers of the university's right-wing orientation only sparked altercations. In 1930, Carl Mierendorff, press adviser of the Hessen provincial administration, had to be protected by the police from angry Nazis who disrupted his speech on students and National Socialism.[33]

In contrast to Frankfurt and Giessen, Geisenheim and many of its neighboring cities remained inhospitable places for the NSDAP during the entire *Kampfzeit*. Still, the Nazis attempted to establish themselves in the region by creating a *Kreisleitung* (county directory) for the entire Rheingau. *Ortsgruppen* surfaced in Eltville, Neudorf, and Rauenthal, and *Ortsgruppenverbände* (regional party associations) were established, uniting branch organizations in Östrich-Winkel with Mittlelheim, in Geisenheim with Johannesberg and Stephanshausen, and in Rüdesheim with Assmannshausen, Eiblingen, Pressberg, and Aulhausen. Party activity in the Rheingau appeared to center around fund-raising rather than street fighting or demonstrating. On 16 July 1932, a note reminded Nazi faithful of an assembly in Eltville at which uniforms, newspapers, postcards, armbands, cigarettes, and pennants were to be sold.[34]

The relative weakness of the Nazi Party in Geisenheim was reflected both in party membership and at the polls. A November 1931 survey revealed that only eight people in the town, out of a population of approximately forty-three hundred, subscribed to the National Socialist *Völkischer Beobachter*. The same was true for three individuals in Östrich, fifteen in Eltville, and sixteen in Rüdesheim. Files at the

Hessian Main State Archives listed only a few National Socialists in Geisenheim by name. They included Arthur Maas, a man by the name of Berg, and Edwin Sulger, who served as Geisenheim's *Ortsgruppen-leiter*.[35] In the end, the Nazis tried, but failed, to convince many in this overwhelmingly Catholic town that the Center Party had become immoral and irreligious. With slogans like "Religion in danger! Vote National Socialist," the Nazis eschewed antisemitism, anti-Bolshevism, and *völkisch* propaganda in favor of an unsuccessful strategy of confessional politics.[36]

What little confidence Germans had in Weimar's economic and political state before 1929 quickly eroded with onset of the Great Depression. The SPD had returned to prominence in Frankfurt, Giessen, and Geisenheim following the national elections of 1928, but after the economic collapse, voters turned away from Social Democrats and the parties of the liberal center, the DVP and DDP. The main victors in the parliamentary elections of 1930 were the Nazis, who took votes away from the DDP, DVP, DNVP, and the communists, who increased their constituent base at the expense of the SPD.

By 1932, 5.6 million people were without work in Germany, an unemployment rate of 29.9 percent. Radicalized by economic misery, many blue- and white-collar workers joined fighting organizations of the extreme left and right. The KPD essentially became a party of those out of work, while the NSDAP developed a broader base of unemployed workers, farmers, and panicked members of the old and new *Mittelstand* (artisans and merchants, civil servants, and white-collar workers).[37] According to Gerald Feldman, the anticommunist slogans of the Nazis proved especially appealing to elements of the impoverished middle class that were antirevolutionary and antiproletarian.[38] But it was the ability of the NSDAP to fashion itself as the savior of both the middle and working classes in Germany that yielded the greatest reward. By promising a national reawakening and immediate relief from the economic crisis, the Nazis offered a "new" alternative to the antiquated worlds of *Bürgertum* and socialism.[39]

Central to Nazi ideology was the belief that Jews were responsible for Germany's disorder.[40] Although this idea was by no means new to the antisemitic right, the unprecedented success with which the Nazis were able to exploit the various themes of antisemitism was unique. It was the "Jew," who, as liberal, championed the weak, corrupt, and decadent democratic order. It was the "Jew," who, as Social Democrat, had "stabbed Germany in the back" and had robbed it of its national pride by signing the Versailles Treaty. It was the "Jew," who, as communist, led the Bolshevik revolution, played a part in the Spartacist revolt in Berlin and in the short-lived Bavarian Soviet Republic, and threatened Gemany with a Marxist revolution. It was the "Jew," who, as eastern European refugee, was lazy, cunning, and parasitic. It was the "Jew," who as cosmopolitan, embraced secularism and modern art and scorned "traditional values." It was the "Jew," who, as capitalist and merchant, oppressed farmers, bankrupted shopkeepers and artisans, and brought on the depression. And, most important, it was the "Jew," who, as Jew and non-German, was the "parasitic bloodsucker" draining Germany of its entire life force.[41]

According to German Jewish sociologist Eva Reichmann, Nazi attacks on Jews were unique in another way. Reichmann differentiated between two "Jewish Questions," one that pitted majority demands for social homogeneity against Jewish separatism and a more dangerous one that had roots in latent personal aggressiveness and group tensions. The Nazi revolt against the "mythical" Jew exploited both, but more so the latter, appealing to primitive impulses and hatred. I agree and would additionally point out, as Gavin Langmuir does, that Nazi antisemitism was chimerical, entailing the acceptance of beliefs attributing to Jews characteristics and conduct that were never empirically verified.[42] Although entirely unjustified, the problem of antisemitism was nevertheless real. Yet the Nazis were aware of the limits of antisemitic invective and tailored their message to suit their audience, often relying on the unwillingness of the general public to condemn the party for its anti-semitic inclination.

Among the German peasantry, small landholders in the Protestant north gave the Nazis their first successes outside of Bavaria. There, the Nazis combined religious antisemitism with *völkisch* ideology, glamorizing the bucolic world of the peasant and extolling the connection between farmers and Germanic "blood and soil." More crucial to the broader success of the NSDAP was its ability to link this traditional animosity toward Jews to the peasants' dislike of the republic. According to John Weiss, peasant support for urban, democratic, and cosmopolitan values was not surprisingly weak and their antisemitism not surprisingly strong, fueled by religious fundamentalism and a fear of the market system.[43] After World War I, farmers were forced to sell produce at low prices because of a postwar international glut of agrarian products; during the depression, meat and dairy prices collapsed and farm foreclosures increased. Casting Jews as "rogue" capitalists and international financiers in cahoots with the leaders of the republic proved the most expedient strategy for the Nazis in their rural campaigning.

Artisans and small shopkeepers of the old *Mittelstand*, who confronted rising bankruptcies and sales that plunged 40 percent between 1928 and 1932, directed their animosities toward Jewish-owned department stores. The Nazis incorporated into their propaganda longstanding accusations from such groups as the Schutz und Trutz Bund (the League of Defense and Defiance), which held that the entire system of retail marketing was a Jewish "scam." Echoing guild myths of the past, the Nazis alleged that the swift expansion of Jewish department stores resulted from "un-Christian methods" that harmed German Christian retailers who were "too honest" to "stoop to Jewish tricks." During the depression, many Gentile retailer organizations joined the Nazis, led by activists recruited from merchants' sons for whom conservative associations had become too passive.[44]

Students and civil servants (the latter constituting the new *Mittelstand*) also voted for the Nazis in relatively high numbers. Although students from upper-class backgrounds tended to remain loyal to the conservative parties of their elders, lower-middle and middle-class students moved further to the right over the course of the republic because economic uncertainty made a university degree no longer a guarantee of employment. Students were attracted to nationalism, racism, and eugenic science as well. They reserved a special anger for supporters of the Versailles Treaty, and German student associations were quick to applaud the murder of Foreign Minister Walther Rathenau and Catholic Center Party leader and Versailles signatory Matthias Erzberger.[45] Civil servants, meanwhile, resented the opening of the civil service to Jews and Social Democrats (although few of either ever rose to positions of leadership); anxious *Angestellten* turned to National Socialism during the depression, when austerity measures intensified competition and threatened job security.

The Nazis achieved far less success among the working and elite classes but more than has been traditionally assumed, especially in the latter group. While most factory workers saw their struggle in economic, not racial, terms and thus remained loyal to the left (drifting ever leftward), many old elites in the Prussian aristocracy and army deserted the conservative parties in favor of the NSDAP. Although the bulk of conservatives remained wary of the populist and lower-middle-class element of National Socialism, conservative campaign rhetoric began to include some of the more invidious antisemitic elements of the Nazi Party. With respect to gender, the Nazis managed to attract some middle-class women who had supported conservative or Catholic candidates before 1930, and in 1932 Protestant women voted for the NSDAP in greater proportion than men.[46]

Both Protestants and Catholics applauded efforts to recapture traditional values allegedly lost during Weimar and frequently condemned the cultural and aesthetic sensibilities of the era as left-wing and decadent.[47] As a group, however, Protestants demonstrated a greater susceptibility to Nazi antisemitism than Catholics, whose political party was often denounced for its support of the "Jewish Republic." During the Depression, Protestant theologians such as Tübingen professor Adolf Schlatter urged Jews to convert to Christianity, and Wilhelm Stapel, editor of the conservative Protestant monthly journal *Deutsches-Volkstum*, cast doubts on Jewish patriotism.[48] A group of fringe Evangelicals calling themselves German Christians went so far as to denounce the Old Testament, deny the Jewishness of Jesus, and combine medieval prejudices against Jews with new forms of racist antisemitism. In Hessen, the Protestant *Evangelisches Sonntagsblatt* served as a mouthpiece for radical antisemites.

Silence and diffidence characterized the response of most German Catholics to Nazi Jew-bashing, especially attacks on Jews as Bolsheviks (to no great surprise). More disturbing was that Heinrich Brüning as leader of the Catholic Center Party and chancellor from 1930 to 1932 consistently ignored pleas to take a stand against antisemitic campaign rhetoric.[49] Hessen's main Catholic newspaper, the *Rhein-Mainische Volkszeitung*, also muted protests against antisemitism during the depression years, although it was often openly hostile to the radical right.[50]

By no means did all Protestant or Catholic leaders endorse or excuse Jew-hatred. Pastor Eduard Lamparter of Stuttgart retired in 1924 to devote his energies to the Gentile Association to Resist Antisemitism (Verein zur Abwehr des Antisemitismus). Cardinal Faulhaber of Munich also assailed antisemitism in numerous sermons, even though he was an ardent foe of the republic and became a wary collaborator with the Nazis during Hitler's reign.[51] Some Democratic, Socialist, and Catholic politicians condemned antisemitic rhetoric as well, but by and large, antidefamation aroused little interest among ordinary Gentiles.[52] Both the Zionist *Jüdische Rundschau* and the *Central-Verein Zeitung* lamented this development although criticism from the latter was more indirect.[53] The *Frankfurt Israelitisches Gemeindeblatt* reasserted the basic claims of Jewish civil rights following the July 1932 elections, but an article that appeared after the November elections anxiously sought to erase the linkage between Judaism and "rationalism."[54]

In Frankfurt, the onset of the Depression signaled the beginning of the end for the Great Coalition of the DDP, Zentrum, SPD, and DVP when representatives from the latter party began an assault on Lord Mayor Landmann's fiscal policy. Following communal elections in November 1929, DVP delegate Richard Merton led a vote of no-confidence against the city administration. Merton's illegal action prompted alderman Heinrich Scharp, editor of the Catholic *Rhein-Mainische Volkszeitung* and Center Party representative, to launch into a tirade against the radical left and right: "Where do you get the moral courage to bring forward a majority group that is exceptionally capable of destroying many exceptional things, but which . . . could not produce one single positive accomplishment!"[55]

Between 1929 and 1932, industrial production in Frankfurt decreased by 65 percent, while the number of unemployed rose to 70,917, creating a jobless rate of over 26 percent.[56] By 1932, nearly thirty-five thousand unemployed workers were no longer eligible for unemployment compensation. The city's growing deficit, resulting from expanding welfare rolls and falling tax revenues, hindered Landmann's ability to cope with unemployment by expanding public works programs. Shrinking revenues from taxes and increasingly meager subsidies from the state and national government also raised the possibility of financial default. Nevertheless, Landmann rejected austerity and stayed his faltering course, cutting construction projects to free up money for welfare and selling off city property to avoid defaulting on loans.[57]

The Nazis benefited from this fiscal chaos and increased their representation on the Frankfurt city council from four in 1924 to eight in 1929. Gains for the NSDAP were partially owing to its portrayal of Frankfurt as a center of "world Jewry."[58] The party capitalized on preexisting animosities toward Jewish-owned department stores and issued a condemnation of city treasurer Bruno Asch, who in December 1929 was elected to the Jewish Agency, the international Zionist organization based in Palestine: "So long as the representative of Frankfurt's communal policy, city treasurer Asch . . . is in the position to lead the finances of world Jewry, we are convinced that he is unfit [for the job]."[59] In preparing for the September national elections, however, the Nazis diluted their antisemitic rhetoric by mixing it with a more acceptable anticommunist and antitax message. On 3 August

Table 25. Results of the Parliamentary Elections of 1928, 1930, 1932, and 1933 (in percent)

Year Place	NSDAP	DNVP	DVP	DDP	Z	SPD	KPD
1928							
Germany	2.6	14.3	8.7	9.4	12.1	29.8	10.0
Hessen-Nassau	3.6	10.0	10.2	5.7	14.8	32.2	8.0
Hessen-Darmstadt	1.9	3.5	11.3	7.6	16.0	32.3	8.7
Frankfurt	4.5	8.6	12.0	8.9	11.1	33.9	12.5
Giessen	1.9	10.8	26.4	8.3	5.8	33.3	4.8
Geisenheim	0.7	3.7	8.3	9.2	36.7	40.4	1.0
1930							
Germany	18.3	7.0	4.9	3.5	14.8	24.5	13.1
Hessen-Nassau	20.8	3.3	5.6	4.0	14.1	25.8	10.0
Hessen-Darmstadt	18.5	1.6	6.7	7.5	N.A	28.9	11.3
Frankfurt	20.7	2.2	8.7	5.8	10.8	27.1	15.0
Giessen	19.4	5.5	13.8	7.0	4.7	26.2	9.1
Geisenheim	9.9	1.8	6.5	4.0	35.7	39.5	2.4
1932 (July elections—percentages in parentheses are for November elections)							
Germany	37.3	5.9	1.2	1.0	15.7	21.6	14.3
	(33.1)	(8.5)	(1.8)	(1.0)	(15.0)	(20.4)	(16.9)
Hessen-Nassau	43.6	4.0	1.6	0.7	15.0	22.4	10.5
	(41.2)	(5.0)	(2.9)	(0.9)	(14.0)	(20.2)	(13.5)
Hessen-Darmstadt	43.1	1.9	1.5	0.6	15.6	26.2	10.2
	(40.2)	(3.0)	(3.0)	(0.7)	(16.1)	(23.3)	(13.7)
Frankfurt	38.7	2.6	2.3	0.7	13.8	25.9	13.6
	(34.2)	(3.8)	(5.3)	(1.4)	(11.8)	(23.0)	(18.0)
Giessen	49.0	5.1	3.6	1.1	7.2	25.5	7.1
	(42.2)	(9.9)	(7.0)	(1.5)	(6.1)	(21.4)	(9.3)
Geisenheim	18.6	1.8	1.7	0.6	37.1	35.7	4.4
	(15.3)	(3.2)	(3.6)	(0.6)	(37.5)	(30.3)	(9.5)
1933							
Germany	43.9	8.0	1.1	0.9	15.5	18.3	12.3
Hessen-Nassau	49.4	4.9	1.7	1.0	13.9	18.7	9.0
Hessen-Darmstadt	47.4	2.9	1.7	0.8	13.6	21.7	10.9
Frankfurt	44.1	3.7	2.7	1.8	12.4	20.9	12.9
Giessen	51.9	8.9	4.1	1.6	6.4	19.5	7.6
Geisenheim	22.9	3.8a	1.9	—	36.6	29.9	4.9

Sources: Dieter Rebentisch, "Zwei Beiträge zur Vorgeschichte und Machtergreifung des Nationalsozialismus in Frankfurt," in *Hessen unterm Hakenkreuz: Studien zur Durchsetzung der NSDAP in Hessen,* ed., Eike Hennig, (Frankfurt, 1983), 286-87; Lothar Bembenek et al., eds., *Materialien zum Unterricht: Sekundärstufe 1 Heft 34:*

1930, one month before Reichstag elections, Hitler greeted seventeen thousand constituents in the Frankfurt Festival Hall, railed against "Jewish" Bolshevism, and promised a German cultural reawakening.[60]

Nazi political activity bore fruit in the 14 September elections when the NSDAP received 20.8 percent of the vote in Frankfurt, compared to 18.3 percent nationally, making it the second most popular political party in the city after the SPD. Electoral analyses have since shown that the Nazis succeeded not only in taking votes away from parties of the center-right but also in mobilizing previous nonvoters who had come to the conclusion that the NSDAP was the last hope for economic recovery.[61] Liselotte F. and Alexander L., Gentiles from Frankfurt, remembered their parents' belief that only Hitler could end unemployment and the chaos of Weimar's multiparty system.[62] But as the August 1930 rally demonstrated, the Nazis chose to cultivate images of a mythical German past and to find scapegoats rather than offer practical solutions to Germany's fiscal problems. Clearly, many of the economically desperate who turned to the NSDAP did not care about specifics, finding the Nazi message palatable enough and Nazi anti-semitism not sufficiently repellent.

Emboldened by their showing in the September elections, Nazis and communists in the Frankfurt city assembly worked to halt the functioning of the town administration by disrupting debates and bombarding the assembly with a deluge of useless proposals. Although only the fifth and fourth largest parties respectively in the city hall after the 1929 communal elections, the NSDAP and the KPD proposed 466 out of the 615 bills that came before the house in 1931. Most of these proposals simply demanded an end to Landmann's administration and the dismantling of Frankfurt's system of government.[63] Fistfights between communists and Nazis in the assembly gallery were also common. The house chairman, Social Democrat Leonard Heisswolf, was frequently forced to call in security and to adjourn meetings because of alterca-

---

Table 25 *sources (cont'd.)*

Nationalsozialismus, Unterrichtsvorschläge und Materialien 1 (Wiesbaden, 1985), 288-97; Karl Demandt, *Geschichte des Landes Hessens* (Darmstadt, 1972), 595; Erwin Knauss, "Die politischen Kräfte und das Wählerverhältnis im Landkreis Giessen während der letzten 60 Jahren," *Mitteilungen des Oberhessischen Geschichts-Vereins 5* (1961): 47-49, 73; Wolf-Heino Struck, *Geschichte der Stadt Geisenheims* (Frankfurt, 1972), 250-51.
a In 1933, the DNVP became the Kampffront Schwarz-Weiss Rot.

tions between right- and left-wing extremists. Even the mayor's office was not safe from violence; on 28 July 1932, the city's chief secretary, Josef Hoffmann, threw a rubber stamp at the *Verwaltungsinspektor* and was later censured for this act and for antisemitic remarks such as "shitty Jews," "the Jewish pig, Landmann," and "Jew pigs will be tossed out!"[64]

In spite of their refusal to function as "normal" political parties, both the KPD and NSDAP increased their constituent bases in 1932, a year that saw the end of Heinrich Brüning's austerity chancellorship, the appointment of Franz von Papen to that office, and his coup against the Prussian state government led by Social Democrat Otto Braun. Yet the popular shift to the National Socialist right undercut efforts by the conservative, antirepublican forces that had assumed control in 1930 to reestablish a pre-1918 order. The presidential elections of March and April 1932 offered glimpses into the decay and political fragility of the traditional right. Incumbent president Paul von Hindenburg defeated Hitler, but only after a run-off election (53 percent to 36.8 percent) and with the help of SPD constituents, fostering the association of the old right with forces of the unpopular "Judenrepublik."[65]

Overshadowing this "victory" was the emergence of the NSDAP as the largest single political party following parliamentary balloting on 31 July 1932 (See Table 25). The Nazis received 37.3 percent of the votes nationally, 38.7 percent in Frankfurt. By the November elections support for the Nazi Party had fallen to 33.1 percent nationally and 34.2 percent in Frankfurt because many voters returned to the DDP, DVP, and DNVP, tiring of the Nazi approach to political and economic problem solving.[66] The KPD upped its vote total to 16.9 percent nationally in the November elections (18 percent in Frankfurt) to replace the Center as the third largest party in Germany after the reeling SPD.[67] The NSDAP in Frankfurt had its strongest showing in the lower-middle-class districts of Outer Sachsenhausen (48.9 percent in July, 40.9 percent in November) and the western Neustadt (46.4 percent in July, 39.7 percent in November).[68] Where the more affluent, assimilated Jews lived, especially in the northwestern Aussenstadt and the western Aussenstadt, the Nazi vote was generally below the citywide percentage, and it was either slightly above or below the average in the working-class eastern districts, home to the poorer *Ostjuden*.[69]

Gentile-Jewish interaction, good, bad, or otherwise, may not have had much influence on the overall voting pattern. It would be absurd to explain the marginally lower vote totals for the Nazis in the West End as a consequence of better Jewish relations with non-Jews. The fact remains that in all Frankfurt districts, the NSDAP enjoyed a plurality by 1932. Historians cannot easily quantify the importance or influence of Gentile-Jewish social contact on electoral behavior, but this does not mean that relations, or their absence, had no effect. Where Jews were few in number, in Outer Sachsenhausen and the Western Neustadt, support for the Nazis was greatest.[70] Antisemitism at the university, manifested in tense relations between Gentile and Jewish students, was also a mobilizing force, as was Nazi propaganda that played on popular disdain of *Ostjuden*, hatred of Landmann's modernism, and fears of financial domination by world Jewry.[71] The relationship between Jews and the DDP experienced a major transformation as well after 1930. Jews from both the West and East Ends deserted the Democrats for the SPD and Center because of the DDP's increasing irrelevance, especially after its reformation as the German State Party (or DStP) and its shift to the right, which brought efforts to distance the party from its Jewish constituency.[72] In July 1932, the former DDP vote was evenly divided between the Center and SPD, but by November more went to the left.[73]

Until 1930, the popularity of the Nazis in Giessen was limited to its poverty-stricken rural districts.[74] As unemployment swelled to over 20 percent in the city, the popularity of the NSDAP grew.[75] Accordingly, public support for Mayor Karl Keller's centrist coalition dwindled once it demonstrated that it had neither the money nor the borrowing power to meet rising welfare costs. In the September 1930 elections, the NSDAP became the second largest force in the city, receiving 19.4 percent of the vote. The Nazis owed much of their success to the muting of antisemitic and anti-Bolshevik rhetoric in preelection rallies, but attacks on Jews and communists resurfaced in subsequent campaigns.[76] In balloting for the Hessian state parliament on 15 November 1931, the NSDAP received nearly 48 percent of the citywide vote in Giessen.[77] Out in the countryside, the Nazis shattered the constituent base of Hessen's farmer organization, the Hessian Landbund, and received 60.6 percent of the peasant vote, partially because they were more vicious than their rivals in attacks against *Viehjuden* and *Bankjuden* (Jewish cattle traders and bankers).[78]

Giessen county's rural areas stood behind Hitler in the March 1932 presidential elections, and the NSDAP, at 49.1 percent, nearly attained an absolute majority from the town in July balloting for Reichstag seats. At the same time, the collective vote total for the DDP,

DVP, and DNVP was 9.9 percent, down radically from 42.8 percent in 1928. The left was also down, but only marginally; the SPD and KPD totaled 35 percent in 1928, 32.8 in July 1932, and 30.8 in November. But SPD losses were offset by gains for the communists, who opposed democracy as much as the Nazis did. Students at the Ludwigs University again voted disproportionately for the Nazi Party, and like everywhere else in Germany, National Socialists attracted a broad spectrum of voters in Giessen. In the July parliamentary elections, the NSDAP received its greatest support (55.9 percent) from the *bürgerlich* or middle-class districts where white-collar, service, and state employees lived. In worker districts like Ward Five, encompassing the streets Hammstrassse, Lahnstrase, Mühlstrasse, and Neustadt, among others, the Nazis did not fare as well, but they still managed 42 percent of the vote. Overall, there does not appear to be any connection between voting for the NSDAP and living in neighborhoods with a concentrated Jewish population. As in Frankfurt, though, antisemitism constituted a mobilizing force for Nazis in the town on the Lahn. Giessen was similar to Frankfurt in two additional ways: the NSDAP obtained a plurality in all of the town's main precincts by 1932, with the exception of the worker quarter of Wieseck, and Jews gradually lost faith in the DDP, turning to either the Zentrum or the SPD.[79]

Despite an unemployment rate of over 20 percent and the collapse of revenues from wine sales, the Nazis encountered difficulties drumming up support for their platform in Geisenheim.[80] Political developments in the Rhenish town may have been exceptions to the general right-wing pattern taking shape throughout Hessen and Germany.[81] But a focus on Geisenheim allows one to move away from a monolithic assessment of the German polity and to point to instances when the Nazis did not achieve electoral success during the depression. In all of the parliamentary elections from 1928 to 1933, including the 5 March elections held a little over a month after Hitler was appointed chancellor, the Center and SPD remained the two most popular parties in the town. In 1928 and 1930, Social Democrats received the highest number of votes in Geisenheim. Thereafter, the Catholics ousted the SPD from its position at the top. The Nazis placed third in the four elections held between 1930 and 1933. After the success of the Zentrum in the July 1932 elections, six Social Democrats refused to take part in the reelection campaign of Mayor Franz Stahl, claiming that he was out of touch with workers and those in need. SPD opposition notwithstanding, Stahl carried nine out of ten Catholic votes on the city council and won his bid for reelection.[82]

Nazi losses in the November election demonstrated that they lacked sufficient electoral backing to assume power on their own. By the same token, Germany's conservative elites were aware that they could no longer sustain presidential regimes without mass support. Despite lingering ambivalence between the old and new right, President Hindenburg appointed Adolf Hitler to the office of chancellor on 30 January 1933, hoping at once to control him and to bind him to a government based on a majority in the Reichstag.[83] The coalition of Nazis and Nationalists was still well short of a majority—247 out of 583 seats in parliament. Hitler soon asked the president to dissolve the Reichstag and call for new elections. After "assurances" from Hitler that the cabinet would remain unchanged regardless of the election outcome, Hindenburg acquiesced, and a national election was set for 5 March.[84]

What followed this decision nationally is well-known: the Reichstag fire on 27 February, the arrest and imprisonment of communist and Social Democratic leaders, the Nazis' 44 percent showing in the March elections, the implementation of the Enabling Act, the beginning of Nazi party coordination with state institutions (*Gleichschaltung*), and nascent manifestations of state-sponsored antisemitism. Less well-known is what happened at the provincial and local levels of German politics. In Frankfurt, Landmann's administration ended with the flight of the lord mayor into hiding in March. In Giessen, Mayor Karl Keller resigned on 31 March 1934 and was replaced by longstanding Nazi Party member Heinrich Ritter. Geisenheim's mayor Franz Stahl was able to retain his office until his death in 1940.[85]

Without denying ideological or political antecedents, it is clear that National Socialism emerged in the context of a particular time and place. Whether one focuses on Germany as a whole, on provinces like Hessen-Darmstadt or Hessen-Nassau, or cities like Frankfurt, Giessen, or Geisenheim, one must conclude that the rise of Nazism was more than an extension of Germany's tradition of political authoritarianism. It was, if anything, a popular rejection of establishment politics, especially of the left but also of the right. Driven to the radical right after a decade of postwar economic trauma, political disarray, and the worst economic depression of the century, a broad yet shallow constituency chose National Socialism as Germany's last hope for "*Arbeit und Brot*—Work and Bread."[86] One must remember, however, that while Hitler was personally popular and while the NSDAP held an electoral plurality, neither actually achieved a majority in the national elections between 1930 and 1932. Accompanying the rise of the Nazis was the growth in popularity of the German Communist Party. The two parties worked against the republic and demonstrated the extent to which extremist options on both sides of the ideological spectrum had risen in appeal by the beginning of the 1930s.[87]

The evidence suggests that in Hessen in general, and in Frankfurt and Giessen in particular, many voters were drawn to Nazism for a variety of reasons. Some liked the populist, antiestablishment message of National Socialism while others found the NSDAP's emphasis on community (*Volksgemeinschaft*), nationalism, and economic rebirth more compelling than anything its rivals on the right had to offer. Still others developed an affinity for Hitler and the larger-than-life scale of Nazi ritual. In regions such as Frankfurt, propaganda work on behalf of the Nazis overwhelmed efforts by their political enemies. In Giessen, where no propaganda machine initially existed, the strength of National Socialism was attributable to a popular base of support that developed on its own. By contrast, in Geisenheim and in much of rural, Catholic Hessen, National Socialism failed to make significant inroads.

Overall, antisemitism played an uneven role in the electoral "success" of the Nazis in Hessen between 1930 and 1932. Historian Richard Hamilton has concluded that opportunism vis-à-vis Jew-hatred was the watchword for the NSDAP throughout Germany: "If antisemitism was not a viable theme in a given area, it was played down or abandoned, if it was viable, it was given considerable play."[88] In Frankfurt and Giessen, antisemitism was a useful element of Nazi propaganda, although it was often subsumed under a host of more respectable critiques. And while dysfunctional Gentile-Jewish interaction did not account for the rise of Nazism, antisemitism manifested in sour relations between Jews and certain societal groups (for example, farmers, students, artisans, shopkeepers, and some Christian religious organizations) proved easy to manipulate. Antisemitism also pervaded NSDAP election rhetoric in other regions of Oberhessen, including Marburg and Friedberg, as well as in Fulda, where the Center was identified as the party of the Jews.[89] None of this was the case in Catholic Geisenheim, although the lack of electoral support for Nazism had more to do with the town's tradition of political Catholicism and the strength of the SPD than moral outrage against Jew-hatred.[90] Less disputable than the use or success of Nazi antisemitism in the election campaigns from 1930 to 1932 was the diffidence toward it among a Gentile populace that had little to do with Jews and cared little about their plight.

6

Close to the Edge:
Relations during the Early
Years of the Third Reich

Historians now believe that Hitler's Reich was less a monolithic party-state and more a polycracy of competing satrapies with which the central government had to seek some modus vivendi. The focus of researchers has therefore shifted to the role of local authorities in administering Nazi legislation and the impact of public opinion on Nazi policy, specifically on state-sponsored antisemitism. This chapter contributes to this historiographical trend through an analysis of Gentile-Jewish relations in Frankfurt am Main, Giessen, and Geisenheim from 1933 to 1938, before the pogroms of Reichskristallnacht. Much of the current work on responses to antisemitism in the Nazi period has concluded that ordinary Germans were not so much radically antisemitic as apathetic. This investigation also shows that although Gentile behavior patterns were complex, most non-Jews remained indifferent or latently ill-disposed to Jews during the early years of the Third Reich, a time when public opinion factored highly in the centralization efforts of the Nazi elite. More important, German citizens condoned and sometimes actively participated in the Nazi antisemitic program, abetting a process of marginalization that made Jews vulnerable to more violent forms of persecution.

The initial implementation of the Nazi platform was only partially achieved from above in the weeks after Hitler's appointment as chancellor on 30 January 1933. The coalition cabinet of National Socialists and Nationalists still lacked a majority in the Reichstag, representing 247 out of 583 parliamentary seats. Hitler therefore petitioned President Paul von Hindenburg to dissolve parliament and call new elections. The president reluctantly assented after Hitler agreed not to tamper with the makeup of the existing coalition. The Reichstag fire on 27 February, allegedly set by communists, prompted Hindenburg to grant a more extreme request from his new chancellor, namely the suspension of seven sections of the Weimar constitution safeguarding individual and civil liberties. Following the decree, the Nazis arrested most communist leaders and many Social Democrats. Despite their intimidation, the Nazis failed to attain a majority in the 5 March elections, winning only 44 percent of the votes. The Social Democratic Party came in a distant second with 18.2 percent of the vote, and the communists, unable to campaign, still received 12.2 percent. The Nazis, with 288 seats in the Reichstag, joined forces with the 52 Nationalists in parliament (who had since renamed themselves Kampffront Schwarz-Weiss-Rot) to form a governing majority.[1]

Yet Hitler needed a two-thirds majority to pass an obscure clause of the constitution which permitted the government to assume dictatorial powers. A two-thirds vote was achieved when 441 delegates (including those from the Center Party) voted in favor of the Enabling Act on 23 March. Only 84 representatives, all Social Democrats, voted against it. The Nazis soon forced the liquidation of all other political parties and began the process of interning political opponents in concentration camps, dissolving trade unions, and subjecting the states to federal authority in an unprecedented policy of coordination (*Gleichschaltung*).[2] On 14 July, with the passage of the Law Against the Formation of New Parties, a one-party state was officially established.[3]

The Hitler administration's seizure of power was met with both violence and mute resignation in Hessen. On 6 March 1933, weeks before the passage of the Enabling Act, SA and SS columns usurped the disposition of armed auxiliary police units and then took control of the streets in the Hessian capital of Darmstadt with the cooperation of the regular police. The public soon realized that National Socialist combat leagues were part of the new order. Sporadic fighting occurred when SA and SS troops enforced the raising of Nazi flags on government buildings and when the Nazi Party headquarters tried to force the regular police to relinquish power. Armed SA posts prevented Minister President Adelung and Minister of the Interior Leuschner from leaving their homes, and Reich Commissioner Heinrich Müller assumed the leadership of the Hessian Interior Ministry. Müller appointed Werner Best, an SS member, state parliament deputy, and legal adviser to the Nazi Party, as special commissioner for the Hessian police. Ironically, according to Robert Gellately's analysis of Best's postwar testimony, there was no significant purge of the regular police force. As evidence, Best stated that Hessen's deputy police chief was allowed to remain in office even though he was a known Freemason and Democrat.[4]

Between 8 and 13 March, National Socialist state governments were legally elected in Hamburg, Württemberg, and Hessen, but only after numerous abstentions from the SPD and the removal of communist deputies.[5] In Hessen, Professor Ferdinand Werner, the National Socialist president of the State Parliament (Landtag), assumed the posts of minister president and Hessian minister of culture, and *Gauleiter* Jakob Sprenger took office as governor (*Reichsstatthälter*) following a decree on April 7.[6] Hessen-Nassau proved easier to coordinate, mainly because it belonged to Prussia and thus had been under national authority since von Papen's July 1932 coup d'état. Prince Philipp of Hessen, a Nationalist turned Nazi, was appointed its president.[7]

Similarly, in Frankfurt am Main, the Nazi takeover occurred swiftly. Enthusiastic crowds of ordinary citizens, party members dressed in civilian clothing, and SA and SS officials marched through the streets of the city to cries of "Sieg Heil" on the day of Hitler's appointment.[8] On 4 February, Prussian minister of the interior Hermann Göring dissolved the Frankfurt city council[11] and nine days later fired the city's Social Democratic police chief, Ludwig Steinberg.[10] Protests by the *Frankfurter Zeitung*, demonstrations by Social Democrats, and street clashes between communists and National Socialists led to an increasing Nazi police presence in the city. After the Reichstag fire, the Nazis banned all local KPD newspapers and the SPD *Volksstimme*.[11] Buoyed by their 48 percent showing in the elections of 12 March, Nazi officials issued a warrant for Mayor Ludwig Landmann's arrest, but he had already fled the city. SA troops managed to occupy the Frankfurt city hall and take Social Democratic *Bürgermeister* Karl Schlosser and several other aldermen into "protective custody." In Landmann's place, they installed Friedrich Krebs, a lawyer and Nazi *Alter Kämpfer*. Under his tenure, Frankfurt languished economically, cut off from the world's financial markets as a result of Hitler's policy of autarky.[12]

In Giessen and Geisenheim, the speed and thoroughness of Nazi coordination varied. In Giessen, SA and SS troops made a sweeping arrest of trade unionists, communists, and Social Democrats on 13 March, but Mayor Karl Keller remained in office for over a year, until 31 March 1934.[13] Heinrich Ritter, a member of the NSDAP since 1924, succeeded him. Nationally imposed coordination in Geisenheim was slower than in Frankfurt and Giessen, largely because Geisenheim was a small, rural town, but also through the political cunning of the Catholic mayor, Franz Stahl.[14] Social Democrat Martin Killian lost his position as an administrator in Geisenheim's Institute for Viticulture and Horticulture in June 1933, well after the Nazis had begun their assault on the SPD. Still, three months earlier—on the same day as the SA's *Aktion* in Giessen, local Nazi officials forced the resignation of five Social Democrats from the Rüdesheim city council, including Geisenheim resident Peter Spring, who was later incarcerated in the Dachau concentration camp.[15]

In general, unlike the relative swiftness with which the Nazis acquired positions of power at the national level and in large cities like Berlin and Frankfurt, the coordination of state and local bureaucracies from above was more erratic and the actual implementation of Nazi legislation much less uniform.[16] Policy toward Jews also lacked clarity and direction in the first two months of Hitler's regime. Michael Kater has argued that state-sponsored antisemitism was frequently initiated at very low command levels of the party with the approval of ordinary Germans.[17]

The Nazi regime's first major assault on Jews was the boycott of Jewish stores, professionals, and cultural institutions held on 1 April 1933 and sponsored by the party's paramilitary wing, the Sturmabteilung.[18] In Frankfurt, on the day before the boycott, Nazi officials broke up a meeting of Jewish merchants and took several into custody. The next day, descriptions of relative calm by the *Frankfurter Zeitung* notwithstanding, SA members raided various institutes of the university and detained Jewish students and professors, including Werner Lipschitz, the director of the Pharmacological Institute. Margarete Sallis, in her memoirs, recounted how ordinary people cursed Jewish merchants, doctors, and lawyers as they walked along Frankfurt's city streets. And Settie Sonnenborn described the scene as tense: "The storm troopers came at 9 o'clock and stayed in front of the entrance. They didn't let anybody in. 'It's a Jewish store,' they said. So my husband said, 'We don't stay here. We close.' He took everything in from the sidewalk, and we closed in the morning, till the afternoon, when they were gone."[19] Reports from Giessen and Geisenheim indicate that the boycott was relatively free incidents although there was less public enthusiasm for the measure in the town on the Rhein.[20]

Although few Gentiles protested the boycott, the undertaking ended the same day it began, partially because it proved to be as much an attack on the German economy as on Jews.[21] Nazi officials had failed to define clearly what constituted a Jewish store and had ignored the fact that several "Jewish" department outlets were in the hands of German banks and that almost all had Gentile employees. Many Germans also objected to restrictions on their already limited buying power and, as a result, continued to conduct business with Jews.[22] Max, Liebmann, and Georg Strauss in Geisenheim retained many of their Gentile customers, and Elizabeth Bamberger remembered how a Catholic family, the Grupps, risked arrest by patronizing her husband's clothing boutique in Frankfurt. Martha Brixius, from Marburg, recalled a similar situation: "[My mother] always went into Jewish stores, even when the SA stood out front to see who entered. Once I went in with her. SA men in uniform stood outside. My mother really gave me courage. . . . It was so terrible—such a very large store and completely empty. The owner came over to us. He was so thankful that someone came. My mother really had nothing to buy, but wanted to show him, I'm still coming. So she bought two small spools of thread."[23]

Gentiles also demonstrated sympathy for Jews in less overt ways. A Reform Evangelical pastor wrote a letter to Margarete Sallis in Frankfurt, expressing his outrage at the boycott and letting her know that Jews were not alone in the fight against Nazi persecution. A Gentile friend of Leo and Settie Sonnenborn, who had recently become an official in the Nazi elite guard or SS, offered more chilling advice: "My old friends, you are Jewish. But you know now I am a Nazi. Have you read *Mein Kampf*? You have to read it. You know what is going on. You have to go away." For people like Meyer Harth, the boycott was all too successful; no longer patronized by non-Jews, Harth's tailor business soon folded.[24]

Following the disappointment of the party's 1 April endeavor, the government announced the first in a series of antisemitic decrees. The April laws were merely the first of some four hundred pieces of anti-Jewish legislation issued by Hitler's regime between 1933 and 1939. In retrospect, legislation turned out to be the least important phase of the Nazi attack on German Jewry, but in the early years of the Reich, law-making was the only approach sanctioned by both party leadership and the general public.[25] The Law for the Restoration of the Professional Civil Service and the Law Concerning Admission to the Legal Profession, decreed on 7 April 1933, represented a limited attack upon Jewish professionals, although they targeted a wide group of "undesirable elements," including communists, socialists, and liberals. The first law, however, confronted the fact that very few Jews, communists, and socialists had ever achieved high positions in the civil service, even during the liberal interlude of Weimar. To that extent, the civil service needed little restoring. And after an entreaty from President Hindenburg, Hitler exempted from dismissal anyone who had fought in World War I or whose father or son had served.[26] The statute concerning the legal profession, unlike the civil service law, affected more Jews, threatening the jobs of approximately three thousand lawyers.

On 22 April, the government enacted a law excluding Jewish medical doctors from the National Health Service, and three days later, restrictions on the number of Jewish students in public schools came into effect.[27] Hitler had exempted Jewish doctors from the application of any "Aryan clause," but his subordinates ignored his wishes. Local Nazi authorities banned Jewish doctors from health insurance panels on their own initiative, prompting the Reich minister of labor to issue a national regulation on 22 April.[28] The same process affected the Law Against the Overcrowding of German Schools, decreed on 25 April with the intention of reducing Jewish attendance to a maximum of 5 percent at any one school or university and 1.5 percent overall.[29]

In Frankfurt on 28 March, before passage of the 7 April law, Lord Mayor Krebs fired eighty-one city employees because they were "Jewish."[30] Several months later, Eduard Schreiber, a judge and World War I veteran who was demoted in position but not immediately fired, reported that Gentile students converged on the city courthouse and assaulted two lawyers. One of the lawyers was a Jewish veteran who had been reinstated; the other was a Gentile who apparently looked Jewish.[31] Almost one-third of the professoriate at Frankfurt University was purged.[32] As a result of a numerus clausus, Jewish student attendance at the university dropped from nearly 10 percent to 1.5 percent.[33] The *Frankfurter Zeitung* responded to the entire "Cleansing Action" with a subtle denunciation: "It is only ours to thank all of those who were fired, who served their discipline with honest intent, and to convey human sympathy for their fate, to each one who fell either for his conviction or without personal guilt."[34] In a letter to the Ministry of Science, Art, and Education, the Jewish historian Ernst Kantorowicz offered a more biting attack, inveighing against those who regarded Jews by their very existence as racial enemies and traitors.[35]

Unlike the situation for Jews at the university, Jewish elementary school children in Frankfurt were not immediately affected by the spring laws. In June 1933, the city school board reported to Lord Mayor Krebs that Prussian law required the 662 Jewish pupils in the metropolitan region to continue their education at one of the city's public schools.[36] In the summer of 1935, this right was rescinded and all

Jewish children were required to attend publicly funded Jewish institutions. Financial difficulties arising from this decree led the mayor to propose that Jewish students be concentrated in two of the city's larger public schools—the Holzhausen Schule and the Varrentrapp Schule.[37]

Overall, Gentile opposition to the spring 1933 measures in Frankfurt was low, and subsequent experiences of instructors at the university and the city's trade school revealed that many people considered the laws too lenient. In January 1934, a group of students in civilian clothing and SS garb jeered Kurt Riezler during a lecture at the university, accusing him of "Jew-friendly behavior" (*judenfreundliches Verhalten*). On 1 October 1935, students at the Handelsschule nearly rioted to force the dismissal of a Jewish teacher, Frohlich, who had not been fired in 1933 because of his status as a war veteran.[38]

In Giessen and Geisenheim, the move against Jews and political opponents in the professions mirrored the situation in Frankfurt. The few Jewish civil servants in Giessen were fired, as were Jewish doctors and lawyers in both towns. Dr. Siegfried Nathan, a physician from Geisenheim, suffered under the restrictive health insurance law, but it was not until 1935 that he left the village altogether for his home state of Lower Saxony.[39] In Giessen, Jews at the university and other educational institutions were hardest hit. Thirty-three professors at Ludwigs University, sixteen of whom were Jewish, lost their posts in the spring purge.[40] Hedwig Burgheim, dismissed as director of the Fröbelseminar's Pedagogical Institute, also endured a personal denunciation: "The Seminar is under the Jewess, Ms. Burgheim and the Democratic teacher Fischer. . . . The children are not allowed to sing certain patriotic songs, the Jewess does not want to hear the Horst Wessel Lied. . . . In the court, a bath was built . . . boys and girls often bathe naked in it, and the Seminar girls, 18 to 20 years of age, stand around it and splash the children with a hose at the behest of the teacher, Fischer. . . . I ask you, Mr. Principal, to bring an end to the abuses in the Kindergarten of the Fröbelseminar."[41] Giessen's deputy mayor eventually ruled that the charges against Burgheim were unfounded.

Despite their popularity, the April laws were almost as ineffective as the boycott. The Nazis failed to remove Jews entirely from the civil service, law, and medicine. Of 717 non-Aryan judges and prosecuting attorneys, fewer than half, 336, or 47 percent, fell under the exclusion provisions, and no more than a quarter of the 4,500 Jewish doctors participating in the National Health Service were excluded.[42] In addition, defining what constituted a Jew remained problematic. Early on, the Nazis introduced the term "non-Aryan" to cover every person, Jewish or Gentile, who had at least one Jewish grandparent.[43] But this created more confusion than clarity. Professor Neisser, the director of Frankfurt's Institute of Hygiene, contested his dismissal order, which had labeled him a Jew, and insisted that he was a devout Protestant.[44] Faculty at the university's Institute of Physics debated whether to admit Hans Goldstein, a Christian "half-Jew": "Two doctoral candidates declared that they would not attend if this "half-Jew" were present. To the credit of the remaining doctoral students . . . the opponents found no support for their demand. . . ."[45] Giessen academicians Werner Schmidt, Franz Kirchheimer, and Franz Soetbeer also experienced discrimination as alleged "half-Jews."[46] Because of the ambiguities in the application of the April laws, most Nazi policy makers came to regard them as inadequate solutions to the "Jewish Question."[47]

The next major wave of Nazi antisemitic legislation came in autumn 1933. On 29 September, a Hereditary Farm Law prohibited Jews from owning farmland or engaging in agriculture. Jews suffered exclusion from film, theater, music, fine arts, and literature as well after a law ensured their regulation by Goebbels's Propaganda Ministry. A more specific law dealing with journalists, passed on 4 October, required government permission to work in broadcasting or in the press.

The effect of the farm law on Jews was minimal because few engaged in farming. The initial effects of laws against Jews in crafts, industry, and commerce were also uneven.[48] Karl Schleunes argues that those who sought the quick exclusion of Jews from German economic life initially lost out to individuals like Economics Minister Hjalmar Schacht, who favored continued Jewish participation in critical aspects of the economy to protect it from disruptive pressures.[49] My reseach confirms Schleunes's assertion to a certain extent.

Secret State Police (Gestapo) reports for Kassel indicate that Jewish economic activity in Hessen, and specifically Jewish trade with Gentiles, did not begin to wane until 1935.[50] In Frankfurt, where, as of February 1934, Jews and other "non-Aryans" owned 1,713 out of 4,955 (34.6 percent) stores, efforts to boycott Jewish businesses and to remove Jews from key areas of the town economy were low priorities for the city and state governments before 1938.[51] Friedrich Weil, a Jew convicted of customs fraud in 1934, served as wine commissioner between 1935 and 1938.[52] On 11 May 1934, Lord Mayor Krebs ruled in favor of an Orthodox Jewish woman seeking permission to operate a ritual slaughterhouse.[53] And in September 1935, Krebs entered into a dispute with *Der Stürmer*, Julius Streicher's antisemitic "newspaper," after it published a copy of an invoice sent from a Jewish shoe store to city hall, requesting payment for shoes ordered under the mayor's authority for welfare recipients.[54] Yet legal and sometimes violent attacks on Jewish economic life did occur, and *Gauleiter* Sprenger felt compelled to inform Hitler in February 1934 of the burden placed on Frankfurt as a result of the closing of numerous Jewish shops.[55]

Likewise in the summer of 1933, Jews in many German cities encountered difficulties obtaining permits to participate in trade fairs (*Messen*). Giessen city officials banned Jews from taking part in the upcoming horse market in September.[56] Hans Nathan Goldschmidt protested his exclusion on the grounds that he was a veteran and that his children belonged to a Gentile gymnastics club.[57] In the end, the only Hessian town that afforded Jews unfettered access to village fairs in 1933 was Alsfeld.[58] Responding to these local initiatives, the Reich Economics Ministry issued a belated directive on 23 September prohibiting the exclusion of Jews from autumn markets.[59]

As early as April 1933, Nazi officials at the state and local levels began removing Jews from the cattle trade and punishing those who failed to sever business ties with Jewish *Viehhändler*.[60] Efforts to create a Jew-free cattle trade in an efficient manner were impeded, however, by non-Jewish pogromists who assaulted Jewish traders and Gentile scofflaws who continued to conduct business with Jews. Lord Mayor Ritter placed Giessen's market centers under surveillance to assure party faithful that he was taking every step to solve the problem.[61] In July 1935, communiques from the underground Social Democratic resistance (Sopade) reported a series of pogroms carried out by the SA against Jewish cattle dealers in several Hessian towns.[62] In Giessen, attacks on Jewish traders followed the buildup of resentment by Gentile cattle dealers who accused Jews of selling cattle to buyers in eastern Prussia for resale to butchers in Baden and Württemberg.[63] Commenting on the violence in August 1935, the Kassel Gestapo proposed that *Volksgenossen* should be instructed simply to sever business ties with Jews and not to harass them.[64]

Jewish merchants suffered numerous incidents of economic discrimination in Frankfurt and Geisenheim as well before 1938. On Christmas Day 1934, party members staged another boycott of Jewish stores in Frankfurt.[65] In late May 1935, the head master of the Frankfurt Bakers' Guild warned members not to buy flour from Jews.[66] In August, representatives from the Frankfurter Boots-Vertrieb GmbH (FRABO), a sporting goods store, demanded that Lord Mayor Krebs prevent the opening of a similar store by a Jew.[67] That same year, Nazi thugs intimidated a Gentile cafe owner who refused to display a sign confirming that his saloon was a *Deutsches Geschäft*—a German store.[68] In Geisenheim, Georg Strauss received an increasing number of threats to his store after the summer of 1933.[69]

In cultural affairs, efforts to single out Jewish artists, writers, and performers in Frankfurt preceded the September 1933 legislation when demands for the expulsion of Jews from the prestigious Höchsche Conservatory surfaced in April: "All Jews must be removed from this institution because the . . . 'Jewish economy' has ruined the Höchsche Conservatory. . . . Herr Salomon . . . this Jewish . . . 'Advocate of German Art' must disappear first. To the Jews, Adolf Rebner, Paul Meyer . . . Walli Kirsamer, and any ally of this motley group . . . disappear is the motto! The time has come to bring the 'national revolution' to the Höchsche Conservatory. And without one single Jew!"[70] One month after the failed boycott, Nazi officials removed books written by Jews from Frankfurt's libraries and burned them.[71] Also in May, the city began firing Jewish employees of the City Theater, even Herbert Graf, a baptized Jew who had become a communist.[72] Following the September decrees, the sculptor Benno Elkan, who had sold his World War I memorial to the city in 1920, and others were deprived of the right to pursue careers in the arts.[73]

Six months after the September decree, Frankfurt's city administration embarked on a crusade to change street names deemed Jewish or "non-Aryan." This decision followed complaints by a female Nazi Party member in December 1933 that her street, Jakob Schiff Strasse, had been named after a Jew.[74] The Börne Platz soon became Dominikaner Platz, Heine Strasse became Rudolf Jung Strasse, and Sonnemann Strasse became Max Eyth Strasse. Not all streets had a "Jewish" connection, however. Because of its association with the Weimar Republic, Stresemann Allee was renamed Wilhelm Strasse, its appellation before 1918.[75]

In Giessen, Joseph Würzburger, founder and director of the Giessen Choir Association, lost his post, and the program director of the city theater, Wolfgang Kühne, a Gentile who had married a Jew, became the target of personal denunciation.[76] In May 1935, Kühne was accused by a *Betriebsobmann* of singing, "Goebbels and Hitler . . . are middlemen best seen from behind," at a theater-sponsored event. That Kühne's wife was Jewish made matters worse, and, despite protestations from Lord Mayor Ritter, Kühne ultimately lost his position in 1937.[77]

Not all non-Jewish cultural organizations or leaders supported the purge of Jews. Fending off accusations that he was Jewish, Frankfurt *Oberspielleiter* Jacob Geis, a Catholic, condemned Jew-hatred as fundamentally un-German.[78] The city's Senckenberger Nature Research Society, too, issued a statement of support for Jews in the summer of 1933, although it sounded more like a plea: "We declare that the Senckenberger Society does not make any distinction between its members, but guarantees, unchanged, equal rights. That goes for our members and friends as well as for our employees. . . . The retaining of Jewish employees will become easier if the [Jews] do not withdraw from the circle of contributing members and friends."[79]

With respect to sport, local and private efforts to expel Jews from German recreational associations also preceded national initiatives. In March 1933, the city administration of Cologne prohibited Jews from using Gentile sporting facilities, and on 4 April Jews were summarily expelled from the German Boxing Association.[80] Three weeks later, the national sport commissioner, Hans von Tschammer und Osten, issued a decree instructing Gentile sporting associations to add an "Aryans only" paragraph to their charters.[81] In the wake of this directive, Martin Harth, from Giessen, and Alex Strauss, from Geiseinheim, could no longer play soccer with their Gentile friends.[82] Hans Schlesinger, who belonged to the Frankfurt soccer club "1880" was not invited to a match between Frankfurt and Heidelberg after protests from members of the Heidelberg team.[83] Nevertheless, a uniform application of Tschammer und Osten's order remained elusive. Olympic fencer Helene Mayer was expelled from her fencing club in Offenbach in November 1933, although her membership in the national German Fencing Association was not affected, and she was later reinstated on the German Olympic team as a concession to the International and American Olympic Committees.[84]

On 2 June 1933, the Prussian minister for science, culture, and education prohibited all Jewish organizations from obtaining permits to stage events. Tschammer und Osten overturned this decree in the fall and granted Jewish sporting unions permission to operate legally. In July 1934, however, he limited state sanction to the patriotic Verein Schild, sponsored by the Jewish veterans group (the Reichsbund jüdischer Frontsoldaten), and the Zionist Makkabi Sports Union.[85] Neither organization had sufficient access to public gymnasia, and restrictions on the two eased only slightly during the preparations for the Olympic Games which were to be held in Berlin in August 1936.[86]

Hessian *Gauleiter* Sprenger did his part to defuse international

Olympic boycott efforts in January 1935 by ordering Frankfurt mayor Krebs to keep city sport facilities open to Jews.[87] Despite this facade of benevolence, Jewish athletes in Frankfurt continued to suffer discrimination. On 25 July 1935, the Ortsgruppe Bahnhof boycotted the city stadium for allowing Jews to use its facilities.[88] In May 1936, three months before the Olympic Games opened in Berlin, Frankfurt's Jews were prohibited from Gentile swimming pools and shunted to a segregated beach in Niederrad.[89]

After the Olympics, Hitler brought his policy in line with those who sought to deny Jews access to sporting arenas and to rescind the legal status of Jewish sport *Vereine*. On 9 October 1936, Himmler placed restrictions on the activities of the Imperial Union of Jewish Front Soldiers. Nearly three months later, the Gestapo officially banned all remaining Jewish associations, except for religious ones.[90]

Hopes for a more radical anti-Jewish policy from the SA were dealt a blow when its leadership was purged by Hitler and the SS in June 1934, and legislative action against Jews was renewed on a subdued scale in the spring of 1935 with the announcement of a new Military Service Law. The law reintroduced general conscription and made "Aryan" ancestry a prerequisite for entry into the armed forces. Like previous legislation, the Military Service Law represented little progress in the ongoing problem of defining what constituted a Jew. If anything, its definition of a "non-Aryan" was less precise than it had been in the 1933 April laws. Complicating matters was a rise in violence against Jews during the summer of 1935, sponsored by Nazi radicals and local party authorities frustrated with the slow pace of antisemitic legislation.

To resolve problems in Jewish policy, the Nazis promulgated a series of laws at the party's September 1935 rally in Nuremberg. The decrees, which quickly became known as the Nuremberg Laws, were intended to regulate Jewish and non-Jewish relations, intermarriage in particular. With the passage of the new laws, the Nazis brought Jewish policy in line with their assumptions that Jews were evil because of their blood and that their most heinous crime had been the defilement of Aryan racial purity, not the infiltration of the civil service, the various professions, or the German economy.[91]

The Law for the Protection of German Blood and Honor, passed on 15 September, outlawed marriages between Jews and "citizens of the state with German or related blood."[92] Extramarital sexual relations between Jews and Gentiles likewise became illegal and punishable by a prison sentence. In addition, the law forbade Jews to employ Gentile housemaids who were under the age of forty-five. The issue of citizenship was also addressed. On 26 April, Interior Minister Wilhelm Frick had announced plans for a change in the Reich citizenship laws based on racial criteria. But a law which appeared on 15 May dealt only with the question of the adoption of German nationality by foreigners and remained inadequate from the point of view of Nazi militants. The Reich Citizenship Law of 15 September redefined Jews as *Staatsangehörige*, or subjects of the state, rescinding their status as *Reichsbürger*, or citizens, without removing any concrete political rights from them.[93]

The First Supplementary Decree to the Reich Citizenship Law, enacted on 14 November, officially revoked voting rights for Jews and tackled the issue of Jewish categorization. Determining who was a Jew became a question of ancestry as the focus shifted away from individuals themselves and toward their grandparents. Racial Jews (*Rassejuden*) included full Jews (*Volljuden*) and "Christian" half-breeds (*Mischlinge*). *Volljuden* were identified as those who belonged to one of the Jewish religious communities (*Glaubensjuden*), crossbreeds who had Jewish spouses, the children of marriages involving one Jewish partner, or the offspring of illegitimate unions between Jews and Gentiles. If individuals had three or more Jewish grandparents, regardless of their or their parents' religious affiliation, they were also full Jews (*Volljuden*) in the eyes of the Nazis.[94] Someone with two Jewish grandparents who did not satisfy the above preconditions was legally a *Mischling* Grade One, someone with one Jewish grandparent, a *Mischling* Grade Two.[95]

According to Nazi estimates, in early 1936, there were four to five hundred thousand full, three-quarter, one-half, or one-quarter Jews in Germany who fit the legal concept of "Jew" and another three hundred thousand one-half and one-quarter "Christian" Jews who fell into the *Mischling* category. The 1939 census revealed 1,866 *Mischlinge* Grade One and 821 *Mischlinge* Grade Two in Frankfurt, 42 *Mischlinge* Grade One and 22 *Mischlinge* Grade Two in Giessen, 9 *Mischlinge* Grade One and 20 *Mischlinge* Grade Two in the entire Rheingau. By making it illegal to marry or consort with the newly defined Jew, the framers of the Nuremberg Laws sought not only to protect "German blood" but also to pave the way for the disappearance of all crossbreeds over time.[96]

As early as October 1933, however, officials in Mainz began discouraging marriages between Jews and Gentiles, a development that prompted the Hessian Gauleitung to persuade other city administrations to follow a similar course of action.[97] According to a December 1933 report from the American consul in Berlin, a Jewish lawyer in Giessen was taken into custody because he allegedly made sexual advances to an Aryan girl. Records indicate that intermarriage was also on the decline in both Frankfurt and Giessen well before the legislation of September 1935.[98]

The Nuremberg Laws brought Hitler's Jewish policy to the end of a major legal phase, evoking a mixture of anxiety and relief among Germany's Jews. Immediately following the September 1935 legislation, antisemitic harassment from the national government abated, partly because of the 1936 Olympic Games. In giving top priority to rearmament, Hitler also had to take into account Economics Minister Schacht's warnings that antisemitism damaged Germany's efforts to acquire raw materials.[99]

Yet legal and extralegal measures to squeeze Jews out of German life persisted at the state and local levels, and national assaults increased after the summer of 1936, as higher-ups in the government in Berlin began challenging the status quo on the "Jewish Question." Many simply felt that there were too many laws, some of which had the effect of protecting Jews, and that the occasional "good laws" were too slow in coming.[100] Further affecting the intensification of efforts to marginalize Jews was the displacement of state structures such as the Reich Chancellery and the Interior Ministry by more radical party institutions like the SS. Although the role of ordinary popular sentiment in the radicalization of Nazi Jewish policy after 1936 is unclear, and the majority of German Gentiles continued simply to assent to antisemitic measures that involved no violence, a growing number of non-Jews were willing to accept physical harassment against Jews and to take an active role in policing the "racial" state as informants.[101]

The earliest reaction to Hitler's regime by Germany's Jewish communal leaders was not as irresolute as many in the postwar era came to believe. Admittedly, many Jews did not perceive Nazi antisemitism as the dire threat it became. Frankfurt rabbi Georg Salzberger insisted that no one could guess what Hitler's coming to power meant, not even the greatest pessimist.[102] Still, the Orthodox Agudas Israel reacted with a call to strengthen Jewish life and culture, and on 30 March 1933, Frankfurt's IG council issued a bold statement reasserting its commitment to civil rights for Jews: "In these difficult times, it is necessary to address our community. Everyone must know that we will exercise all of our power, in association with all of the other communities in Germany, to speak up for the civil and political rights of German Jews."[103] And after initially condemning foreign anti-Nazi sentiment, the editors of the liberal *Central-Verein Zeitung* denounced the May book burnings as a "new Inquisition."[104]

The quickness of the Nazi assault, along with the inclusion of both foreign and native-born Jews in the new laws, brought Germany's diverse Jewish communities together. In mid-June 1933, Jewish community leaders in Berlin created a special cultural union, the Israelitischer Kulturbund, to promote Jewish pride and to ameliorate the effects of discriminatory legislation. Also that summer, new Jewish schools began emerging throughout Germany and in the Hessian towns of Wiesbaden, Darmstadt, and Worms.[105] In September, Germany's Jewish communities banded together to form the Reichsvertretung der deutschen Juden (National Representation of German Jews, RV). Founded by the Central Union of German Jews and the Zionist Federation to represent the collective interests of all Jewish organizations in Germany, the RV functioned as the sole source of German Jewish welfare and cultural activity after the fall of 1933. Seeking to transcend the ideological differences that had divided previous organizations, the RV chose two individuals who commanded enough respect to hold together German Jewry's warring factions. Leo Baeck, Berlin's well-known Reform rabbi, became the RV's president, and Otto Hirsch, a lawyer from Stuttgart, took the reins as executive director. Under their leadership, the RV aided emigration and revived a general charitable campaign known as Winter Help (Winterhilfe) that had originated during the Weimar period.[106]

In Frankfurt, where nearly one-fifth of Gemeinde members—mostly *Ostjuden*—lived on the edge of poverty, Jewish Winter Help provided food and clothing. A Jewish Work Program for young apprentices and adults offered courses in metalwork, woodwork, and mechanics. The Philanthropin, too, absorbed Jewish students expelled from city schools and expanded its curriculum to include different foreign languages, notably English. Finally, the Jewish House of Learning became a haven for Jewish intellectuals who had lost their jobs in the spring purge, including Ernst Kantorowicz, Caesar Seligmann, and Bertha Pappenheim. Martin Buber directed the activities of the Lehrhaus until his emigration to Palestine at the beginning of 1938.[107]

The Frankfurt Cultural Association (Kulturbund), founded in 1934 by Cologne conductor Hans Wilhelm Steinberg, offered art courses and maintained an orchestra of nearly fifty members. At its first concert in May of that year, the Kulturbund orchestra played symphonies of Beethoven and Schubert and Mendelssohn's violin concerto.

During Hanukkah, the Cultural Association even obtained permission to stage an art exhibit for unemployed Jewish artists and to perform Stefan Zweig's *Jeremias*.[108] To the Nazis, the Kulturbund served as a convenient facade of "tolerance" that facilitated Nazi control over Jewish cultural activities: "What could at first be taken for a gesture toward cultural self-determination was exposed as a means of restricting more and more the intellectual basis of Jewish existence and forcing Jews into a sort of cultural ghetto."[109] For Jews, however, the work of Jewish cultural centers in Berlin, the Rhein-Ruhr, and the Rhein-Main regions turned out to be a source of inner consolidation and pride.

The smaller Jewish communities of Giessen and Geisenheim, like their larger neighbor on the Main, tried to preserve a sense of normality in the early phase of Nazi persecution. In Giessen, as a consequence of a 1933 restriction, Erich Neumann could no longer serve as *shochet* (ritual butcher), but he continued to work as cantor and a religious instructor and even fulfilled certain rabbinical functions in the wake of the death of IRG head Leo Hirschfeld.[110] Despite falling demographic tallies, Giessen-Jewish *Verein* life in the 1930s endured as organizations such as the Jewish Cultural Association, the Jewish Central Welfare Office, and the Front Soldier Union remained active until the war.[111] In both Giessen and Geisenheim, normalcy for Jews meant observing the Sabbath, conducting business, obtaining some form of education (whether secular or Jewish), or simply holding to an established routine.

Jews also responded to Nazi persecution through emigration. Between 1933 and 1938, approximately 169,000 Jews left Germany, the largest number migrating initially to Palestine and then, after 1936, to the United States.[112] The Zionist Association, whose membership jumped from 7,500 in 1931 to 57,000 in 1934, initiated a program that helped German Jews leaving for Palestine to take with them some of their otherwise blocked funds. Under the terms of the Haavara Transfer Program, the German government permitted departing Jews to buy German goods with their funds and ship them to Palestine for resale. The ebb and flow of Jewish emigration from Germany corresponded to the various phases of Nazi persecution, falling from a peak of 37,000 in 1933 to 21,000 in 1935, rising to 25,000 in 1936, falling once again in 1937, and reaching its final crescendo in 1938, before and after the pogroms of Kristallnacht.[113] Not surprisingly, in the early years of the Nazi regime, German Jewish émigrés tended to be single individuals between the ages of twenty and thirty who were already predisposed to migrate within Germany.[114]

In Frankfurt, the local branch of the German Jewish Relief Association worked closely with the Palestine Office of the Jewish Agency to facilitate the emigration of more than eleven thousand Jews from the city between 1933 and 1937, the majority of whom left Germany altogether. The pattern of Jewish emigration from Frankfurt corresponded to the general pattern of German Jewish migration in the 1930s, falling from a high in 1933 to a low in 1935 and rising again to an even higher point in 1939.[115] As a consequence of migration and other demographic factors, fewer than fifteen thousand Jews (out of a 1933 population of twenty-six thousand) remained in Frankfurt by 1939.[116]

After losing his position in the Prussian Justice Service in April 1933, Paul Arnsberg left for Palestine. Martin Buber was forced from his home in 1938 and also emigrated to Palestine. Activist Henriette Fürth moved to Bad Ems following her removal from public office. Former politicians Hugo Sinzheimer and Bruno Asch, like Ludwig Landmann, went to Holland—Sinzheimer in 1933, Asch in 1938. The Franks emigrated to Holland as well, in 1933. Finally, following Kristallnacht, Ruth Westheimer went to Switzerland and Leo and Settie Sonnenborn fled to England.

In Giessen, 198 Jews emigrated to the United States, 82 to Palestine, 32 to South America, 16 to Africa, 2 to Asia, 2 to Australia, 33 to Holland, 13 to Belgium and Luxembourg, 27 to France, 37 to England, 7 to Italy, 1 to Denmark, 6 to Austria, and 330 to elsewhere in Germany (110 to Frankfurt).[117] In the decade, 1933 was the largest single year of Jewish emigration from the town, falling to a low in 1935, rising in 1937, and then dropping off because there were fewer Jews in Giessen. According to census reports, as of 1939, only 272 Jews were left in Giessen.[118]

In October 1937, Erich Neumann went to Eschwege; less than a year later, in September 1938, Martin Harth emigrated to the United States, and in March 1939 Harth's parents left for Johannesburg, South Africa. Josef Stern was able to leave in 1936, but his parents, Julius and Claire, were not as lucky. Opting to remain in Giessen, they were ultimately deported to Poland in 1942.

In Geisenheim, 1933 was not as big a year for emigration as 1934, perhaps because of the slightly delayed effects of antisemitic persecution in the town. In January 1934, Alex Strauss went to Frankfurt and eventually emigrated to San Francisco. Dr. Nathan returned to his home state of Lower Saxony in 1935 before moving permanently to Chicago. The next significant wave of emigration occurred in 1938 and

1939. Max and Auguste Strauss, Alex's parents, left for Johannesburg in May 1939. Six months earlier, Emma and Georg Strauss had emigrated to São Paulo. Seeking greener pastures and anonymity in a larger city, the elder Strausses, Liebmann and Karoline, went to Wiesbaden in August 1939.[119]

One of the more well-known opponents of the Nazi dictatorship, former Leipzig mayor Carl Friedrich Goerdeler, resigned his post as price commissioner one year after Hitler's appointment in protest against the antisemitic actions of Nazis in Leipzig. For their part, Social Democratic and communist resistance cells in Germany dealt more with the struggle against fascism than with the plight of Jews. This was the case for SPD and KPD groups in Frankfurt, Giessen, and Geisenheim, including the Socialist Worker Youth (SAJ), the Communist Opposition (KPO), the International Socialist Fighting Union (ISK), the Socialist Worker Party of Germany (SAP), and the Central Association of Officials (ZdA). The rhetoric of the "Red Help" movement in Giessen, the KPD District Leadership Hessen-Frankfurt, and the SPD District Leadership Hessen-Nassau was similarly narrow, targeting only workers, farmers, and young people in pamphlets distributed in 1933.[120] Even Emil Carlebach, a Jewish Marxist from Frankfurt, was arrested for distributing procommunist, not pro-Jewish, literature.[121] In Geisenheim, SPD member Martin Killian insisted that he and fellow Social Democrats had little time to dwell on the persecution of German Jewry. But Killian, like several Geisenheim Jews, felt threatened enough to seek anonymity in Wiesbaden after he was fired for political unreliability.[122]

Within the clergy, most Evangelical Protestant leaders avoided direct confrontations with the regime over antisemitism, and the small German Christian sect within the Evangelical church was unabashedly antisemitic, condemning the Old Testament and promoting a Nordic vision of Jesus. German Christians also called for the establishment of a national "people's" church. The numerous local bodies into which the Protestant church was divided hoped to deflect the issue of a national church by promulgating a centralized constitution on 27 May 1933. However, elections to the church synod held on 23 July produced a majority for the German Christians and enabled them to install Ludwig Müller, a military chaplain and acquaintance of Hitler, as Reich bishop.

Responding to this development and to the more onerous aspects of German Christian theology were such Protestant dissidents as the Swiss theologian Karl Barth and Berlin pastor Martin Niemöller.[123]

Mass demonstrations by Protestant faithful in the fall of 1934 followed the arrest of two politically conservative and orthodox Lutheran state bishops, Hans Meiser of Bavaria and Theophil Wurm of Württemberg. On 21 October, Niemöller's group, the Pastors' Emergency League, formally rejected the Reich church and created the Confessing Church. Hitler became concerned about the schism and decided to drop the attempt to control the Protestant church directly through Reich Bishop Müller and official support for the German Christians.

Meiser and Wurm were eventually reinstated, but the change had little effect on German Jewry. Cooperation between the Protestant church and the Nazi regime continued under their leadership.[124] Racist pitches also continued to find a receptive audience among many everyday Protestants. Anna Katterfield wrote in 1934 in the Protestant journal *Der Bote* that mixing races was against divine will: "It is the sacred obligation of our leaders to build a dam and put an end to any additional, ominous dilution of Aryan blood, even when in the process harsh measures cannot be avoided."[125] In June 1933, a commentary on the "Jewish Question" by Tübingen theologian Gerhard Kittel enraged Martin Buber and prompted him to respond:

> I no longer found it possible to acknowledge that you really do justice to Judaism as such, as you put it. . . . But what is even more important to me is your restriction of the "guest people"—"precisely because it is a guest," you wrote on page forty-two. Do you perhaps wish to extend this conclusion to the German minorities around the world? For surely the *lack of protection* by a unified nation living in a neighboring country (page eleven) cannot be a motivation for discriminating against the Jews. Does the status of a resident alien legitimize discrimination? You cite Deuteronomy 24:14 and 27:19 (page fifty-seven) but not Deuteronomy 10:17ff., or Leviticus 19:33f. ("love him as yourself"), not Leviticus 24:22 or Numbers 15:16 ("one standard for stranger and citizen alike" . . . one law for you and for the resident alien). Are these words supposed to apply only to Israel in relation to the heathens and not also to the Christian nation in regard to Israel?

In a rare show of support, theologian Ernst Lohmeyer wrote to Buber in August: "I have just read your 'Open Letter to Gerhard Kittel' and feel impelled to tell you that your every word expresses my deepest feelings. But what really impels me is not just this sense of spiritual affinity, . . . but, quite frankly, something like shame that fellow theologians are capable of thinking and writing as they do, and that the Protestant church can keep silent as it does."[126]

Like their counterparts in the Confessing Church, several priests and Catholic politicians who supported the prodemocratic Center Party rejected the Nazi agenda. But many Catholics agreed to coexist with Hitler's regime because of its anticommunism. As a result of the concordat signed between Hitler and the Vatican in the summer of 1933, German Catholics retained the right to publish encyclicals, worship in peace, and maintain Catholic schools, although they could no longer organize politically through the Center Party. At the same time, because the government consistently gave the concordat the narrowest of interpretations, conflicts arose over provisions concerning Catholic schools and youth organizations. The struggle between Catholics and the Nazi state reached a climax in March 1937 following the issuance of the papal encyclical *Mit brennender Sorge* (With Burning Concern), which assailed the main tenets of National Socialism. After its publication, many priests were sent to forced labor camps.[127]

Early on, Protestant church leaders in Frankfurt lent enthusiastic support to the Nazi regime. In a March 1933 sermon delivered at St. Paul's Church, Pastor Karl Veidt warmly greeted Hitler's nationalist, anticommunist agenda. By November he was speaking out against it—not so much because he opposed the persecution of Jews, socialists, or communists, but because he opposed the National Socialist, and specifically German Christian, concept of Christianity.[128] In late May 1934, a Confessing Church congregation emerged in Frankfurt, and several of its more radical members eventually sent letters of protest against antisemitic persecution. By and large, however, Frankfurt's Protestant clergy remained silent on the issue of Nazi antisemitism during Hitler's reign. With some exceptions, notably Father Alois Eckert, so too did most Catholic priests. In fact, Eckert was one of the few spiritual figures in Germany who criticized Nazi Jewish policy in its earliest phases. In an article published in the *Rhein-Mainische Volkszeitung* on 4 April 1933, Eckert argued that no person should be persecuted because of race. On his initiative, a circle of dissident priests, the Main-Rhein Clerical Front, formed in Frankfurt in the summer of 1934. In 1936, this group sent a memorandum to the German Conference of Bishops decrying the government's persecution of Jews and the arbitrary incarceration of dissenters in concentration camps. The bishops offered no response.[129]

One of the few religious dissidents who had any connection to Giessen was Protestant minister Paul Schneider, who received much of his theological training there. At a funeral of an eighteen-year-old Hitler Youth member on 11 June 1934, Schneider incurred the wrath of the NSDAP county director, Karl Moog, for minimizing a reference to Wessel, the SA thug killed in a street brawl with communists in 1930 and later immortalized by Nazis in a rallying anthem. For the next three years, Schneider endured arrest numerous times following clashes with Nazi authorities that sometimes involved protests against antisemitism. In November 1937, he was sent to Buchenwald for "anti-governmental utterances." He died there on 18 July 1939.[130]

In Geisenheim and environs, Margot Freimuth remembered a nun who cared for her dying grandfather during the Hitler years, and Martin Killian cited a Jesuit priest who was executed because he refused to enlist in the army. Killian pointed out, though, that there was little overt protest against antisemitism from Catholic priests in the Rheingau. Wilhelm Hesse, the priest of Geisenheim Cathedral from 1935 to 1961, remained silent on the issue and avoided confrontations with the Nazis at all cost to preserve his parish and its network of cultural and social organizations.[131]

An interesting footnote to the story of responses to Nazi antisemitism was the reaction of Christians of Jewish descent. Months after the concept of "non-Aryan" emerged, Christian "non-Aryans" created the Reich Association of Christian German Citizens of "non-Aryan" or Not Purely Aryan Descent. The founders emphasized "German thinking," "Christian sentiment," "national principles," and the "Führer idea." In 1935, following the Nuremberg Laws, they renamed themselves the Reich Association of Non-Aryan Christians, and later, emphasizing the Jewish origins of the apostle Paul, they became the Paulus Federation Reich Association of non-Aryan Christians. The organization essentially provided members with legal consultation, employment referrals, and educational advice. In 1937, it was prohibited from accepting individuals classified as *Volljuden*. Christian half-Jews and quarter-Jews, the so-called *Mischlinge*, composed the association's remaining members, and its title was changed once again, to Association 1937. Since Christian half-Jews needed special permission to marry a "pure German," and marriage to a "pure Jew" elevated half-Jewish status to that of *Volljude*, *Mischlinge* advertised secretly for mates in their own news bulletin. In 1939, just before the outbreak of the war, Association 1937 folded.[132]

Relations between "Christian Jews" and Jewish community members were complicated by the fact that for many Jews, conversion constituted apostasy. For many secessionists, their reclassification as Jews was an equally grievous insult. In the end, as involuntary Jews, Christian *Mischlinge* maintained the maximum separation from Jewish communal institutions and leaders.

While most German Gentiles reacted to state-sponsored antisemitism with a mixture of tacit acquiescence and indifference, there was considerably more room for popular initiative and active public support in policing the regime than past historians have assumed. Many non-Jews responded to the Nazi regime by immediately severing all contact with Jewish friends and acquaintances in January and February 1933. Ernst Valfer, a student in Frankfurt at the time, remembered losing friends once they joined the Hitler Youth.[133] And according to a secondhand account from Martin Killian, Gentile friends of the Geisenheim physician Dr. Siegfried Nathan dissociated themselves from him after Hitler took office.[134] In Giessen, following Hitler's appointment, Eva Steinreich's dancing-class girlfriends looked away as they passed her on the street, even though days before they had all danced together.[135] One of Alfred Gutsmuth's schoolmates also quickly turned against him: "A real friend [of Alfred's], with whom he had gone from Wieseck to Giessen every day . . . donned the black uniform on 31 January 1933 and knew Alfred no more."[136]

Martin Scheuer remembered that the friendship between his father and the eventual mayor of Friedberg did not affect the latter's position on the predicament of Germany's Jews: "By 1933, the mayor and the rest would not help. They would not lift a finger when it started. They all turned Nazi and said, 'We're sorry.' If you had a chance to corner them, 'We're sorry, but we have to make a living. What can we do?' They had no civil courage. There were very few [who did]." Similarly, Lili Hahn from Frankfurt lamented that an old friendship of her mother's fell apart, although admittedly later—in the summer of 1934: "A few days ago, we had our regular evening of chamber music. After playing, the evening ended with the usual social hour. Tea with rum was served. The conversation began about new literary publications and then turned to musical events. Mrs. Rapp related that [conductor Otto] Klemperer had a horrible mishap. Mrs Graber said 'I wish he had broken his neck because he's a Jew.' In the awkward silence that followed, mother said in a voice choked with emotion, 'You don't seem to know that my father was also a Jew!"[137] The severing of ties between Jews and Gentiles in the wake of Hitler's appointment was not without significance. Much of this upheaval came well before the establishment of the Nazis' one-party dictatorship.

Reports from the Sopade and Gestapo also show that verbal and physical outbursts against Jews occurred sporadically from 1933 to 1938. In September 1934, the Kassel Gestapo reported that Jew-hatred in Hessen-Kassel was on the rise, one month after it had asserted that antisemitic outbursts were rare occurrences. Communiques from both the Frankfurt and Kassel Gestapos revealed an increase in SA and party-inspired assaults against Jews and Jewish property between September 1934 and September 1935.[138] The Sopade reported incidents of pogroms in Hessen during the summer of 1935 and argued in September 1935 that all means were being employed to carry out the fight against Hessian Jews.[139] The September report specifically described how members of the Hitler Youth marched through many towns in Hessen singing, "when Jewish blood flows from a knife, then everything will be good."[140] Margot Freimuth, from Östrich-Winkel near Geisenheim, remembered a time when she was physically assaulted by classmates who resented her refusal to give the Hitler salute.[141]

A tiny minority of Gentiles weathered the increasingly radical pressures of Nazi dictatorship and continued to maintain contact with Jews.[142] Elizabeth Bamberger, from Frankfurt, recalled how some non-Jewish acquaintances became staunch Judeophiles after the "seizure of power." One of her son's professors at the Goethe Gymnasium, a conservative no less, planned a long boat trip in protest against Nazi Jewish policy. Gentile friends of Frankfurt cantor Joseph Levy privately spoke out against Hitler and antisemitism as well. Erich Decker, a compatriot of Franz Kirchheimer, a half-Jew who was fired from Giessen's Geological Institute, stood up for his friend when he was cornered by a drunken SA official in a pub. Dora Scheuer even had a female friend in Giessen who was a Nazi but who hid Jews in her home. Annelise Schnabel's mother worked secretly for Georg and Emma Strauss in Geisenheim, and Donald Strauss remembered the bond between his father, Alex, and a former soccer mate from the town by the name of Dillmann: "Alex was from a Jewish family and Herr Dillmann from a Catholic family. Their friendship continued into the late 1930s. Herr Dillmann was an employee of the German Post Office and as I understand, he was required to join the Nazi Party. About 1937, Alex was visiting Herr Dillmann in his apartment in Frankfurt. Herr Dillmann was married and had a family at this time. It was possible for them both to be jailed for 'fraternizing.' Herr Dillmann said to my father that conditions for the Jews would get even worse and that my father should leave the country."[143]

Some Jewish memoir writers recounted instances when help was offered by strangers. Alice Oppenheimer described how her brother-in-law occasionally disappeared from Frankfurt for days because an official who accepted bribes had warned him of raids by party members. Some survivors, like Martin Harth and Joseph Levy, were remindful that many non-Jewish friends, fearful for their own lives, privately expressed frustration over their inability to do anything about Nazi antisemitic legislation or pogroms. In the same breath, Levy told a story about an elderly Gentile woman he encountered on the street who said that Levy belonged to a small minority of "decent Jews" (*anständige Juden*)." Some interviewees pointed to a further distinction made by Gentile friends, acquaintances, and strangers between an individual Jew and "the Jews."[144]

Although indifference and inaction typified Gentile conduct toward Jews between 1933 and 1938, I would like to focus here on two behavior patterns that characterized the extremes—*Rassenschande* and denunciation. Memoirs and interviews make it clear that many non-Jews demonstrated and risked punishment for "Jewish-friendly behavior" (*judenfreundliches Verhalten*).[145] Reports from SA Group Hessen and Hessian *Kreisleitungen* also listed prosecutions of Nazis who continued to conduct business and socialize with Jews. Karl Brinkwerth, SA *Obersturmführer* in Frankfurt, was expelled from the party because he had personal contact with Jews. The same fate befell SA *Oberscharführer* Karl Raab for consulting a Jewish doctor.[146]

Sexual relations between a Jew and a non-Jew, the basis for *Rassenschande* (or race defilement) charges, constituted a more radical, if not more marginal, act. The Sopade listed 179 cases of *Rassenschande* from October 1935 to December 1936. Most of the 68 reported cases between October 1935 and August 1936 involved Jewish men accused of having longstanding relations with Gentile women. These cases were frequently precipitated by a third party denunciation, but they occasionally followed an unwed couple's desire to obtain a marriage license.[147] Those who committed *Rassenschande* tended to receive longer sentences than those who merely came to the aid of or socialized with Jews (*Judenfreunde*) because the former was a clear violation of the law while the latter was not, per se. *Judenfreunde* were prosecuted under laws covering slander, conspiracy, and treason. Initially, sentences for *Rassenschande* involved terms in a normal prison (*Gefängnis*), but by 1937, a growing number of convicts were being sent to harsher penitentiaries (*Zuchthäuser*) and then, upon their release, to concentration camps.[148]

All eight instances of *Rassenschande* in Frankfurt between 1935 and 1938, published by Ernst Noam and Wolf-Arno Kropat, dealt with Jewish men and Gentile women, and the average time span of their acquaintance was five and a half years. The cases included a Jewish cattle dealer who was accused of having sexual relations with a long-standing lover, an unemployed worker who was also charged with having sex with his non-Jewish former wife, a Jewish writer whom the Frankfurt county court indicted on two counts of *Rassenschande*, and a merchant brought up on charges of masturbating in front a Gentile prostitute. In only one of the eight cases was the non-Jewish female sentenced, and six of the eight Jewish male convicts were sent to *Zuchthäuser*. Their sentences were also much harsher than ones involving terms in regular jails, averaging over two years.[149] On a more everyday level, Martin Scheuer of Friedberg remembered how the new racial laws affected his social life:

> "I had a few girl friends—Jewish and Gentile, *Shiksas*. The one *Shiksa* I remember. I went out with her and then one night she told me, "I can't see you anymore because my boyfriend is a Nazi, the highest storm trooper in Hessen (!)." And she was afraid. "I'm going to get into trouble. I better stay away from you." I always got with the wrong people.
>
> And then I went out with another girl, a blonde. Jews weren't allowed to go out with Gentile girls anymore. They were not allowed to go to any restaurants. The only restaurant you could go to was at the railway station . . . so we went there for some refreshments. Then I took her to a movie. When I came out, we were confronted by a group. They weren't dressed up as storm troopers, but they were Nazis. I knew what they were going to do. I didn't enjoy that scene. They said, "We have to take you to the police station." I was willing to go along, but somebody who knew the girl said, "You're making fools of yourselves. The girl is Jewish too."[150]

Using *Rassenschande* to assess Gentile behavior toward Jews is problematic because it constituted a form of deviance. One could also commit "race defilement" without resistance-driven motivations. An interesting case involved Richard Limpert, director of the Frankfurt Musicians' Orchestra. In August 1935, the Gestapo accused him of failing to sever ties with his allegedly Jewish former wife. Limpert lodged a protest with the mayor's office, insisting that his former wife was a Gentile and that he had never socialized with Jews in his entire life. But his complaint fell on deaf ears and the city personnel office decided not to renew his contract.[151]

Historians disagree about denunciations of Jews to the Gestapo in Frankfurt. Walter Otto Weyrauch, in an analysis of still classified Frankfurt Gestapo files on twelve hundred paid informants, so-called V-persons (*Vertrauensleute*), has concluded that the secret police recruited foreigners living in Germany (Swiss citizens and eastern Europeans) and enemies of the regime (Jews and Catholic priests) to inform on suspicious individuals.[152] Heinrich Baab, SS-*Untersturmführer* and criminal secretary in Frankfurt, argued that Emil Schott, one of the town's Jewish community leaders in the late 1930s, lent his cooperation in the search for Gentiles who sustained relations with Jews and cross-breeds. According to historian Reinhard Mann, however, only 15 percent of all Gestapo cases were initiated by V-persons while most followed leads of volunteer informers.[153]

Because of new German laws dealing with confidentiality, informant files in Frankfurt remain classified. As a result, the small number of cases to which I had access more than likely paint a skewed picture of voluntary denunciation. Nonetheless, in several instances an interesting twist surfaced. Gentile informers often denounced other Gentiles who refused to suspend relations with Jews: a health care provider's wife was accused of patronizing a Jewish store, a Jew by the name of Westheimer came under scrutiny for socializing with a Gentile female in a Frankfurt pub, and a police sergeant was denounced because his wife continued to do work cleaning for the Jewish community center. In Geisenheim, Annelise Schnabel's mother risked denunciation for a similar reason; a doctor apparently knew that she was moonlighting at Georg and Emma Strauss's feed store.[154]

Available accounts of denunciations from elsewhere in Hessen concur with the spotty pieces of information from Frankfurt, Giessen, and Geisenheim, although summaries of those denuciations in the catalogs of the Hessian Main State Archives in Wiesbaden do not distinguish voluntary from paid informants. A denunciation to *Der Stürmer* prompted the investigation of an Eschwege family who continued to buy clothes from a Jewish merchant. An SA member from Limburg was also denounced for buying from Jews. And in Frankenberg, a priest suffered denunciation for preaching that hatred of Jews was un-Christian. In other instances, denunciations came against Jews, as was the case with Hedwig Burgheim in Giessen, or against individuals suspected of being Jewish. In Frankfurt, a priest denounced an opera singer whom he believed to be a Jew, and a nurse informed on a female doctor at the university's Ophthalmology Clinic for the same reason.[155]

Determining the motives of informants, an issue frequently raised by researchers, is a difficult if not impossible task. Some individuals denounced for opportunistic reasons or out of personal and antisemitic malice, or a combination of all three. Moreover, according to Robert Gellately, not everyone in a Gestapo dossier, nor everyone brought to court because of alleged political criminality, was found guilty. Hans Robinsohn pointed out that courts in Hamburg, Cologne, and Frankfurt acquitted over 10 percent of *Rassenschande* defendants. As many as 16 percent of all those brought to trial in Frankfurt were declared innocent. There were many additional charges that did not come to court, a not surprising development given the large number of "amateur helpers on the trail of crime." Despite its shortcomings, denunciation proved indispensable to the Terror by fostering fear, paralyzing opposition, and harnessing personal resentment and spite for the purposes of the Nazi state.[156]

In the early stages of Hitler's regime, the different atmospheres for Jews in Frankfurt am Main, Giessen, and Geisenheim began to assume a shared quality of hostility. Overall, from 1933 to 1935, the majority of Gentiles in the three cities acquiesced passively to antisemitic legislation, although evidence from my research suggests that violence against Jews was not uncommon and that popular denunciations played a useful role in the enforcement of Nazi antisemitic policy. Between 1935 and 1938, a minority of Germans, mainly party members and the SA but also some nonparty members, sought a more brutal policy, while another minority opposed antisemitism and maintained ties with Jewish acquaintances. These minorities remained polarized around a compliant majority that deviated little from previous modes of conduct toward Jews.[157]

Although the relational context behind Gentile thought and action vis-à-vis Jews in the three towns did not always produce uniform results, many patterns of Gentile-Jewish interaction that predated 1933 influenced behavior during Hitler's reign. Friendships that survived a rupture in 1933 often provided a well of support for Jews while consistently negative interrelations tended to foster convictions of disregard or tacit approval of antisemitic restrictions. The latter two sentiments were by far more commonplace, and by aiding in the marginalization of German Jewry in the early years of the Third Reich, they removed obstacles in the way of harsher anti-Jewish measures in the immediate period before the outbreak of World War II and during its course.

7

Relations During
the "Final Solution"

The destruction of European Jewry at the hands of the Nazis during World War II may not have been the inevitable result of centuries of anti-semitism on the continent. Even the intensification of persecution against Jews in Germany before the invasion of Poland in September 1939 did not necessarily foreshadow genocide. Clearly, though, the situation for German Jews had become more violent and life-threatening well before the beginning of the war. Reports on the Jewish Question from the Nazi Party's Security Service (Sicherheitsdienst, or SD), admittedly biased and sometimes unreliable sources, implied that public opinion had also shifted in favor of more brutal measures. Yet in Frankfurt am Main, Giessen, and Geisenheim, the number of proponents and *opponents* of antisemitic barbarism increased between 1938 and 1945, while most Gentiles simply continued to turn a blind eye to Jews.

The winter months of 1937-38 marked a turning point in both the development of Hitler's Reich and the direction of Nazi Jewish policy. Conservatives such as Foreign Minister Konstantin von Neurath, Economics Minister Hjalmar Schacht, and Generals Werner von Blomberg and Werner von Fritsch lost their posts, and Hitler personally assumed the duties of commander-in-chief of the armed forces by taking over the War Ministry. Radical antisemites were especially pleased by the departure of Schacht, who had impeded efforts to remove Jews from the German economy.

The replacement of Schacht by Air Force Minister Hermann Göring in December ushered in an era of heightened antisemitic activity. Julius Streicher organized a boycott of Jewish stores in Nuremberg during Christmas week 1937. In January 1938, Göring codified the prohibition of contract extension to firms whose governing boards were 25 percent Jewish. SS head Heinrich Himmler ordered the expulsion of foreign-born Soviet Jews in February, and the 28 March Law Regarding the Legal Status of Jewish Communities deprived Jewish religious congregations of the legal protection accorded to "bodies of public law." On 26 April, another decree required Jews to register all property holdings, an obligation that portended the outright seizure of Jewish property. Fifteen hundred Jews were arrested and sent to the Buchenwald and Sachsenhausen concentration camps in a major roundup in June. And finally, in August, all Jews were forced to take the names Sarah and Israel, and the stamping of Jewish passports with a red "J" began on 5 October.

The exclusion of Jews from the few remaining social arenas open to them gathered speed as well in 1938. The NSDAP county leader in Hessen sent the following letter to Frankfurt's Lord Mayor Krebs on 27 July:

> Complaints from the population are multiplying day by day concerning the use by Jews of the Niederrad bathing area. In particular, the inhabitants of Niederrad and of those parts of the city near the bathing area complain that they are being forced to go a relatively long way when they want to swim, because the bathing areas near them are continually being used by Jews. Moreover, on warm days the trams to and from Niederrad are so full of Jews that it often results in unpleasant incidents. With regard to the fact that the bathing facilities here are not adequate for the German population, it is no longer acceptable that the Jews should have a bathing area at their disposal. I therefore request the Jews be forbidden to use the Niederrad bathing area as soon as possible.[1]

On 2 November, Krebs decreed that the Niederrad beach would no longer be open to Jews.[2]

Although antisemitic persecution increased during the winter of 1938, emigration remained the main goal of Nazi Jewish policy. The German annexation of Austria in March and the acquisition of two hundred thousand Jews, however, more than canceled out German Jewish emigration totals from 1933 to early 1938.[3] Prospects of an even larger deluge of Jews fleeing from Austria to the United States prompted President Franklin D. Roosevelt to call for the convening of an international conference on refugees. In July, thirty-two countries responded by sending delegates to the French town of Evian, a move that did little to resolve the refugee problem.[4] Subsequent British decisions to restrict Jewish emigration to Palestine actually removed options for German Jews. By the autumn of 1938, only 150,000 to

170,000 Jews had left Germany, one-third of the approximately 500,000 German *Glaubensjuden* counted by the 1933 census.

Complicating matters was the emergence of a conflict over Jewish policy among Göring, the SS (specifically, Himmler and Reinhard Heydrich), and radicals in the SA. Dissension festered until November, when problems arising from the Kristallnacht pogroms convinced Hitler that the objectives of Nazi Jewish policy were unattainable without centralized control and a more "rational," that is, less violent, approach.[5]

Intraparty discord over Jewish policy was ill-timed, coming on the heels of Hitler's foreign policy "triumph" at the Munich Conference.[6] In September, Hitler, Italian leader Benito Mussolini, French premier Eduard Daladier, and British prime minister Neville Chamberlain met in the Bavarian capital to settle a dispute over the German-speaking Sudeten region of Czechoslovakia. In what has been attacked as the quintessential act of appeasement, Chamberlain agreed to the German annexation of the Sudetenland, miscalculating Hitler's desire for war. On 21 October, Hitler notified his military chiefs that the dismantling of Czechoslovakia had become a short-range goal of German foreign policy. After the Munich agreement, the Germans also expelled nearly three thousand *Ostjuden*. This act served as a prologue to events that culminated in the anti-Jewish rioting of 9 and 10 November, commonly known as Kristallnacht or the "Night of Broken Glass," during which synagogues were destroyed, Jewish businesses were ransacked, ninety-one Jews were killed, and nearly twenty-six thousand were sent to concentration camps.

The roots of the November pogroms actually lay in a broader conflict between the German and Polish governments over Polish Jews living in Germany. In March 1938, the cabinet of Marshal Rydz-Smigly, prime minister of Poland, issued an Expatriates Law that threatened to void the citizenship of Polish nationals living outside of Poland as of 31 October 1938 unless they received a special passport stamp. But when Polish Jews went to their consulates in Germany, they were refused the dispensation, mainly because the Polish government had no desire to see Jews return to their native land. In angry retaliation, on 28 October, the Nazis began deporting seventeen thousand of Germany's seventy thousand Polish Jews. Because Poland refused to admit them, they were forced to live in no-man's-land—the area between the official boundaries of Poland and Germany—in terrible weather and without shelter.

In the early morning of 7 November, a Jewish youth whose parents were among those rounded up by the Gestapo shot the third secretary in the German embassy in Paris, Ernst vom Rath, who died two days later. The assassin, Herschel Grynzspan, was a seventeen-year-old former Yeshiva student from Frankfurt am Main living with relatives in Paris. For years, historians saw vom Rath's assassination as the spark for Kristallnacht. Yet according to Karl Schleunes, the Night of Broken Glass was neither an act of vengeance coordinated by the government in Berlin nor a spontaneous venting of popular rage against vom Rath's assassination. In Schleunes's opinion, the pogroms were a failed attempt by Propaganda Minister Josef Goebbels, the SA, and party radicals to seize control of Nazi Jewish policy. Seeking to regain Hitler's lost favor following an embarrassing love affair with a film star, Goebbels envisioned pogroms of revenge occurring on the anniversary of the November 1923 Beer Hall Putsch, and, with Hitler's blessing, he enlisted the help of the SA for one "final fling against the Jews." Schleunes believes that Goebbels's scheme was ruined by a popular backlash against the violence and strong opposition from Himmler, Heydrich, and Göring, who preferred the controlled terror of the police state to the chaotic fervor of the SA.[7]

In Hessen, the pogroms began before vom Rath's death and Goebbels's agitation and were not solely the responsibility of the SA. SA-and SS-inspired violence in Kassel during the nights of 7 and 8 November was considered model behavior by the minister of propaganda in his incendiary speech in Munich on the ninth.[8] In Marburg and Fulda, SS and SD men gave orders to torch the synagogues of their respective towns independently of the Munich communique.[9] Goebbels's commendation of the events in Hessen followed admissions of ignorance on the part of town mayors and overt protests against the pogroms from Hessen *Gauleiter* Jakob Sprenger and Kurhessen deputy *Gauleiter* Solbrig.[10]

Kristallnacht in Frankfurt capped off a year of escalating violence toward Jews. In the spring of 1937, Orthodox IG rabbi Jakob Hoffmann was arrested and deported.[11] At the end of April 1938, party radicals staged another boycott of Jewish stores, and in September, Gestapo agents took the community's other Orthodox rabbi, Jakob Horovitz, into custody. The Gestapo eventually released Horovitz and allowed him to emigrate to Holland, but he died soon afterward from injuries suffered during his incarceration.[12] When news reached Frankfurt of the attempted assassination of von Rath on 7 November, local NSDAP officials fumed. Vom Rath, after all, had come from Frankfurt, and his assassin, Grynzspan, had studied at the city's Yeshiva. At 5:00 in the morning of 10 November, SA and Hitler Youth members began torching the city's synagogues and vandalizing Jewish stores. At 6:30, the Gestapo began arresting Jewish men. Later that morning, various party functionaries in civilian clothing took to the streets shouting "Down with the Jews, " "Germany awaken!" In an effort to maintain calm, the Reich Main Security Office of the SS (the RSHA) ordered all Jewish stores to close, but throngs of party members, including SS and SA men, and non-Nazi mob enthusiasts quickly turned order into anarchy by plundering shops and adjacent apartments of Jews and trashing the Museum of Jewish Antiquity.[13] The Sopade described the scene as simply horrifying:

> All of the synagogues are completely destroyed. They offer a grisly picture of devastation. . . . The big synagogue on Friedberger Anlage, a beautiful and quite recent construction, burned to the ground. Firefighters looked on without making an attempt to extinguish the fire. The large West End synagogue, just like all other old synagogues, became a prey of the flames. Windows in all Jewish stores were broken, and everything inside, large and small, smashed. It looked tragic at Ehrenfeld's, a gift store on the Zeil. Expensive radios and photographic devices lay destroyed in the demolished shop window. . . . Windows and shutters at Voltz-Eberle, a wine store chain, were [also] destroyed and wine was poured into the alley. . . . Shops previously owned by Jews and now under Gentile management affixed signs reading "Now Aryan Property." At Reta, a sundries store, it was written that ownership of the business was falling into Gentile hands. In front of many stores also stood police detachments. They appeared, however, only after the destruction had finished. It [the pogrom] looks like a premeditated undertaking.[14]

The fire department eventually extinguished the fires in the city's synagogues, but at 5:00 P.M., when factories and offices closed and the number of rabble-rousers in the streets increased, fires were set again, this time to blaze unchecked until the buildings were completely gutted.[15] Frankfurt's East End, where the bulk of *Ostjuden* lived, then suffered the first in a series of attacks against Jews citywide. On the evening of the tenth, hundreds of Jewish men were arrested and incarcerated in the Frankfurt Festhalle. From there, they were brought to the South Train Station and deported to concentration camps. Those arrested included Yeshiva director Willy Mainz and teachers from the Philanthropin. The arrests stopped on Monday morning, 14 November, only to begin again thirty-six hours later. Pairs of SS troopers roamed the streets stopping pedestrians and entering homes on the pretext of looking for Jewish males who might have been hiding. In all, 2,621 Frankfurt Jews ended up in Buchenwald following the pogrom.[16]

In Giessen, Kristallnacht played itself out in similar fashion. SS and SA men (among them future academicians) stole furniture, books, carpets, and precious ritual objects from the synagogues on Sudanlage and on Steinstrasse, torched the buildings, and instructed firefighters merely to prevent the spread of the blaze.[17] As in Frankfurt, Jewish stores in Giessen were plundered and numerous Jewish men were sent to concentration camps, among them Martin Harth's father. Storm troopers also led away an individual who was taking pictures of the scene and assaulted a Jewish man who tried to save burning Torah scrolls.[18] Like newspapers in Frankfurt and throughout Germany, both the *Oberhessische Tageszeitung* and the *Giessener Anzeiger* asserted that the pogrom was a spontaneous venting of anger on the part of Giessen *Volksgenossen*.[19]

Reports for Geisenheim maintained that the 9-10 November attack on Jews was less severe in the Rhenish village than in Frankfurt, Giessen, and other Hessen towns (including some in the Rheingau).[20] Max and Liebmann Strauss, however, would have taken issue with this claim. On the night of the pogrom, an SS official led SA men in civilian clothing and students from the Viticulture Research Institute to the Strauss's store located in the center of the village. Shouts of "shitty Jews" and the sound of storefront windows being shattered brought numerous village residents out of their homes and into the streets. Storm troopers, accompanied by a few onlookers, proceeded to raid the Strauss's place of business, trash their apartments, and take both Max and Liebmann into custody. Liebmann's wife, Karolina, and Ferdinand and Ludwig Mayer were also detained by the police for several days. Because Ludwig Mayer was sick and because the rest were over sixty years old, none of them were sent to a concentration camp. But the piles of silverware, furniture, and sundry merchandise from the Strauss store which lay strewn in the road served as a lasting reminder that

Jews, even in the smallest of villages, were no longer safe from physical assault.[21]

According to Sarah Gordon, Ian Kershaw, and David Bankier, the vast majority of Germans disapproved of Kristallnacht because it involved murder and the destruction of property.[22] In Germany's Catholic and urban regions (the south and west) outrage over the violence was stronger than in the Protestant rural north. Otto Dov Kulka and Aron Rodrigue have warned, however, against overstating the moral outrage aroused by Kristallnacht and have insisted that economic concerns were the primary motives behind any opposition to the pogroms.[23] Much of the evidence from the three towns points to a complex conclusion, suggesting that citizens may have raised objections in the privacy of their homes but did little to protest the carnage openly, that many joined the SA and SS in their orgy of destruction, and that most returned to a state of indifference toward Jews and the "Jewish Question" after the pogrom.

The SD's annual report for 1938 disclosed that most church groups refrained from criticizing the violence.[24] Bishop Antonius Hilfrich of Limburg said that it was inappropriate for him to raise his voice in protest, and he went to great lengths to deny the Jewish origins of Christianity in sermons delivered after Kristallnacht.[25] Three years later he stood at the forefront of church remonstrance against the Nazi euthanasia program that gassed terminally ill and handicapped persons.

Accounts of ordinary Gentiles and Jews in Frankfurt, Giessen, and Geisenheim varied in their description of Kristallnacht, but by and large, they shared a perception of the violence as party-sponsored mob aggression that encountered only pockets of resistance. Rabbi Georg Salzberger asserted that "no fireman would put out the blaze." Alice Oppenheimer argued in her memoirs that the "people [of Frankfurt] were drunk with power, drunk with their misguided authority, and obsessed with hooliganism to destroy and ruin" during the night of 9-10 November. But she also told a story of a mysterious caller, likely a former patient of her husband's, who asked to meet with her secretly to secure the release of her incarcerated spouse:

> I crossed the open square and reached the beginning of the promenade. Nor far from a street lantern stood a man in a cap. His face was hidden by a woolen scarf. . . . I took a few steps back, then I believed that the man in the scarf was the one who had called me, and I swung my glove back and forth. He came to me as if I were a prostitute. Suddenly

another man whispered. . . . He raised a finger and waved me to him. . . . Like an old acquaintance, he shook my hand strongly. With the same hoarse voice as on the telephone, he said "Hello, Frau Oppenheimer. I am in a hurry. We have to do this fast." "Yes," I answered, "I know that we are being watched. Let us go down this dark street." "O.K., give me your husband's passport!" "Can you rescue him?" I asked. "Yes, but don't ask me so much. Do you have his passport with you?" "Yes, but I don't want to give it to you." "Don't you believe me?" "No!" I said without hesitating. "If I show you your husband's key as proof that I am telling the truth, then will you believe me?" He took a key ring from his pants pocket and showed it to me. . . . I compared it to one of the keys on my ring, and it matched. . . . Hesitatingly, I gave him the passport. "Do you have any money with you? This will cost much!" I gave him everything that I had with me, to the last penny.[26]

Alice's husband, Siegfried, was eventually freed and later joined his wife, who had already emigrated to Palestine.

Elizabeth Bamberger, also from Frankfurt, cited examples of Gentile friends (of her friends) who likewise lent their support: "A friend had returned from a concentration camp, and his sister-in-law went to visit him. The cook who had been in his employment for many years grabbed her by the arm and cried out, 'Mrs. H., how can a man be so mistreated?' Other friends had visits from a Christian couple who embraced them in tears and the man cried, 'I am ashamed to be a German.'" Cantor Joseph Levy remembered a Christian notary who visited during the "horrible November days," blasting all of the "scoundrels, rogues, and murderers" involved in the violence. The journalist Artur Lauinger, too, recalled that the widow of an army official friend used her late husband's influence and her own ingenuity to free several Jews languishing in Gestapo prisons. Finally, while struggling to secure exit visas from Germany, Settie Sonnenborn was sustained by the kindness of a few good Gentiles:

One neighbor had a grocery store, and one had a butcher shop. They all used to call me, to talk on the telephone. They knew that Leo was in a concentration camp, and that my father was in bed, sick. From the grocery store, they asked me, "Mrs. S., call me Mrs. Smith, not my real name." She said, "I will call you everyday and write down what you need. Then I'll open the door and ring the bell, and put them on the steps. You come down and pick it up." My butcher did the same. They all had signs—"No Jews allowed to go in." You couldn't get anything anywhere. But this one butcher always gave me sweetbreads. I went to the butcher in the morning, despite the sign. I was standing in the back. He looked at me, and said I should stay in the back. In front, there were four women, and one woman said, "Did you hear what was going on last night? They took all the Jews in the *Sporthalle.* Then they took them in the train and beat them." I knew my husband had been beaten. One woman said, "I think it is awful." They didn't know I was a Jew, but the butcher said, "Listen, you come later, or my wife will come to you."[27]

Clearly, one of the common denominators linking these cases was a friendship between a Gentile and a Jew. In each of those instances, intimate ties affected non-Jewish opposition to Kristallnacht.

Still, most Jewish eyewitnesses from Frankfurt maintained that the overall sentiment toward Jews during the November pogrom was one of hostility and disregard.[28] Kurt Blaum was struck by the refusal of city authorities to rein in the violence. Sidney Baumann described how a group of thugs raided his orphanage, smashed furniture, beat him up, and dragged him off to Gestapo headquarters. Rabbi Salzberger, Baumann, Lauinger, Josef Berolzheimer, and Hans Berger remembered that an angry mob bombarded them with stones as they were led through the streets of the city to the Festival Hall and then to the train station: "On the same evening, in severe cold, we were taken in trucks to . . . the Festhalle, where we arrived at eleven at night. A howling mob [of both men and women] received us at the entrance to the Festhalle—abusive shouts, stone-throwing, in short the atmosphere of a pogrom."[29]

Perceptions of Kristallnacht in Giessen and Geisenheim (particularly, but not exclusively, Gentile ones) have implied that there was less popular support for the pogrom than in Frankfurt.[30] Apart from the SA and SS, only firefighters routinely came under attack in memoirs and interviews for their conduct. Auguste Wagner, from Giessen, reported that every eyewitness to the torching of the Steinstrasse synagogue cursed the arsonists. More credible accounts from Dora Scheuer and Erich Deeg called to mind several residents who privately expressed their disgust with the Nazi action. Deeg pointed out that the synagogue fire did not inspire the formation of a large mob, leaving the impression that most Giesseners tried to ignore the pogrom.[31]

Yet according to a study of Nazi war crimes in Hessen, there was not a single documented case of Gentile aid for a Jewish family in the region during Kristallnacht. And even Deeg admitted that gang attacks against Jewish store owners occurred in the area of the Neustadt. Martin Harth's father, Meyer, was one such victim of random violence. According to the testimony of his son, Harth was assaulted by his barber on the night of 10 November.[32] The assertion that Giesseners were unanimously opposed to Kristallnacht is therefore questionable. If anything, as in Frankfurt, most residents of Giessen chose to look the other way, or, if they still had Jewish friends, to express their disapproval tacitly and in confidence. Alfredo Strauss could not recall Gentile friends or strangers in Geisenheim coming to the aid of his parents or relatives during the carnage.[33] Despite proof that numerous rabble-rousers in Geisenheim were students at the village Lehranstalt, non-Jewish and even Jewish interviewees held to the misconception that the pogromists had all come from out of town.[34]

In the immediate aftermath of Kristallnacht, German officials confronted the problem of paying for the damage, estimated at between twenty-five and several hundred million marks. Since most of the property owners were insured, Göring argued that insurance companies should make reimbursements—not to Jews but to the "true" victim of the pogroms, the Reich government. The state then ordered Jewish store owners to repair their shops and to clear rubble from the streets at their own expense. After dealing with the insurance issue, discussion among the Nazi elite turned to the future of Reich Jewish policy. Two days after the pogroms, Hitler and Reich Marshal Göring engaged in lengthy talks concerning the overall implications of Kristallnacht. Out of these meetings came a change in Hitler's previously favorable position toward Goebbels and the assumption of greater influence over Jewish policy by Göring. Revealing the content of his discussions with Hitler to a gathering of Nazi leaders at the Air Ministry, Göring declared that the Führer had issued an order "requesting that the Jewish Question be now, once and for all, coordinated or solved in one way or another." For the Reich marshal, this meant an end to pogrom antisemitism and wild Aryanization and the implementation of more "rational" measures, specifically, forced emigration and state-monitored seizures of Jewish property.[35]

Effective on 1 January, 1939, Jews were prohibited from operating retail and wholesale establishments as well as independent artisan shops. The law also prevented Jews from having employees and selling their wares on the market. Under these new pressures, Jewish merchants sold their businesses to "Aryans" at an unparalleled rate. As a result of Göring's forced Aryanization program, 80 percent of the Jewish businesses that had managed to stay in existence until 1938 fell into Nazi hands by April 1939. Alf Krüger, an Economics Ministry official, noted that of the 39,552 Jewish businesses operating on 1 April 1938, nearly 6,000 had been "Aryanized" by April 1939, nearly 15,000 had been liquidated altogether, and another 11,000 were either in the process or on the verge of being "Aryanized."[36] Moreover, some 78,000 Jews left Germany in 1939, reducing the community to 213,000, less than half its size in 1933.

The change in Nazi policy also hastened the end of Jewish communal autonomy. Under the Tenth Decree Supplementing the Reich Law on Citizenship, passed on 4 July 1939, a new organization called the Reichsvereinigung der Juden in Deutschland (Reich Association of Jews in Germany) replaced the old Reichsvertretung. Membership in the new organization was compulsory for all Jews. Charged first with facilitating emigration and secondarily with providing schools and welfare relief, the Reichsvereinigung was not initially the administrative equivalent of a Nazi-controlled ghetto forced to preside over its own liquidation. New research has shown that the initiative to transform the Reichsvertretung from a federal umbrella organization into a centralized institution came from the Reichsvertretung itself in the summer of 1938.[37]

After the pogroms in Frankfurt, the city administration tightened the noose on its Jewish communities by seizing the assets of the largest Jewish welfare agency, removing the remaining Jewish students from "Aryan" schools, and purging the town economy of its Jewish element. Jews were forced to leave their homes and move into designated "Jewish" dwellings as early as 30 January 1939.[38] The joint stock company Wolf, Netter, and Jacobi lost a forty-million mark turnover following its dissolution by the Mannesmann-Tube Works.[39] And through so-called Jewish contracts, Lord Mayor Krebs forced the newly merged IG/IRG community to sell its real estate to the city at the lowest possible price.[40] Included in the deal were the various synagogue grounds, the Gagernstrasse hospital, the building of the Philanthropin, and all of the various Jewish cemeteries (on Battonstrasse, Rat-Beilstrasse,

Eckenheimer Landstrasse, and in Böckenheim, on Sophienstrasse). Then the city council reneged on its initial payment of 1,819,395 marks, as set by a 3 April 1939 contract. After subtracting communal debts, mortgages, and interest, the city transferred one-third of the original sum to an account controlled by Nazi administrators instead of to the Jewish community. On a more personal note, Settie Sonnenborn recalled how the city's takeover of Jewish cemeteries added to her grief in the wake of Kristallnacht:

> Then my father died. The next day, the Jewish cemetery went over to Gentile hands. . . . I wanted a burial for my father. The officials said you had to wait five days. The urns were coming from all over—Buchenwald, Dachau. They didn't have enough workers to dig the graves. On the fifth day, they buried him. I went to the cemetery with my brother-in-law who was a friend of ours. There was no service at all. Leo's brother-in-law was very religious. He was a teacher in Frankfurt and was on his way home during Kristallnacht, so he wasn't arrested. On that day, he just came by accident to us. He didn't know my father had died. He wanted to pray, just to say *Kaddish*, but the cemetery workers wouldn't let him. They said, "It's not allowed here. It's not Jewish anymore." They wouldn't even let us throw a little bit of soil on the grave. They said, "Here we don't do that."[41]

Finally, in the ten months between the November pogroms and the start of World War II, forced emigration resulted in the departure of 6,367 Jews from Frankfurt, 5,438 (85.4 percent) of whom left Germany altogether.[42] Two of the many Frankfurt Jews who made it to the United States were Leo and Settie Sonnenborn. To facilitate their emigration, Settie had to renounce any claim to her father's estate. She went to a Gentile lawyer who informed her that her husband could be released at a price: "I went to a lawyer who was a Nazi in Berlin. He said whoever paid him 700 marks each month, he would work it so [that] their relatives [could be released]. So we gave him some money. . . . Leo was four weeks in the concentration camp, and then he came home . . . he had lost weight, and his head was shaved. He looked awful, and he stank. He said, 'I didn't have my suit off in four weeks.' He didn't explain why he was set free. They told him only, 'You go home.' Maybe it helped that I went to the Nazi lawyer." That same night, Settie called her brother in England and asked him to transfer four hundred pounds into the Sonnenborn's account. In the morning, Leo went to the Gestapo and signed an affidavit promising that he would take no more than ten marks out of the country. He then called his nephew, who had been in a concentration camp for two years and who had come home with him, and gave him power of attorney over the house. After the war started, they never heard from him again. When Leo and Settie finally made the Channel crossing from Calais they had barely enough money to buy food.[43]

In Giessen, much of the Aryanization of Jewish businesses and the selling off of Jewish property actually preceded the events of 9-10 November. Of the 130 stores owned by Jews in July 1936, only 53 remained in Jewish hands by October 1938.[44] By May 1939, there were only 81 Jews registered in the entire Rheingau. Half of them ended up in concentration camps.[45] In Geisenheim, Max and Liebmann Strauss' furniture store was demolished, but apart from that, there was little need for an intensification of Aryanization in the wake of the pogroms. No Jews lived in the town after the summer of 1939, a situation common to many German villages by then.[46] Max and Auguste went to Johannesburg, South Africa, in May 1939, and Liebmann and his wife moved to Wiesbaden in August. Georg and Emma Strauss had already emigrated to São Paulo, Brazil, on 17 December 1938.

The outbreak of war in September 1939, sparked by Germany's attack on Poland, did not bring immediate changes in Nazi Jewish policy. Emigration remained the central goal of the German government, and, as late as the summer of 1940, Nazi officials were considering the possibility of resettling Jews in Madagascar.[47] A complete ban on Jewish emigration did not come until October 1941, a little over three months after the German invasion of Russia. The start of the war was not without repercussion for Germany's remaining two hundred thousand Jews, however, for they were prohibited from using radios, buying food from German stores, and being seen in public after a certain time (9:00 P.M. in the summer, 8:00 P.M. in winter). In addition, Nazi officials reduced the supply of food, clothing, and other daily needs to Jews, incarcerated *Ostjuden* still living in Germany in concentration camps, and deported Jews from Stettin and southwest Germany to the occupied territories in February and October 1940 respectively.[48]

At best, Nazi leadership was ambivalent toward Jews in the initial phase of the war. Consistency demanded that the fighting both be blamed on world Jewry and represented as a crusade against the Jewish "race." But many Nazi policy makers felt that Jewish manpower could be used in the war effort.[49] Several historians now feel that the decision to exterminate Jews did not come until 1941, either during the planning of the Russian campaign or at some stage of the actual invasion.[50] Most German Gentiles ignored rumors of genocide and worried more about their own survival as the war progressed.[51] Nazi propaganda fell short of whipping the German public into a supportive frenzy over extermination, but, as it turned out, the Nazi elite needed only acquiescence on the part of the general populace to carry out the Final Solution.

In the months preceding the start of World War II, Frankfurt am Main experienced the largest out-migration of Jews to date as 4,287 Jewish residents left the country and 541 moved to other towns in Germany. Emigrating to England in April 1939, Georg Salzberger was the last rabbi to leave Frankfurt.[52] Between 1939 and 1941, Nazi officials tightened their grip on the most mundane aspects of daily Jewish existence in Frankfurt, prohibiting the purchase of radios by Jews and establishing "Jews only" grocery markets.[53] Elizabeth Bamberger remembered that Gentile storekeepers would often "slip something to old customers," but primarily, she recalled only hardship during the early years of the war. Her new landlord was, by her account, a "stupid, uneducated man," who harassed her constantly during the blackout times.[54] An example of how miserable conditions had become for the city's Jews by the fall of 1941 can be found in a complaint filed by the *Kreisleiter* of Frankfurt-Höchst that detailed the discovery of twenty Jewish workers who had hidden apples in their backpacks. The *Kreisleiter*'s letter implored the Höchst city council to address this unacceptable behavior.[55] Of the 17,197 *Rassejuden* living in the Frankfurt according to the 1939 census (including 14,461 *Glaubensjuden* and 2,736 *Mischlinge*), only 10,592 Jews remained by the time of the first deportations in October 1941.[56]

The noose around the neck of Giessen Jewry tightened as well between 1939 and 1941. According to the census of 1939, only 273 Jews, including *Mischlinge*, were left in Giessen by the end of the decade.[57] In contrast to Frankfurt, Jewish emigration totals from the town on the Lahn were rather low, largely because most of Giessen's Jews had either already left Germany or had migrated to larger cities like Frankfurt seeking a more tolerable, if not more anonymous, existence. Twelve Jews emigrated to Palestine in 1939, and only two left between 1940 and 1941. Those who stayed behind were gradually forced to move into "Jewish houses" on Liebigstrasse, Marburgerstrasse, Asterweg, and Wetzlarer Weg. In 1942, three "ghetto residences" on Walltorstrasse 42 and 48 and Landgrafenstrasse 8 absorbed what remained of Giessen's Jewish community.[58] Like their counterparts in Frankfurt and elsewhere, Jews in Giessen endured increasingly restrictive legislation, ranging from curfews and public transportation bans to the wearing of the yellow star. Eyewitness reports and memoirs from Giessen Jews tell similar tales of heightened support for more radical ordinances, of heightened resistance, and of pervasive apathy. There were many instances when Gentiles supplied Jewish friends with food, and there was also a noticeable increase in the severity of punishments for public disobedience.[59] Accompanying these trends, however, was a rise in the number of denunciations.[60] Equally disturbing, and perhaps more representative of the behavior of most Giessen residents, was an incident that occurred on 14 January 1940. Leopold and Fanni Borngässer, sixty-seven and sixty-eight years old respectively, perished in a fire that swept through their apartment. They could have been saved had it not been for the callous inaction of neighbors and city officials.[61]

The turning point in the Nazi persecution of Jews during the war was the German invasion of Russia on 22 June 1941, a campaign designed as the apocalyptic struggle against communism, Slavs, and Jews. The decision to exterminate the Jews probably came during the planning of the attack on Russia in March 1941, but an exact date may never be known. Even the orders that Reinhard Heydrich received from Göring to that effect on 31 July 1941 have sparked debate, partially because they are linguistically vague but also because the killing of Soviet Jews was already well under way:

In completion of the task which was entrusted to you in the Edict dated January 24, 1939, of solving the Jewish Question by means of emigration or evacuation in the most convenient way possible, given the present conditions, I herewith charge you with making all necessary preparations with regard to the organization of practical, and financial aspects for an overall solution [*Gesamtlösung*] of the Jewish Question in the German sphere of influence in Europe. Insofar as the competency of other central organizations are affected, these are to be involved. I further charge you with submitting to me promptly an overall plan of the preliminary organizational, practical, and financial measures for the execution of the intended final solution [*Endlösung*] of the Jewish Question.[62]

Regardless of the ambiguities of the Göring communiqué, the killing of Soviet Jews was under way within the first week of the German invasion. Charged with this grisly task were mobile firing squads known as *Einsatzgruppen*. The vast area stretching from the Baltic Sea to the Black Sea was divided into four regions, A, B, C, and D, with one Einsatzgruppe in each. Manpower for the squads came primarily from the SS and police units (Security Police, Sipo, and Order Police, Orpo), while commanding officers were by and large members of the SD.[63] The *Einsatzgruppen* followed advancing army brigades into Soviet territory, rounded up Jews, conveyed them outside towns and villages, and murdered them beside antitank trenches or pits dug specifically for executions.

In the autumn of 1941, preparations began for the deportation of Jews from the Greater German Reich to the East. On 1 September, the Nazis revived a medieval tradition and forced Jews to wear a yellow star, in part to humiliate them, in part to paint them as a potential third column in collaboration with the Soviets. SD reports noted that the measure received a favorable response from radical antisemitic circles and that some Germans went so far as to oppose the exemptions made for Jews living in mixed marriages.[64] The Confessing Church, by contrast, denounced the labeling of Christian *Mischlinge* and Jewish converts to Christianity as Jews, while Catholic leaders opted to hold separate services for their "Jews." It appears from the SD that the regulation encountered less support from religious leaders and more from ordinary churchgoers who protested having to receive communion next to *Rassejuden* (racial Jews).[65]

Punishments for not wearing the star were often severe. E.D. Oswalt, a sixty-five-year-old half-Jewish publisher who had been married to a Jewish woman, frequently forgot to wear the star. He was ordered to appear before the Frankfurt Gestapo and never returned.[66] An uncle of Helmut S. from Giessen was apparently denounced by a neighbor for not wearing the yellow badge. His family later received his ashes in an urn.[67]

Numerous memoirs and eyewitness accounts from survivors suggest that the predominant public response to the yellow badge was opposition. Ernst Bukofzer, Klaus Scheurenberg, Leo Baeck, Jacob Jacobsen, and Inge Deutschkron asserted that the typical German reacted with a mixture of pity and shame.[68] Other testimonies from the time held to a similar line: "A Jewish schoolteacher who was in Berlin until the end of October 1942 and wrote her memoirs immediately after leaving Germany for Palestine noted that the labeling initially caused quite a stir. In time, however, people became used to it. There were antisemitic remarks, especially from children who evinced contempt for Jews, but adults turned away, apparently out of embarrassment."[69] Despite inconsistencies in these sources, one should not conclude that the perceptions of the SD or eyewitnesses were either fraudulent or mutually exclusive. The general response to the yellow star was mixed, ranging from mild distaste to overwhelming disregard.

On 14 October, nearly one month after the yellow star decree, the chief of the Order Police, Kurt Daluege, ordered the deportation of 19,827 German Jews to the Lodz ghetto in Poland. Of those, over half came from Vienna and Prague, the rest from Berlin, Cologne, Hamburg, Düsseldorf, and Frankfurt am Main.[70] Deportations focused attention on the Jews' status as *Staatsangehörige* and on the means of stripping them of that status. This was done, according to Rogers Brubaker, by making the loss of "subject" status for Jews the consequence of "taking up" (or being forced to take up) "residence" (even in a concentration camp) "abroad" (defined broadly for the purpose of the law so as to include most destinations for Jewish deportation).[71] This permitted the creation of the legal fiction that it was not German *Staatsangehörige* who were killed but stateless persons of Jewish descent.

Even with this legal charade, in all cases the Gestapo used a pretext to arrest and deport Jews. Often this pretext involved the maintenance of illegal contact between Jews and non-Jews:

(From case 63 [c]): The Jewish wife was ordered to appear before the defendant for a discussion. He arrested her because she had gone to an Aryan hairdresser. She was sent to Auschwitz, where she died.

(from case 8): "Your wife, who is Jewish, has not shown the necessary reticence in her relations with Aryans, and despite repeated warnings has not changed her behavior."

(from case 14-15): "[The Jewish wife] was accused of having visited an Aryan physician."

(from case 73): "She was accused of visting Aryan shops and of failing to use the obligatory first name of Sara."[72]

Among those Jews sent to Lodz were 1,125 from Frankfurt am Main. On the day of the deportations, Gestapo agents and SA men rousted Jews from their homes and assembled them at a central point. The Gestapo chose potential deportees from lists of Jews prepared by Jewish community officials under orders from the Secret State Police. Lina Katz described the scene in her memoirs:

> On Sunday morning at seven o'clock, the SA rounded up specific people determined by a list. They had some time to pack some things and then were led through the city by foot to the Central Market Hall (*Grossmarkthalle*). I saw all of this myself because I lived with six other Jewish families in the former Reinemann Villa, Böckenheimer Landstrasse 73. Everyone in the house was rounded up except me, because I worked for the Jewish community. My husband was in the hospital at the time. I helped my neighbors with their packing. I also went to other apartments of people who were on the list, to bid farewell to them; but an SA man threatened that if I didn't get lost, I would be taken away.
>
> I accompanied the march to the Great Market Hall, tried to take the tram, but was thrown off because of my Jewish star. The march went through the city on a clear day. Right and left stood people [Gentiles] who looked on silently in dense queues. I could not go into the Great Market Hall. There the SS took over the SA led procession. . . . The SA-Leute said that the destination was Lodz, a very orderly and pretty ghetto.[73]

The "evacuation" of Frankfurt was not entirely without problems. An SA *Sturmbannführer* complained that SA men often waited alongside Jewish deportees in their apartments for hours until Gestapo agents arrived to finish paperwork and take them to the train station.[74]

Katz's eyewitness account clashed with the questionable, hearsay-based testimony of Antonius Hilfrich, bishop of Limburg, who asserted that non-Jewish opposition to the transports was high.[75] Both sources, however, agreed on the extent of public knowledge of the deportations. In Frankfurt, as well as in Giessen, deportees marched through the streets to their respective assembly points in broad daylight.[76] Even information on the killings in the occupied East was so widespread that foreigners and many ordinary German citizens knew of the hideous work of the murder squads. One such foreigner was Edwin van D'Elden: "Of the five convoys leaving Frankfurt prior to his departure, he learned from incontestable sources that only one reached Lodz and that three never reached [their] destination. The Jews of these three [convoys] were compelled to leave the train in Poland, were stripped of their clothing and then were summarily executed by Nazi firing squads who mowed down the victims by machine-gun fire. He learned of these events from friends who secured the information from soldiers who actually participated in the executions in Poland and who subsequently returned to Frankfurt on leave."[77]

Whether or not all German Gentiles had knowledge of the *Einsatzgruppen* is almost immaterial. Only the most myopic could have believed that nothing bad awaited the deportees.[78] First, Jews and non-Jews were well aware of the extensive network of concentration camps within Germany. In Hessen alone during the war there were 532 forced labor camps, and as early as May 1933, the general public in Oberhessen was informed of the internment of four hundred political opponents at Osthofen near Worms.[79] During the war, the Nazis established a work camp in Frankfurt-Heddernheim, an auxiliary camp (*Aussenkommando*) for Buchenwald outside of Giessen, and similar branches for Natzweiler in Frankfurt and in Geisenheim. The Geisenheim camp held approximately two hundred prisoners, most of them Jewish women from Poland assigned to work details in either the Johannisberg Machine Factory or the Krupp works, both visible on the outskirts of town.[80] Second, accounts of Jewish suicides were widely publicized, and they often elicited popular sympathy when they involved major celebrities. Such was the case with Joachim Gottschalk, a famous German actor who had repeatedly refused to divorce his Jewish wife. The night before his wife and son were to be deported, they all committed suicide.[81]

When the plan to "resettle" Jews from the Reich in the Lodz ghetto met with difficulties, the Nazis decided to send them farther east into Russian territory, to Riga and Minsk. This decision marked the beginning of the systematic annihilation of German Jewry. On 24 October, Daluege issued another deportation order, the day after Himmler instructed the head of the Gestapo, Heinrich Müller, to issue a comprehensive ban on German Jewish emigration. The new deportation writ called for the removal of 50,000 Jews from sixteen cities in the Reich to the vicinity of Riga and Minsk. That number included 2,042 Jews from Frankfurt am Main. To make room for the incoming transports of German Jews, 27,000 Jews from the Big and Little Ghettos in

Riga were executed in the wooded killing grounds outside the city limits.[82]

The deportations of Reich Jews to the East coincided with the decision to explore the use of poison gas in the extermination process. The model for the process was a series of euthanasia experiments conducted on individuals with terminal illnesses or mental retardation between January 1940 and August 1941. In that time, 70,273 people were exterminated either through lethal injections or use of carbon monoxide. Leaders of the Catholic and Protestant churches protested to government ministries, and some, including several bishops, even raised their voices in public protest. Bishop Hilfrich sent a letter to the minister of justice on 13 August 1941 protesting experiments at a nearby installation in Hadamar. Local children, he wrote, recognized the buses with blacked-out windows that transported victims to the sanatorium, often saying, "Look, there's the murder-box coming again," or "You're crazy. They'll take you to the oven at Hadamar."[83] Such protests and an increasing number of appeals made to the courts by relatives of the deceased persuaded Hitler to suspend the euthanasia operation on 24 August. Even though some killing continued afterward in secret, opposition from church leaders such as the bishop of Limburg helped effect a change in government policy. There was no similar protest when the extermination involved Jews.

Gassing became the method of choice for the extermination of Jews by the fall of 1941. Following the deportation of Reich Jews to the occupied East in October, a meeting took place between Judge Alfred Wetzel, Victor Brack of Hitler's chancellery, and Adolf Eichmann to discuss the construction of gas installations. For the operation of these extermination factories, Eichmann and Brack availed themselves of experts who had managed the euthanasia scheme. In early December 1941, the use of gas trucks began in the Chelmno extermination camp about forty miles northwest of Lodz. By the spring, gassing became employed in the Belzec, Sobibor, and Treblinka camps. The same was true of Auschwitz-Birkenau in Eastern Upper Silesia although there, as later in Majdanek near Lublin, the Nazis used prussic acid, a chemical marketed as a disinfectant by the well-known trade name of Zyklon-B. At the Wannsee Conference held on 20 January 1942, RSHA chief Heydrich harnessed the relevant authorities of the Reich to ensure the smooth coordination of the Final Solution.

Documentary evidence reveals that foreigners and ordinary German citizens must have had some knowledge of the gassings.[84] Following the entry of the United States into the war, an American newspaper correspondent reported that Jews and hundreds of Russian prisoners had been either shot or gassed, adding that "when typhus had broken out in one camp in Poland, it was checked by herding Russian prisoners into rooms by scores and gassing them on the pretext of delousing their clothes and bodies."[85] In addition, data on euthanasia gathered by British intelligence included information from a German railway guard that trains with wounded soldiers entered a tunnel in which they were gassed.[86] The story of a gassing tunnel spread rapidly: Lili Hahn mentioned that in November 1941, two transports of Frankfurt Jews were gassed in a tunnel near Minsk.[87] A member of the Berlin Philharmonic Orchestra, questioned by British authorities in Lisbon, also gave details of the extermination process: "Deportations to Poland and Russia were equivalent to a death sentence, for Jews were being gassed there."[88] Finally, Salazar Sorinao, a Bolivian engineering student who left Frankfurt in March 1943 and was subsequently interviewed by the British in Lisbon, maintained that the Nazis deported and executed four thousand Frankfurt Jews in June 1942.[89]

In the late spring of 1942, the first mass deportations of Jews from the Reich to extermination camps began. The destination for many was the Sobibor death camp, located outside the Polish town of Lublin. The eventual stop for most Reich Jews was the so-called privileged camp of Theresienstadt, a way station to Auschwitz forty kilometers northwest of Prague. Of the approximately 109,000 Jews whom the Nazis had sent to Theresienstadt by the end of 1942, 16,000 had died in the camp and 40,000 had been deported to the occupied East, initially to Lublin and Minsk, later to Auschwitz.

On 8 May 1942, the deportations of Frankfurt Jews to Lublin began with a roundup of 938 individuals.[90] Between August 1942 and January 1944, the Nazis deported over three thousand Jews from Frankfurt to either Theresienstadt or an unspecified location in the occupied territories, most likely to Auschwitz.[91] Magda Spiegel, a popular opera singer in the city during the years of the republic, was one of the deportees who died at Auschwitz.[92] Arthur Weinberg, an executive with I.G. Farben and friend of the director, Georg von Schnitzler, died in Theresienstadt in 1943.[93] Former Frankfurt residents who had emigrated to other European countries but who ultimately lost their lives in concentration camps included Anne Frank and her family and Rabbi Menachem Mendel Kirschbaum, former director of the Frankfurt rabbinical council living in exile in Belgium. The Nazis arrested Kirschbaum for not carrying his identification papers on a Sabbath day in September 1942.[94] The former mayor of the Frankfurt suburb of

Table 26. Jews Deported from Frankfurt from 1941 to 1944

Date	Destination	Number of Jews
19 October 1941	Lodz	1,125
11 November 1941	Minsk	1,052
22 November 1941	Riga	992
8 May 1942	Lublin	938
24 May 1942	Lublin	930
11 June 1942	Lublin	1,016
18 August 1942	Theresienstadt	1,020
1 September 1942	Theresienstadt	554
15 September 1942	Theresienstadt	1,378
24 September 1942	"to the East"	234
1 March 1943	"to the East"	11
16 March 1943	Theresienstadt	41
12 April 1943	Theresienstadt	12
19 April 1943	"to the East"	17
16 June 1943	Theresienstadt	19
28-29 October 1943	Auschwitz	5
	Theresienstadt	3
	Ravensbruck	7
	Buchenwald	5
8 January 1944	Theresienstadt	56

Source: Übersicht über die Transporte, die von Frankfurt am Main aus abgingen, 1941-1944, Nach den Listen der Geheimen Staatspolizei Frankfurt, ergänzt aus den Akten des Polizeipräsidenten, Document XIV15, in *Spuren, des Faschismus in Frankfurt: Das Alltagsleben in Frankfurt am Main, 1933-1945* (Frankfurt, 1988), 95.

Höchst, Bruno Asch, committed suicide in Amsterdam following the Nazi invasion of Holland. Hugo Sinzheimer and Ludwig Landmann, Jewish political figures in Frankfurt in the 1920s, also died in Holland, but at the end of the war.[95]

In January 1942, there was a roundup of Jews in Giessen for deportation to Riga. Hedwig Burgheim, the former leader of the Fröbelseminar, was not on the list but a friend was. Burgheim became clinically depressed afterward. The next major roundup in the town occurred in September when 141 Jews were deported. They, along with 9 Jews from neighboring Wieseck, were assembled at the Goetheschule, taken via bus to the train station, and from there dispatched to either Theresienstadt or Auschwitz via Darmstadt. On 1 November,

Josef Stern's father, Julius, and stepmother, Claire, became victims of the "evacuation." They were sent to Poland and were never heard from again.[96] Burgheim was deported to her death in February 1943.[97] In Geisenheim, no Jews remained by the time of the deportations. Former village residents Liebmann and Karolina Strauss lived in a Gestapo-monitored *Judenhaus* in Wiesbaden before being sent to Theresien-stadt, where they eventually perished.[98] According to Martin Killian, the fact that all Jews had left Geisenheim by 1940 aroused little interest among its Gentile residents.[99] It may be meta-historical to inquire about rescue options for Geisenheim's Jews before and after 1938, given their visibility in the town. But one conceivable, albeit life-threatening option could have been harboring them in one of the monastic wineries located in the surrounding hills.

In the initial phase of the "evacuations," the Nazis made excep-tions for *Mischlinge*, Jews living in mixed marriages, Jews not fit for transport, and Jews in work details, but the bestowal of privileged status did not guarantee exemption from discrimination or, worse, deporta-tion. At Wannsee, Heydrich proposed sterilizing Jews living in mixed marriages and categorizing second-degree crossbreeds, or individuals with one Jewish grandparent, as Jews if they had an "unfavorable ap-pearance." Conferences on 6 March and 27 October 1942, under the auspices of Eichmann, postponed the sterilization plan and resolved that intermarried Jews and their offspring would remain in a special ghetto until the end of the war.[100] But during a roundup in Berlin facto-ries at the end of February 1943, intermarried Jews were arrested alongside other Jews while at work. Protests by church leaders and the Gentile wives of those incarcerated resulted in their eventual release.[101] Himmler continued to reverse the trend of protecting *Mischlinge* in October 1944 by conscripting first-degree crossbreeds into forced labor and then, on 13 January 1945, decreeing that all Jews living in mixed marriages (basically Christians of "non-Aryan" descent) be sent to Theresienstadt.

The Nazis deported all intermarried Jews from Frankfurt follow-ing an ordinance on 8 February 1945.[102] Five days later, twelve indi-viduals from mixed marriages in Giessen were sent to Frankfurt for deportation to Theresienstadt.[103] *Gauleiter* Sprenger and Administrative Inspector Ernst Holland, commissioner of the Gestapo's Department of Jewish Welfare in Frankfurt, reportedly targeted intermarried Jews and *Mischlinge* as early as 1943.[104] The experiences of Johanna Fraenkel, a *Mischling* who was not able to secure an exit visa for herself and her family to join her Jewish husband in exile in 1942, suggest that the threat of deportation came even earlier:

> In May 1942, Mrs. Fraenkel was leaving her home when she met an officer from the Jewish community in Frankfurt entering the house. As the community had to compile the lists for the transports and had to break the news to the deportees, Mrs. Fraenkel feared the worst. Indeed, she was on the list of the next transport. She went immediately to see the lawyer who represented the Jewish community and who happened to be a relative of Mrs. Fraenkel. The lawyer suggested that the only way to escape deportation was to divorce her Jewish husband (who had managed to flee to England). . . . The rest of the day was spent running from office to office (Jews were, of course, not allowed to use public transport) until a document was obtained stating officially that proceedings had been begun. Mrs. Fraenkel then took this to the Gestapo who, at first refused to accept it and asked why she had waited until the last moment to begin proceedings and why she had married a Jew in the first place. Mrs. Fraenkel answered that if the Gestapo had any humanity, they would understand that she wanted to give her daughter a home and had married for her sake. This evidently had some effect on the the Gestapo officer who passed Mrs. Fraenkel's application not to be deported. . . . After the war, she joined her "divorced" husband in London where they re-married.[105]

In Giessen, too, the move against Jews living in mixed marriages started well before 1945. Max Walldorf, a *Mischling* Grade One married to a Catholic, was reclassified as a *Volljude* following orders from the mayor's office dated 16 February 1940.[106] And after receiving tips from jealous neighbors in early 1944, the Nazis deported to Theresienstadt a Jewish widow from Giessen who had married a Gentile.[107] Although popular outrage against the persecution of *Mischlinge* occurred periodically, what ultimately saved those of mixed parentage from complete annihilation was Germany's impending defeat in the war, resistance from such Nazi officials as Bernhard Lösener, desk officer for racial affairs within the Interior Ministry, and Hitler's own ambivalence towards *Mischlinge*, which produced a stream of contradictory impulses.[108]

Research has suggested that personal ties between Gentiles and Jews were an important factor for those who were rescued. Sometimes non-Jews rescued Jews because they were fellow members of a group, occasionally because they were influenced by a particular person or group to do so. Samuel and Pearl Oliner found that rescuers overall had more Jewish friends before the war than did nonrescuers (59 percent versus 34 percent) and were less likely to have heard anti-Jewish slurs in homes than bystanders (3 percent to 16 percent). The Oliners found no difference between rescuers and nonrescuers in the communication of positive opinions of Jews—only in the absence of negative ones and an emphasis on the common humanity of all people.[109]

Many Jews from Frankfurt recounted instances of aid from Gentile friends during the war. A skat player who associated with socialists and communists in a Frankfurt pub was executed in 1942 for helping Jews.[110] Margarete Josefine Speier and an English girlfriend suffered a brief period of incarceration in a concentration camp for discussing illegal emigration possibilities with a Reichsvereinigung member.[111] Otto Neuland, a shoemaker, continued to repair shoes for Jewish customers during the war, and his wife, Franziska, gave a Jewish woman her identity papers so that she could cross into Switzerland. Elsgert Braun hid a Jewish neighbor in his apartment so effectively that he eluded discovery by the Nazis.[112] Others who helped Jews in wartime Frankfurt included Karl and Fanny Ofer, Adolf Rückdeschel, and former police officer Karl Bierwirth, who had refused to divorce his Jewish wife in 1935. Finally, the daughters of Karl Wolf, the Reichsvereinigung functionary responsible for drawing up lists of potential deportees in Frankfurt, warned Jews of their intended fate and often concealed their valuables with Gentile friends. For breach of trust, Wolf was sent to Buchenwald, and his daughters, Else and Maria, to Auschwitz.[113]

Giessen, too, had its share of small-time resisters. Following tips from a Swede named Imgart, the Gestapo arrested two Evangelical pastors, Alfred Kaufmann and Ernst Steiner, six other Gentiles, and a Jew for listening to foreign radio broadcasts in February 1942.[114] Heinrich Will, a painter and leader of one of the seven resistance groups in the town, and his Jewish wife were also executed for subversive activities.[115] Among those whose defiance proved more successful were Wolfgang Meier and Erwin Franke, who kept their Dutch Jewish wives hidden from Nazi authorities, Otto and Irmgard Christ, who smuggled groceries to Jewish friends, and a Jewish woman named Siesel, who survived the war by living with a former employee under a false name. Dora Scheuer, a Catholic convert whose parents were Jewish, remembered how a friend who happened to be a party member helped her and her family shortly before her deportation: "She even made her bedroom available to us. Later she took in still more people. She took in three families, gave us beds, and slept on the floor herself."[116]

On balance, however, resistance constituted an unsuccessful, marginal experience. SA and SD reports for Frankfurt and Giessen emphasized that while deportation procedures in the two towns may have encountered technical problems, they did not meet with significant opposition from the public.[117] During the September 1942 "evacuation" of Giessen, Jews even suffered parting insults from ordinary citizens on the way to the train station, slurs like "It's time that the cancer is finally eliminated" (es würde ja Zeit, daß endlich das Krebsgeschwür ausgebrannt wird)."[118] Moreover, opposition to the expulsion of Jews may have had wholly pragmatic, non-humanitarian roots. In a diary entry made four days after the deportations in Giessen had begun, Georg Edward rued only that the persecution of Jews would inevitably bring terrible revenge, which was for him the "true" Hebrew God.[119] And then there were Nazis who criticized the untidy application of Reich Jewish policy after 1942 but not its ultimate goal. The editor of the SS mouthpiece, Das Schwarze Korps, simultaneously decried brutality against Jews and called for propriety in the handling of the Final Solution: "For after all, we do not want to look like frenzied sadists."[120] Finally, apart from isolated incidents, neither the political underground nor church leadership did much to rescue Jews in Frankfurt, Giessen, Geisenheim, Hessen, or Germany as a whole.[121] In fact, when protests from spiritual leaders occurred, they rarely specified the extermination of Jews. On 19 August 1943, Catholic bishops circulated a pastoral letter that condemned the murder of innocents but made only a buried, oblique reference to "human beings of foreign races and tribes."[122]

As defeat in the war loomed, German Gentiles exhibited an even greater disregard for the predicament of Jews.[123] Robert Jay Lifton and Eric Markusen argue that action on behalf of Jews did not occur partially because non-Jews possessed a fragmentary awareness of genocide and were therefore unable to overcome the human tendency to look away from brutal behavior.[124] But to conceive of apathy solely in those terms would be to ignore both the particular in-group–out-group nature of antisemitic persecution and instances of comparable levels of awareness, such as the euthanisia controversy, when the murder of mentally ill and disabled Protestants and Catholics drew widespread condemnation. As a way of dealing with Jews and the "Jewish Question," indifference had been a long-standing pattern of Gentile thought and behavior. It should come as no surprise that the majority of Germans turned away from Jews in the context of an ever-worsening wartime situation under a dictatorship.

According to Sarah Gordon, the extermination of European Jewry was possible because of the Nazi centralization of power and World War II, not, as Daniel Goldhagen believes, a particular form of "eliminationist" antisemitism allegedly unique to Germany.[125] At the same time, the Nazis attempted to marshal public support for the physical destruction of Jews and succeeded in co-opting huge sections of the military, bureaucracy, and the general populace in the day-to-day process of organized murder.[126] Most German Gentiles rejected mass killing, but for a host of reasons—fear of the Terror, concern for survival, varying degrees of antisemitic prejudice, or simple disregard—did little to stand in the way of the implementation of that policy. In Frankfurt and Giessen, towns with well-rooted antisemitic traditions, reactions to Nazi Jewish policy after 1938 were characterized primarily by apathy but also by an increase in both support for and resistance to genocide. The situation for the few remaining Jews in Geisenheim, meanwhile, had become unbearable by the end of 1938, prompting their departure. It is difficult to say whether action on behalf of Jews during the war was possible or whether large-scale protest would have had any effect on government policy. Having failed to repudiate Nazi antisemitism in its early stages, however, ordinary Germans became unwitting accomplices to genocide.

Epilogue

On Thursday, 29 March 1945, National Socialist rule in Frankfurt came to an end, and its occupation by the U.S. army began. Greater Hessen itself came into being in May 1945 as the occupying U.S. forces merged Hessen-Darmstadt with the Prussian province of Hessen-Nassau.[1] Jakob Sprenger, the Nazi *Reichsstatthalter* of Hessen during the Third Reich, left Frankfurt before the arrival of the American army and committed suicide in a Bavarian forest.[2] Of the major Nazis in Frankfurt's city administration, only one official, Gestapo criminal secretary Heinrich Baab, received a life sentence in prison for his involvement in the Final Solution as the head of Division IIB2, which dealt with Jews. No eyewitnesses could be found to testify against either Reinhard Breder, head of the Frankfurt Gestapo, or Ernst Grosse, leader of Division II, and Gestapo official Oswald Poche lived in the city under a false name until his death in 1962.[3] Even former Mayor Friedrich Krebs enjoyed a brief return to political life in the early 1950s as a member of a small right-wing party.[4]

Allied and Jewish organizations estimated that between 160,000 and 180,000 German Jews were murdered by the Nazis during World War II. After the war, 200,000 Jewish survivors from across Europe ended up as displaced persons (DPs) in internment camps established on German soil by the occupying British and American forces. By 1955, only 15,000 remained after the majority emigrated to either Palestine or the United States. In Hessen, as of 1946, there were 34,578 DPs, and the largest Jewish DP camp was located in Zeilsheim, outside of Frankfurt.

At the beginning of the U.S. occupation of Frankfurt, there were only 140 "racial Jews" (*Rassejuden*) left in the city, *Glaubensjuden* having long since been deported.[5] In April, the American forces set up a relief agency for Jews in Frankfurt, and Leopold Neuhaus, rabbi of the IG during the deportations, returned to the city in July 1945 to aid in the process of Jewish communal reconstruction. On 9 November 1946, members of the nascent community gathered at the old Jewish cemetery on Rat-Beil Strasse to remember the dead. One survivor later offered a poignant observation of the ceremony: "I am not a religious

Jew. I don't know the contents of pious hymns. It was noise until the cantor began reciting the names of the concentration camps. That tore at my soul. I crept away slowly from the service, crying."[6]

As for Giessen, U.S. infantryman John Houston Hill reported his unit's capture of the town and the discovery of a concentration camp near Kinzenbach on 29 March 1945:

> As a member of the 99th, while we were trying to capture Giessen, Germany, my company was involved in a separate mission to circle the city and come in from the mountain side (northern) so that we could infiltrate the city at night and occupy several key places near the bridges. During the daylight hours, we were on our "approach march," crossed the Lahn river, and went up into the high ground overlooking the city. We had departed the city of Wetzlar on 29 March 1945 and started our climb to the high ground. I'm not sure where we were, but we came to a camp of "political" prisoners while en-route to Kinzenbach. This camp had ovens for cremation, barracks full of people who were near death by starvation and other sicknesses. There was nothing we could do but to continue our mission. We also came across a prisoner camp of Russian women who were very anxious for freedom, and as soon as we broke open their gate, they fled for the little mountain town which was below us and executed the *Bürgermeister* and his whole family. We later saw the results when we continued on our mission.[7]

By 1950, there were twenty Jews in Giessen, a portion of whom had survived deportation. Its mayor, Social Democrat Albin Mann, was a survivor as well, of Dachau.[8] On 9 November 1966, the city commemorated the twenty-eighth anniversary of Kristallnacht by unveiling a memorial on the grounds of the former Südanlage synagogue. According to statistics from the end of that year, only twenty-four Jews resided in Giessen. Most had come from Russia, and with the exception of two, most were tavern keepers.[9] Finally, by 1946, there were no Jews living in Geisenheim. Four years later, one solitary Jew resided in the town, and there were only ten Jews in the entire Rheingau.[10] During that time a little-known Jewish American soldier, Earl Friedman, courted and wed Elisabeth Meyer, a Catholic from Geisenheim, fostering one of the many transatlantic connections to the village that endure to this day.

Currently, eastern European Jews form the core of the Jewish communities in Germany, and only one-third of all German Jews can claim German descent. From the mid-1950s to the end of the 1980s, there were around thirty thousand Jews living in Germany, and despite an aging population and low fertility rates, this number remained fairly constant, primarily because of immigration from the east. Since the beginning of the 1990s, a wave of Jewish immigrants from the former Soviet bloc has pushed the official population tally of Jews in Germany to approximately forty-three thousand. In addition to the number of registered Jews, there are ten thousand unregistered, bringing the total to more than fifty thousand. As before, Jews in the postwar era have concentrated in large cities: Berlin (ten thousand), Frankfurt (six thousand), Munich (four thousand), and Hamburg, Cologne, and Düsseldorf (each with two thousand.) The rest are scattered in communities throughout the country. In all, there are just under eighty *Gemeinden*, some of which are extremely small.[11]

On 29 August, 1994, Frankfurt's West End synagogue was inaugurated for the third time, fifty-six years after its destruction by the Nazis on Kristallnacht. At the opening festivities, the prime minister of Hessen called the synagogue "a sign of hope" and a testimony of Jewish cultural survival. By contrast, the mayor of Frankfurt spoke more somberly about the rise of right-wing xenophobia and called for moral courage in the face of increasing intolerance.[12] The reemergence of the radical right in the fin de siècle is not limited to Germany, but World War II and the Holocaust have made a recurrent focus on its political scene almost unavoidable.

For five decades after the defeat of Hitler, the German memory of its Nazi past came in two forms: a communist recollection (from the Soviet-backed German Democratic Republic of East Germany), which saw antisemitism as a marginal element in the Nazis' assault on the working class;[13] and the vexing take on history by the democratic Federal Republic (West Germany), which used reparations to Jews and the state of Israel in the 1950s as a salve on the German public conscience,[14] turned a more critical lense on its past in the 1960s,[15] and finally cultivated more defiant positions in the context of a conservative-nationalist revival in the 1980s.[16] For some, the rise of neo-Nazism, antisemitism, and violent antiforeign sentiment following West Germany's absorption of communist East Germany in the "reunification" of 1990 constituted yet another sign of Germany's inability to escape its past.[17]

Today, growing numbers of Germans refuse to confront the Nazi legacy, precisely because they feel inundated by references to the extermination of the Jews. From films to schoolbooks, the Third Reich and the Holocaust seem all-consuming, spawning a move for closure with that period in German history.[18] Yet the call for a *Schlußstrich*, or final conclusion, is nothing new. Former president Ronald Reagan and current chancellor Helmut Kohl committed more than just a political blunder when they honored German casualties of war at Bitburg cemetery in 1985. They confirmed a rhetorical turn toward the "relativization" of the Third Reich and, more specifically, of the perpetrators and victims of that era, a move that ignited the so-called *Historikerstreit*, or historians' debate, in 1986. This "relativization" or "historicization" was initially associated with left-wing historians such as Martin Broszat, who proposed viewing Nazism in the wider context of German economic and political "modernization." Historians of the right, such as Ernst Nolte, have taken "relativization" to mean downplaying the singularity of Nazi fascism, antisemitism, and genocide.[19]

For all the talk of closure, legislation has encumbered means to that end by restricting access to certain files from the Nazi years under the guise of confidentiality, evoking scenes from the German film, *The Nasty Girl*. Suspicions of pervasive German dishonesty have been fanned further by the recent discovery that archivists in Hamburg had destroyed (and intended to continue destroying) documents pertaining to the persecution of Jews, Gypsies, and homosexuals in the city during the Nazi period.

Polls may suggest that only 15 percent of Germans are overtly antisemitic, but few Gentiles have ever knowingly met one of Germany's fifty thousand Jews, and most regard them as vaguely exotic creatures, treating them with everything from exaggerated friendliness to suspicion and mistrust.[20] The fact that vestigial prejudice, discomfort, and anxious philosemitism characterize current Gentile attitudes toward Jews demonstrates that the experience of the Holocaust has not resulted in a normalization of Gentile-Jewish relations. If anything, a variant of the "Jewish Problem" has emerged, in which Jews form a new type of outsider to Germany, not because they are rejected by Gentiles inasmuch as they are accepted for tenuous reasons—as a lasting reminder of Germany's brutal past.

Conclusion

Enduring references to Leo Baeck's alleged proclamation in 1945 of the end of German Jewry's thousand-year history underscore the centrality among historians in the post-Holocaust era of the question, Did the Nazi genocide reveal the symbiosis between German Gentiles and German Jews to be a tragic illusion?

Detlev Peukert has argued that the rise of antisemitic discrimination and the role of anti-Jewish racial hatred within National Socialist ideology were not the outcomes of events within the history of the Jews in Germany but were solely part of the evolution of the German radical right.[1] I would argue that one cannot easily separate the two. Concentrating on developments within Germany's Jewish communities, however, has led some academicians, such as Gershom Scholem and S.M. Bolkosky, to attack German Jewry's liberal leadership for clinging to an overly sanguine view of German society before 1933. This book has attempted to shift the argument back to non-Jewish prejudice toward Jews and to assess the role of Gentile-Jewish social relations in the rise of Nazism and the implementation of antisemitic legislation.

Unfortunately, Gentile behavior patterns were rarely of a piece. Lines between apathy, latent antisemitism, and more radical forms of Jew-hatred were often blurred, and the fact that someone may have been antisemitic did not predetermine a certain mode of anti-Jewish behavior at any given time. Above all, the transition from everyday Jew-hatred to state-sponsored antisemitism after 1933 was a tortuous process, and the jump from legal exclusion and de-emancipation to genocide was even more complicated.

Centering on German antisemitism begs an additional question: Why did genocide occur under the aegis of Germany, which had emancipated Jews, and not Poland or Russia, where antisemitism was much stronger? Sarah Gordon correctly insists that prejudice alone cannot explain the slaughter of Jews: "No matter how much or how little antisemitism existed in Germany, systematic extermination, as opposed to sporadic pogroms, could be carried out only by an extremely powerful government, and probably could have succeeded only under the cover of wartime conditions."[2] While agreeing that the Holocaust was committed by a totalitarian elite in wartime and that conditions during the Weimar period or even the early years of the Third Reich did not necessarily foreshadow genocide, I reject both a rosy assessment of German Jewish integration before 1933 and efforts to downplay the complicity of ordinary Gentiles and everyday antisemitism in the demise of Germany's Jews.

The problem with the thesis of Scholem and Bolkosky, along with its determinism, is its predication on the belief that German Jews refused to accept the harsh realities of their enviroment before and, to a certain extent, during the Third Reich. Both historians overlook the fact that Jews from a variety of stations in life lamented Germany's schizoid social and political environment between 1919 and 1933, felt that tolerance from Gentiles remained elusive, and attempted to alter their surroundings through education and antidefamation. That the Nazis achieved success through Weimar's electoral process does not mean that Jews had failed to address the issue of prejudice adequately or that their inability to purge the republic of its antisemitic elements was inevitable. It does, however, reflect the relative powerlessness of German Jewry and the weakness of Gentile support for Jewish civil and political rights before 1933.

Indeed, non-Jews carried their insensitivity to Jews into the Third Reich, aiding in the consolidation of the Nazi terror state and in the elimination of options for assistance and rescue. In Frankfurt and Giessen, a sufficient number of Gentiles had been too ill-disposed or apathetic to work toward the eradication of Jew-hatred in the Weimar period and then remained indifferent to antisemitic legislation under Hitler. The situation for Geisenheim's Jews also worsened quickly after the Nazis came to power despite the town's more tolerant environment and the slowness of the Nazi *Gleichschaltung.* In many respects, the turn for the worse in all three communities was occasioned by local forces that either predated or acted outside the dictates of the Nazis' national policy of coordination.

All of this suggests a greater importance of the Weimar period in any assessment of the Third Reich. The persistence of the "Jewish Question" in the discourse of German politics during the republican era had tragic consequences and revealed the extent to which Germany lacked an adequate remedy to anti-Jewish prejudice. A greater effort on the part of Gentile political and religious leaders and ordinary citizens to interact with their Jewish neighbors and to infuse within the general German psyche a fundamental acceptance of Jews as human beings may have aided the search for an antidote.[3]

Notes

Introduction

1. See Karl Schleunes, *The Twisted Road to Auschwitz: Nazi Policy Toward German Jews, 1933-1939* (Urbana, 1970).

2. See Lawrence Stokes, "The German People and the Destruction of the European Jews," *Central European History* 6 (1973): 167-91; Marlis Steinert, *Hitler's War and the Germans: Public Mood and Attitude During the Second World War*, ed., and trans. Thomas de Witt (Athens, Ohio, 1977); Falk Weisemann "Judenverfolgung und nichtjüdische Bevölkerung," in *Bayern in der NS-Zeit*, ed. Martin Broszat et al. (Munich, 1977), 1:427-86; Ian Kershaw, "The Persecution of the Jews and German Popular Opinion in the Third Reich," *Leo Baeck Institute Yearbook* 26 (1981): 262-82; Kershaw, *Popular Opinion and Political Dissent in the Third Reich: Bavaria, 1933-1945* (Oxford, 1983); Otto Dov Kulka, "Public Opinion in Nazi Germany and the Jewish Question," *Jerusalem Quarterly* 25 (1982): 121-44, and 26 (1983): 34-45; Sarah Gordon, *Hitler, Germans, and the Jewish Question* (Princeton, 1984); Michael Kater, "Everyday Antisemitism in Prewar Nazi Germany: The Popular Bases," *Yad Vashem Studies* 16 (1984): 129-59; and David Bankier, *The Germans and the Final Solution: Public Opinion Under the Nazis* (Oxford, 1992).

3. *Alltagsgeschichte*, or "history of the everyday," is largely an extension of the "history from below" movement that began in the 1960s among historians in the United States, Great Britain, France, and West Germany who drew inspiration from Marxist and Weberian social theories. In Germany, the shift to social history initially resulted in studies of social structure and demography. As more scholars focused their efforts on "everyday" life, investigations of cultural matters assumed greater significance. Monographs and essays by historians of the everyday include Detlev Peukert's *Inside Nazi Germany* (New Haven, 1987), his *Weimar Republic: Crisis of Classical Modernity* (New York, 1992); Richard Bessel, ed., *Life in the Third Reich* (Oxford, 1987); and Alf Lüdtke, "Formierung der Massen, oder mitmachen und hinnehmen: Alltagsgeschichte und Faschismusanalyse," in *Alltagsgeschichte: Zur Rekonstruktion historischer Erfahrungen und Lebensweisen* (Frankfurt, 1988). See also Geoff Eley, "Labor History, Social History, *Alltagsgeschichte*: Experience, Culture, and the Politics of the Everyday—a New Direction for German Social History?" *Journal of Modern History* 61 (June 1989): 297-343.

4. Like many studies of the everyday, the theoretical underpinnings of this book can be traced to the Italian theoretician Antonio Gramsci, who

conceptualized power relationships as products not only of coercion and force "from above" but also of negotiated and active consent "from below." Central to my thesis is the belief that ordinary German Gentiles played a role in both the undermining of the Weimar Republic, as an antidemocratic electoral force, and in the functioning of the Third Reich, as participants in the Nazi *Volksgemeinschaft.* Focusing on Germany does not mean that I regard Germans as somehow unique or that I deny the broader European context of antisemitism and fascism. The phrase "Gentile-Jewish symbiosis," however, has been a subject of intense debate ever since it was "coined" by the German Jewish philosopher Hermann Cohen in the early part of the twentieth century. See Gramsci, *Selections from the Prison Notebooks of Antonio Gramsci,* trans. Quinton Hoare (New York, 1977); Rudy Koshar, *Social Life, Local Politics, and Nazism: Marburg, 1880-1935* (Chapel Hill, 1986), 16-17. On the symbiosis issue, see Enzo Traverso, *The Jews and Germany: From the "Judeo-German Symbiosis" to the Memory of Auschwitz* (Lincoln, Neb., 1995); Hermann Cohen, "Deutschtum und Judentum," reprinted in C. Schulte, ed., *Deutschtum und Judentum* (Stuttgart, 1993).

5. Some of these documents, mainly SD reports and memoirs, raise problems because they are sometimes biased and inaccurate. One must, of course, corroborate their content by employing a broad spectrum of contemporary and eyewitness accounts.

6. Karl Demandt, *Die Geschichte des Landes Hessen* (Kassel, 1972), 20.

7. The district of Wiesbaden included both the cities of Wiesbaden and Frankfurt am Main and the counties *(Landkreise)* of Biedenkopf, Dillkreis, Limburg, Main-Taunus, Oberlahn, Obertaunus, Oberwesterwald, Rheingau (Geisenheim's county), Sankt Goarshausen, Unterlahn, Untertaunus, Unterwesterwald, Usingen, and Wetzlar. The district of Kassel was made up of the cities of Fulda, Hanau, Kassel, and Marburg and the counties of Eder, Eisenberges, Eschwege, Frankenberg, Fritzlar-Homberg, Fulda, Gelnhausen, Hanau, Schmalkalden, Hersfeld, Hofgeismar, Hunfeld, Kassel, Marburg, Melsungen, Rotenberg, Schlüchtern, Twiste, Wiztenhausen, Wolfhagen, and Ziegenhain. Hessen-Darmstadt was divided into three provinces, Starkenburg, Oberhessen, and Rheinhessen. Starkenburg encompassed the cities of Bensheim, Darmstadt, and Offenbach and the counties of Bensheim, Darmstadt, Dieburg, Erbach, Gross-Gerau, Heppenheim, and Offenbach. Oberhessen included the cities of Giessen and Friedberg and the counties of Alsfeld, Büdingen, Friedberg, Giessen, Lauterbach, and Schotten. Rheinhessen comprised the cities of Bingen, Mainz, and Worms and the counties of Alzey, Bingen, Mainz, Oppenheim, and Worms.

8. The Jewish population of Frankfurt in 1925 was 29,385. See Paul Arnsberg, *Die Geschichte der Frankfurter Juden seit der französischen Revolution* (Darmstadt, 1983), 2:481, *Statistik des deutschen Reiches: Provinz Hessen-Nassau,* Vol. 405, Issue 26 (Berlin, 1928), 84.

9. Giessen's Jewish population in 1925 was 1,017. See Paul Arnsberg, *Die jüdischen Gemeinden in Hessen* (Frankfurt, 1971), 1:254, Erwin Knauss, *Die jüdische Bevölkerung Giessens, 1933-1945: Eine Dokumentation* (Wiesbaden, 1976), 17; *Statistik des deutschen Reiches: Land Hessen*, Vol. 405, Issue 34 (Berlin, 1928), 72.

10. The Duchy of Nassau did not recognize Geisenheim as a city until 1864. Its overall population in 1925 was 4,252, its Jewish population, 25. See *75 Jahre Rheingaukreis: Herausgegeben vom Landrat Leopold Bausinger im Auftrag des Kreistages und des Kreisausschusses* (Rüdesheim, 1962), 199; Wolf Heino Struck, *Geschichte der Stadt Geisenheims* (Frankfurt, 1972), 252, 274-75.

11. See Hans Ulrich Wehler, *Das deutsche Kaiserreich, 1871-1918* (Göttingen, 1973); Wehler, "Probleme der modernen deutschen Wirtschaftsgeschichte," in his *Krisenherde des Kaiserreichs, 1871-1918* (Göttingen, 1970); Jürgen Kocka, *White Collar Workers in America, 1890-1940* (Beverly Hills, 1980); Kocka, "Organisierter Kapitalismus im Kaiserreich," *Historische Zeitschrift* 230 (1980): 613-31; Hans Jürgen Puhle, *Politische Agrarbewegungen in kapitalistischen Industriegesellschaften: Deutschland, USA, und Frankreich im 20. Jahrhundert* (Göttingen, 1976); Heinrich Winkler, *Von der Revolution zur Stabilisierung: Arbeiter und Arbeiterbewegung in der Weimarer Republik, 1918 bis 1924* (Berlin, 1984). For criticism of the *Sonderweg*, see David Blackbourn and Geoff Eley, *The Peculiarities of German History* (Oxford, 1984).

12. *Civis Germanus Sum: Von Einem Juden deutscher Nation* (Berlin, 1890), 16, as cited in S.M. Bolkosky, *The Distorted Image: German-Jewish Perceptions of Germans and Germany, 1918-1936* (New York, 1975), 7-8.

13. Franz Oppenheimer, *Erlebtes, Erstrebtes, Erreichtes: Erinnerungen* (Berlin, 1931), 214, also cited in Bolkosky, *Distorted Image*, 9.

14. H.G. Adler, *Die Juden in Deutschland von der Aufklärung bis zum Nationalsozialismus* (Munich, 1960).

15. Gershom Scholem, "On the Social Psychology of Germans and Jews," in *The Problematic Symbiosis: Germans and Jews, 1880-1933*, ed. David Bronsen (New York, 1981), 9-32; Traverso, *The Jews and Germany*; and Bolkosky, *Distorted Image*, 3-48.

16. Donald Niewyk, *Jews in Weimar Germany* (Baton Rouge, 1980); Monika Richarz, *Jüdisches Leben in Deutschland: Selbstzeugnisse zur Sozialgeschichte, 1918-1945* (New York, 1982).

17. This is essentially the premise of Peter Pulzer, *The Rise of Antisemitism in Germany and Austria* (New York, 1964). More recently, Shulamit Volkov has placed the question of rising antisemitism within the overall context of rising antimodernism in the late nineteenth century in *The Rise of Popular Antimodernism in Germany: Urban Master Artisans, 1873-1896* (Princeton, 1978).

18. Bahr suggested the theory in 1894, and it has reappeared in a variety of manifestations since. See Hermann Bahr, *Der Antisemitismus* (Berlin, 1894); Erich Kuttner, *Patholgie des Rasseantisemitismus* (Berlin, 1930); F. Bernstein, *Der*

Antisemitismus als Gruppenerscheinung: Versuch einer Soziologie des Judenhasses (Berlin, 1926); R.N. Coudenhove-Kalergi, *Das Wesen des Antisemitismus* (Vienna, 1929), as cited in Niewyk, *Jews in Weimar Germany*, 43.

19. Hannah Arendt, *The Origins of Totalitarianism*, rev. ed. (New York, 1966), 3-120; Hans-Joachim Schoeps, *Unbewältigte Geschichte: Stationen deutschen Schicksals seit 1763* (Berlin, 1964). Marxist historians have attacked Jews for supporting capitalism and economic liberalism. See Walter Mohrmann, *Antisemitismus: Ideologie und Geschichte im Kaiserreich und in der Weimarer Republik* (Berlin, 1972); *Jews in Weimar Germany*, Niewyk, 45. See also Reinhard Rürup, *Emanzipation und Antisemitismus: Studien zur "Judenfrage" der bürgerlichen Gesellschaft* (Göttingen, 1975).

20. Jacob Katz, *From Prejudice to Destruction* (Cambridge, Mass., 1980); Peter Pulzer, *The Jews and the German State: A Political History of a Minority, 1848-1933* (Oxford, 1992); Uriel Tal, *Christians and Jews in Germany: Religion, Politics, and Ideology in the Second Reich, 1870-1914* (Ithaca, 1975).

21. Pulzer, *Jews and the German State*, 14-15.

22. Rogers Brubaker, *Citizenship and Nationhood in France and Germany* (Cambridge, Mass., 1992), 51.

23. Milton Gordon, *Assimilation in American Life: The Role of Race, Religion, and National Origins* (New York, 1964).

24. See Marion Kaplan's introduction to her "Tradition and Transition: The Acculturation, Assimilation, and Integration of Jews in Imperial Germany, a Gender Analysis," *Leo Baeck Institute Yearbook* 27 (1982): 4-7.

25. David Sorkin, *The Transformation of German Jewry, 1780-1870* (Oxford, 1987), 3-9; Tal, *Christians and Jews in Germany*, 290.

26. Niewyk, *Jews in Weimar Germany*, 104.

27. Germany's Jewish population in 1925 was approximately 564,000.

28. Research into majority-minority relations in the United States today reaches similar conclusions about interaction of whites with non-white ethnic groups. See Albert Ramirez, "Differential Patterns of Intra and Interethnic Interaction in Social Power Systems," *Journal of Social Psychology* 133 (1993): 307-16, Frances Henry, *Victims and Neighbors: A Small Town in Nazi Germany Remembered* (South Hadley, Mass., 1984), 149-52; Rachel Heuberger, *Hinaus aus dem Ghetto: Juden in Frankfurt am Main, 1800-1950* (Frankfurt, 1988), 150.

29. Henry, *Victims and Neighbors*, 150.

30. Heide Hermanns Holde, unpublished memoir, 1, Leo Baeck Institute, ME 864.

31. Helen Fein, *The Persisting Question: Sociological Perspectives and Social Contexts of Modern Antisemitism* (New York, 1987), 74.

32. Allport lists further characteristics of majority-minority relations that complement the above criteria, further affecting attitudes and the structure of interethnic contact. There is, for instance, a status aspect to minority-majority contact, that is, whether the minority member has inferior, equal, or

superior status to the majority member or whether the minority group as a whole has high or low status socially, economically, politically, or culturally. The roles held by minority groups or individuals belonging to a minority group vis-à-vis majority groups and individuals is equally significant. For example, whether a relationship is competitive or cooperative or whether the minority or majority is in a subordinate or superordinate role influences the qualitative and quantitative aspects of and ideas toward that relationship. Allport also considers the social atmosphere in which contact occurs. Here, he asks whether segregation between groups and individuals has always been present in a particular society, whether contact is voluntary or involuntary, whether contact is perceived as in-group or out-group relations, whether a relationship is typical or exceptional, and, like the qualitative distinctions, whether contact is important and intimate or trivial and transient. Finally, Allport shows how the personalities of individuals and groups experiencing contact with minorities help shape the contours of an interethnic relationship. He asks whether the initial prejudice of a majority member toward a minority member (or vice versa) is high, medium, or low. Is said prejudice of a surface, conformity type or is it deeply rooted in one's character structure? Are the majority groups and individual members of the majority secure or insecure in their position in society? What is the previous experience of a majority individual or group with a minority group or member? What are the age, religious, political, occupational, and educational backgrounds of the majority and minority individuals? Each of these variables affects the way an interethnic relationship develops and how prejudices against certain ethnic groups who happen to be in a minority either grow or dissipate. See Allport, *The Nature of Prejudice*, 25th ed. (Reading, Mass., 1979), 262.

33. Sander Gilman confuses the matter further by using the term "Aryan," rather than Christian or Gentile, as the antithesis to Jew. See Gilman, *The Jew's Body* (New York, 1991); Michael Meyer, "Jews as Jews Versus Jews as Germans, Two Historical Perspectives: Introduction to Year Book 36," *Leo Baeck Institute Yearbook* 36 (1991): xvii.

34. Michael Marrus, "Theory and Practice of Antisemitism," *Commentary*, August 1982, 38-42; and Allport, Nature of Prejudice, 14.

35. See especially Dietz Bering, *The Stigma of Names: Antisemitism in German Daily Life, 1812-1933*, trans. Neville Plaice (Ann Arbor, 1992), 278-79, Henry, *Victims and Neighbors*, 154-55. Bering argues that the Nazis were able to steer the history of the Jews toward a gruesome end first by weakening the resistance to antisemitism through the condescending mockery of names, then through the ostracism of names to the point of personality destruction, and, finally, through an assurance of precision of access on the part of the murderous antisemites via name signals.

36. Karl Dietrich Bracher, *The German Dictatorship: The Origins, Structure, and Effects of National Socialism* (New York, 1970); Eberhard Jäckel, *Hitler's Weltanschauung: A Blueprint for Power* (Middletown, Conn., 1972); Jacob

Talmon, *The Origins of Totalitarian Democracy* (London, 1952); Arendt, *Origins of Totalitarianism;* Eva Reichmann, *Hostages of Civilization: The Social Sources of National Socialist Antisemitism* (London, 1950).

37. Martin Broszat, *Der Staat Hitlers: Grundlegung und Verfassung seiner inneren Entwicklung* (Munich, 1969); In English *The Hitler State: The Foundations and Development of the Internal Structure of the Third Reich* (New York, 1981); Hans Mommsen, "The Realization of the Unthinkable: The Final Solution of the Jewish Question in the Third Reich," in *The Polities of Genocide: Jews and Soviet Prisoners of War in Nazi Germany,* ed. Gerhard Hirschfeld (London, 1986).

38. The first analysis of these sources can be found in Aryeh Unger, "The Public Opinion Reports of the Nazi Party," *Public Opinion Quarterly* 29 (1965): 565-82. See also Otto D. Kulka and Aron Rodrigue, "The German Population and the Jews in the Third Reich: Recent Publications and Trends in Research on German Society and the 'Jewish Question,'" *Yad Vashem Studies* 16 (1984): 421-35.

39. Stokes, "The German People and the Destruction of the European Jews," 167-91; Michael Marrus, "History of the Holocaust: A Survey of Recent Literature," *Journal of Modern History* 59 (1987): 131; Steinert, *Hitler's War,* 145; Aron Rodrigue, "German Popular Opinion and the Jews Under the Nazi Dictatorship" (B.A. thesis, University of Manchester, 1978), Kershaw, *Popular Opinion;* Gordon, *Hitler, Germans, and the Jewish Question;* Bankier, *Germans and the Final Solution.*

40. Jeremy Noakes, *The Nazi Party in Lower Saxony, 1921-1933* (Oxford, 1971), 206-10, Marrus, "History of the Holocaust," 132; William Sheridan Allen, *The Nazi Seizure of Power: The Experience of a Single German Town, 1930-1935* (Chicago, 1965), 77; Kater, "Everyday Antisemitism," 129-59; Kulka, "Public Opinion," 121-44; Kulka, ed., *Changes in the Status and Activities of the Jews Under the Impact of the Third Reich, 1933-1939* (Jerusalem, 1966); Daniel Goldhagen, *Hitler's Willing Executioners: Ordinary Germans and the Holocaust* (New York, 1996); John Weiss, *Ideology of Death: Why the Holocaust Happened in Germany* (Chicago, 1996). Goldhagen's book stands in contrast to Christopher Browning's *Ordinary Men: Reserve Police Battalion 101 and the Final Solution in Poland* (New York, 1992), which argues that antisemitism was not the major factor motivating police battalions charged with executing Jews.

41. Marrus, "Theory and Practice of Antisemitism," 38-42.

Chapter 1

1. See Jacob Katz, *Out of the Ghetto: The Social Background of Jewish Emancipation* (New York, 1973).

2. For a consideration of the stop-and-go nature of Jewish emancipation during the nineteenth century, see Reinhard Rürup, "The Tortuous and Thorny Path to Legal Equality—'Jew Laws' and Emancipatory Legislation in Germany from the Late Eighteenth Century," *Leo Baeck Institute Yearbook* 31

(1986): 3-34; Michael Graetz, "From Corporate Community to Ethnic-Religious Minority, 1750-1830," *Leo Baeck Institute Yearbook* 37 (1992): 71-82.

3. Jacob Toury, "Types of Municipal Rights in German Townships: The Problem of Local Emancipation," *Leo Baeck Institute Yearbook* 22 (1977): 56.

4. German authorities consistently opposed efforts by German Jews to establish a national representative organization. (This policy extended to Catholics as well.) See Robert Liberles, "Emancipation and the Structure of the Jewish Community in the Nineteenth Century," *Leo Baeck Institute Yearbook* 37 (1986): 62.

5. There were hundreds of rural Jewish communities in Germany, but most German Jews lived in urban areas.

6. Arnsberg, *Die jüdischen Gemeinden*, 1:11, 239, 254; Knauss, *Die jüdische Bevölkerung*, 9.

7. Katz, *Out of the Ghetto*; Sorkin, *Transformation of German Jewry*; Jonathan Frankel and Steven Zipperstein, eds., *Assimilation and Community: The Jews in Nineteenth Century Europe* (Cambridge, 1992), explore various aspects of Jewish emancipation in Europe, the first two works focusing on the pace of ideological transformation, the third on social and economic change. Ulrich Friedrich Kopp, "Juden in Hessen," in *Bruchstücke zur Erläuterung der deutschen Geschichte und Rechte* (Kassel, 1799), 1:155, cited in Wolf-Arno Kropat, "Die Emanzipation der Juden in Kurhessen und in Nassau im neunzehnten Jahrhundert," in *Neunhundert Jahre Geschichte der Juden in Hessen: Beiträge zur politischen, wirtschaftlichen, und kulturellen Leben* (Wiesbaden, 1983), 325.

8. *75 Jahre Rheingaukreis*, 177.

9. Kropat, "Die Emanzipation," 340-41.

10. Knauss, *Die jüdische Bevölkerung*, 11.

11. Heuberger, *Hinaus aus dem Ghetto*, 64, 66; Kropat, "Die Emanzipation," 340-41.

12. See Niewyk, *Jews in Weimar Germany*, 97-105, 195-200; David Sorkin, "Emancipation and Assimilation: Two Concepts and Their Application to the Study of German Jewish History," *Leo Baeck Institute Yearbook* 35 (1990): 17-33.

13. According to Dietz Bering, the imposition of last names on Jews was a major way in which German Jewry was socially stigmatized (*Stigma of Names*, 278-79).

14. David Sorkin, "The Impact of Emancipation on German Jewry: A Reconsideration," in ed. Frankel and Zipperstein, *Assimilation and Community*, 179-80; Jacob Toury, *Soziale und politische Geschichte der Juden in Deutschland, 1847-1871* (Düsseldorf, 1977), 114, 277; Helga Krohn, *Die Juden in Hamburg, 1880-1950* (Frankfurt, 1967), 49-50.

15. See Sorkin, *Transformation*, 107-72.

16. Even Moses Mendelssohn, the father of the Haskalah, was not permitted to join a Gentile social lodge.

17. According to Jakob Petuchowski, Frankfurt had some connection

to all of the major religious trends in modern Judaism—Reform, Conservatism, and Neo-Orthodoxy. See his "Frankfurt Jewry: A Model of Transition to Modernity," *Leo Baeck Institute Yearbook* 29 (1984): 405-17.

18. Jost was a historian, writer, and reformer who taught at the Philanthropin (Frankfurt's liberal Jewish school) from 1835 to 1860. Geiger, the "Father of Reform," became Frankfurt's leading rabbi in 1863. See Heuberger, *Hinaus aus dem Ghetto*, 44, 73; Knauss, *Die jüdische Bevölkerung*, 11-13; Arnsberg, *Die jüdischen Gemeinden*, 1:255. The Frankfurt synagogue was rededicated in 1860; the Giessen synagogue was built in 1867 and expanded in 1892.

19. Heuberger, *Hinaus aus dem Ghetto*, 74.

20. According to Katz, the decision of the Neo-Orthodox to declare themselves a separate religion was tactical. In so doing, they won the right to establish separate communal organizations under government auspices (*Out of the Ghetto*, 210). See also Robert Liberles, *Religious Conflict in Social Context: The Resurgence of Orthodox Judaism in Frankfurt am Main, 1838-1877* (Westport, Conn., 1985).

21. Knauss, *Die jüdische Bevölkerung*, 13, 15.

22. Scholem, "Social Psychology," 13.

23. Liberal Judaism found a home in the cities in large part because of their more cosmopolitan environments and because of the weakening effects of urban migration on traditional ties. See Steven Lowenstein, "The Pace of Modernization of German Jewry in the Nineteenth Century," *Leo Baeck Institute Yearbook* 21 (1976): 47, and both volumes of Arnsberg, *Die jüdischen Gemeinden*.

24. Both Conservative Judaism and *Gemeindeorthodoxie* had connections to Frankfurt am Main. *Gemeindeorthodoxie* originated there, and Conservative Judaism began as the result of a protest by its founder, Zechariah Frankel, over the diminution of Hebrew by the 1845 Frankfurt Rabbinical Conference. See Petuchowski, "Frankfurt Jewry," 405.

25. Since few official records for the Jewish community of Geisenheim exist, information about it has come from memoir testimonies and interviews. The information concerning the degree of Geisenheim Jewry's religious observance is confirmed by a 10 October 1993 interview with Geisenheim resident Berhnarde Wilhelmy and correspondence dated 20 December 1993 with Gretel Strauss, a descendant of Geisenheimer Jews. Initially, because of its central location between Rüdesheim and Winkel, Geisenheim was to have its own synagogue. But the Jewish community there did not have the wherewithal to erect one, and in 1842, five Jews from Rüdesheim and one from Geisenheim helped build a new temple in Rüdesheim (Arnsberg, *Die jüdischen Gemeinden*, 1:240).

26. Heuberger, *Hinaus aus dem Ghetto*, 134; Arnsberg, *Die jüdischen Gemeinden*, 1:255.

27. Leo Baeck, "Kulturzusammenhang," *Der Morgen* 1 (1925): 72-83;

Baeck, "The German Jews," *Leo Baeck Institute Yearbook* 2 (1957): 35-36; Niewyk, *Jews in Weimar Germany*, 100.

28. From Leopold Zunz's Science of Judaism to later institutions such as the Centralverein, Jews referred decreasingly to the unifying ties of Judaism and increasingly to a Jewish community of shared destiny *(Schicksalgemeinschaft)*. See Niewyk, *Jews in Weimar Germany*, 103, his citation of Ludwig Hollaender's *Deutsch-jüdische Probleme der Gegenwart* (Berlin, 1929), 14, and "Warum sind und bleiben wir Juden?" *Central-Verein Zeitung*, 16 December 1932.

29. See Tal, *Christians and Jews in Germany*.

30. David Rausch, "The Church and the Holocaust," in *Holocaust Literature: A Handbook of Critical, Historical, and Literary Writings* (Westport, Conn., 1993), 125; Rausch, *Legacy of Hatred: Why Christians Must not Forget the Holocaust* (Grand Rapids, Mich., 1990); Edward Flannery, *The Anguish of the Jews: Twenty-Three Centuries of Antisemitism* (New York, 1985).

31. Eleanore Sterling, *Judenhass: Die Anfänge des politischen Antisemitismus in Deutschland, 1815-1850* (Frankfurt am Main, 1969).

32. The words "antisemite" and "antisemitic" required, of course, the prior emergence of the terms "Semite" and "Semitic." Credit for this terminology has been given to A.L. von Schloezer, who used the term in his *Fortsetzung der allgemeine Welthistorie* (Halle, 1771) to describe a family of languages as well as the community and culture (but not race) of Jews. See Thomas Nipperdey and Reinhard Rürup, "Antisemitismus," in *Geschichtliche Grundbegriffe*, ed. Otto Brunner et al. (Stuttgart, 1972), 1:129-31. Peter Pulzer argues that the shortcomings of liberalism and the identification of Jews as liberals fueled the rise of antisemitism in the fin de siècle. Similarly, George Mosse and Fritz Stern have implied that antisemitism was a symptom of a conservative and proto-fascistic reaction against Enlightenment values in the late nineteenth century. Shulamit Volkov, too, has postulated a link between the popular revulsion of modernity and the hatred of Jews. Paul Lawrence Rose, however, has suggested that modern German antisemitism may have had stronger roots in the German Enlightenment and more relevant spokesmen in revolutionaries such as Johann Fichte. Jacob Katz, David Rausch, and Edward Flannery see the persistence of traditional religious antisemitism as a major factor in the popularity of new forms of Jew-hatred. James Harris has also shifted the focus away from antisemitic ideologues in the late 1800s to popular opinion in the mid-century as a way of assessing continuities in public discontent with emancipation. See Pulzer, *Rise of Antisemitism*; George Mosse, *The Crisis of German Ideology: The Intellectual Origins of the Third Reich* (New York, 1964); Fritz Stern, *The Politics of Cultural Despair: A Study in the Rise of the Germanic Ideology* (Berkeley, 1961); Volkov, *Rise of Popular Antimodernism*; Paul Lawrence Rose, *Revolutionary Antisemitism in Germany from Kant to Wagner* (Princeton, 1990); Katz, *From Prejudice to Destruction*; Rausch, *Legacy of Hatred*; Flannery, *Anguish of the Jews*; James Harris, "Public Opinion and the Proposed Emancipation of the Jews in

Bavaria, 1849-1850," *Leo Baeck Institute Yearbook* 34 (1989): 68-80, Harris, *The People Speak! Antisemitism and Emancipation in Nineteenth Century Bavaria* (Ann Arbor, 1994).

33. Other racial-cultural antisemites such as Richard Wagner argued that as a cultural force, Jews had contributed nothing to German life. See Wagner, *Das Judentum in der Musik* (Leipzig, 1869).

34. Racists pointed to the growing presence in Germany of more traditional Jews from eastern Europe (*Ostjuden*) to buttress their claim that all Jews were inherently different.

35. See Wolfgang Wippermann and Michael Burleigh, *The Racial State: Germany, 1933-1945* (Cambridge, 1990); Gilman, *The Jew's Body*, 235.

36. Koshar, *Social Life*, 65.

37. Schweitzer was a Social Democrat who supported Lassalle and became president of the General German Workers' Union in 1867. His three-volume work *Lucinde oder Kapital und Arbeit* assailed the alleged connection between Jewry and liberalism. The Association of Academics (Verein akademisch gebildeter Lehrer) excluded teachers from both Frankfurt's liberal and Orthodox Jewish communities. See Heuberger, *Hinaus aus dem Ghetto*, 119-21.

38. Niewyk, *Jews in Weimar Germany*, 60.

39. See Richard Levy, *The Downfall of the Antisemitic Parties in Imperial Germany* (New Haven, 1975).

40. See Ismar Schorsch, *Jewish Reactions to German Antisemitism, 1870-1914*, (New York, 1972).

41. Heuberger, *Hinaus aus dem Ghetto*, 124-26.

42. For a consideration of this development, see Jehuda Reinharz, *Fatherland or Promised Land? The Dilemma of the German Jew, 1893-1914* (Ann Arbor, 1975).

43. Stephen Poppel, *Zionism in Germany, 1897-1933: The Shaping of a Jewish Identity* (Philadelphia, 1977), Table 3. Between 1918 and 1933, nearly two thousand German Jews, primarily Ostjuden, left for Palestine (Richarz, *Jüdisches Leben*, 35-36).

44. According to Stephen Poppel, an additionally problematic aspect of German Zionism was its usage of discourse and rhetoric that often paralleled its contemporary counterpart, the German *völkisch* movement (Poppel, *Zionism in Germany*, 127-30, Heuberger, *Hinaus aus dem Ghetto*, 126-27).

45. Excerpts from "A Letter to Michael from His Uncle Martin," 16 July 1971, 23, Leo Baeck Institute, ME 449.

46. Poppel, *Zionism in Germany*, 77-78.

47. The Frankfurt CV organized protests against the Judenzählung, and the Frankfurter Zeitung assailed it in numerous editorials. The protests of the Frankfurt CV actually ran counter to the wishes of then CV chairman, Eugen Fuchs, who insisted that Jews remain silent for the sake of the Fatherland. See Fuchs, "Deutschtum und Christentum," *Im deutschen Reich* 34 (July–August 1918): 280; Pulzer, *Jews and the German State*, 206; Heuberger, *Hinaus aus dem Ghetto*, 132.

48. Franz Oppenheimer, *Die Judenstatistik des preussischen Kriegsministeriums* (Munich, 1922); Jakob Segall, *Die deutschen Juden als Soldaten im Kriege, 1914-1918* (Berlin, 1922); Pulzer, *Jews and the German State*, 206.

49. In April 1918, for example, the eastern frontier of Prussia was closed to all Polish Jewish immigrants, ostensibly to prevent a typhus epidemic (Pulzer, *Jews and the German State*, 206). See also Jack Wertheimer, *Unwelcome Strangers: Eastern European Jews in Imperial Germany* (New York, 1987); Steven Aschheim, *Brothers and Strangers: The East European Jew in German and German-Jewish Consciousness, 1800-1923* (New York, 1982).

50. Heuberger, *Hinaus aus dem Ghetto*, 132; Arnsberg, *Die jüdischen Gemeinden*, 1:239, 254.

51. Richarz, *Jüdisches Leben*, 13.

52. *Der Schild*, 7 June 1926, as cited in Niewyk, *Jews in Weimar Germany*, 40.

53. As Peter Gay put it, the culture of Weimar was created by groups on the margins of German society, "perennial" outsiders like Jews, who became easy targets for the radical right. See Gay, *Weimar Culture: The Outsider as Insider* (New York, 1968); and Traverso, *Jews and Germany*, 32.

Chapter 2

1. Peukert, *Weimar Republic*, 7-9; D. Petizina, *Materialien zur Statistik des Deutschen Reiches, 1914-1945: Sozialgeschichtliches Arbeitsbuch III* (Munich, 1978).

2. The number of 615, 021 counted only those who openly proclaimed themselves Jews. According to Gershom Scholem, the number of Jews among dissidents or those listed as *sonstige* cannot be ascertained. Jews in this category were likely very small in number, although their numbers increased during the 1920s (Scholem, "Social Psychology," 10; Richarz, *Jüdisches Leben*, 14).

3. The picture at the micro level was more complex. The population of Hessen rose from 1,282,051 in 1910 to 1,429,048 in 1933, in Hessen-Nassau from 2,286,871 in 1910 to 2,584,828 in 1933. In 1910, Jewish percentages ran 1.88 percent and 2.33 percent in Hessen and Hessen-Nassau respectively. Table 2 shows that Jews constituted greater proportions of the population in the Hessian lands than in Germany as a whole. But here again, percentages declined before numbers. In Hessen-Darmstadt, the Jewish population added 1,373 people between 1871 and 1880 and still sank in percentage from 2.97 to 2.86. By 1933, Jews were only 1.25 percent of the population in Hessen and 1.82 percent in the Prussian province of Hessen-Nassau. Numerically, there was a noticeable ebb as well. In 1933, there were 6,000 fewer Jews in Volkstaat Hessen (or Hessen-Darmstadt) than there had been in 1910, falling from approximately 24,000 to less than 18,000. Almost two and a half times more Jews resided in Hessen-Nassau than in Hessen-Darmstadt (because of Frankfurt), but between 1910 and 1933, their numbers dropped from 51,781 to 46,923.

Over the same time period, the total population of Hessen-Darmstadt increased by nearly 150,000, Hessen-Nassau by almost 300,000. See Arnsberg, *Die jüdischen Gemeinden*, 1:18, *Statistik des deutschen Reiches: Die Bevölkerung des deutschen Reiches nach den Ergebnissen der Volkszählung 1939. Stand, Entwicklungs-, und Siedlungsweise der Bevölkerung des deutschen Reiches*, Vol. 552, Issue 1 (Berlin, 1943), 26, 34.

4. *Statistisches Handbuch der Stadt Frankfurt am Main: Zweite Ausgabe Enthaltend der Statistik der Jahre 1906/07 bis 1926/27* (Frankfurt, 1928), 70.

5. *Statistik des deutschen Reiches: Die berufliche und soziale Gliederung der Bevölkerung des deutschen Reiches: Süddeutschland und Hessen*, Vol. 456, Issue 33 (Berlin, 1935), 36; Arnsberg, *Die jüdischen Gemeinden*, 1:254-55.

6. *Statistik des deutschen Reiches: Die Bevölkerung des deutschen Reiches nach den Ergebnissen der Volkszählung 1933: Die Glaubensjuden im Deutschen Reich*, Vol. 451, Issue 5 (Berlin, 1936), 7, 9, 35, 36, 41; "Verzeichnis der abgemeldeten Personen, Mai 1928 bis April 1942," and the city's "Einwohnerliste," Stadtarchiv Geisenheim, 123-03.

7. Richarz, *Jüdisches Leben*, 14.

8. Lawrence Schofer argues that German Jews may have internalized a different ideal family size earlier than their Gentile neighbors ("Emancipation and Population Change," in *Revolution and Evolution: 1848 in German-Jewish History*, ed. Werner Mosse, Arnold Paucker, and Reinhard Rürup (Tübingen, 1981), 88-89. See also Lowenstein, "The Pace of Modernization of Germany Jewry," 41-56; Jacob Toury, *Soziale und politische Geschichte der Juden in Deutschland* (Düsseldorf, 1977); and Avraham Barkai, "The German Jews at the Start of Industrialization: Structural Change and Mobility, 1835 to 1860," in *Revolution*, ed. Mosse, Paucker, and Rürup, 123-56.

9. Mortality rates revealed that Evangelicals accounted for 64.1 percent of all deaths, Catholics for 32.05 percent, and Jews for 1.23 percent. These numbers may be skewed because only three years (1919-21) are offered for consideration in Julius Rothholz, *Die deutschen Juden: In Zahl und Bild* (Berlin, 1925), 10.

10. The Jewish birth rate in Hessen-Darmstadt also failed to keep pace with mortality. This assertion is verifiable only for the early years of the republic to 1925, when Jewish deaths in Hessen outnumbered births by an average of 296 to 267. This would have meant that the death rate of Hessen Jewry was about 1.45 percent, and the birth rate was 1.3 percent, leaving a growth rate of negative 0.15 percent (Paul Troschke, *Evangelisches Kirchenstatistik Deutschlands: Kirchenstatistik* Issues 2 and 3 [Berlin, 1929], his table "Jüdische Sterblichkeit").

11. Richarz, *Jüdisches Leben*, 15, 67; *Statistik des deutschen Reiches: Die Glaubensjuden im deutschen Reich*, 17; Ezra Ben Nathan, "Die demographische und wirtschaftliche Struktur der Juden," in *Entscheidungsjahr 1932: Zur Judenfrage in der Endphase der Weimarer Republik*, ed. Werner Mosse (Tübingen, 1965), 95.

12. Richarz, *Jüdisches Leben*, 15, 67; and Arthur Ruppin, *The Jews in the Modern World* (London, 1934), 318-19.

13. *Statistik des deutschen Reiches: Die Bewegung der Bevölkerung, 1925-1927*, Vol. 360, Issue 1 (Berlin, 1929), 17; *Statistik des deutschen Reiches: Die Bewegung der Bevölkerung 1932-34*, Vol. 495, Issue 1 (Berlin, 1936), 32.

14. Marriages among German Gentiles declined as well between 1929 and 1932 (from 585,742 to 558,764). In 1930 marriages between German Jews and either Protestants or Catholics totaled 1,384. In 1932 the number of similar intermarriages was 1,029. Interestingly, the number of such intermarriages in 1933, following the Nazi takeover, was 1,425. The increase may have been owing to the belief among Jews that marriage to Christians provided a degree of immunity from persecution. See *Statistik des deutschen Reiches: Die Bewegung der Bevölkerung, 1932-34*, 32; *Statistisches Jahrbuch für das deutsche Reich, 1931* (Berlin, 1931), 30; *Statistisches Jahrbuch für das deutsche Reich, 1932* (Berlin, 1932), 30.

15. "Nondenominationalism" became popular among both Jews and Christians over the course of the Weimar period. The number of individuals classified as *sonstige* or "none of the above" in religious affiliation grew accordingly, as did the number of marriages between Jews and *sonstigen* (Arthur Ruppin, *The Jewish Fate and Future* [London, 1940], 282).

16. Only if we add the number of births by mixed marriages do we obtain a birth overflow of 524, but we do not know if these unions necessarily produced Jewish offspring. Moreover, Jewish birth rates moved in a wavelike pattern from 1906 to 1926, totaling 375 in 1906, 174 in 1917 (during the war), and 517 in 1923. The number of deaths was higher in the 1920s than in the first decade of the twentieth century (averaging about 400 annually as compared to 330). These statistics are calculated by an analysis of the *Statistisches Handbuch der Stadt Frankfurt a, M.: Zweite Ausgabe Enthaltend die Statistik der Jahre 1906/07 bis 1926/27* (Frankfurt, 1928), 79, 83. W. Hanauer counted the mortality surplus at around 600 in these years in his "Bilanz der jüdischen Bevölkerung Frankfurts, 1910-1925," *Frankfurt Israelitisches Gemeindeblatt* 6, no. 5 (1927-28): 136, but it appears he did not include Jewish births out of wedlock. See also Arnsberg, *Die Geschichte der Frankfurter Juden*, 2:494.

17. The numbers were down from 2,760 (1,388 boys, 1,372 girls) in 1900 to 1,156 (599 boys, 557 girls) in 1925 (*Statistisches Handbuch der Stadt Frankfurt der Jahre 1906/07 bis 1926/27*, 70).

18. At 137, the number of endogamous marriages between Jews in 1932 was up slightly from 133 in 1931. In the wake of the Nazi seizure of power in 1933, the intermarriage rate jumped to nearly 40 percent. It then dropped to 25 percent in 1934 and to 12 percent in 1935 before being outlawed. See *Frankfurt Israelitisches Gemeindeblatt* 6, no. 5 (1927/28): 136; *Beiträge zur Statistik der Stadt Frankfurt: Tabellarische Übersichten Betreffend den Zivilstand der Stadt* 15 (Frankfurt, 1931), 46; *Beiträge zur Statistik der Stadt Frankfurt: Tabellarische Übersichten Betreffend den Zivilstand der Stadt* 16 (Frankfurt, 1937), 2, 26, 50, 74, 98.

19. Some sources as cited in note 18; *Beiträge zur Statistik der Stadt Frankfurt: Tabellarische Übersichten Betreffend den Zivilstand der Stadt* 16

(Frankfurt, 1937), 79; *Statistische Jahresubersichten der Stadt Frankfurt am Main, 1928*, 168, 175; Arnsberg, *Die Geschichte der Frankfurter Juden*, 2:492.

20. Under German law, it was possible for Jews to leave the Jewish community structure without adopting Christianity. In 1929, 105 Frankfurt Jews withdrew from the community but only one Jewish man officially converted to Christianity. By contrast, in 1933, 34 Jews left the city's Gemeinde and 73 left Judaism. In 1929 8 individuals reentered the IG, while in 1933, 37 did, perhaps realizing that conversion did little to protect Jews from Nazi persecution. See Lothar Bauer, "Gemeindestatistik in Zahl und Wort," *Frankfurt Israelitisches Gemeindeblatt* 13, no. 9 (1934-35): 343.

21. Ostjuden chose the IG because they received a cold shoulder from the IRG and had little desire to endure the process of communal secession.

22. Trude Maurer, *Ostjuden in Deutschland, 1918-1933* (Hamburg, 1986), 72, 75-76; Richarz, *Jüdisches Leben*, 14; Heuberger, *Hinaus aus dem Ghetto*, 134-35.

23. In 1925, the number of foreign-born Jews in Frankfurt increased by 2,282 (3,451 to 5,733, 13.5 percent to 19.6 percent of the city's Jewish population) (Maurer, *Ostjuden in Deutschland*, 75-76; Heuberger, *Hinaus aus dem Ghetto*, 134-35).

24. Arnsberg, *Die Geschichte der Frankfurter Juden*, 2:495, 497-98, Bauer, "Gemeindestatistik," 343; Wilhelm Hanauer, "Die Bevölkerungsbewegung der Frankfurter Juden," *Frankfurt Israelitisches Gemeindeblatt* 8, no. 10 (1929-30): 394-96.

25. *Beiträge zur Statistik der Stadt Frankfurt: Tabellarische Übersichten Betreffend den Zivilstand der Stadt* 15 (1931): 46; *Beiträge zur Statistik der Stadt Frankfurt: Tabellarische Übersichten Betreffend den Zivilstand der Stadt* 16 (1937): 2, 26; Bauer, Gemeindestatistik," 343.

26. Arnsberg, *Die jüdischen Gemeinden*, 1:254; Knauss, *Die jüdische Bevölkerung*, 17.

27. *Mitteilungen der hessischen Zentralstelle für Landesstatistik, 9/10 Oktober/Dezember 1931* (reporting for 1930), 148-49, ibid., *1932* (reporting for 1931), 11, 48, 91, 92; ibid., *1933* (reporting for 1932), 108, Hessisches Staatsarchiv Darmstadt.

28. *Mitteilungen der hessischen Zentralstelle für Landesstatistik*, 255, 260.

29. Knauss, *Die jüdische Bevölkerung*, 112-18, 153-77.

30. None of the Catholic churches in Giessen which I consulted reported a conversion by a Jew in that period, although anecdotal information suggests that there may have been a few. Paul Arnsberg lists, for example, Max Walldorf, who was classified by the Nazis as a "full Jew" (*Volljude*) even though he no longer belonged to the Jewish community and had married a Catholic. See Konfessionswechsel: Tabellen über Austritte und Übertritte zu der evangelischen Landeskirche, 1909-1928, Stadtkreis Giessen, Zentralarchiv der evangelischen Kirche Hessen, Darmstadt, 17-470; "Eheschliessungen nach Glaubenskenntnis der Eheschliessenden," in *Mitteilungen der hessischen*

Zentralstelle für Landesstatisitk, 1923 to 1930, Hessisches Staatsarchiv Darmstadt; Arnsberg, *Die jüdischen Gemeinden*, 1:255.

31. Comparing marriage rates in Frankfurt and in Giessen in 1931, for instance, shows that there was one marriage per 130 Jews in Frankfurt, but only one marriage per 250 Jews in Giessen (*Mitteilungen der hessischen Zentralstelle für Landesstatistik*, 1932, 91, 92; *Beiträge zur Statistik der Stadt Frankfurt: Tabellarische Übersichten Betreffend den Zivilstand der Stadt*, 2).

32. One of the members of the Strauss family is recorded to have left for St. Louis in 1931 ("Verzeichnis der abgemeldete Personen Mai 1928 bis April 1942," Stadtarchiv Geisenheim, 123-03).

33. No Jewish records for the community in Geisenheim exist, and city records do not register a Jewish birth, death, conversion, or intermarriage in these years ("Einwohnerliste der Stadt," Stadtarchiv Geisenheim, 123-03).

34. The only record I have found of an intermarriage comes from *Der Rheingaukreis in den Jahren 1869-1893* (Ansgabe, 1893), 23, in which one child is listed as a product of a union between a Jewish man and a Catholic woman in 1890. See also "Civilstands-Register der Proclamierten und Copulierten in Geisenheim, 1918-1933," Katholisches Pfarramt Geisenheim; "Verzeichnis der Getrauten," in Evangelisches Gemeindehaus Geisenheim.

35. "Einwohnerliste," Stadtarchiv Geisenheim.

36. Although more Jews entered urban areas, migration from the countryside into towns overall began to abate by the 1920s (Peukert, *Weimar Republic*, 10).

37. Richarz, *Jüdisches Leben*, 17; *Statistik des deutschen Reiches: Die Bevölkerung des deutschen Reiches nach den Ergebnissen der Volkszählung 1933; Die Bevölkerung des deutschen Reiches nach der Religionszugehörigkeit*, Vol. 451, Issue 3 (Berlin, 1936), 9-14.

38. Table 5 also reveals that Frankfurt maintained the second largest Jewish community in Germany, second only to Berlin, which held over one-third of the entire German Jewish population. The inclusion of Frankfurt in the Hessen-Nassau tally explains why 66 percent of Jews, but only 35 percent of all Nassauers, lived in regions in excess of 100,000 people. Of the province's total population, 57 percent, compared to 26 percent of its Jews, lived in small villages. By comparison, in Hessen, Jews and Gentiles (51.9 percent and 61.2 percent respectively) were mostly rural or small-town urban.

39. The East End, comprising the östliche and nordöstliche Neustadt and the östliche Aussenstadt, still had slightly more Jews than any other district until 1910, when the number of Jews in the northern and western sections of town surpassed earlier figures. By 1925, the number of Jews in both the West and East Ends were roughly even. Thirty percent of the city's Jews lived in either the west or northwest districts, and 14 percent resided in the northern suburbs, while nearly 44 percent continued to live in the east-northeast part of town. In those areas, the percentage of Jews in relation to the overall population was, in some instances, very different. Only 8.9 percent of the population

in west-northwest Frankfurt (the westliche Neustadt, and the westliche, sud-westliche, and nordwestliche Aussenstadt) was Jewish, but 30 percent of the city's Jews lived there. The reason for the lower proportion of Jews was that few of them settled in the very populous sudwestliche Aussenstadt. If this region is taken out of our computation, we see that 23.1 percent of the population in the remaining three areas combined was Jewish. That is very close to the tally of 25 percent, which was the percentage of Frankfurt Jews who lived in those areas. If we take the westliche Neustadt out of the count, the percentage of the population that were Jewish becomes even greater. In fact, the second largest concentration of Frankfurt's Jews was in the nordwestliche Aussenstadt with 4,410 (15 percent of all Jews in Frankfurt, 30 percent of the overall population there). In the northern suburbs 9.9 percent of the general population was Jewish, but nearly 14 percent of Frankfurt's Jews chose those districts for residence. Finally, in the Ostend (östliche Neustadt, östliche Aussenstadt, nordöstliche Aussenstadt), 15 percent of the total population was Jewish, yet 43.7 percent of the city's Jews lived there. So while in all three areas Jews were a small minority, they were a concentrated and therefore visible one. The largest number of Jews as of 1925 was in the östliche Aussenstadt with 6,384 (21.7 of all Jews in Frankfurt, 20 percent of the district's total population). See *Statistisches Handbuch der Stadt Frankfurt a.M.*, 69, and Heuberger, *Hinaus aus dem Ghetto*, 92.

40. Heuberger, *Hinaus aus dem Ghetto*, 92-93.

41. "Aufstellung der am 30. 1. 1933 und später in Giessen und Giessen-Wieseck wohnhaft gewesenen jüdischen Personen," in Knauss, *Die jüdische Bevölkerung*, 54-111; "Verzeichnis der zur Israelitischen Religionsgemeinde Giessen steuerpflichtigen Personen: Stand Januar 1932" and "Verzeichnis der Mitglieder der Israelitische Religionsgesellschaft, Giessen, Stand vom 13. 3. 1935," ibid., 112-18.

42. "Verzeichnis der Abgemeldete" and "Einwohnerliste," Stadtarchiv Geisenheim, 123-03.

43. The typical urban German Jewish community was divided into four strata. At the top stood wealthy banking families, followed by professionals and well-to-do businessmen, then small merchants, and finally, Ostjuden. The comparison in Table 12 of social standing among Gentiles and Jews shows that while 45 percent of the former were wage laborers (*Arbeiter*), only 8.7 percent of the latter were. Eighty percent of Jews, yet only 34 percent of Gentile Germans, worked as independents (*selbständig*) or salaried employees (*Beamten* or *Angestellten*). In the 1920s, 58 percent of Frankfurt's Jews counted as independents, in contrast to 19 percent of the city's Gentile work force. See Niewyk, *Jews in Weimar Germany*, 16-20.

44. The figures for Hessen and Hessen-Nassau in Table 10 closely mirror the national statistics. During the Weimar period, 51.9 percent of Jews in Hessen-Nassau and 55.2 percent of those in Hessen were involved in trade, whereas the rates for Gentiles in those areas ran 17.6 percent and 14.5 percent respectively. A little more than 2 percent of Jews in both Hessian regions

worked the land, in comparison to over 30 percent of the general population. Yet it is unlikely that this tally included the large number of commercial Jews who had urban residences and traded out in the countryside as cattle dealers. Between 38 and 40 percent of all Hessians worked in industry or crafts, but only 16 to 17 percent of Hessian Jews did. Finally, Jewish engagement in occupations labeled as "other" exceeded general involvement by a two-to-one margin. Jobless independents, not professionals, constituted the bulk of this category.

45. Scholem, "Social Psychology," 13.

46. The ratio of Jewish and Gentile involvement in public service and the free professions was fairly even in Frankfurt and Geisenheim, but a glaring imbalance existed in Giessen, a university town, where approximately 30 percent of the work force (but only 7.3 percent of working Jews) made a living as public servants or professionals. See Table 11.

47. The 1933 figure of 28.9 percent was down from 1907's report of 36.8 percent, indicating that the Gentile population of Germany also was becoming less agrarian.

48. According to Werner Mosse, of the twenty leading taxpayers of Hessen-Nassau, twelve were of Jewish origin. Clearly visible was the wealth of the Rothschilds and Goldschmidt-Rothschilds, with an aggregate fortune of 384 million marks. They were followed by members of the Gans/Weinberg families of Leopold Cassella and Company, worth 108 million marks. Hessen's wealthy Gentile elite essentially consisted of manufacturers (Carl Henschel in Kassel and Herbert von Meister of Farbewerke Hochst), bankers (Carl von Metzler, Albert Mumm von Schwarzenstein), and heirs to fortunes (Lucie Fleischer, Alexander Friedrich Landgraf von Hessen). See Mosse, *The Jews in the German Economy: The German-Jewish Economic Elite, 1820-1935* (Oxford, 1987), 210-11.

49. Heuberger, *Hinaus aus dem Ghetto*, 88.

50. Whereas nearly 75 percent of all Evangelicals in the city and 83 percent of Catholics made three thousand marks or less annually, only 45 percent of Jews did; 16.47 percent of Frankfurt's Jews made more than 12,500 marks, compared with 4.86 percent of Evangelicals and 1.93 percent of Catholics. The city's Jews also paid more taxes than their Gentile neighbors: 427.50 marks to 121 marks for Evangelicals and 59.40 marks for Catholics (*Zeitschrift für Demographie und Statistik der Juden* 4 [1905]: 12; Heuberger, *Hinaus aus dem Ghetto*, 97; Arnsberg, *Die Geschichte der Frankfurter Juden*, 2:491).

51. Economic pressures translated into a high suicide rate among Jews. In Berlin in 1925, the suicide rate for Jews stood at 68 per 100,000, for Protestants, 45 per 100,000, and for Catholics, 32 per 100,000. See Niewyk, *Jews in Weimar Germany*, 20; "Erschütternde Selbstmordziffern," *Der Schild* 4 (1925): 453-54; "Berufsproblematik der Juden," *Central-Verein Zeitung* 6 (December 1923).

52. Alfred Marcus, *Die wirtschaftliche Krise der Juden* (Berlin, 1931);

"Jüdische Arbeitslosigkeit: Statistische Untersuchung über jüdische Arbeitslose in Frankfurt am Main," *Jüdische Wohlfahrtspflege und Sozialpolitik* 3 (April 1932) 4: 113; Donald Niewyk, "The Impact of Inflation and Depression on German Jews," *Leo Baeck Institute Yearbook* 28 (1983): 19-36.

53. Brenario's estimate that Jews paid 45 percent of city taxes before the war but only 15 percent during the first year of the Depression is out of line with Werner Sombart's calculation that they paid 20.8 percent of taxes in the city in 1907. See Niewyk, "Impact," 34; *Verwaltungsblatt des preussischen Landesverbandes jüdischer Gemeinden* 9, no. 5 (October 1931): 31.

54. Tietz became Hertie during the Nazis' "Aryanization" of Jewish businesses.

55. Heuberger, *Hinaus aus dem Ghetto*, 88.

56. Thirty-two percent of Jewish women in the city had outside employment, while 37 percent were housewives, and 31 percent were dependents. See Heinrich Silbergleit, "Die jüdische Wohnbevölkerung am 16. Juni 1925 nach Wirtschaftsabteilungen,-gruppen, und-zweigen sowie nach der Stellung im Beruf," in *Die Bevölkerungs-und Berufsverhältnisse der Juden im Deutschen Reich: Freistaat Preussen* (Berlin, 1930), 232.

57. "Verzeichnisse," 1932, 1935, in Knauss, *Die jüdische Bevölkerung*, 112-18.

58. Map of Jewish stores in Giessen in Kurt Heyne, "Judenverfolgung in Giessen und Umgebung 1933-1945," *Mitteilungen der Oberhessischen Geschichtsvereins Giessen* 69 (1984): 180-81.

59. "Aufstellung," and "Verzeichnisse," 1932, 1935, in Knauss, *Die jüdische Bevölkerung*, 112-18.

60. Verzeichnis," and "Einwohnerliste," Stadtarchiv Geisenheim, 123-03.

61. Richarz, *Jüdisches Leben*, 22.

62. One need only invoke the name Rothschild or other Frankfurt-born bankers like Jakob Schiff to gain a sense of this presence (Heuberger, *Hinaus aus dem Ghetto*, 86). Silbergleit, "Die jüdische Wohnbevölkerung," 231-33, 258; Hans-Dieter Kirchholtes, *Jüdische Privatbanken in Frankfurt am Main* (Frankfurt, 1969). In the nineteenth century, Aron Heichelheim founded a banking institution with the help of the Rothschilds from Frankfurt. His son Siegmund (who eventually became the leader of Giessen's Israelitische Gemeinde) and grand-nephew Albert took over their predecessor's operations and in 1907 merged their branch with the Mitteldeutsche Creditbank, today the Commerzbank. Following the merger, Albert became the director of Creditbank's subsidiary in Giessen. Both Albert and Siegmund died in the early years of the republic. Bankhaus Herz and the Privatbank remained under Jewish direction until the Nazi period. The chairman of Privatbank, Jakob Grünewald, was also the head of the Orthodox community in Giessen ("Verzeichnisse," 1932, 1935, in Knauss, *Die jüdische Bevölkerung*, 112-18). See also Arnsberg, *Die jüdischen Gemeinden*, 1:257.

63. Richarz, *Jüdisches Leben*, 22-23.

64. Heuberger, *Hinaus aus dem Ghetto*, 88; Silbergleit, "Die jüdische Wohnbevölkerung," 231, 233. Silbergleit, 231, states that 579 out of 2,916 Jews in Frankfurt industry were *Arbeiter.*

65. "Verzeichnisse," 1932, 1935, in Knauss, *Die jüdische Bevölkerung*, 112-18, Arnsberg, *Die jüdischen Gemeinden*, 1:257.

66. "Aufstellung," in Knauss, *Die jüdische Bevölkerung*, 54-111.

67. "Verzeichnis," Stadtarchiv Geisenheim, 123-03.

68. Chapter 3 will deal extensively with the integration of Jews in Germany's educational system. See Henry, *Victims and Neighbors*, 149; Richarz, *Jüdisches Leben*, 24.

69. Heuberger, *Hinaus aus dem Ghetto*, 89; Arnsberg, *Die Geschichte der Frankfurter Juden*, 2:500.

70. Notker Hammerstein, *Die Johann Wolfgang Goethe Universität. Von der Stiftungsuniversität zur staatlichen Hochschule. Band 1, 1914-1950* (Frankfurt, 1989), 220; Heuberger, *Hinaus aus dem Ghetto*, 111-12.

71. Michael Kater, *Studentenschaft und Rechtradikalismus in Deutschland 1918-1933* (Berlin, 1974), 147; Heuberger, *Hinaus aus dem Ghetto*, 158.

72. Some of the "Jewish" plays performed at the Neues Theater (*Die Fünf Frankfurter*, for instance) portrayed (and often satirized) the culture of both indigenous and foreign Jews (Heuberger, *Hinaus aus dem Ghetto*, 154).

73. Frankfurt's Moritz Oppenheim was one of the most famous Jewish painters in nineteenth-century Germany, and the twentieth-century painters continued his legacy of assimilating elements of German culture and adapting them to Jewish themes. Both Nussbaum (a Zionist) and Schames painted street scenes of Frankfurt life (*An der Hauptwache in Frankfurt, Frankfurter Opernplatz*) but never ignored their Jewishness (Schames's *Jüdisches Siechenheim*). Benno Elkan's sculpture *Den Opfern* remains a powerful memorial to the German soldiers who were killed in World War I.

74. Heuberger, *Hinaus aus dem Ghetto*, 257.

75. "Aufstellung," and "Verzeichnisse, 1932, 1935" in Knauss, *Die jüdische Bevölkerung*, 54-111, 112-18; Arnsberg, *Die jüdischen Gemeinden*, 1:257.

76. The "Verzeichnisse" also lists twenty-nine Jewish widows and four Jewish women without a profession in Giessen in the early 1930s (Knauss, *Die jüdische Bevölkerung*, 112-18).

77. Heyne, "Judenverfolgung," 32; "Aufstellung," in Knauss, *Die jüdische Bevölkerung*, 61.

78. Knauss, *Die jüdische Bevölkerung*, 32.

79. Alfred Bock's works included "Die Pflastermeisterin," "Aus einer kleinen Universitätsstadt," "Der Flürschutz," "Die leere Kirche," "Grete Fillunger, " "Hessenluft," and "Wege im Schatten." Werner's contributions to literature were "Das ewige Du," "Der Pudel der Frau Barboni," "Blute am Abgrund," "Die beiden Rosen," "Trostung," and "Anthropos." See Knauss, *Die jüdische Bevölkerung*, 33.

80. "Verzeichnis," and "Einwohnerliste," Stadtarchiv Geisenheim, 123-03.

Chapter 3

1. The Zionists were divided between pan-Germanists (Kurt Blumenfeld), spiritual Zionists who tended to see Judeity and Germanness as opposed (Gershom Scholem and, I would say, Martin Buber), or those who were more inclined to socialism (Arnold Zweig). See Traverso, *Jews and Germany*, 34.

2. For instance, Max Naumann's League of German Nationalist Jews.

3. Two prominent Jewish avant-garde intellectuals of the Weimar period were Max Horkheimer and Theodor Adorno. They represented a conspicuous minority, however, and would have been unwilling to acknowledge the slightest Jewish element in their outsider cultural marginality. Between the two poles of self-denial and zealous religiosity stood the mass of Jewish intellectuals who regarded their dual German Jewish identity as a "mission" to be accomplished and as a value to be preserved within German or Austrian society. In the field of politics, they could identify as much with the left (Ernst Toller, Gustav Landauer, Lion Feuchtwanger, Erich Mühsam, and Alfred Döblin) as with the liberal-progressive position (Stefan Zweig and Jakob Wassermann) or with conservatives (Hermann Cohen, Leo Baeck). See Traverso, *Jews and Germany*, 33, 34.

4. For liberal efforts to revitalize Jewish identity during the Weimar period see, Richard Koch, "Das Freie Jüdische Lehrhaus in Frankfurt," *Der Jude* 7 (1923): 116-20; "Mehr Mut!" *Central-Verein Zeitung*, 31 October 1924; Hans Sachs, "Offener Brief an die liberalen Vorsteher der jüdischen Gemeinde zu Berlin," *Jüdische Liberale Zeitung* 12 (15 October 1932); Ludwig Holländer, "Warum sind und bleiben wir Juden," *Central-Verein Zeitung*, 16 December 1932.

5. There were sixty-five students at the Yeshiva in 1930, of whom only twenty-five were native-born German Jews (Heuberger, *Hinaus aus dem Ghetto*, 159-63).

6. The Philanthropin was unique in that most Jewish schools in Germany had ceased to function during the Wilhelmine era. In 1928, 176 boys attended the Philanthropin's high school, while matriculation at the all-girls' school was 208. A Ritual Commission, led mostly by nonseparatist, Orthodox Jews, was also established in Frankfurt. It succeeded in preserving a measure of tradition (especially kosher dietary restrictions) in many communal and private institutions. In 1924, eight Jewish butcheries, four bakeries, and two restaurants went strictly kosher. See *Statistische Jahresübersichten der Stadt Frankfurt* (1930), 53; Arnsberg, *Die Geschichte der Frankfurter Juden*, 1:893, 897, 2:504, his citation of *Frankfurt Israelitisches Gemeindeblatt* 3 (1924-25); *Das Philanthropin zu Frankfurt am Main: Dokumente und Erinnerungen* (Frankfurt, 1964), 103; Heuberger, *Hinaus aus dem Ghetto*, 161-65.

7. A Jewish religious school, located on Unterlindau 21-23, served as an additional Orthodox synagogue (Heuberger, *Hinaus aus dem Ghetto*, 160).

8. Ernst Simon, "N.A. Nobel (1871-1922) als Prediger," 6, Erich Ahrens Collection, Leo Baeck Institute, AR4389 A 11/5.

9. Rudolf Geiger was the leader of the IG's liberal faction, and Napthali Fromm headed up the Orthodox delegation (*Jüdisches Jarhbuch für Hessen-Nassau* [Frankfurt, 1932-33], 67).

10. Heuberger, *Hinaus aus dem Ghetto*, 159-61, 165.

11. Ibid.

12. Simon, "N.A. Nobel," 6.

13. *Jüdische Stiftungen in Frankfurt am Main: Stiftungen, Schenkungen, Organisationen, und Vereine mit Kurzbiographien jüdischer Bürger* (Frankfurt, 1988), 180-85.

14. *Frankfurt Israelitisches Gemeindeblatt*, Jg. 1, Nr. 1 (1922-23); (December 1922): 1.

15. Arnsberg, *Die Geschichte der Frankfurter Juden*, 1:895.

16. According to Donald Niewyk, Liberals also had majorities on the Jewish community councils of Berlin, Breslau, and Duisburg but were much less compromise-oriented (*Jews in Weimar Germany*, 112).

17. Caesar Seligmann, "Mein Leben," 119, Leo Baeck Institute, ME 595.

18. Erich Ahrens to Rabbi J. Seligson, New York, 27 September 1962, 3, Ahrens Collection, Leo Baeck Institute, AR4389 A 11/5.

19. *Jüdische Stiftungen*, 227.

20. Arnsberg, *Die Geschichte der Frankfurter Juden*, 1:897; *Frankfurt Israelitisches Gemeindeblatt* 4 (1925-26).

21. Other prominent non-Zionists, including Leo Baeck, head of Berlin's Jewish community, also lent their support to Jewish emigration to Palestine. See Richarz, *Jüdisches Leben*, 36, Heuberger, *Hinaus aus dem Ghetto*, 165, 166, 168; *Frankfurt Israelitisches Gemeindeblatt* 8, nos. 2, 3 (1929).

22. There were numerous other foundations that promoted Jewish cultural activities and supported Jewish students financially, for instance, the Isaak and Berta Glazier Stiftung, founded in 1909, and the Flora Geisenheimer-Kann, founded in 1922, for female students (*Jüdische Stiftungen*, 17).

23. Erich Ahrens, "Franz Rosenzweig and the Men of the Frankfurt Lehrhaus 1921-1922," 3, Leo Baeck Institute, ME 705; Heuberger, *Hinaus aus dem Ghetto*, 163-64.

24. Jehuda Reinharz, "The Lehrhaus in Frankfurt am Main: A Renaissance in Adult Education," 6, Leo Baeck Institute, MS 128.

25. Ibid., Wolfgang Schivelbusch, *Intellektuellendämmerung: Zur Lage der Frankfurter Intenz in den zwanziger Jahren* (Frankfurt, 1982), 37.

26. Buber-Rosenzweig correspondence, Leo Baeck Institute, AR 3866.

27. The Lehrhaus experienced a forced "renaissance" during the Third

Reich, when Buber reopened it to serve as a center of Jewish culture and education. Heuberger, *Hinaus aus dem Ghetto*, 164-65.

28. At the IRG schools in 1909, 106 students attended the elementary school (*Vorschule*), 249 the boys' *Realschule*, and 245 the girls' *Lyzeum*. In 1927, those numbers fell to 25 for the *Vorschule*, 237 for the *Realschule*, and 206 for the *Lyzeum*. Arnsberg, *Die Geschichte der Frankfurter Juden*, 2:504-5, Festschrift zum 75jährigen Bestehen der Realschule mit Lyzeum der Israelitischen Religionsgesellschaft [Frankfurt, 1928]; Heuberger, *Hinaus aus dem Ghetto*, 162, 166.

29. Heuberger, *Hinaus aus dem Ghetto*, 166-67.

30. Salomon Spiro, "Judenerinnerungen aus hessischen Judengemeinden," 42, Leo Baeck Institute, ME 614.

31. Jakob Rosenheim, *Erinnerungen, 1870-1920* (Frankfurt, 1950), 58, 87, 118.

32. Wertheimer, *Unwelcome Strangers*, 21.

33. Rachel Heuberger mistakenly identifies all of Frankfurt's Orthodox rabbis after Samson Raphael Hirsch (Breuer, Jona Horowitz, Markus Horovitz, Nobel, and Hoffmann) as *Ostjuden* (*Hinaus aus dem Ghetto*, 136, 138-39).

34. "Bruno Ostrovsky: Erinnerungen und Betrachtungen, " in Richarz, *Jüdisches Leben*, 196.

35. Heuberger, *Hinaus aus dem Ghetto*, 139. Not all Frankfurt Jews were wary of *Ostjuden*. Friedel Rothschild Lichtenberg reports that her father invited many to her home on occasion, and later, I shall consider the efforts of SPD delegate and Frankfurt police chief Leopold Harris on behalf of eastern European Jews. These two individuals, however, appear to have been exceptional cases (Lichtenberg, "Reminiscences of a Frankfurt Childhood," 1, Leo Baeck Institute, ME 521; Harris, "Biographie von Leopold Harris," 56, Stadtarchiv Frankfurt, Nachlass S1/18/20/1960).

36. Heuberger, *Hinaus aus dem Ghetto*, 163; *Jüdische Stiftungen*, 125, 260; Arno Lustiger, "Bertha Pappenheim," ibid., 367-70.

37. Arnsberg, *Die Geschichte der Frankfurter Juden*, 2:93.

38. Niewyk, *Jews in Weimar Germany*, 22, and his citation of *Der Israelit*, March 28, 1929, and June 18, 1931.

39. Heuberger, *Hinaus aus dem Ghetto*, 127; Poppel, *Zionism in Germany*, Table 3.

40. Bar Kochba's membership in 1930 was 650. Several other Zionist institutions were also active in the city at the time: the Lema'an Zion-Palestine Relief Association, the Zionist Student Group (Frankfurt office founded in 1930), the Union of Revisionist Zionists (a mouthpiece for the expansive ideology of Ze'ev Jabotinsky and Josef Trumpeldor, founded in 1924, led initially by Paul Arnsberg), the Bet Chalutz (House of Pioneers), Brith-Ha-Olim Young Jewish Hiking Union (Socialist Zionist association founded in 1920), Brith-Trumpeldor (founded in Riga in 1923, in Frankfurt in 1930), Kadimah (another

Zionist youth group, the Frankfurt Ortsgruppe of which was founded in 1925), the Jung-Wizo Circle, the Sport Association Bar Kochba, a branch of Poale Zion Youth, the Mizrachi Organization (Orthodox Jewish/Zionist association, in Frankfurt since 1903), Zeire Mizrachi (Orthodox/Zionist youth group), the Zionist Youth Group, and the Zionist-Revisionist Youth Group Herzliah (in Frankfurt since 1929).

41. "Bruno Ostrovsky," in Richarz, *Jüdisches Leben*, 195.

42. *Jüdische Stiftungen*, 264.

43. Membership in the ZVfD fell from 33,339 in 1922-23 to 9,539 in 1929-30, rising to 17,548 after the first significant electoral showing of the Nazis in 1930-31, and then falling off again to 7,546 in 1931-32. (Poppel, *Zionism in Germany*, Table 3).

44. Heuberger, *Hinaus aus dem Ghetto*, 127.

45. Caesar Seligmann, *Erinnerungen* (Frankfurt, 1975), 159.

46. See especially Bolkosky, *Distorted Image*.

47. Other organizations, however, included the Lodge of the Frankfurt Eagle (founded in 1832, 1928 membership 205), the Lodge of the Rising Sun (founded in 1807, 1932 membership 153), the Imperial Union of Jewish Front Soldiers, Talmud-Torah Association (1929 membership 767), the Jewish Gymnastics Union (founded for Orthodox Jews in 1926, 1932 membership 320), the Sport Association of the Philanthropin (established in 1921, 1936 membership 600), Gymnastic and Sport Association Schild (created in 1925 by the Imperial Union of Jewish Front Soldiers), Union of German University Students of the Jewish Faith (founded in 1896 as Fraternal Convention Nassovia or Kartell-Convent Nassovia), Union of Jewish Academicians (an Orthodox university student group), Jewish Liberal Youth Community of Frankfurt (founded in the city in 1925 emphasizing the positive aspects of Reform), Jewish Youth Union of Frankfurt am Main (founded in 1928, apolitical), Union of Jewish Boy Scouts (founded in Frankfurt in 1928 to instill Jewish pride, also apolitical), Youth Group of the Jewish Women's Union (founded in Frankfurt in 1925), Comrades (a German Jewish youth hiking group), Black Flag (a patriotic German Jewish Boy Scout group that grew out of Comrades), and Association Montefiore (*Jüdische Stiftungen*, 125-410).

48. The 1913 membership of the Frankfurt Lodge was 461 (ibid., 256).

49. Arnsberg, *Die Geschichte der Frankfurter Juden*, 2:49-50.

50. Indifference to issues affecting Jews from several left-wing Jewish politicians (notably Hugo Sinzheimer and Tori Sender) was a lesser concern because many Jews on the Social Democatic left, such as Bruno Asch and Henriette Fürth, fought for Jewish civil rights. The attraction of the SPD to Jews became more intense over the course of the republic because it became the only party that seemed to defend the republic, democracy, and the rights of "people on the margins," including Jews (Heuberger, *Hinaus aus dem Ghetto*, 149). Over the course of the republic, Ludwig Holländer, the leader of the

Centralverein, referred less to the unifying ties of Judaism and increasingly to the Jews' "community of shared destiny." According to Donald Niewyk, by 1933 there may have been as many as sixty thousand ethnic Jews in Germany who "either strove for amalgamation or else acknowledged their Jewishness in purely secular ways" (*Jews in Weimar Germany*, 99, 102). See also Holländer, "Warum sind und bleiben wir Juden?"; Friedrich Rülf, "Untergang der deutschen Juden?," *Israelitisches Familienblatt*, 7 September 1922; Gustav Löffler, "Religiöse Not," *Der Morgen* 2 (1926): 259-71; Arnsberg, *Die Geschichte der Frankfurter Juden*, 1:22, 74-75, 113, 2:492; Hans Salfeld, "Wehmut ums Westend," 128, Leo Baeck Institute, ME 578; *Statistische Jahresübersichten der Stadt Frankfurt am Main*, 1928 (Frankfurt, 1930), 46; *Stadtarchiv Frankfurt; Statistische Jahresübersichten der Stadt Frankfurt am Main, 1931/1932* (Frankfurt, 1933), 17. For an instance of a liberal Jew in Frankfurt who became more traditional, see Margarete Sallis Freudenthal, "Meine Beiden 40 Jahren," 98, Leo Baeck Institute, ME 550, and her *Ich habe mein Land gefunden* (Frankfurt, 1977), 55.

51. By comparison, attendance in Berlin was 49 percent and in Breslau 58 percent. The number of rabbinical students underwent a similar decline. In 1928, only 0.1 percent of Jewish students throughout Germany were studying to be rabbis, as compared to the 2.7 percent of Catholic students and 2.7 percent of Protestant students who were preparing for the clergy. See Niewyk, *Jews in Weimar Germany*, 102-3; *Israelitisches Familienblatt*, 6 September 1928; Kurt Sabatzky, "Hebung des jüdischen Lebens," *Israelitisches Familienblatt*, 5 December 1929.

52. Selmar Spier, "Anfang-Mitte-Ende," 4-5, Leo Baeck Institute, ME 611.

53. See Arnsberg, *Die Geschichte der Frankfurter Juden*, 2:492, 493, 494, and all of Vol. 1.

54. Seligmann, *Erinnerungen*, 159.

55. As we shall see in Chapter 4, Jewish students established their own fraternities and *Vereine* because they were excluded from many Gentile ones. German Jews did, however, belong to many Gentile sporting, recreational, and cultural associations from which they were expelled after the Nazi takeover. Denial of membership to Jews in Gentile clubs was not unique to the German social scene. American Jews and African Americans faced (and continue to face) this discrimination.

56. *Frankfurt Israelitisches Gemeindeblatt* 8 (1929): 80.

57. Novelist Jakob Wassermann echoed this sentiment when he said, "I am a German, and I am a Jew, one as intensely and as completely as the other, inextricably bound together." See Niewyk, *Jews in Weimar Germany*, 100, 108; Kurt Alexander's speech on the occasion of the twenty-fifth anniversary of the "Sprevia" on 3 November 1919, *Kartel-Convent Blätter* 9 (1919): 180; Jakob Wassermann, *Mein Weg als Deutscher und Jude* (Berlin 1921), 126.

58. Arnsberg, *Die jüdischen Gemeinden*, 255, 256, 257.

59. The IRG was recognized as an officially separate religious community in 1923.

60. Arnsberg, *Die jüdischen Gemeinden*, 1:254-56.

61. Interview with Martin Harth by Jonathan Friedman, New York City, 10 July 1993.

62. The 1925 membership of the Jewish Burial Association was 150 and of the Jewish Casino Society 110.

63. Arnsberg, *Die jüdischen Gemeinden*, 1:254, 264; Erwin Knauss, "Kurzgefasste Geschichte der Juden in Giessen: 13es Jahrhundert bis 1945," *Zur Statistik Giessens und seines Umlandes: Aufsätze und Reden* (Giessen, 1987), 380.

64. Erich Neumann, "To Life," unpublished memoir, 174-75, 453.

65. Josef Stern, *Stark wie ein Spiegel* (Giessen, 1989), 39-44. Stern also recounted how he and his family enjoyed singing both German and Hebrew songs. See pp. 51, 52.

66. Ibid., 73-75.

67. Interview with Harth.

68. Henry Buxbaum, "Recollections," in Monika Richarz, *Jewish Life in Germany* (Bloomington, 1991), 301-2.

69. A consideration of the cemeteries in Rüdesheim and Östrich-Winkel (the village immediately east of Geisenheim) provides a tiny clue into the extent of Jewish integration in the Rheingau. Jewish sections within municipal cemeteries were established in Germany for the first time in the 1870s in Düsseldorf, Alzey, Giessen, and Schweinfurt. In each case, Jewish sections were established only after Orthodox Jews managed to make numerous modifications. In Rüdesheim, Jews were buried in a separate annex to the general cemetery, as in Frankfurt and Giessen. Moreover, Jewish gravestones there looked exactly like their Christian counterparts, very similar to the situation in Giessen and Frankfurt. By contrast, Jewish tombstones in the Östrich-Winkel cemetery had Hebrew, not German, inscriptions. See Falk Weisemann, "Jewish Burials in Germany: Between Tradition, the Enlightenment, and the Authorities," *Leo Baeck Institute Yearbook* 37 (1992): 28; Arnsberg, *Die jüdischen Gemeinden*, 1:240; Interview with Elisabeth and Wilhelm Will by Jonathan Friedman, Geisenheim, 15 September 1993.

70. Interview with Elisabeth and Wilhelm Will.

71. See Bolkosky, *Distorted Image*.

Chapter 4

1. Werner Cahnman, "Village and Small Town Jews in Germany" in *German Jewry: Its History and Sociology*, ed. Joseph Maier et al. (New Brunswick, N.J., 1989), 58. At the turn of the century, the German sociologist Ferdinand Tönnies proposed the dichotomy of *Gesellschaft* and *Gemeinschaft* to characterize the rift betwen modern "society" and traditional "community."

2. According to Gordon Allport, the United States in the 1940s was as problematic for Jews as Germany had been in the 1920s because Jews encountered similar prejudices and problems gaining access to Gentile social organizations. Moreover, relations between blacks and whites in the United States were clearly more troubled than the Jewish/non-Jewish relationship because state-sponsored segregation against blacks was commonplace in many regions (Allport, *Nature of Prejudice*, 77).

3. Paul Kluke, *Die Stiftungsuniversität Frankfurt am Main, 1914-1932* (Frankfurt, 1972), 32, 62; Heuberger, *Hinaus aus dem Ghetto*, 107, 109.

4. Although destroyed in World War II, the Budge nursing home was rebuilt in 1960 (*Jüdische Stiftungen*, 98).

5. Interestingly, the loudest opposition to the creation of a Jewish theology department at the university came from its Jewish founders (Franz Rosenzweig to Martin Buber, Frankfurt, 12 January 1923, in Nachum Glatzer and Paul Mendes-Flohr, eds., *The Letters of Martin Buber: A Life of Dialogue* [New York, 1991], 293).

6. Adorno, Horkheimer, Fromm, and Marcuse taught at the university's Institute of Social Research, founded in 1923 (Martin Jay, *The Dialectical Imagination: A History of the Frankfurt School and the Institute of Social Research, 1923-1950* [Boston, 1973], 3-29).

7. One Jew, Leopold Mayer, was a member of Giessen's chamber of commerce, and there was a Jewish privy councillor (*Hofrat*) and a Jewish district commissioner (*Bezirksdirektor*) in town. See "Aufstellung," and "Verzeichnisse," in Knauss, *Die jüdische Bevölkerung*, 54-118; Arnsberg, *Die jüdischen Gemeinden*, 1:258.

8. Heuberger, *Hinaus aus dem Ghetto*, 98-101; James Sheehan, *German Liberalism in the Nineteenth Century* (Chicago, 1978); James F. Harris, *Study in the Theory and Practice of German Liberalism: Eduard Lasker, 1829-1884* (Lanham, Md., 1984); John Snell, *The Democratic Movement in Germany, 1789-1914* (Chapel Hill, 1976).

9. Heuberger, *Hinaus aus dem Ghetto*, 149.

10. These individuals did not exercise much influence beyond their own immediate circle, and the radical left-wing *Frankfurt Volkstimme* failed to attract Jewish readers, who remained loyal to the Liberal-Democratic *Frankfurter Zeitung* (Pulzer, *Jews and the German State*, 253; Heuberger, *Hinaus aus dem Ghetto*, 148-49).

11. Frankfurter Historische Kommission, *Frankfurt am Main: Geschichte der Stadt* (Sigmaringen, 1991), 444; Bericht über die Verhandlungen der Stadtverordnetenversammlung der Stadt Frankfurt am Main 1924, Paragraph 799, p. 634.

12. Dieter Rebentisch, "Frankfurts modernes Fundament stammt von Ludwig Landmann," *Frankfurter Allgemeine Zeitung*, 28 July 1983, and his *Ludwig Landmann: Frankfurts Oberbürgermeister in der Weimar Republik* (Wiesbaden, 1975).

13. Heuberger, *Hinaus aus dem Ghetto*, 102-4; *Jüdische Stiftungen*, 290-97, 367-69.

14. Silbergleit, "Die jüdische Wohnbevölkerung" 261; Knauss, "Aufstellung" and "Verzeichnisse," in *Die jüdische Bevölkerung*, 54-118.

15. *Statistisches Handbuch der Stadt Frankfurt a. M. Zweite Ausgabe: Enthaltend die Statistik der Jahre 1906/07 bis 1926/27* (Frankfurt, 1928), 76.

16. Interview with Martin Harth; Interview with Margot Freimuth by Jonathan Friedman, Geisenheim, 12 September 1993. According to Harth, his father normally used the name Max instead of Meyer in everyday discourse. Apparently, when employees at his tailor business struck, the *Giessener Anzeiger* referred to Meier Harth in an effort (according to his son) to focus on the fact that Harth was a Jew.

17. Georg Salzberger, "Autobiographische Skizze," 7, Leo Baeck Institute, ME 542.

18. Elizabeth Bamberger, "Die Geschichte und Erlebnis," 3-4, Leo Baeck Institute, ME 387; Nora Rosenthal, "Opus One," 27, Leo Baeck Institute, ME 532; Margarete Sallis Freudenthal, "Meine Beiden 40 Jahren," 99, Leo Baeck Institute, ME 550.

19. See Lewis Hertzman, *DNVP: Right-Wing Opposition in the Weimar Republic, 1918-1924* (Lincoln, Neb., 1963), 124-64; Hans-Helmuth Knütter, *Die Juden und die deutsche Linke in der Weimarer Republik, 1918-1933* (Düsseldorf, 1971) 174-205; George Mosse, "German Socialists and the Jewish Question in the Weimar Republic," *Leo Baeck Institute Yearbook* 16 (1971): 134-43; Donald Niewyk, *Socialist, Antisemite, and Jew: German Social Democracy Confronts the Problem of Antisemitism, 1918-1933* (Baton Rouge, 1971), 195-96; Niewyk, *Jews in Weimar Germany*, 50-75.

20. See the collection from the Staatsanwaltschaft bei dem Landgericht Frankfurt a. M., Abteilung 461, Hessisches Hauptstaatsarchiv, Wiesbaden.

21. Arnsberg, *Die Geschichte der Frankfurter Juden*, 3:409.

22. Heuberger, *Hinaus aus dem Ghetto*, 150.

23. Likewise, Toni Sender never once mentioned her Jewish origins in her *Autobiographie einer deutschen Rebellin* (Frankfurt, 1981, reprint from the English, 1939); Heuberger, *Hinaus aus dem Ghetto*, 148-49.

24. Heuberger, *Hinaus aus dem Ghetto*, 102-4.

25. Stadtverordnetenversammlung, 21 Sitzung, 17 December 1929, Paragraph 1588.

26. According to IG council member Selmar Spier, Frankfurt was regarded by the Nazis with hostility as the "New Jerusalem on the Franconian Jordan" (Spier, "Anfang-Mitte-Ende," 34; Ben Lieberman, "Testing Peukert's Paradigm: The Crisis of Classical Modernity in the "New' Frankfurt, 1925-1930," *German Studies Review* 17 [1994], 299-300).

27. Hugo Sinzheimer also failed to obtain Prussian confirmation for the job of police chief. Subsequently bribed by an eastern European Jewish deportee, Harris threatened to leave the SPD for the communists after party

members assailed his transgression (Johanna Harris, "Biographie," Nachlass S1/18/20/1960, 54, 71, Stadtarchiv Frankfurt).

28. Frankfurt City Housing Office, 16 February 1920, as cited by Maurer, *Ostjuden in Deutschland*, 282.

29. Heuberger, *Hinaus aus dem Ghetto*, 138, and her citation of the Magistratsakte R 1376, Stadtarchiv Frankfurt.

30. Magistratsakte R 1376, Stadtarchiv Frankfurt; Wolfgang Wippermann, *Das Leben in Frankfurt zur NS-Zeit: Band I, Die national-sozialistische Judenverfolgung—Darstellung, Dokumente und didaktische Hinweise* (Frankfurt, 1986), 48.

31. Wippermann, *Judenverfolgung*, 48-49; Salomen Adler-Rudel, *Ostjuden in Deutschland, 1880-1940* (Tübingen, 1959), 115.

32. According to Detlev Peukert, the Scheuneviertel riot could be seen as a portent of the anti-Jewish boycott of 1 April 1933, and the Reichskristallnacht of 9-10 November 1938, but there were notable differences. For one, in 1923, the police cleared the antisemitic mob from the streets. Second, the invocation of an abstract, demonized image of the Jew played a far more important part in the latter two events than in the Scheuneviertel episode, an event more akin to an outbreak of traditional antisemitic hostility or a pogrom prompted by mob violence than anything else. See *Vossische Zeitung*, 6 November 1923; Peukert, *Weimar Republic*, 160.

33. Wippermann, *Judenverfolgung*, 49.

34. Heuberger, *Hinaus aus dem Ghetto*, 164; Maurer, *Ostjuden in Deutschland*, 65.

35. Heuberger, *Hinaus aus dem Ghetto*, 105, 162; Arnsberg, *Die Geschichte der Frankfurter Juden*, 1:898.

36. Catholic antisemites did not come just from Bavaria. The vicar general of Mainz agreed with Hitler's accusation that Jews were "poisoning German culture."

37. Walter Hannot shows how apathy toward Jews and the Jewish Question extended to nearly all of the major Catholic newspapers in Germany, while the Austrian ones were more antisemitic. Donald Niewyk, among others, points out that Protestants tended to be more antisemitic than Catholics in Germany. Walter Dirks, section editor of the Catholic *Rhein-Mainische Volkszeitung* until 1933, maintained that he had a close circle of Jewish friends. See Niewyk, *Jews in Weimar Germany*, 55-65; Walter Hannot, *Die Judenfrage in der katholischen Tagespresse Deutschlands und Österreichs, 1923-1933* (Mainz, 1990); Walter Dirks, "Frühe Nahe," in *Das Judentum lebt—ich bin begegnet: Erfahrungen von Christen* (Freiburg, 1985), 64-69. See also Hermann Greive, *Theologie und Ideologie: Katholizismus und Judentum in Deutschland und Österreich, 1918-1935* (Idelberg, 1969), 33-52; Hans-Joachim Kraus, "Die Evangelische Kirche," in Werner Mosse and Arnold Paucker, *Entscheidungsjahr 1932: Zur Judenfrage in der Endphase der Weimar Republik* (Tübingen, 1966), 254-56, 263-66; Eberhard Röhm and Jorg Thierfelder, *Juden-Christen-Deutsche, 1933-1945*

(Stuttgart, 1990), 68-69, 71; Ino Arndt, "Die Judenfrage im Lichte der evangelischen Sonntagsblätter, 1918-1938" (Ph.D. diss. University of Tübingen, 1960).

38. Franz Rosenzweig to his parents, letter of 1917, I Korrespondenz, Franz Rosenzweig Collection, Leo Baeck Insititute, ARC-1935.5043; Dominique Bourel, "Un soupir de Rosenzweig," *Franz Rosenzweig: Les cahiers de la nuit surveillee, no. 1* (Paris, 1982), 176-77.

39. Martin Buber, *Der Jude und sein Judentum: Gesammelte Aufsätze und Reden* (Cologne, 1963), 693; Buber to Robert Weltsch, letter of 1928, in *Juden und Judentum in deutschen Briefen aus drei Jahrhunderten* (Königstein, 1935), 397-99.

40. See also Rosenzweig's wartime correspondence with Eugen Rosenstock-Huessy, a Jewish convert to Christianity, in Rosenzweig, *Briefe* (Berlin, 1935); Huessy, *Judaism Despite Christianity: The Letters on Christianity and Judaism Between Eugen Rosenstock-Huessy and Franz Rosenzweig* (Tuscaloosa, Ala., 1969), 57, 113.

41. Rosenzweig to Buber, Frankfurt am Main, 19 March 1924, in Glatzer and Flohr, eds., *Letters of Martin Buber*, 311.

42. Wurm was arrested in the early phase of Hitler's reign (in 1934), but he was eventually reinstated and went on to cooperate with the Nazi regime. See Jeremy Noakes and Geoffrey Pridham, *Nazism, 1919-1945: A History in Documents and Eyewitness Accounts* (New York, 1983), 1:584.

43. It would be unfair to say that Buber's and Rosenzweig's participation in Jewish-Christian dialogue during the Weimar period was unique. There were animated discussions between Jews and the League of Religious Socialists, between Carl Mennicke, Eduard Heimann, and Paul Tillich, and between Walter Benjamin and the Swiss Christian Socialist Fritz Lieb. Many Jews also contributed to Karl von Ossietzky's left-wing journal *Die Weltbühne*, although not with the direct intention of promoting Gentile-Jewish dialogue within the German intelligentsia. See Traverso, *Jews and Germany*, 36; Rohm and Thierfelder, *Juden-Christen-Deutsche*, 98-101; *Jüdische Stiftungen*, 244.

44. Letter from the Oberbürgermeister Karl Keller, 10 July 1930, Giessen, Handakten der Stadt Giessen 2108/03/2, Akten 1426, Stadtarchiv Giessen.

45. *Giessener Anzeiger*, 30 September 1879; Knauss, "Die jüdische Bevölkerung," 13-14.

46. Knauss, "Kurzgefasste Geschichte der Juden in Giessen: 13es Jahrhundert bis 1945," *Zur Statistik Giessens und seines Umlandes: Aufsätze und Reden* (Giessen, 1987), 390.

47. In 1928, 2,312 Jewish students attended Prussian universities (4.5 percent). Of them, 248 attended Frankfurt University (9.6 percent). See "Das Schicksal Jüdischer Studenten und Studentinnen an der Johann Wolfgang Goethe Universität," in *Die braune Machtergreifung. Universität Frankfurt, 1930-1945* (Frankfurt, 1989), 41; and Kater, *Studentenschaft und Rechtra-*

dikalismus in Deutschland, 147. The rise in the number of foreign-born Jews at German universities resulted in an intensification of preexisting animosities. In 1886, 9.8 percent of all Jewish university students had non-German origins; by 1909, that percentage had increased to 21.7 percent (ibid., 151).

48. The German educational system, particularly the *Gymnasien* and universities, had been closed to women for centuries. They were closed to Jewish females because of gender, not religious affiliation (Kaplan, "Tradition and Transition," 26).

49. Table 17 reveals that one Protestant boy and three Protestant girls were in attendance at the high schools of the Philanthropin in 1928, while one Protestant boy and one Protestant girl received an education at the high schools of the Samson Raphael Hirsch Schule that same year. These numbers may be so minuscule as to be without import, but for Gentiles to have attended any of the city's Jewish high schools was surprising. One might argue that while there was some Jewish integration in public and private education in Frankfurt there was almost no reciprocal Gentile participation in Jewish education, but one cannot juxtapose Jewish attendance at public and private schools with Gentile attendance at Jewish parochial schools. Protestants rarely attended Catholic private schools (and vice versa) let alone Jewish ones.

50. Niewyk, *Jews in Weimar Germany,* 111, 112; M. Kosler, "Mehr Mut!" *Central-Verein Zeitung,* 31 October 1924; *Frankfurt Israelitisches Gemeindeblatt,* September–October 1925.

51. It is also not possible to follow the educational path of converts or marginal Jews who belonged to neither a synagogue nor to one of the various communities.

52. In 1910, there were 197 hours of Jewish religious training in 22 schools set aside for 1,384 Jewish boys and girls. Frankfurt was, however, an exception in Germany. See *Israelitisches Familienblatt,* 7 July 1911; Heuberger, *Hinaus aus dem Ghetto,* 106, 113.

53. Sonnemann's position may have reflected an overzealous, yet subconscious, desire to advance his perception of Jewish assimilation. See Heuberger, *Hinaus aus dem Ghetto,* 101; *Frankfurter Zeitung,* 22 August 1877.

54. Niewyk, *Jews in Weimar Germany,* 111; *Der Israelit,* 19, 30 July, 6 August 1931.

55. Die Magistratsakte der Stadt Frankfurt, S 3646, Stadtarchiv Frankfurt; Arnsberg, *Die Geschichte der Frankfurter Juden,* 1:755.

56. Twelve Jewish teachers held posts at the Helmholtzschule for gifted students during the Weimar period (Silbergleit, *Die Bevölkerungs- und Berufsverhältnisse der Juden im deutschen Reich,* 261; Hans Thiel, *Die jüdischen Lehrer und Schüler der Frankfurter Helmholtzschule, 1912-1936* [Frankfurt, 1994], 4).

57. Elsewhere in Germany, demands for a numerus clausus or quota on Jewish students surfaced in the late 1920s. At the University of Würzburg, Catholic student groups lent their support to restrictive admissions policies.

The perception that Jews, and specifically Ostjuden, were "overrunning" German universities was nothing new. During the Kaiserreich (1871-1918), students facing uncertain futures made an issue of the fact that university attendance of eligible foreign Jews had risen from 9.8 percent in 1886 to 21.7 percent in 1909. Konrad Jarausch also sees academic competition between Jews and non-Jews, the spurious perception of a particular Jewish inability to become German, and the political linkage of Jews with liberalism and modernity as other important factors in the popularity of antisemitism at German universities in the late nineteenth century (*Students, Society, and Politics in Imperial Germany: The Rise of Academic Illiberalism* [Princeton, 1982], 356; Kater, *Studentenschaft und Rechtradikalismus*, 151; Heuberger, *Hinaus aus dem Ghetto*, 122).

58. Dieter Rebentisch, "Zwei Beiträge zur Vorgeschichte und Machtergreifung des Nationalsozialismus in Frankfurt," *Hessen unterm Hakenkreuz. Studien zur Durchsetzung der NSDAP in Hessen* (Meisenheim, 1983), 284.

59. *Die braune Machtergreifung*, 33, 36, 45.

60. According to Rudy Koshar, *Vereine* like the Corps Teutonia and the Association of German Students were either overtly antisemitic or more indirect, simply denying Jews membership in the late nineteenth century. The practice of excluding Jews from student associations endured into the republican period; in 1919, the umbrella group of all student organizations, the German Student Union, prohibited membership to all non-Aryans. Not coincidentally, German Jewish fraternities emerged in the context of fin-de-siècle and early twentieth-century antisemitism (Koshar, *Social Life, Politics, and Nazism*, 121; Heuberger, *Hinaus aus dem Ghetto*, 119-21; Rebentisch, *Ludwig Lardmann*, 284).

61. Even though many Jewish professors in Giessen, Marburg, and elsewhere in Germany sustained good relations with many of their Gentile colleagues and attacks on Jewish professors were rare before 1933, the German professorate never repudiated antisemitism in toto. For an instance of more overt hostility, see information regarding the case of Ernst Cohn in Breslau (Ernst Frankel, "Die schweren Unruhen an der Breslauer Universität," *Central-Verein Zeitung*, 18 November 1932; Kurt Pohlen, "Der Antisemitismus an den Hochschulen," *Mitteilungen aus dem Verein zur Abwehr des Antisemitismus*, 20 July 1929; David Baumgart, "Looking Back on a German University Career," *Leo Baeck Institute Yearbook* 10 (1965): 241, 244; and Niewyk, *Jews in Weimar Germany*, 64-66.

62. The NSDStB defied the ban by continuing to distribute literature and conduct rallies in nearby Böckenheim (*Die braune Machtergreifung*, 46, 48).

63. Between 1933 and 1939, race hygiene institutes were founded only at Frankfurt, Jena, and Königsberg. The universities of Giessen, Hamburg, Leipzig, and Tübingen converted existing anthropological institutes. Although not all eugenicists were antisemites, those who were included Giessen professor Heinrich Wilhelm Kranz, Jena philosopher Max Wundt, Munster sociologist Johann Plenge, Jena zoologist Ludwig Plate, Greifswald philosopher Hermann

Schwarz, and Berlin jurist E. von Möller. See Max Wundt, *Der ewige Jude: Ein Versuch uber Sinn und Bedeutung des Judentums* (Munich, 1926), 3-19, *Central-Verein Zeitung*, 11 November 1927; Baumgart, "Looking Back on a German University Career"; Niewyk, *Jews in Weimar Germany*, 64-67, M. Günther, "Die Institutionalisierung der Rassenhygiene an den deutschen Hochschulen vor 1933" Ph.D. diss., Mainz, 1982), and Robert Proctor, *Racial Hygiene: Medicine Under the Nazis* (Cambridge, Mass., 1988), 339, 513.

64. Bertha Katz, "Autobiography," 17-18, Leo Baeck Institute, *Berichte gegen Vergessen und Verdrängen von 100 Überlebenden jüdischen Schülerinnen und Schülern über die NS Zeit in Frankfurt am Main* (Bonn 1995), 38. Salfeld, "Wehmut ums Westend," 106, Leo Baeck Institute ME578. Ernst Noam, "Erinnerungen und Dialog," 60, Leo Baeck Institute, ME 477; Margarete Sallis Freudenthal, "Meine Beiden 40 Jahren," 128, Leo Baeck Institute.

65. Some of these individuals did not belong to either Jewish religious community, but they found themselves reclassified as Jews by the Nazis.

66. Heyne recalls the irony of Geppert's proclaimed antipathy toward Jews, foreigners, and revolutionaries. He was fired in 1933 because of his Jewish origins ("Judenverfolgung," 43). Mombert and Laqueur were not taxpaying members of Giessen's Jewish community.

67. Dr. Gertrud Engel and Elizabeth Huf-Fischer, both Jews, overlooked this fact in a positive, post-1945 assessment of the town before the rise of Hitler. See Rolf and Brigitte Kralovitz, *Da war nachher nichts mehr da . . . Ein Dokumentationsbericht von Rolf und Brigitte Kralovitz* (Giessen, 1983), 8.

68. Although not in and of itself an antisemitic development during Weimar, the university funded a department of anthropology that served as an institute for race hygiene under the Nazis. Heinrich Wilhelm Kranz, an "authority" on racial science before 1933, promoted euthanasia for "asocials" at the university during the Third Reich. See *Völkischer Beobachter,* 30 April, 29 July 1932; Kranz Collection, Berlin Document Center File; Proctor, *Racial Hygiene,* 513.

69. *Sätzung der Freien Burschenschaft mit den Grundsätzen der ADB Palatia 1927,* in Bruno Reimann et al., eds., *Antisemitismus und Nationalsozialismus in der Giessener Region* (Giessen, 1991), 320.

70. Heyne, "Judenverfolgung," 37.

71. *Akademischer Beobachter,* January 1927; Reimann, et al., eds., *Antisemitismus*, 297.

72. Interview with Martin Harth; interview with Bar Menachem (Alfred Gutsmuth) by Kurt Heyne, 25 May 1984, in Netanya, in Heyne, "Judenverfolgung," 39.

73. Struck, *Geschichte der Stadt Geisenheims*, 277.

74. Interview with Elisabeth Will, Geisenheim, 15 September 1993.

75. Telephone interview with Bernharde Wilhelmy, Geisenheim, 10 October 1993.

76. Interview with Friedrich Schwank, Geisenheim, 11 October 1993.

77. Letter from Alfredo Strauss to Jonathan Friedman, São Paulo, 22 December 1993.

78. But 103 Frankfurt stores with Jewish ownership closed down during the Sabbath, including Schmöller, Hansa, Führlander, Julius Obernzenner, and the city's metalworks Beer, Sondheimer, and Cie, the largest business in Germany that did not conduct business on Saturdays. See Mordechai Breuer, *Jüdische Orthodoxie im deutschen Reich, 1871-1918* (Frankfurt, 1986), 246; Heuberger, *Hinaus aus dem Ghetto*, 91; *Der Israelit*, 20 September 1901, 1672.

79. Bamberger, "Die Geschichte und Erlebnis," 10, 11; Interview with Annelise Schnabel, Geisenheim, 9 October 1993; Trudi Berger, *A Daughter's Gift of Love: A Holocaust Memoir* (Philadelphia, 1992), 39; Charlotte E. Zernik, *Im Sturm der Zeit: Ein persönliches Dokument* (Düsseldorf, 1977), 32; *Anne aus Frankfurt: Leben und Lebenswelt Anne Franks* (Frankfurt, 1990), 46.

80. Cahnman, "Village and Small-Town Jews," 58; Stern, *Stark wie ein Spiegel*, 48. That this relationship was symbiotic is also found in a memoir of Jew from Gemünden, a village about fifteen miles northeast of Giessen, Salomon Andorn, "Wie es in unserer kleinen Welt einst war," 2, 6, Leo Baeck Institute, ME 8/9.

81. Cahnman, "Village and Small-Town Jews," 59.

82. An interview with two sisters by Alison Owings reveals that whenever two Christians were involved in a trade dispute, they referred to themselves by name, whereas in cases involving a Jew and a non-Jew, the Jewish individual was almost always referred to as "the Jew" behind his back. See Owings, *Frauen: German Women Recall the Third Reich* (New Brunswick, N.J., 1993), 282, 496. See also Franz Joseph Rohr, "Die freien erwerbwirtsschaftlichen und wirtschaftspolitischen Organisationen der pfälzischen und saarländischen Landwirtschaft in der Kriegs-und Nachkriegeszeit" (Ph.D. diss., Heidelberg University, 1922), 3-7, 14-17; Jonathan Osmond, *Rural Protest in the Weimar Republic: The Free Peasantry in the Rhineland and Bavaria* (New York, 1993), 17.

83. Interview with Frau Erna Tietz, in Owings, *Frauen*, 282-83.

84. Koshar, *Social Life, Local Politics, and Nazism*, 64-65. See also Rudiger Mack, "Otto Böckel und die antisemitische Bauernbewegung in Hessen, 1887-1894," in *Neunhundert Jahre Geschichte der Juden in Hessen*, 113-47; and Levy, *The Downfall of the Antisemitic Parties in Imperial Germany* (New Haven, 1975).

85. *Giessener Anzeiger*, 18 July 1932.

86. *Oberhessische Zeitung*, 3 May 1924; the recollections of a farmer named Bergmann in NSDAP Marburg, *Festschrift*, 22; Koshar, *Social Life, Local Politics, and Nazism*, 182, 191, 339, 341.

87. From older studies of antisemitism offered by Gordon Allport (T. W. Adorno's *Authoritarian Personality* [New York, 1950], for instance), the findings suggested that the same people who accused Jews of being seclusive or

unassimilated also tended to accuse them of being intrusive, i.e., too assimilated. See Allport, *Nature of Prejudice*, 194.

88. Bankers and banking corporations that chose mostly Jewish partners included Fischel, Mannheimer, Loeb, Melchior Jeidels, Paul Kempner, Bieber, and Paul Wallich (Mosse, *Jews in the German Economy*, 382, 403).

89. Heuberger, *Hinaus aus dem Ghetto*, 153-57.

90. Knauss, "Die jüdische Bevolkerung," 32-33.

91. Heuberger, *Hinaus aus dem Ghetto*, 154-56; *Frankfurter Nachrichten*, 10 October 1927; Heilbrunn in Klaus Gallwitz, ed., *Max Beckmann in Frankfurt* (Frankfurt, 1984), 23.

92. "Before the Storm: A Portrait of a Way of Life Set Between Two Friday Nights," 1, 8, 9, 15, 23, 24, anonymous memoir, Leo Baeck Institute, ME 37. Marion Kaplan describes how the exclusion of German Jewish women from important communal and synagogue affairs had led to their important domestic role in preserving a more personal connection to Judaism ("Tradition and Transition," 23).

93. Literally, "Gentile joy." See "Before the Storm," 1.

94. The acknowledgment of Jewish rituals and holidays by Gentiles was also relatively uncommon. I could not find a single mention of Jews or Jewish activities in any of the issues of the Geisenheim newspaper, the *Lokal Anzeiger*, which I surveyed for the Weimar period. Still, it is interesting that the Reform temple in Giessen had a Gentile organist and choir director (Hessisches Landesbibliothek, Wiesbaden; interview with Harth).

95. Margarete Sallis Freudenthal, *Ich habe mein Land gefunden*, 83; *Anne aus Frankfurt*, 46; interview with Annelise Schnabel; interview with Martin Harth. Margot Freimuth also referred to similar cultural exchanges in Östrich and Geisenheim during Purim, Passover, Easter, Christmas, and Hanukkah (interview with Freimuth).

96. Freudenthal, "Meine Beiden 40 Jahren," 98, 127; Ibid., *Ich habe mein Land gefunden*, 55; *Anne aus Frankfurt*, 39; interviews with Wilhelmy and Harth; Naomi Lacqueur, *A Memoir, 1920-1995* (Frankfurt, 1996), 10-11.

97. Stern, *Stark wie ein Spiegel*, 35; Salomon Spiro, "Judenerinnerungen aus hessischen Judengemeinden," 3; *Anne aus Frankfurt*, 46; interview with Freimuth.

98. Letter from Eva Steinreich, Hollywood, Florida, 3 November 1989, cited in Heyne, "Judenverfolgung," 21; Saul S. Friedman, *Amcha: An Oral Testament of the Holocaust* (Lanham, Md., 1979), 30; interview with Harth; Letter from Gretel and Donald Strauss to Jonathan Friedman, San Francisco, 20 December 1993. Fritz Hallgarten, in an interview conducted by Horst Dickel in 1988, also spoke of Jewish participation in Gentile *Vereine* in his town of Eltville (telephone interview with Fritz Hallgarten, conducted by Horst Dickel, London, 23 June 1988, and interview with Elizabeth Will). Charlotte Zernik also mentions in her memoirs that her father was the president of an

Odd Fellow Lodge, but she does not clarify whether it was a Gentile or Jewish lodge (*Im Sturm der Zeit*, 32).

99. Richard Plant, *The Pink Triangle: The Nazi War Against Homosexuals* (New York, 1986), 3.

100. This was done by a decree of the *Reichssportkommissar*. Clubs everywhere in Germany, including 12,852 gymnastics associations, were affected by the law. In the end, some forty thousand Jews were affected by the Nazi purge of German sport (Paul Yogi Mayer, "Equality-Egality: Jews in Sport in Germany," *Leo Baeck Institute Yearbook* 25 [1980]: 227; Wippermann, *Judenverfolgung*, 72).

101. Letter from the NSDAP Gau of Hessen, 26 November 1934, Abteilung 483, Nr. 1629, Hessisches Hauptsaatsarchiv, Wiesbaden.

102. The Zionist Makkabi sports club, the patriotic Schild, and the clubs associated with the liberal Centralverein were among the groups to which Jewish athletes often turned. German Jews had been denied membership in dueling societies in the 1800s, and Frances Henry tells us that Jews were excluded from a Casino club, a literary society, and a tennis club in her town of Sonderburg during the 1920s. See Kevin McAleer, *Dueling: The Cult of Honor in fin-de-siècle Germany* (Princeton, 1994), 255; Henry, *Victims and Neighbors*, 58-59.

103. Henry, *Victims and Neighbors*, 56.

104. Interviews with Martin Harth, New York City, 10 July 1993; Margot Freimuth, Geisenheim, 12 September 1993; Annelise Schnabel, Geisenheim, 9 October 1993; Dr. Fritz Hallgarten, Geisenheim, 1988; and Martin Killian, Geisenheim, 24 September 1993; Heilbrunn, in Gallwitz, ed., *Max Beckmann in Frankfurt*, n.p.; Simon cited in Wolfgang Schivelbusch, *Intellektuellendämmerung: Zur Lage der Frankfurter Intelligenz in den zwanziger Jahren* (Frankfurt, 1985), 47; Henry, *Victims and Neighbors*, 56-57.

105. Lily von Schnitzler, "Frankfurt Zwischen den beiden Weltkriegen," tape recording, 1962, Stadtarchiv Frankfurt; Owings, *Frauen*, 469; Scholem, "Social Psychology," 19-20.

106. Ruth Westheimer, *All in a Lifetime* (New York, 1987), 7, 18; Freudenthal, *Ich habe mein Land gefunden*, 83; Bamberger, "Die Geschichte und Erlebnis," i, ii; Holde, n.t., 7, 38; Salfeld, "Wehmut ums Westend" 9, 128; Letter from Jenny Apolant to a friend, 24 November 1918, in *Jenny Apolant zum Gedächtnis* (Frankfurt, 1926), 50; Heuberger, *Hinaus aus dem Ghetto*, 102-3.

107. Interview with Florence Neumann, New York, 20 July 1993; Joseph Levy, "Mein Leben," 12-14, Leo Baeck Institute; Karl Albert K., a Gentile from Frankfurt, spoke of contact with Jewish friends in the Ostend, but did not make clear whether they were *Ostjuden*. See Erinnerungen Karl Albert K., JG 1925, *Jugend im Nationalsozialistische Frankfurt* (Frankfurt, 1987), 319; Maurer, *Ostjuden in Deutschland*, 86; Erinnerungen Gustav L., JG 1929, in *Jugend im NS Frankfurt*, 318.

108. Bertha Katz, "Autobiography," 19; Noam, "Memoirs," 63, 65, 100; Lichtenberg, "Memoirs," 1, 2.

109. Interview with Harth; Stern, *Stark wie ein Spiegel*, 35.

110. There is, however, a record of a marriage in 1890 between a Jewish man and a Catholic woman. One birth is also listed from this union (*Der Rheingaukreis in den Jahren 1869-1890* [Ansgabe, 1893], 23).

111. Interviews with Annelise Schnabel and Friedrich Schwank.

112. Alfredo Strauss to Jonathan Friedman, 22 December 1993.

113. Gretel and Donald Strauss to Jonathan Friedman, 20 December 1993.

114. Reasons for this congenial interaction may have been that the village was a Catholic town in a primarily Protestant region and that none of its Jewish residents engaged in the much maligned cattle trade, were conspicuously wealthy, or were visibly different, as were the Jews from eastern Europe. (Interviews with Killian and Freimuth).

115. See especially my interviews with Harth, Schwank, Schnabel, Killian, Freimuth, and Elisabeth Will. See also the interview with Rabbi Henry B., 5 March 1985, HVT-539, Yale University Library, *Holocaust Video Testimonies* (New York, 1990), 1:63. One of the few testimonies to come to the opposite conclusion was the report of two so-called *Mischlinge* from Giessen, who argued that antisemitism in the town was minimal before Hitler: "Betty and Jenny Student, London: Would the Germans Really Do Anything Wicked?," unpublished memoir, 1, Wiener Library Testimonies, 021683, Yad Vashem, Jerusalem.

116. This was in marked contrast to the situation in eastern Europe and in several regions of central and western Europe. In Hungary, for instance, the rate of intermarriage in 1929 was only 11.97 percent, in Galicia, 0.83 percent, in Russia, 6.8 percent. The rates for Vienna and Amsterdam were not much higher, 12.95 percent and 14,83 percent respectively. See Arthur Ruppin, *The Jews in the Modern World* (London, 1934), 318-19; Henry, *Victims and Neighbors*, 62; *Mitteilungen des Hessischen Landesstatistischen Amtes* (hereafter *MdHLA*), Nr. 9, October 1924, 83; *MdHLA*, Nr. 8, August 1926, 99; *MdHLA*, Nr. 9, September 1929, 115; *MdHLA*, Nrs. 9-10, October–December 1931, 147; *MdHLA*, Nr. 4, January 1933, 91; *MdHLA*, Nr. 5, December 1933, 107; Kaplan, "Tradition and Transition," 16.

117. *MdHLA*, Nr. 4, January 1933, 91.

118. Kaplan, "Tradition and Transition," 15-16. Kaplan argues that in rural districts where Jewish women outnumbered eligible men, there was a greater tendency for women to marry out of their religion. For Hessen, she cites an August 1905 issue of *Zeitschrift für Demographie und Statistik der Juden* (hereafter *ZDSJ*), 7. This may have been the case in the Wilhelminian period, but in the 1920s and early 1930s, Jewish men more than Jewish women intermarried in Hessen, according to my calculations from various issues of *MdHLA*.

119. According to Kaplan, these statistics tell us how many men and women were willing to marry out of their faith. They do not tell us how many of these people married converted Jews (Kaplan, "Tradition and Transition," 15-16; *ZDSJ*, January–February 1924, 25; October 1930, 54).

120. The percentage of Jewish women intermarrying in Frankfurt increased to 17 percent in 1931, before falling to 12 percent in 1932.

121. Kaplan, "Tradition and Transition," 15-16; Max Marcuse, *Über die Fruchtbarkeit der Christlich-jüdischen Mischehe* (Bonn, 1920), 16; *ZDSJ*, February–March 1914, 52-54. Kaplan offers an additional source, Felix Theilhaber's *Die Schädigung der Rasse durch soziales und wirtschaftliches Aufsteigen bewiesen an den Berliner Juden* (Berlin, 1914), 87-88. His statistics reveal that of 563 Jewish women marrying Jews in Berlin, 359 (63 percent) had never been employed for a living. Of 116 Jewish women entering a mixed marriage, 37 (31 percent) had never been employed.

122. Maurer, *Ostjuden in Deutschland*, 86; Marsha Rozenblit, *The Jews of Vienna, 1867-1914: Assimilation and Identity* (Albany, 1983), 129; Marshal Sklare, *America's Jews* (New York, 1971), 201.

123. Admittedly, during my interviews and in memoirs, individuals referred to intermarriage much too broadly, without the analytical style of a sociologist, and church records, which normally would have provided assistance in this area, were either basic, fragmentary, or nonexistent. I refer to my interviews with Martin Harth and Margot Freimuth, plus an interview with Rev. Matthias Kloft of the Frankfurt Cathedral, Frankfurt, 14 October 1993, and an interview with Professor Walther Hell, Östrich-Winkel, 30 September 1993. For memoirs, see Holde, n.t., 7; Levy, "Mein Leben," 12-14; Bamberger, "Die Geschichte und Erlebris," i-ii.

124. Scholem, "Social Psychology," 21-22.

125. Henry, *Victims and Neighbors*, 63.

126. Heine and Marx were among the more prominent Jews who underwent baptism in the nineteenth century. But not all potential converts obtained permission to change religious affiliations; for instance, David Friedländer in 1799 did not. Others encountered difficulties if they tried to convert back to Judaism. In Geisenheim, the only conversion on record that I could find dealt with an individual by the name of Eduard Levitha, who, in 1885, failed in his attempt to undo his secession. See Rozenblit, *Jews of Vienna*, 133; Arnsberg, *Die jüdischen Gemeinden*, 1:240; and Korrespondenz Levitha, Abteilung 405, Hessisches Hauptstaatsarchiv, Wiesbaden.

127. From 1900 to 1932, approximately fifteen thousand German Jews converted to various branches of Christianity, primarily Protestantism. See Ruppin, *The Jews in the Modern World* (London, 1934), 330; Arnsberg, *Die Geschichte der Frankfurter Juden*, 2:497.

128. The tradition was different in Austria, where either the Jewish or non-Jewish partner had to convert before they could marry.

129. The Nazi census of Jews in Germany, Austria, and the Sudetenland, held on 17 May 1939, found that 84,674 of the 330,539 racial Jews (*Rassejuden*) were *Mischlinge* who had only one or two Jewish grandparents. Whereas 91.5 percent of the full-blooded Jews (*Volljuden*) identified themselves as adherents of Judaism (*Glaubensjuden*), only 6.6 percent of the *Mischlinge* did so. See Bruno Blau, "The Jewish Population of Germany, 1939-1945," *Jewish Social Studies* 12 (1950): 161-172, Niewyk, *Jews in Weimar Germany*, 99; Ruppin, *The Jews in the Modern World*, 330-31.

130. Arnsberg, *Die Geschichte der Frankfurter Juden*, 2:492, 496-97; *Statistische Jahresübersichten der Stadt Frankfurt a.M. 1928* (Frankfurt, 1928), 168, 175.

131. Conversely, most converts to Judaism entered the IG and not the Orthodox IRG.

132. According to Scholem, the overwhelming majority of Jewish conversions to Christianity occurred in the lowest, poorest stratum, which expected to better its economic position, and the highest, which hoped to attain a final emancipation from Judaism. Some underwent baptism out a conviction that sprang from a genuine religious motivation and not a social one, but Scholem has maintained that this was a small minority. We should keep in mind, however, that Maurer and Mosse have taken issue with Scholem and point out that the Jewish upper and lower classes were much less uniform in demographic movement. See Scholem, "Social Psychology."

133. Again, church dispensations obviated the need for espousal conversion so long as any children were reared as Christians. Intermarried couples may have also left Giessen altogether (as many other Jews did), leaving no information about their home life.

134. Interview with Dora Scheuer, 15 October 1982, Giessen, cited in Heyne, "Judenverfolgung," 195-96.

135. Nathan Samter, *Judentaufen im Neunzehnten Jahrhundert* (Berlin, 1906); Michael Marrus, *Les juifs de France a l'epoque de l'affaire Dreyfus* (Paris, 1972); Rozenblit, *Jews of Vienna*, 138.

136. Arnsberg, *Die Geschichte der Frankfurter Juden*, 2:496.

137. "Konfessionswechsel: Tabellen uber Austritte und Übertritte zu der evangelischen Landeskirche," file 17-470; "Kirchlich," 1930-32, file 17-500; Zentralarchiv der evangelischen Kirche Hessen, Darmstadt, 9.

138. While citing Ruppin, Donald Niewyk makes a more optimistic estimate, believing that nearly 25 percent of children from mixed marriages in Weimar Germany were raised as Jews (Ruppin, *The Jews in the Modern World*, 324-25, Niewyk, *Jews in Weimar Germany*, 98; R.E. May, "Die Entwicklung der jüdischen Mischehen und ihre Wirkung auf die jüdische Gemeinschaft," *Gemeindeblatt der deutsch-israelitischen Gemeinde zu Hamburg* 8 [1932], 1-3).

139. Arnsberg, *Die Geschichte der Frankfurter Juden*, 2:495; *Frankfurt Israelitisches Gemeindeblatt*, Jahrgang 6, Nr. 5 (1927-28), 136.

140. *Beiträge zur Statistik der Stadt Frankfurt am Main: Tabellarische Übersichten Betreffend den Zivilstand der Stadt*, Heft 13 (Frankfurt, 1926), 114, 118.

141. *Beiträge zur Statistik der Stadt Frankfurt am Main: Tabellarische Übersichten Betreffend den Zivilstand der Stadt*, Heft 16 (Frankfurt, 1937), 30.

142. Ruppin suggests that birth control was also a more pressing threat to Jewish demography than mixed marriage. See Ruppin, *The Jews in the Modern World*, 325; *Beiträge zur Statistik der Stadt Frankfurt am Main: Tabellarische Übersichten Betreffend den Zivilstand der Stadt*, Heft 13, 74; *Beiträge zur Statistik der Stadt Frankfurt am Main: Tabellarische Übersichten Betreffend den Zivilstand der Stadt*, Heft 16, 30.

143. *MdHLA* 9-10 (October–December 1931): 148; "Kirchlich," 1930, 15, 16, 17/500; Zentralarchiv der Evangelischen Kirchen Hessen, Darmstadt.

144. Birth tallies for Giessen's Jews varied yearly, however, like their marriage statistics. In 1930, records show births from both intermarriages and endogamous Jewish marriages and then, in 1932, only births from purely Jewish marriages. See "Kirchlich," 1932, 15, 16; *MdHLA*, 1931, 148, and 1933, 108.

145. *MdHLA* 9-10 (October–December 1931): 148-49; *MdHLA*, 1932, 11, 48, 92; *MdHLA*, 1933, 108.

146. For more on the sociology of this phenomenon, see Allport, *Nature of Prejudice*, 261-81.

147. Employing statistical methodology, Hilde Weiss concludes that antisemitic attitudes do in fact weaken as the extent of contact to Jews increases ("On the Significance of Personal Contact to Jews," in *Error Without Trial: Psychological Research on Antisemitism*, ed. Werner Bergmann [Berlin, 1988], 449).

Chapter 5

1. Thomas Childers, *The Nazi Voter: The Social Foundations of Fascism in Germany, 1918-1933* (Chapel Hill,1984); Broszat, *Hitler and the Collapse of Weimar Germany* (Leamington Spa, 1987); Allen, *Nazi Seizure of Power*; Noakes, *Nazi Party in Lower Saxony*; Koshar, *Social Life, Local Politics, and Nazism*; Peter Fritzsche, *Rehearsals for Fascism: Populism and Political Mobilization in Weimar Germany* (New York, 1990).

2. After a reexamination of autobiographical statements made by 581 early Nazis, Peter Merkl was struck by how little the Nazi movement was motivated by shared goals of any kind, even antisemitic ones. Sarah Gordon further observed that the majority of antisemites in the party were moderate, nonaggressive bigots. Among voters, Jew-hatred played an uneven role. William Sheridan Allen has argued that those who were drawn to antisemitism were drawn first to Nazism, not the other way around. See Peter Merkl, *Political Violence Under the Swastika* (Princeton, 1975), 498-527; Gordon, *Hitler, Germans, and the Jewish Question*, 56; Allen, *Nazi Seizure of Power*, 77.

3. Two-thirds of these communities had less than five hundred inhabitants. In regions that were more than 70 percent agrarian, the Nazis received 84 percent of the popular vote in the July 1932 national elections. In those where agriculture amounted to no more than 20 percent, Nazi success was lower but still relatively high at 46 percent. See Eike Hennig, "Der Hunger näht—Mittelstand wehr Dich—Wir Bauern misten aus," in *Hessen unterm Hakenkreuz: Studien zur Durchsetzung der NSDAP in Hessen*, ed. Hennig (Frankfurt, 1983), 387.

4. Oded Heilbronner, "The Role of Nazi Antisemitism in the Nazi Party's Activity and Propaganda: A Regional Historiographical Study," *Leo Baeck Institute Yearbook* 35 (1990): 417. On Lenz and Sprenger, see Dieter Rebentisch, "Persönlichkeitsprofil und Karrierverlauf der nationalsozialistischen Führungskader in Hessen, 1928-1945," in *Hessisches Jahrbuch für Landesgeschichte* (1983): 310, 313-14. On Böckel and Werner, see Koshar, *Social Life, Local Politics, and Nazism*, 63-70.

5. See Eike Hennig, "Einleitung: Die NS Bewegung in Hessen und ihre Erforschung," in *Hessen unterm Hakenkreuz*, ed. Hennig; Eberhard Schön, *Die Entstehung des Nationalsozialismus in Hessen* (Meisenheim, 1972), who argues that antisemitism was only a factor for the Nazis in Marburg. Rudy Koshar, who also focuses on Marburg, implies that antisemitism was useful to the Nazis throughout Hessen.

6. For this development in general see Robert Moeller, *German Peasants and Agrarian Politics, 1914-1924: The Rhineland and Westphalia* (Chapel Hill, 1968); Heinrich Winkler, *Mittelstand, Demokratie, und Nationalsozialismus: Die politische Entwicklung von Handwerk und Kleinhandel in der Weimarer Republik* (Cologne, 1972).

7. Social Democrats also made up the largest faction in the provincial diets of Prussia and Hessen, as well as in the Frankfurt city assembly.

8. In 1919, 1923, and 1924 there were abortive coup attempts in Wiesbaden, the central headquarters of the Allied occupying force, by separatists who called for the establishment of a Rhenish republic. A "Great Hessen" movement accompanied the emergence of separatists in Hessen-Nassau, promoting unification with Hessen-Darmstadt. Unfortunately for the supporters of Hessian unity, Nassauer associations such as the Grossdeutsch-Hessischer Bund and its mouthpiece, the *Hessische Zeitung*, failed to agree on much of anything and disappeared from the political scene in the late 1920s. See Demandt, *Geschichte des Landes Hessen*, 588-90, 604-5.

9. The hyperinflationary excesses of 1922-23 left a profound mark on the German psyche. Even though inflation had begun as a problem as early as 1914, the dramatic image of breakdown in 1923 was significant. The extreme right and left benefited from the sudden upsurge in unemployment, the persistence of low living standards among workers, and the loss of savings and long-term investments on the part of much of the middle class. According to Gerald Feldman, the inflation of 1923 spawned protest against the system from the old

Mittelstand (artisans) and from parts of the new *Mittelstand* (white-collar workers and civil servants) that was revealed in the 1924 elections and then spearheaded the Nazi success of 1930-32. See Feldman, "Inflation and Depression as Hitler's Pace-Makers," *Leo Baeck Institute Yearbook* 28 (1983): 40; Peukert, *Weimar Republic,* 64-65. See also Feldman, *The Great Disorder: Politics, Economy, and Society in the German Inflation, 1914-1924* (New York, 1993); Feldman and H. Homburg, *Industrie und Inflation* (Hamburg, 1977); Feldman, *Die Nachwirkung der Inflation auf die deutsche Geschichte 1924-1933* (Munich, 1985); C.D. Krohn, *Stabilisierung und ökonomische Interessen: Die Finanzpolitik des deutschen Reiches, 1923-1927* (Düsseldorf, 1974); M. Schneider, "Deutsche Gesellschaft in Krieg und Währungskrise, 1914-1924: Ein Jahrzehnt Forschungen zur Inflation," *Archiv für Sozialgeschichte* 26 (1986): 301-19; William Hubbard, "The New Inflation History," *Journal of Modern History* 62 (1990): 552-62.

10. *Jüdische Rundschau,* 12 March 1920; *Frankfurter Zeitung,* 7 November 1923; and Niewyk, *Jews in Weimar Germany,* 51; Lewis Hertzman, *DNVP: Right-Wing Opposition in the Weimar Republic, 1918-1924* (Lincoln, Neb., 1963), 124-64.

11. Peukert, *Weimar Republic,* 76.

12. *Statistisches Handbuch der Stadt Frankfurt a.M. 1906/07 bis 1927/28,* 451.

13. Frankfurter Historische Kommission, *Frankfurt am Main,* 441.

14. Rosenthal, "Opus One," 35; interview with Martin Scheuer, in Friedman, *Amcha,* 30.

15. *Statistisches Handbuch der Stadt Frankfurt,* 451.

16. Frankfurter Historische Kommission, Frankfurt am Main, 444; Bericht über die Verhandlungen der Stadtverordnetenversammlung der Stadt Frankfurt am Main 1924, Paragraph 799, p. 634.

17. Lieberman, "Testing Peukert's Paradigm"; Frankfurter Historische Kommission, *Frankfurt am Main,* 444-65.

18. Erwin Knauss, "Die politischen Kräfte und das Wahlerverhältnis im Landkreis Giessen während der letzten 60 Jahren," *Mitteilungen des Oberhessischen Geschichtsvereins* 5 (1961): 48-49, 73; Lothar Bembenek et al., eds., *Materialien zum Unterricht: Sekundärstufe 1 Heft 34: Nationalsozialismus, Unterrichtsvorschläge und Materialien* (Wiesbaden, 1985), 291.

19. Akten des Bürgermeister Giessens, 82/163, Stadtarchiv Giessen.

20. *Giessener Anzeiger,* 10 October 1932.

21. The same could be said for Rüdesheim but not for Eltville and other areas of the Rheingau (Struck, *Geschichte der Stadt Geisenheims,* 249-51).

22. *Statistik des deutschen Reiches: Ergebnisse der Reichstagswahl 6 Juni 1920,* Vol. 292, Issue 2 (Berlin, 1922); 54.

23. Frankfurter Historische Kommission, *Frankfurt am Main,* 470.

24. Obersturmführer F. K., "Kampferlebnis am 3.12.1926," Bundesarchiv Koblenz, NS 26/531; Dieter Rebentisch, "Zwei Beiträge zur Vorgeschichte und Machtergreifung des Nationalsozialismus in Frankfurt," in *Hessen unterm Hakenkreuz,* ed. Hennig, 282-83.

25. Rebentisch, "Zwei Beiträge,"286.

26. Sprenger grew up near Bergzabern and served as a lieutenant in World War I. At forty-three, he was one of the older members of a party that prided itself on its youthful image (ibid., 283-84). *Frankfurter Zeitung*, 4 July 1929. Many German university rectors took a stand against antisemitism, including those from Cologne, Würzburg, and Munich. See *Mitteilungen aus dem Verein zur Abwehr des Antisemitismus*, January 1930; *Der Israelit*, 17 May 1928; Niewyk, *Jews in Weimar Germany*, 67.

27. There were only ten members in the Giessen SS (Schutzstaffel) or elite guard of the NSDAP before 1930. In party membership, the entire province of Oberhessen, with only 1,268 Nazi Party members by 1931, stood behind the Hessian provinces of Rheinhessen and Starkenburg. In addition, the Oberhessian contribution of 900 men to the services of the SA fell below the overall regional average of 1,100 (Akten 327/2b from the Stadtarchiv Marburg; Jorg-Peter Jatho, "Zur Durchsetzung des Nationalsozialismus in der Provinz Oberhessen—unter besonderer Berücksichtigung der Stadt Giessen," in *Hessen unterm Hakenkreuz*, ed. Hennig, 181-82).

28. *Völkischer Beobachter*, 10 October 1927.

29. While serving as a councilman, Lotz attempted to influence the repertoire of the city theater by insisting that there be more performances of German classical music and plays with traditional values (Jatho, "Zur Durchsetzung," 184).

30. Bruno Reimann, "Die Giessener Studentenschaft und Professorenschaft im Zeichen der Rechtspolitisierung und der Durchsetzung der Nationalsozialismus," in *Antisemitismus und Nationalsozialismus*, ed. Reimann et al., 96.

31. Ibid., 258, 320; Paragraph 3 of the Charter der Burschenschaft Palatia 1927, UAG PrA 100; *Akademischer Beobachter*, January 1927.

32. Among these professors were Jakob Friedrich Zimmer, who wrote that the Jewish question was not a religious but a racial question in "Zur Ausländerfrage an den deutschen Hochschulen," *Deutschlands Erneuerung* 9 (1920): 557, and a Professor König, Julius Geppert, H. C. Karl Berger, Herzog, Hummerl, and Kühn. Under Hitler, Georg Bertram, a professor of theology at Giessen became the director of the Institute for Research into Jewish Influence on Church Life. He held a post at Frankfurt University after 1945. See Reimann, et al., eds., *Antisemitismus und Nationalsozialismus*, 341-42, 345, 340; *Völkischer Beobachter*, 6, 30 April, 29 July 1932, 3 March 1933; *Das braune Buch: Kriegs-und Naziverbrecher in der Bundesrepublik Deutschland und West Berlin* (Berlin, 1968), 351, a problematic source from communist East Germany.

33. On balance, Giessen was similar to Marburg, its small-town neighbor to the north, where Nazis also enjoyed support at the university and exploited antisemitism in electoral propaganda. A Nazi pastor named Munchenmayer delivered antisemitic sermons in Marburg and in other parts of Germany. See *Frankfurter Zeitung*, 9 February 1930; Jatho, "Zur Durchsetzurg,"

192-96; Heilbronner, "Role of Nazi Antisemitism," 419; Schon, *Entstehung*, 182-83, Hennig, "Einleitung," 30; Koshar, *Social Life, Local Politics, and Nazism*, 63-70, 182-83, 191-92; Heiko Boumann, "Zur Entwicklung des Antisemitismus und der rechtsradikalen Gruppen in der Giessener Region, 1890-1933," in *Antisemitismus und Nationalsozialismus in der Giessener Region*, 31-64.

34. Abteilung 483/2630a/P86, Letter to Party Members, 16 July 1932, Eltville, 194, Hessisches Hauptstaatsarchiv Wiesbaden.

35. Abteilung 483/2630b, Parteipresse und Bevölkerung, 28 November 1931, 8, 281, and Abteilung 483/2632/P88, Ortsgruppenleiter Geisenheim, 11, Hessisches Hauptstaatsarchiv, Wiesbaden.

36. Abteilung 483/2630b, "Die Religion in Gefahr! Wählt NS!" July 1932, 242, Hessisches Hauptstaatsarchiv Wiesbaden.

37. Thomas Childers maintains that white-collar workers turned to the Nazis much later than historians have traditionally assumed. See Childers, "National Socialism and the New Middle Class," in *Die Nationalsozialisten: Analysen faschistischer Bewegungen*, ed. *Reinhard Mann* (Stuttgart, 1980), 19-30; R. Vierhaus, "Auswirkungen der Krise um 1930 in Deutschland. Beiträge zu einer historisch-psychologisichen Analyse," in *Staats und Wirtsschaftskrise* eds. Werner Conze et al. (Stuttgart, 1967), 155-75; Peukert, *Weimar Republic*, 253-55.

38. Feldman, "Inflation and Depression," 14.

39. Eckhard Wandel, "Germany's Morale and Morals During the Great Depression," *Leo Baeck Institute Yearbook* 28 (1983), 15.

40. Martin Killian, a Social Democrat from Geisenheim, insisted in an interview that Gentiles just did not care about Jews one way or the other (*"Die haben sich nicht für Juden interessiert"*).

41. With respect to left-wing radicalism in particular, many Jews, like Joseph Levy from Frankfurt, feared the political implications of this popular association of German Jewry with the cause of the left. After the Russian Revolution, the Sparticist revolt in Berlin, and the short-lived Bavarian Republic (in all of which a large number of Jews, among them Paul Levi, Rosa Luxemburg, Kurt Eisner, Gustav Landauer, Ernst Toller, and Eugen Levine, participated), the hunt for Jewish Bolsheviks became a central element not only of the radical right but of the conservative right as well. See Traverso, *Jews and Germany*, 30; and Levy, "Mein Leben," 25.

42. Reichmann, *Hostages of Civilization*; Gavin Langmuir, "Toward a Definition of Antisemitism," in *Persisting Question*, ed. Helen Fein, 126.

43. Weiss, *Ideology of Death*, 272-75.

44. Ibid., 278-81.

45. Ibid., 225-27.

46. Ibid., 283-85.

47. John Weiss correctly asserts that a focus on the influence of the Weimar avant-garde has led us to miss the significance of the far more popular

culture of those years, which relied on traditional aesthetics and prefigured much of Nazi artistic style (*Ideology of Death*, 249).

48. Adolf Schlatter, *Wir Christen und die Juden* (Velbert-im-Rhinelnad, 1930), 6-21; Wilhelm Stapel, *Antisemitismus und Antigermanismus: Über das seelische Problem der Symbiöse des deutschen und des jüdischen Volkes* (Hamburg, 1928); Stapel, *Sechs Kapitel über Christentum und Nationalsozialismus* (Hamburg, 1931); Niewyk, *Jews in Weimar Germany*, 56, 58.

49. Curt Prufer to Brüning, 30 March 1931, Reich Chancellery Documents on Jewish Affairs, R 431/2193 L. 382281-84, Bundesarchiv Koblenz; Niewyk, *Jews in Weimar Germany*, 72.

50. Eberhard Röhm and Jorg Thierfelder, *Juden-Christen-Deutsche, 1933-1945* (Stuttgart, 1990), 68-69, 71; Ino Arndt, "Die Judenfrage im Lichte der evangelischen Sonntagsblätter, 1918-1938" (Ph.D. diss., University of Tübingen, 1960); Walter Hannot, *Die Judenfrage in der katholischen Tagespresse Deutschlands und Österreichs 1923-1933* (Mainz, 1990). In Hannot, especially, one sees the relative neutrality and indifference of all major German Catholic news publications toward Jews and antisemitism.

51. Eduard Lamparter, *Evangelische Kirche und Judentum: Ein Beitrag zu christlichem Verständnis von Judentum und Antisemitismus* (Berlin, n.d.); Lamparter, *Das Judentum in der Kultur und Religionsgeschichtlichen Erscheinung* (Gotha, 1928); Günter Lewy, *The Catholic Church in Nazi Germany* (New York, 1964), 5; *Israelitisches Familienblatt*, 16 October 1930; *Mitteilungen aus dem Verein zur Abwehr des Antisemitismus*, 12 September 1922; Niewyk, *Jews in Weimar Germany*, 58-60.

52. Some of the protest by Social Democrats can be found in Jost Müller's "Sozialdemokratische Arbeiterkultur in Frankfurt, 1925-1933," in *Gewerkschaften, Sozialdemokraten, und Friedensfreunden in Frankfurt, 1900-1935*, ed. Fritz König et al. (Frankfurt, 1985), 190. See also Niewyk, *Socialist, Antisemite, and Jew*, and *Jews of Weimar Germany*, 55-81; Rudolf Morsey, *Die deutsche Zentrumspartei, 1917-1923* (Düsseldorf, 1966); P.B. Wiener, "Die Parteien der Mitte," in *Entscheidungsjahr 1932: Zur Judenfrage in der Endphase der Weimar Republik*, eds. Mosse and Paucker (Tübingen, 1965), 306-14.

53. "Deutscher Nationalismus und Jüdischer Intellektualismus," *Jüdische Rundschau*, 17 June 1932; "Vor den Reichstagswahlen," *Jüdische Rundschau*, 8 July 1932; "Verteidigen oder fordern?" *Jüdische Rundschau*, 12 July 1932; and "Nach den Reichstagswahlen," *Jüdische Rundschau*, 2 August 1932. For the reaction of the CV, see "Bindet den Helm fester," *Central-Verein Zeitung*, 26 September 1930.

54. Eduard Strauss, "Unser deutsches Schicksal," *Frankfurt Israelitisches Gemeindeblatt* 11 (July 1932); Edith Falk, "Rationales Denken—eine jüdische Grundhaltung?" *Frankfurt Israelitisches Gemeindeblatt* 3 (November 1932).

55. Communal ordinances prohibited the use of a no-confidence vote in the Frankfurt city assembly (Frankfurter Historische Kommission, *Frankfurt am Main*, 476). Scharp quoted in Bericht über die Verhandlungen der Stadt-

verordnetenversammlung der Stadt Frankfurt am Main 1929, Paragraph 1588, p. 1287.

56. *Statistik des deutschen Reiches: Die berufliche und soziale Gliederung der Bevölkerung des Deutschen Reiches: Provinz Hessen-Nassau,* Vol. 456, Issue 25 (Berlin, 1936), 37.

57. The city's financial crisis ended only after the extension of a Prussian loan on 27 January 1933, three years after the Nazis had begun their electoral rise and three days before the appointment of Hitler to the office of chancellor (Frankfurter Historische Kommission, *Frankfurt am Main,* 478-79).

58. According to Dieter Rebentisch, the Nazis reserved their more vicious attacks against Jews for the streets and not the city assembly (*Ludwig Landmann,* 269).

59. The Nazis employed rhetoric similar to the Schutz und Trutz Bund, which, in 1920, had accused Jews of dominating the Frankfurt economy and urged a boycott of Jewish stores. See letter from the Schutz und Trutz Bund to the Frankfurt Jewish Women's Union, 14 January 1920, Akten der IHK, Mappe 1284/161, Stadtarchiv Frankfurt; Heuberger, *Hinaus aus dem Ghetto,* 122, 141, 152; Stadtverordnetenversammlung, 21 Sitzung, 17 December 1929, Paragraph 1588.

60. A Nazi placard read, "Frankfurter Wehrt Euch! Steuerlasten!" See Rebentisch, *Ludwig Landmann,* 287-88.

61. See Childers, *Nazi Voter;* Allen, *Nazi Seizure of Power.*

62. Erinnerungen Liselotte F., JG 1920, and Erinnerungen, Alexander L., JG 1924, in *Jugend im nationalsozialistischen Frankfurt,* 236.

63. The KPD and NSDAP, for instance, disrupted the debates over the replacement of city treasurer Bruno Asch in December 1931. Of these proposals, 251 came from the KPD, 215 from the NSDAP (Frankfurter Historische Kommission, *Frankfurt am Main,* 475-76).

64. Personalakten 6/119, Josef Hoffmann, Oberstadtssekretär, 165, Stadtarchiv Frankfurt.

65. Ernst Thälmann, the communists' choice for president, received 10.2 percent of the votes in the April run-off. Colonel Theodor Duesterberg, who represented the German nationalists and specifically the Stahlhelm, received 6.8 percent in the first election but was not a candidate in the run-off. In Frankfurt, Giessen, and Geisenheim, Hindenburg prevailed over Hitler in the elections, but in Kreis Giessen (or Giessen county) and in Oberhessen, Hitler won a plurality over the incumbent Hindenburg (49.4 to 47.4 and 52.7 to 43.2 respectively).

66. Hitler's popularity waned among conservative voters who opposed his entreaties to workers. His support of brown shirts who had murdered a communist miner in August did not help his standing with the public either.

67. Childers, *Nazi Voter,* 209, 211; and Rebentisch, *Lugwig Landmann,* 287.

68. *Frankfurter Zeitung,* 2 August, 8 November 1932.

69. In the northwest Aussenstadt, the NSDAP vote in July was 35.9 percent, in November 29.5 percent, while in the western Aussenstadt the Nazi vote in July was 30.7 percent, in November 26.1 percent. Admittedly, in the northern Aussenstadt, the Nazis, at 42.7 percent in July and 38.6 percent in November, had a showing higher than the citywide percentages of 38.7 percent and 34.2 percent. In the Östliche Neustadt, the Nazis received 34 percent of the vote in July, 31.8 percent in November. In the Östliche Aussenstadt, the NSDAP received 38.4 percent of the vote in July, 35.9 percent in November, tallies that were above the city average. See Pulzer, *The Jews and the German State* 304-15, *Statistische Jahresübersichten der Stadt Frankfurt am Main 1927/1928*, 15, 162-63; *Statistische Jahresübersichten der Stadt Frankfurt am Main 1931/1932*, 19.

70. Jews in Outer Sachsenhausen were only 2.1 percent of the population, in the Western Neustadt, 4.7 percent. By contrast, Jews were 22.9 percent of the population in the northwest Aussenstadt and 16.7 percent in the eastern Aussenstadt. Pulzer, 310, 314; *Statistische Jahresübersichten*).

71. Lieberman, "Testing Peukert's Paradigm," 299-300.

72. Niewyk, *Jews in Weimar Germany* 73; Pulzer, *The Jews and the German State*, 308-12; and Jürgen Falter et al., *Wahlen und Abstimmungen in der Weimarer Republik: Materialien zum Wahlverhalten, 1919-1933* (Munich, 1986), 163-70. Falter's regression analysis argues that the Jewish population correlated more positively with DDP strength from 1924 to 1933 than with that of any other party. But, as Niewyk points out, once the DDP shrank into insignificance, became the DStP, and began distancing itself from its Jewish constituency, with assertions that it was "a-Semitic," it lost the Jewish vote. According to Pulzer, a survey from 1924 to 1932 shows that Jews of the East End moved left earlier, so that their predilections could not be picked up so easily once the depression had set in. Over this period, the vote for the left went up by 0.5 percent in Frankfurt. All of the Jewish districts went up by substantially more, ranging from 3.7 percent in the Östliche Aussenstadt to 11.8 percent in the Nordwestliche Aussenstadt. In the western districts that was due entirely to the rise after 1928. In the eastern districts the same applied to the Östliche Neustadt, which had a left-wing performance similar to that of the West End but a poor SPD performance. Yet, in the Östliche Aussenstadt the greater part of the left's improvement, particularly for the SPD, came before 1928. In this respect it resembled the working-class districts, with the difference that it retained the greater part of the left's gains during the depression.

73. Perhaps the clearest indication of how metropolitan Jews voted can be gained from the districts with the highest Jewish concentrations in Berlin (Wilmersdorf), Hamburg (Harvestehude), and Frankfurt (Nordwestliche Aussenstadt). All had high DDP showings up to 1928, all had high Center gains in 1930 and July 1932, and all showed gains by the left at a time when it was in decline nationally, and particularly for the SPD at a time when that party lost a third of its voting share nationally (Pulzer, *The Jews and the German State*, 312).

74. There was not even a National Socialist newspaper in town at the time (Jatho, "Zur Durchsetzung;" 185).

75. *Statistik des deutschen Reiches: Hessen*, Vol. 456, Issue 33 (Berlin, 1936), 36; *Materialien zum Unterricht*, 204, and its citation of *Giessener Anzeiger*, 4 October 1932.

76. When interviewed by Jorg Peter Jatho, Nazi Party member in Giessen Hone Horn agreed that antisemitism was a major part of Nazi rhetoric but argued that he and his comrades could not have foreseen where the results of Jew-hatred would lead. Martin Scheuer describes the prominence of anti-semitism in the village of Friedberg, twenty-miles south of Giessen: "I had no fights as a kid, but later on, when the Nazis came, in 1930, I had my firstfight, in the main street in Friedberg. . . . Some guy—I don't know who he was—tried to beat me up. The town youth stood around, and he attacked me with a belt. It had a Nazi insignia. I took that belt away from him and beat him up. It was in broad daylight. Nobody came to help, even though it was in my own home town." See Bundesarchiv Koblenz, NS 26/528-533; Jorg Peter Jatho, *Wenn es hoffentlich bald nach Blut und Eisen riecht: Ein NS Bericht aus der Kampfzeit in Giessen, 1927-1933* (Giessen, 1986), 18-19, 24, 31, 39-40; Heilbronner, "Role of Nazi Antisemitism," 420-21; interview with Scheuer, in Friedman, *Amcha*, 30-31.

77. Protests from the Wirtschaftspartei, and the Reichspartei der deutschen Mittelstandes led to the holding of a second election on 19 June 1932, in which NSDAP support in Giessen ran 52.5 percent (Bembenek et al., eds.; *Materialen Zum Unterricht*, 288).

78. Wolfgang Egerer, "Die Entwicklung des Nationalsozialismus im Kreis Friedberg und seine Beziehungen zu den bauerlichen Organisationen," in *Hessen unterm Hakenkreuz*, 216-217. Egerer also emphasizes the continuity of the antisemitic tradition in the region by focusing on Ferdinand Werner, a central activist in the antisemitic movement before World War I, but does not consider the figure F. Dreher, who also served the Nazi Party as a speaker outside the area (Heilbronner, "Role of Nazi Antisemitism," 420).

79. Interview with Harth; Bembenek et al., eds.; *Materialen Zum Unterricht*, 290-95; Jatho, "Zur Durchsetzung," 190-95. Jatho specifically concentrates on districts ten and eleven, areas on the southeast side of the old city, including Lonystrasse, Löberstrasse, Stephanstrasse, and Bleichstrasse. See also Map 4 in Chapter 2 for Jewish population distribution in Giessen.

80. *Statistik des deutschen Reiches: Hessen Nassau*, Vol. 456, Issue 25 (Berlin, 1936), 44; Struck, *Geschichte der Stadt Geisenheim*; 289.

81. The Rheingau was not electorally homogeneous. Rüdesheim was similar to Geisenheim in that the Center remained the most popular party even after the March 1933 elections. The SPD was not as popular in Rüdesheim as it was in Geisenheim, however, presumably because of the latter's larger industrial base. In Eltville, success for the NSDAP mirrored national developments as the Nazi Party became the largest vote-getter after the July 1932 elections (Struck, *Geschichte der Stadt Geisenheims*, 249-52).

82. Ibid., 250-51, 261. According to interviews with Freimuth and Killian and letters, the Strauss family was loyal to the DDP.

83. Peukert, *Weimar Republik*, 269-72.

84. For a general analysis in English, see William Shirer, *The Rise and Fall of the Third Reich: A History of Nazi Germany* (New York, 1969), 189.

85. Akten 82/206, Akten Oberbürgermeister, 15, Stadtarchiv Giessen; *Giessener Anzeiger,* 19 May 1934; Struck, *Geschichte der Stadt Geisenheims,* 261-62.

86. Hennig, "Der Hunger näht," 420.

87. Germany was not unique in succumbing to fascism during the 1920s and 1930s—consider Italy, Spain, and eastern Europe.

88. Richard Hamilton, *Who Voted for Hitler?* (Princeton, 1982), 606; Heinrich August Winkler, "Die deutsche Gesellschaft der Weimarer Republik und der Antisemitismus," in *Antisemitismus: Erscheinungsformen der Judenfeindschaft gestern und heute,* ed. Gunther Ginzel (Bielefeld, 1991), 189.

89. Studies of the town of Wetzlar, where the Nazis made electoral inroads, and the hamlet of Vilbel, where leftist organizations successfully fought off the Nazi threat, do not mention the use of antisemitic propaganda by the NSDAP. See Kurt Wagner, "Dorfleben im Dritten Reich: Körle in Hessen," in *Hessen unterm Hakenkreuz,* 115-16; Ulrich Mayer, *Das Eindringen des Nationalsozialismus in did Stadt Wetzlar* (Wetzlar, 1970); K. Schoenekaes, "Christenkreuz über Hakenkreuz und Sowjetstern. Die NSDAP im Raum Fulda," in *Hessen unterm Hakenkreuz,* 159, 162; R. Mann, "Entstehen und Entwicklung der NSDAP in Marburg," in *Hessisches Jahrbuch für Landesgeschichte* 22 (1972): 330; Koshar, *Social Life, Local Politics, and Nazism,* 63-70, 182-83, 191-92; Heilbronner, "Role of Nazi Antisemitism," 420.

90. Interviews with Killian, Freimuth, and Schnabel.

Chapter 6

1. See Bracher, *German Dictatorship;* Shirer, *Rise and Fall of the Third Reich,* 194-96.

2. Volker Berghahn, *Modern Germany: Society, Economy, and Politics in the Twentieth Century* (New York, 1982), 126-31; Broszat, *Hitler State,* 96.

3. The same day, the Law for the Prevention of Hereditary Defective Offspring authorized the sterilization of mentally retarded persons, schizophrenics, asocials, Gypsies, Jewish *Mischlinge,* and the children of black soldiers in the French occupation army and native German women (the so-called Rhineland Bastards), sixty-six of whom had been born in Hessen. Schools for backward and handicapped children were also subject to disgraceful treatment in the context of Nazi racial policy. Special schools became institutions of racial selection because it lay within their competence to decide whether disabled pupils should be compulsorily sterilized. How frequently this occurred can be inferred from a denial published on 9 April 1936 by the Municipal Health Office in Frankfurt: "The Municipal Health Department declares that the rumors to the effect that all backward pupils are to be sterilized are false. . . . Examinations carried out to date in Germany have shown that almost half of backward

schoolchildren are not hereditarily ill, and therefore do not come into consideration for compulsory sterilization" (Städtischer Anzeigenblatt, 9 April 1936; Burleigh and Wippermann, *Racial State*, 215).

4. The Nazis generated a fierce campaign against the Social Democratic minister of the interior, Leuschner, who was charged with contravening the intentions of the emergency decrees passed after the Reichstag fire. See Broszat, *The Hitler State*, 98-103; Best in *Trials of the Major War Criminals Before the International Military Tribunal* (Nuremberg, 1947-49), 20:125-26; Robert Gellately, *The Gestapo and German Society* (Oxford, 1990), 50.

5. In all other Länder, "appointed" National Socialist police deputies forestalled the constitutional formation of new governments and instead put in National Socialist special commissioners for the separate governmental departments (Broszat, 103).

6. Sprenger went on to strip Werner of his post in 1935 in a consolidated effort to merge the offices of governor and minister president (ibid., 49, 98-103, 109, 117).

7. Ibid., 194.

8. Lili Hahn, *White Flags of Surrender* (Washington, D.C., 1974), 14.

9. The city council did, however, meet on 7 February because of a legal technicality, and when it convened, the Nazis and the Nationalists left and the communists continued to attack the SPD as worse than the fascists (Frankfurter Historische Kommission, *Frankfurt am Main*, 481).

10. Steinberg's successor was General von Westrem from Wiesbaden, an NSDAP member since 1931 and former member of the Union of Front Soldiers, who came out of retirement to become SA *Sturmbanfürher* (ibid., 482).

11. Catholic newspapers and the liberal *Frankfurter Zeitung* were allowed to function independently for a while longer. See Sybil Milton, "Mass Media and Censorship in Nazi Germany," United States Holocaust Memorial Museum Brief, 23 July 1995.

12. Landmann fled to Berlin and then to Holland. He hid in Amsterdam during World War II and died on 5 March 1945 of heart failure brought on by malnutrition. It took Krebs almost four years to understand the workings of city bureaucracy and administration. Karl Lindner served as Frankfurt's *Bürgermeister.* See Frankfurter Historische Kommission, *Frankfurt am Main*, 481-88, 496.

13. Heyne, "Judenverfolgung," 49.

14. Catholic leaders in Geisenheim were able to prevent nearly three-quarters of the boys and girls belonging to Catholic youth associations in the village from being dragooned into Nazi organizations, but the Nazis managed to turn the city kindergarten into a Nazi school in 1937, to take over the local newspaper, the *Geisenheimer Lokal Anzeiger,* that same year, and to close down the girls' school in 1940. Stahl was able to stay on as mayor until his death in

1940. He was succeeded by Adolf Wollschlager, who served as mayor until April 1945 (Struck, *Geschichte der Stadt Geisenheims*, 263, 275, 297, 284).

15. Letter from the Office of the Mayor (*Bürgermeister*) to Martin Killian, Geisenheim, 1 June 1933; Struck, *Geschichte der Stadt Geisenheims*, 262, 275.

16. A look at the implementation of race-hygiene programs at German universities shows how slow some aspects of coordination were. Four universities, Danzig, Jena, Frankfurt, and Tübingen, had institutes for racial hygiene that also functioned as NSDAP Racial Political Offices for the local *Gau*. Such an identification of party political functions was the exception rather than the rule, although many institutes for anthropology and hygiene adjudicated on race and paternity. Between 1933 and 1939 racial hygiene institutes were founded only at Frankfurt, Jena, and Königsberg. The universities of Giessen, Hamburg, Leipzig, and Tübingen converted existing anthropological institutes. Other universities extended the responsibilities of teachers in hygiene or psychiatry. By 1945, less than half of the universities in the Reich had a special institute for race hygiene or human heredity. Hence, despite immense political pressure, the institutional development of race hygiene was slow. See H.W. Kranz, "Zur Entwicklung der Rassenhygienischen Institute an unseren Hochschulen," *Ziel und Weg* 9 (1939): 286-90, Proctor, *Racial Hygiene*, 513.

17. After 30 January 1933, Nazi policy against the Jews came to resemble a pattern of interaction between private initiative, semilegal activities, and government legislation. More often than not, SA *Scharführer* or *Sturmführer*, the equivalents of sergeant and second lieutenant respectively, initiated raids and pogroms on their own authority, frequently in the absence of their immediate superiors. The SA was made up of approximately two million men over the age of seventeen, roughly 10 percent of the entire civilian male population. According to Kater, if one assumes that the SA, by virtue of its historic and contemporary self-perception, was violently antisemitic, the conclusion is inevitable that in the early summer of 1933 every tenth male adult German was inimically disposed toward Jews. This figure does not take into account members of the NSDAP, the SS, the Nazi Motor Corps, or other party affiliates who in all likelihood were antisemitic to some degree. Therefore, any anti-Jewish infringement commenced by the activist representatives of Germany's known antisemitic 10 percent gained the approval of a much larger segment of the entire Gentile population. See Kater, "Everyday Antisemitism," 142-43, and his citation of, among other documents, the Halbmonatsbericht des Regierungspräsidenten von Oberund Mittelfranken, 7 April 1933, in Martin Broszat and Elke Fröhlich, eds., *Bayern in der NS-Zeit II: Herrschaft und Gesellschaft im Konflikt*, Teil A (Munich, 1979), 291-308. See also Kater, "Ansätze zu einer Soziologie der SA bis zur Röhmkrise," in *Soziale Bewegung und politische Verfassung: Beiträge zur Geschichte der modernen Welt*, ed. Ulrich Engelhardt et al., (Stuttgart, 1976), 799; Eric Reiche, "From Spontaneous to Legal Terror: SA, Police, and the Judiciary in Nurnberg, 1933-34," *European Studies Review* 9

(1979): 240; Hans Mommsen, "Der nationalsozialistische Polizeistaat und die Judenverfolgung vor 1938," *Vierteljahrshefte für Zeitgeschichte* 10 (1962): 68-77; Mommsen, "Die Realisierung des Utopischen: Die Endlösung der Judenfrage im Dritten Reich," *Geschichte und Gesellschaft* 9 (1983): 381-420; Uwe Dietrich Adam, *Judenpolitik im Dritten Reich* (Düsseldorf, 1979).

18. The Nazis tried to justify the boycott as a reaction to international anti-Nazi campaigns, particularly those organized by American Jews. Originally planned for a week, the boycott was shortened to one day, and a weekend day at that, in response to criticism at home and abroad. According to Robert Weltsch, editor of the Zionist *Jüdische Rundschau*, the impact of the boycott on Jews was considerable nonetheless. "Many Jews on this Saturday were depressed," he wrote in an editorial on 4 April. They had been "forced to admit their Jewishness," not "for an inner conviction, not for loyalty to their people, not for their pride in a magnificent history" but by "the affixing of a red placard or a yellow badge." Weltsch went on to utter his now famous quote: "Jews, take it upon yourselves, that Star of David, and honor it anew" (*Jüdische Rundschau*, 4 April 1933; Adam, *Judenpolitik im Dritten Reich*, 60-61, 86; Kater, "Everyday Antisemitism," 140-43).

19. *Frankfurter Zeitung*, 31 March, 2, 5 April 1933; Document I 3 in *Dokumente zur Geschichte der Frankfurter Juden, 1933-1945* (hereafter *DGF*) (Frankfurt, 1963), 21; Der Prorektor in Vertretung des Rektors der Universität an den Minister fur Wissenschaft, Kunst, und Volksbildung, 1 April 1933, Document III 39 in *DGF*, 96; Schleunes, *Twisted Road*, 84-87; Freudenthal, "Meine Beiden," 158; interview with Leo and Settie Sonnenborn, in Friedman, *Amcha*, 43. See also Arno Lustiger, "Die Steine dieser Stadt mögen für uns zeugen: Mit dem Judenboykott am 1. April 1933 begann der Leidensweg," in *Frankfurter Allgemeine Zeitung*, 31 March 1983.

20. *Giessener Anzeiger*, 2 April 1933; *Geisenheimer Lokal Anzeiger*, 4 April 1933.

21. David Bankier offers reports from the Gestapo in Magdeburg, Münster, and Dortmund to buttress this argument: Gestapo Magdeburg, Report August 1935, REP/90 P, Gestapo Münster, Report July 1935, REP/90 P, and Gestapo Dortmund, Report July 1935, REP/90 P, all in Geheimes Staatsarchiv, Berlin; see Bankier, *Germans and the Final Solution*, 75, 171.

22. Schleunes, *Twisted Road*, 86-89.

23. Interviews with Schnabel and Freimuth; Bamberger, "Die Geschichte und Erlebnis," 10; interview with Martha Brixius, in Owings, *Frauen*, 199-200.

24. Freudenthal, "Meine Beiden," 159; interview with Leo and Settie Sonnenborn, in Friedman, *Amcha*, 43; interview with Harth; Betty and Jenny Student "voluntarily" sold their bankrupt clothing store later, in 1936 (Betty and Jenny Student, Wiener Library testimony, 02/683).

25. Schleunes, *Twisted Road*, 109-10.

26. See Hans Mommsen, *Beamtentum im Dritten Reich: Mit aus-*

gewählten Quellen zur nationalsozialistischen Beamtenpolitik (Stuttgart, 1966), 39-61; Adam, *Judenpolitik im Dritten Reich*, 51-64, 114-44; Schleunes, *Twisted Road*, 103-5, 109, 110.

27. The firing of Jewish doctors in Hessen was particularly fierce in Wiesbaden, ruthlessly pursued by the director of the Nazi Union of Doctors there, Dr. Althen. Early in 1934, Frankfurt's mayor Krebs began threatening city workers with disciplinary action if they sought treatment from Jewish doctors. As of 2 June, Jewish dentists were no longer insured. See Kropat, "Die hessischen Juden im Alltag der NS Diktatur," in *Neunhundert Jahre Geschichte der Juden in Hessen*, 416-18; Die Rundverfugung des Oberbürgermeisters, 3 February 1934, Document V12, in *DGF*, 226-27. For Frankfurt, see Siegmund Drexler, *Ärztliches Schicksal unter der Verfolgung, 1933-1945, in Frankfurt am Main und Offenbach* (Frankfurt, 1990).

28. This law was extended to Jewish dentists and dental technicians in June 1933.

29. Jeremy Noakes and Geoffrey Pridham, eds., *Nazism, 1919-1945: A History in Documents and Eyewitness Accounts* (New York, 1983), 1:528.

30. The 81 individuals represented 1.4 percent of Frankfurt's civil service. According to Nazi sources, between April 1933 and May 1934, 121 out of 275 "non-Aryan" lawyers in Frankfurt were forced to resign. See Verfügung des beauftragten Oberbürgermeisters, durch den Personaldezernenten weitergegeben, 28 March 1933, Document III 3, in *DGF*, 65-66; Aktennotiz des Personaldezernenten zur Kenntnis des beauftragten Oberbürgermeisters" 13 April 1933, Document III 5, in *DGF*, 67-68. For the stat on lawyers, see, Alfred Vogel, *Erblehre und Rassenkunde in bildlicher Darstellung* (Stuttgart, 1935), 69.

31. Schreiber was eventually forced into retirement (Eduard Schreiber, "Erlebnissen eines deutschen Richters 1993/34," Document III 2, in *DGF*, 62-64).

32. Out of 355 professors, 109 were fired. They included Hermann Heller (law), Werner Lipschitz (pharmacology), Max Horkheimer (social philosophy), Adolf Löwe (economics), Karl Strupp (law), Max Wertheimer (philosophy), Carl Grünberg (economics), Franz Oppenheimer (sociology), Karl Pribaum (economics), Carl Mannheim (sociology), Ernst Cahn (law), Hugo Sinzheimer (law), Ludwig Wertheimer (law), Ludwig Benda (chemotherapy), Fritz Mayer (chemistry), Joseph Igersheimer (ophthalmology), Georg Ludwig Dreyfus (internal medicine), Karl Altmann (dermatology), Hugo Braun (bacteriology), Edgar Goldschmid (pathology), Marcel Traugott (gynecology), Raphael Weichbrodt (psychiatry), Wilhelm Hanauer (social medicine), Richard Koch (medicine history), Walter Lehmann (surgery), Joseph Berberich (ear, nose, throat), Martin Sommerfeld (german philology), Fritz Heinemann (philosophy), Otto Szasz (mathematics), Walter Frankel (physical chemistry), Friedrich Hahn (chemistry), Edmund Speyer (chemistry), Siegfried Budge (economics), Gottfried Salomon (sociology), Walter Sulzbach (sociology), Fritz Neumark (economics), Ernst Eduard Hirsch (law), Franz Hermann (dermatology), Emmy Klieneberger (bacteriology), Ernst Herz (psychiatry), Ernst

Metzger (ophthalmology), Martin Plessner (semitic philology), Theodor Wiesengrund (philosophy), Hans Weil (pedagogy), Gottfried Fraenkel (zoology), Erich Heymann (physical chemistry), Friedrich Pollock (economics), Eugen Altschul (economics), Norbert Glatzer (judaism), Ernst Kahn, Ernst Kantorowicz (history), Hendrik de Man (social psychology). Far from considering the release of so many intellectuals a brain drain, the Nazis condemned the fact that the education of Germans was in "Jewish hands." See *Der Weltkampf*, Heft 119, November 1933; Heuberger, *Hinaus dus dem Ghetto*, 174; Hammerstein, *Johann Wolfgang von Goethe Universität*, 220; Gerda Stuchlik, *Goethe im Braunhemd: Universität Frankfurt, 1933-1945* (Frankfurt, 1984), 90-100.

33. At the beginning of the summer semester in 1933, SA men tried to prevent Jewish students from entering classroom buildings, and soon thereafter, the German Student Association expelled all of its Jewish members. Jewish doctoral candidates were also casualties of the April decree. Oddly enough, the historian Jakob Katz, a foreign Jew from Hungary, managed to complete his doctorate at the university. A law passed on 11 January 1934, and another on 15 April 1937, decreed that Jews could no longer graduate with a university degree ("Das Schicksal jüdischer Studenten," in *Die braune Machtergreifung, Universität Frankfurt, 1930-1945* (Frankfort, 1989) 50-56, 62.

34. *Frankfurter Zeitung*, 27 April 1933, Document III 41, in *DGF*, 97.

35. Enzo Traverso asserts, I believe wrongly, that Kantorowicz protested only because the Nazis included him on the list of Jewish professors to be fired. See Professor Dr. Ernst Kantorowicz an den Minister für Wissenschaft, Kunst, und Volksbildung, 20 April 1933, Document III 42, in *DGF*, 99-100; Traverso, *Jews and Germany*, 88.

36. Prussian law mandated primary education for all citizens and dependents of the state (Das Schulamt an den Oberbürgermeister, 20 June 1933, Document III 52, in *DGF*, 105).

37. Der Bürgermeister an den Regierungspräsidenten, 24 June 1935, Document III 58, in *DGF*, 112-13.

38. Professor Dr. Kurt Riezler an den Rektor der Universität, 15 January 1934, Document III 45, in *DGF*, 101-2; Der Leiter der Handels-und Höheren Handelsschule fur Knaben an das Schulamt, 1 October 1935, Document III 56, in *DGF*, 111.

39. Nazis also frequently picketed outside Dr. Nathan's residence (interview with Dr. Horst Dickel, Geisenheim, 3 October 1993).

40. The thirty-three professors discharged constituted nearly 20 percent of the university's *Ordinariat*. The Jewish contingent included Professors Margarete Bieber (archaeology), Julius Geppert (pharmacology), Georg Jaffe (physics), Julius Levy (semitic philology), Paul Mombert (economics), Egon Pribaum (medicine), Ludwig Schlesinger (mathematics), Franz Soetbeer (medicine), and Erich Stern, *Privatdozenten* Fritz Heichelheim (archaeology and history) and Alfred Storch, and lecturers Ernst Adler, Samuel Bialoblocki, Wilhelm Grünberg, Franz Kirchheimer, and Egon Winter. Jewish students at

the university also suffered discrimination. Bernhard Teitler could no longer continue his doctoral studies in mathematics after 1933 so he emigrated to Palestine. Alfred Gutsmuth was luckier; after being denied admission for an eighth semester of law school, Gutsmuth found tutelage under Wolfgang Mittermeier, who was later dismissed for political unreliability. See Heyne, "Judenverfolgung," 39-45; Bruno Reimann, "Entlassung und Emigration: Die Universität Giessen in den Jahren nach 1933," in *Zwischen Unruhe und Ordnung: Ein deutsches Lesebuch für die Zeit von 1925-1960 am Beispiel einer Region: Mittelhessen*, ed. Gideon Schuler (Giessen, 1989), 186.

41. "Kleinkinderschule, Kindergarten des Fröbelseminars, 1918-1934," Akte Nr. L 1315-1, Stadtarchiv Giessen, a letter from the Bürgermeister, Giessen, 15 August 1933, Akte Nr. L 1315-1, Stadtarchiv Giessen; Brigitte Kralovitz et al., *Hedwig Burgheim oder die Reise nach Giessen: Bericht über das Leben einer Lehrerin* (Giessen, 1981); Heyne, "Judenverfolgung," 33.

42. Schleunes, *Twisted Road,* 109.

43. Raul Hilberg, *Perpetrators, Victims, Bystanders: The Jewish Catastrophe, 1933-1945* (New York, 1992), 150.

44. Professor Neisser, Direktor des Städtischen Hygienischen Universitäts-Instituts, an den Personaldezernenten, Frankfurt, 29 March 1933, Document III 8, in *DGF,* 70.

45. *Die braune Machtergreifung,* 56.

46. Schmidt encountered difficulties finishing his medical degree. Kirchheimer lost his post at the Geological Institute, and Soetbeer was dismissed from the university clinic (telephone interview with Kirchheimer, Freiburg, 13 January 1983; interview with Ida Hahn, 20 January 1983; telephone interview with Werner Schmidt, December 1982 and January 1983, all in Heyne, "Judenverfolgung," 158-67).

47. A 14 July 1933 law providing for the denaturalization of any individual who had received citizenship from the Weimar government followed the April legislation. Because so few *Ostjuden* were German citizens, the denaturalization law was largely a meaningless gesture. For eastern Jews who held German citizenship, however, its revocation undermined their ability to emigrate. A decree of expulsion for denaturalized persons came in March 1934. This order laid the legal foundation for the expulsion of eastern European Jewish refugees, but no such action occurred until mid-1938 (Schleunes, *Twisted Road,* 111-12).

48. In October 1933, the National Association of Craftsmen prohibited Jews from assuming leadership positions in guilds, although it did not yet deny them guild membership (Schreiben des Reichsverbands der Handwerker, 18 October 1933, in Josef Walk, ed., *Das Sonderrecht für die Juden im NS-Staat* [Heidelberg, 1981], 56).

49. Schumacher Archiv, Folder 240 I, Berlin Document Center; Schleunes, *Twisted Road,* 140.

50. Lagebericht für December 1935, Lageberichte Staatspolizeistelle

Kassel, in Thomas Klein, ed., *Die Lageberichte der Geheimen Staatspolizei über die Provinz Hessen-Nassau, 1933-1936* (Cologne, 1986), 1:365.

51. Denkschrift des Wirtschaftsamtes, 17 February 1934, Document IV2, in *DGF,* 178-85.

52. "Friedrich Weil," in Richarz, *Jüdisches Leben,* 269.

53. Wirtschaftsamt an den Oberbürgermeister, 25 April 1934, Document IV 5, in *DGF,* 188; Die Entscheidung des Oberbürgermeisters, 11 May 1934, Document IV 5, in *DGF,* 188; Denkschrift des Wirtschaftsamtes, 17 February 1934, Document IV 2, in *DGF,* 178-85.

54. Deutschland Bericht der Sopade, 2 September 1935, A II: Die Judenverfolgung, in *Deutschland-Berichte der Sozialdemokratischen Partei Deutschlands* (Paris and Prague, 1934-40) 1033-34; hereafter *Sopade.*

55. Jews were also excluded from leadership positions in many economic associations in Frankfurt as a result of a ruling from the local Fighting Union for the Employed Middle Class. See Richtlinien des Kampfbundes für den gewerblichen Mittelstand, 25 April 1933, in Walk, ed., *Das Sonderrecht,* 162; Sprenger, as cited in Kropat, "Die hessischen Juden im Alltag der NS-Diktatur," 420.

56. Anordnung des Oberbürgermeisters, as reprinted in the *Frankfurter Zeitung,* 17 September 1933.

57. Some Jews who had been front soldiers in World War I, were able to participate in Giessen's trade fairs. In fact, an *alter Kämpfer* complained that city officials had rejected his application for permission to take part in the 1934 fall market but had granted a permit to the Jewish individual who had previously owned the Nazi's store. See Schreiben der Bürgermeisterei vom 3 August 1933 und 9 April 1934, Schreiben von Hans Nathan Goldschmidt vom 15 August 1933 in Akten 9506/8, Stadtarchiv Giessen; Schreiben der Bürgermeisterei Giessen vom 1 September 1933 an den Hessischen Gemeindetag, Mainz in Akten 5605, Stadtarchiv Giessen; Schreiben Olga Schumann an den Bürgermeister, 24 August 1934, in Heyne, "Judenverfolgung," 58-59, 233.

58. In July 1933, Jews in Aachen, Büdingen, Darmstadt, Koblenz, Konstanz, Mainz, Ludwigshafen, and Worms were all denied permission to participate in the annual *Messen.* Kassel and Lauterbach allowed a restricted number of Jews to take part in their trade fairs, however. See Akten des Bürgermeister Giessens, Akten 9506/8 (1933), Stadtarchiv Giessen.

59. Schreiben von dem Reich Ministerium der Wirtschaft, 23 September 1933, in Walk, *Das Sonderrecht,* 52.

60. See the directive of the Reichsverband des nationalen Viehhandels in *Central-Verein Zeitung,* 7 September 1933. In Baden Jews were excluded from the cattle trade in April. See the directive of the Baden Ministry of Interior, 19 April 1933, in Walk, *Das Sonderrecht,* 15.

61. Schreiben des Oberbürgermeister Ritters, Giessen, 30 January 1937, Akten 2138, Stadtarchiv Giessen; *Oberhessische Tageszeitung,* 2 January

1935; Michael Breitbach et al. eds., *Beamte im Nationalsozialismus: Dokumente und Erläuterungen zur Giessener Ausstellung Oktober 1988* (Giessen, 1988), 15-19.

62. The most well-known pogroms that summer occurred on 15 July on Berlin's Kurfürstendamm.

63. Bericht der Sopade, 2 July 1935, A IV: Der Terror, in *Sopade*, 804.

64. A factory owner in Hessen also protested the erection of a sign with the slogan "Jews are not wanted here" (Bankier, *Germans and the Final Solution*, 99; Lagebericht für August 1935, Staatspolizeistelle Kassel, in *Die Lageberichte*, 1:309).

65. A year earlier, on 28 November 1933, two Jewish merchants in the Frankfurt suburb of Buern were taken into custody because the population supposedly demanded it. In December, an ordinance forbade Jewish stores to use Christian symbols during Christmas. Einzelhandelsverband Frankfurt, 1 December 1933, cited in *Jüdische Rundschau*, 8 December 1933; Bericht der italienischen Zeitung, Mattino, über den Boykott jüdischer Geschäfte in Frankfurt am Main, Weinachten 1934, 30 December 1934, Document I 7, in *DGF*, 24-26).

66. Deutschland Bericht der Sopade, 2 July 1935, A IV: Der Terror, in *Sopade*, 803.

67. Der Frankfurter Boots-Vertrieb GmbH (FRABO) an den Oberbürgermeister, 26 August 1935, Document IV 6, in *DGF*, 189.

68. A Sopade report from May 1935 indicated that most stores in Frankfurt bore signs reading, "Deutsches Geschäft" or "Deutsches Gastwirtschaft." Rarer, but not nonexistent, were stores that had signs proclaiming, "Jews are not welcome." The case of a Frankfurt Jew who sued his company in March 1935 for firing him to remain true to its *Deutsches Geschäft* epithet was thrown out of court. In 1936, Robert Ley, head of the Nazi German Workers Front, declared that signs bearing such an inscription would no longer be distributed (Die Kreisleitung an den Oberbürgermeister, 1935, Document IV 11, in *DGF*, 193; Deutschland Bericht der Sopade, Prague, 2 May 1935, in *Sopade*, 534; Bericht der Frankfurter Zeitung über die Entlassung eines nichtarischen Büroangestellten im Zusammenhang mit dem Schild, "Deutsches Geschäft," 23 March 1935, Document IV 9, in *DGF*, 191).

69. Interview with Schnabel, a secondhand recollection from her mother.

70. Die Schriftleitung des *Frankfurter Volksblattes* bringt dem Ober-bürgermeister eine anonyme Zuschrift, unterzeichnet, "Die Pg. der NSDAP," zur Kenntnis, 3 April 1933, Document III 32, in *DGF*, 88-89.

71. One year later, in June 1934, the Hessian Cultural Association decreed that the Old Testament would no longer be included in religious education (*Frankfurt Israelitisches Familienblatt*, Nr. 19, May 1933, 9; Verfügung der Hessischen Kultusverwaltung, 21 June 1934, as cited in *Israelitisches Familienblatt*, 21 June 1934).

72. Der Magistrat an den Regierungspräsidenten, May 1933, Document III 22, and Die Gauleitung der Gaubetriebszellenleiter an den kommissarischen Oberbürgermeister, 3 April 1933, Document III 23, in *DGF,* 80, 81.

73. Der Präsident der Reichskammer der bildenden Kunste an Benno Elkan, 12 February 1935, Document III 34, in *DGF,* 93-94; Der Präsident der Reichsschrifttumskammer an Benno Elkan, 2 March 1935, Document III 35, in *DGF,* 94. The famous painter Max Beckman also lost his job in Frankfurt because the Nazis regarded his work as degenerate.

74. Eine Parteigenossin an das *Frankfurter Volksblatt,* 17 December 1933, Von der Schriftleitung des Frankfurter Volksblättes an die Stadtkanzlei weitergeleitet, Part A, Document III 88, in *DGF,* 163; Der Strassenbennenungsausschuss an den Oberbürgermeister, 6 March 1934, Part B of Document III 88, in *DGF,* 163.

75. Das Bauamt, Strassenbennenungsausschuss an den Oberbürgermeister, 3 February 1935, Document III 93, in *DGF,* 167-73; Das Bauamt, Strassenbennenungsausschuss an den Oberbürgermeister, 18 February 1936, Document III 95, in *DGF,* 173-77.

76. Brief vom Irmgard Christ and Dr. Erwin Knauss, 25 August 1983, in Heyne, "Judenverfolgung," 64.

77. Schreiben vom 4 May 1935 an den Oberbürgermeister, Akten Nr. 1151; Dienstleistungszeugnis des Oberbürgermeisters vom 30 August 1937, Document 5, Akten Nr. 1141; Documents 6, 7, 8, in Akten Nr. 1141; Interessant sind die Begründungen der einzelnen Stellen, Documents 9, 10, in Akten Nr. 1141, all in Stadtarchiv Giessen.

78. Die Schriftleitung der "Hessischen Volkswacht" an der Gauleitung, Abteilung für Volksbildung, des Schreiben des Oberspielleiters Jacob Geis von April 1932 zur Kenntnis, 14 August 1933, Document III 25, in *DGF,* 82-83.

79. Aufruf der Senckenbergischen Naturforschenden Gesellschaft, Frankfurt am Main, 25 June 1933, Document III 31, in *DGF,* 88.

80. Rundschreiben Stadtverwaltung Köln, March 1933, in Walk, *Das Sonderrecht,* 8. For the boxing directive, see *Dokumentensammlung über die Entrechtung, Ächtung, und Vernichtung der Juden in Deutschland seit der Regierung Adolf Hitler* (N.p., 1936), 139.

81. The German Gymnastics Association issued its own "Aryan" paragraph on 24 May 1933 (Richtlinien der Reichssportkommissar, 25 April 1933, in Walk, *Das Sonderrecht,* 18; Bekanntmachung des Führer der deutschen Turnerschaft, 24 May 1933, ibid., 25).

82. Interview with Harth; phone interview with Donald and Gretel Strauss by Jonathan Friedman, 21 December 1993.

83. Report of John Slade, formerly Hans Schlesinger, in *Bericht gegen Vergessen,* 115.

84. Mayer was studying law at the University of Southern California at

the time (*New York Times*, 24 November 1933; Richard Mandell, *The Nazi Olympics* [New York, 1971], 63-64).

85. In 1933, Makkabi had a membership of three thousand and Schild of seven thousand. By 1935, total membership in both organizations neared forty thousand. Osten issued a decree in September 1934 asserting that the prohibition of contact between Jews and Gentiles did not apply to the realm of sports (Richtlinien der Reichsportführer, 18 July 1934, and Schreiben des Reichsportführer, 17 September 1934, in Walk, *Das Sonderrecht*, 88, 92; "Die Olympische Spiele," Exhibit of the Landessportbund Nordrhein-Westfalen, 1986; Wippermann, *Judenverfolgung*, 72-73).

86. The Olympics went off despite international protests over the Nuremberg Laws of the fall of 1935, the German reoccupation of the Rhineland in March 1936, and continued discrimination against German Jews. See Count Baillet-Latour to Avery Brundage, 17 November 1935, Avery Brundage Collection, University of Illinois; Schreiben an die Gauleiter, Munich, 29 January 1936, RG-11.001M.01, Reel 4, Folder 261, United States Holocaust Memorial Museum Archives; Kropat, "Die hessischen Juden im Alltag der NS Diktatur," in *Neunhundect Jahre Geschichte der Juden in Hessen*, 426-27.

87. Officials in Koblenz also urged Germans not to harass Jewish sport organizations, if only to deflect foreign criticism (Tagebuch Friedrich Krebs, 24 January 1935, 26, Stadtarchiv Frankfurt, S1/50; Verfügung der Staatspolizeistelle Koblenz, 31 August 1935, in Walk, *Das Sonderrecht*, 125).

88. Erlass der Gestapo, Berlin, 9 August 1935, in Kropat, "Die hessischen Juden im Alltag der NS Diktatur," 426; Brief der Ortsgruppe Bahnhof an die Stadion GmbH, Frankfurt, 25 July 1935, Document VII 28, in *DGF*, 363.

89. On 2 November 1938, just days before Kristallnacht, Lord Mayor Krebs decreed that the Niederrad beach would be closed to Jews during the next summer season. In some cities, the exclusion of Jews from swimming pools and beaches came earlier. In Fulda, Berlin-Wannsee, Beuthen, and Speyer, restrictions emerged in August 1933, while in Schweinfurt, Karlsruhe, Friedberg, Gladbach, and Dortmund, exclusive policies surfaced in 1935. Pools in Düsseldorf were declared off limits to Jews on 11 February 1936, in Baden on 27 May 1936. See Protokoll der Amtsleiterbesprechung, 12 May 1936, in *DGF*, 365; Niederschrift des Sportamtes uber die Besprechung beim Oberbürgermeister, Frankfurt, 2 November 1938, Document VII 34, in *DGF*, 368; *Central-Verein Zeitung*, 7 September 1933; Oberbürgermeister Düsseldorf, 11 February 1936, in Walk, *Das Sonderrecht*, 154; Erlass von dem badischen Ministerium des Innern, 27 May 1936, ibid., 164; Deborah Lipstadt, *Beyond Belief: The American Press and the Coming of the Holocaust, 1933-1945* (New York, 1986), 66.

90. The Reichsbund continued to function until after Kristallnacht (9-10 November 1938). See Kropat, "Die hessischen Juden im Alltag der NS Diktatur," 427.

91. See Adam, *Judenpolitik im Dritten Reich*, 51-64, 114-44; Schleunes, *Twisted Road*, 116-20; Kater, "Everyday Antisemitism"; Gerd Rühle, *Das Dritte Reich: Dokumentarische Darstellung des Aufbaues der Nation: Das dritte Jahr* (Berlin, 1935), 254-58, 277-82.

92. Jews were also forbidden to fly the Nazi flag. Legal commentaries broadened the law´s application to include Gypsies and blacks.

93. Noakes and Pridham, *Nazism*, 536.

94. Crucial to the official Nazi definition of the "Jew" was the matter of religion. Karl Schleunes argues that Nazi medical science had made no progress in isolating a specific Jewish blood type. Nazi legislators therefore had to assume that religion somehow determined blood or that an equally mystical process forced someone with Jewish blood to accept Judaism. The absurdity of these assumptions bothered neither Nazi doctors nor legislators. Interestingly, too, the Nazis did not force the dissolution of pre-existing mixed marriages, and they rarely treated non-Jewish partners in mixed unions as Jews, unless they fit the categorization of Nuremberg (Adam, *Judenpolitik im Dritten Reich*, 114-44; Schleunes, *Twisted Road*, 129).

95. The term *Mischling* was not a Nazi invention. It appeared in German eugenics publications before World War I and was applied to the offspring of Germans and colonial blacks (Annegret Ehmann, "The Mischlinge and Their Neighbors," paper presented at the American Historical Association Convention in Alanta, January 1996).

96. *Statistik des deutschen Reiches: Die Bevölkerung des Deutschen Reiches nach den Ergebnissen der Volkszählung 1939: Die Juden und jüdischen Mischlinge im Deutschen Reich*, Vol. 552, Issue 4 (Berlin, 1944), 21, 32, 120-30.

97. Bürgermeisterei der Stadt Mainz an das Standesamt Mainz, 31 October 1933, Document V1B, in *DGF*, 216-17; Die Gauleitung, Gaupersonalamt, Abteilung für Judenfragen an die Kreisleitung, 14 November 1933, Document V1A, in DGF, 216.

98. National Archives, College Park, Md., Raymond Geist to Secretary of State Cordell, December 1933, RG-59. Records show a marriage between a Protestant man and a Jewish woman in Giessen in 1934. In Frankfurt in 1933, there were forty-one cases of Jewish men marrying Protestant women, fourteen cases of Jewish men marrying Catholic women, eight cases of Jewish women marrying Protestant men, and eight cases of Jewish women marrying Catholic men. In 1934, there were seventeen cases of Jewish men marrying Protestant women, nine cases of Jewish men marrying Catholic women, five cases of Jewish women marrying Protestant men, and three cases of Jewish women marrying Catholic men. In 1935, there were eight cases of Jewish men marrying Protestant women, six cases of Jewish men marrying Catholic women, two cases of Jewish women marrying Protestant men, and three cases of Jewish women marrying Catholic men. At the same time endogamous Jewish marriages increased from 123 in 1933 to 153 in 1935. See Kirchlich-statistische

Haupttabelle, 17/500 Dekanat Giessen 1934, 9, Zentralarchiv der Evangelischen Kirchen Hessen; *Beiträge zur Statistik der Stadt Frankfurt am Main: Tabellarische Übersichten Betreffend den Zivilstand der Stadt, 1931-1935*, Heft 16 (Frankfurt, 1937), 26, 50, 74, 98, Stadtarchiv Frankfurt.

99. Rearmament had begun shortly after the reintroduction of conscription in March 1935. Hitler's move into the Rhineland occurred one year later. See Lipstadt, *Beyond Belief*, 84; Bankier, *Germans and the Final Solution*, 53.

100. Schleunes insists that Nazi Jewish policies from 1933 to 1939 did not prefigure the Final Solution but were policies that the Nazis themselves saw as failures. David Bankier points to similar discontent from Dortmund, Koblenz, and Bielefeld Nazis. See Gestapo Dortmund, Report September 1935, R 58/514, Bundesarchiv Koblenz; Gestapo Bielefeld, Report September 1935, R 58/513, Bundesarchiv Koblenz; Gestapo Koblenz, Report November 1935, REP/ 90 P, Geheimes Staatsarchiv, Berlin; Bankier, *Germans and the Final Solution*, 78-79, 171; Schleunes, *Twisted Road*, 132; Schleunes, "Retracing the Twisted Road: Nazi Policies Toward German Jews, 1933-1939," in *Unanswered Questions: Nazi Germany and the Genocide of the Jews*, ed. François Furet, (New York, 1989), 61.

101. According to David Bankier, ordinary Gentiles became increasingly indifferent not only to Jews but to the Nazi regime as well after the Olympics. After 1936, large sections of the urban population, who had facilitated the party's success, betrayed visible signs of weariness and lack of faith. The farmers became even more indifferent than in previous months. The Münster Gestapo reported that farmers were staying away from political meetings. In Wesermünde, they also refused to wave flags. Meanwhile, the Frankfurt Gestapo reported that the public mood after 1936 reached its lowest ebb since the party came to power. See Gestapo Frankfurt am Main, Report February 1936, R 58/1151, Bundesarchiv Koblenz; Gordon, *Hitler, Germans, and the Jewish Question*, 206; Bankier, *Germans and the Final Solution*, 52, 53; Gellately, *Gestapo*, and his paper, "The Role of Informers: Popular Participation in Policing the Nation," presented at the American Historical Association Convention, Atlanta, January 1996.

102. Gordon, *Hitler, Germans, and the Jewish Question*, 48; Gordon's citation of the quote from Leonard Baker, *Days of Sorrow and Pain: Leo Baeck and the Berlin Jews* (New York, 1978), 124; Georg Salzberger, *Leben und Lehre* (Frankfurt, 1982).

103. *Frankfurt Israelitisches Gemeindeblatt* 8 (April 1933), 1; *Der Israelit*, 9 February 1933.

104. "Unser Kampf für Deutschland: Gegen die Gruelpropaganda im Ausland," *Central-Verein Zeitung*, 30 March 1933; "Schwarze Liste der deutschen Literatur," ibid., 4 May 1933.

105. Emigration drained the number of school-age children from many areas in rural Hessen, forcing the closure of numerous small-town Jewish schools (Kropat, "Die hessischen Juden im Alltag der NS Diktatur," 429).

106. See Ruth Gay, *The Jews of Germany: A Historical Portrait* (New Haven: 1992), 257-60.

107. Heuberger, *Hinans aus dem Ghetto*, 180-84.

108. Der Kulturbund Deutscher Juden an Staatskommissar Hinkel, 1 November 1934, Document VII 17A, and Staatskommissar Hinkel an den Kulturbund Deutscher Juden, 7 November 1934, Document VII 17B, in *DGF,* 350.

109. Herbert Freeden, *Jüdisches Theater in Nazideutschland* (Tübingen, 1964), 51-52; Kurt Düwell, "Jewish Cultural Centers in Nazi Germany: Expectations and Accomplishments," in *The Jewish Response to German Culture: From the Enlightenment to the Second World War*, ed. Jehuda Reinharz and Walter Schatzberg (Hanover, 1985), 314.

110. The Nazi ban on ritual slaughtering was issued on 21 April 1933 (Reichgesetzblatt, I, 21 April 1933, 203, Walk, *Das Sonderrecht*, 15; Erich Neumann, "To Life," unpublished memoir, 173).

111. Der Vorstand der Jüdischen Kultusvereinigung Giessen an die Gestapo, 1 February 1940 und 1 November 1940, Abteilung 612, Konv. 23, Faszikel 12, Mappe 16, and Faszikel 10, Mappe 25, Hessisches Staatsarchiv, Darmstadt.

112. Heuberger, *Hinans aus dem Ghetto*, 187.

113. Strauss, "Jewish Emigration from Germany: Nazi Policies and Jewish Responses," *Leo Baeck Institute Yearbook* 25 (1980), 330.

114. Kropat, "Die hessischen Juden im Alltag der NS Diktatur," 434.

115. In 1933, 3,479 Jews left Frankfurt, falling to a low of 996 in 1935, picking up to over 2,600 in 1936, falling again in 1937 to 1,700, and rising to over 3,800 in 1938 and 4,800 in 1939 (Frankfurt Zuzug und Abwanderung der Juden in den Jahren 1933/1934, Document IX 18, in *DGF,* 418; Der Polizeipräsident an den Oberbürgermeister, 20 January 1936, Document IX 19, in *DGF,* 418; Frankfurt Zuzug und Abwanderung der Juden von Januar 1936 bis September 1939. Zusammengestellt nach den Monatsberichten des Polizeipräsidenten an den Oberbürgermeister, Document IX 20, in *DGF,* 418).

116. There were 20,252 Jews (including 1,092 *Mischlinge*) remaining in Hessen-Nassau and 6,068 Jews (including 353 *Mischlinge*) in Hessen as of 1939 (*Statistik des deutschen Reiches*, Vol. 552, Issue 4, pp. 6, 8, 21).

117. Arnsberg, *Die jüdischen Gemeinden*, 1:259.

118. "Aufstellung" in Knauss, *Die jüdische Bevölkerung Giessens*, 54-110; *Statistik des deutschen Reiches*, Vol. 552, Issue 4, 32.

119. Ferdinand Mayer was the second to last Jew to leave Geisenheim, moving on 19 July 1939 ("Verzeichnis der Abgemeldeten," Stadtarchiv Geisenheim).

120. Interview with Martin Killian; Wolfgang Wippermann, *Das Leben in Frankfurt zur NS-Zeit: Band 5, Der Widerstand, Darstellung, Dokumente, didaktische Hinweise* Band 5, (Frankfurt, 1986), 35-60; Aus einem Ende 1933 durch Walter Deeg in Giessen verteiltes illegales Flugblatt der "Roten

Hilfe Deutschlands," Document M 16 a, in *Faschismus in der Provinz: Lokalgeschichtlicher Unterricht am Beispiel von Giessen* (Kassel, 1985), 62; Gemeinsamer Aufruf der KPD-Bezirksleitung Hessen-Frankfurt und der SPD-Bezirksleitung Hessen-Nassau 5 September 1934, Document M 16 b, ibid., 62.

121. In all fairness, during his incarceration in Buchenwald, Carlebach engaged in sabotage, came to the aid of Jewish prisoners, and smuggled goods in for them (Arnsberg, *Die Geschichte der Frankfurter Juden*, 3:75).

122. Killian even received restitution after the war for his suffering, although Annelise Schnabel has pointed to inconsistencies in his personal history as well as to instances of alleged collaboration on his part (Martin Killian, Antrag auf Wiedergutmachung, 22 November 1948, Schlussbescheid der Regierungspräsident-Entschädigungsbehörde, Wiesbaden, 8 October 1956; interviews with Killian and Schnabel).

123. Protestant opponents of the Reich suffered a variety of fates. Some, like Barth and Paul Tillich, lost posts at universities, some, like Martin Niemöller, ended up concentration camps, and some, like Dietrich Bonhöffer, were executed. But many of those who turned to resistance initially blunted criticisms against the introduction of an Aryan paragraph into church administration and the removal of "Jewish" elements from the Bible by welcoming Hitler's decision to leave the League of Nations. See James Bentley, *Martin Niemöller, 1892-1984* (New York, 1984); Edwin Robertson, *The Shame and the Sacrifice: The Life and Martyrdom of Dietrich Bonhöffer* (New York, 1988).

124. Noakes and Pridham, *Nazism*, 583-85.

125. *Der Bote*, 31, no. 7, 18 February 1934, 76; Michael Phayer, *Protestant and Catholic Women in Nazi Germany* (Detroit, 1990), 85, 256.

126. Buber to Kittel, undated, is a reply to Kittel's letter of 13 June 1933. Buber's public response, "Offener Brief an Gerhard Kittel," appeared in the *Theologische Blätter* 12 (August 1933): 4-6. See Glatzer and Mendes-Flohr, eds., *Letters of Martin Buber*, 403; Lohmeyer to Buber, Glasegrund bei Habelschwerdt, 19 August 1933, ibid., 406.

127. Hajo Holborn, *A History of Modern Germany, 1840-1945* (Princeton, 1969), 742-43.

128. Erklärung der Pfarrerschaft der Frankfurter Landeskirche zur gegenwärtigen Lage in Frankfurt am Main, 26 February 1933, in *Dokumentation zum Kirchenkampf in Hessen und Nassau* (Darmstadt, 1974), 1:370, 410, cited in Wippermann, *Widerstand*, 61-66, 154.

129. *Rhein-Mainische Volkszeitung*, 4 April 1933, cited in Wippermann, *Widerstand*, 67, 155; report from Wippermann, ibid., 68.

130. Biographische Daten zu Pfarrer Schneider, Document M5, in *Faschismus in der Provinz*, 40-41.

131. Interviews with Freimuth and Killian; *Geschichte der Stadt Geisenheims*, Struck, 284.

132. Hilberg, *Perpetrators, Victims, Bystanders*, 153; Files of the Reich

Association of Non-Aryan Christians in the Staatsarchiv Leipzig, Collection Polizeipräsident Leipzig V, Folders 4537 and 4538.

133. The overwhelming majority of the one hundred Jewish students interviewed in *Berichte gegen Vergessen*, 39, had the impression that their social environments soured quickly after 30 January 1933.

134. Interview with Killian.

135. The same thing happened to Ursula K. and her family later in 1934 (interview with Ursula K., January 1983, and letter from Eva Steinreich, Hollywood, Florida, 3 November 1983, in Heyne, "Judenverfolgung," 21-23).

136. Dr. Werner Schmidt, a half-Jew by Nazi classification, encountered a similar problem, and at a reunion of his 1932 *Abitur* class, he issued a harsh critique of his fellow schoolmates (telephone interview with Dr. Werner Schmidt by Kurt Heyne in December 1982, Heyne, "Judenverfolgung," 40; Gutsmuth as recalled by Erwin Knauss, ibid., 40).

137. Interview with Martin Scheuer, in Friedman, *Amcha*, 30; Hahn, *White Flags*, 26-27. For similar experiences, see Erinnerungen Arthur St., JG 1921, in *Jugend im Nationalsozialistischen Frankfurt*, 313; Erinnerungen Liselotte F., JG 1920, ibid., 318.

138. Lagebericht Staatspolizeistelle Kassel, August, September 1934, in *Die Lageberichte*, 153, 168. Only in December 1935 did the Kassel Gestapo mention that a portion of the Hessian population viewed the government's policy toward Jews as too radical (ibid., and Lageberichte Staatspolizeistelle Kassel, October 1934, August, September, December 1935, Lageberichte Staatspolizeistelle Frankfurt am Main, September 1935, in *Die Lageberichte*, 182-83, 308-9, 364-65, 367, 485).

139. Bericht der Sopade, July, September 1935, in *Sopade*, 802-5, 1033.

140. Strangely, in January 1936, the Sopade declared that the Hessian population as a whole was not antisemitic (Bericht der Sopade, September 1935, January 1936, in *Sopade*, 1033, 26).

141. Interview with Freimuth.

142. David Gushee, "Many Paths to Righteousness: An Assessment of Research on Why Righteous Gentiles Helped Jews," *Holocaust and Genocide Studies* 7 (1993): 385. Some high-ranking Nazis allegedly maintained ties with Jews. In his memoirs, Albert Speer claimed that he had Jewish friends and was never an antisemite, as did Adolf Eichmann, the administrator of the Final Solution (Speer, *Inside the Third Reich: Memoirs* [New York, 1970], 19-20; Hannah Arendt, *Eichmann in Jerusalem: A Report on the Banality of Evil*, rev. ed. [New York, rev. ed., 1992]).

143. Bamberger, "Die Geschichte und Erlebnis," 11-12; Levy, "Mein Leben," 36; interview with Erich Decker, Giessen, 1976, by Kurt Heyne, in Heyne, "Judenverfolgung," 38-39; interview with Dora Scheuer, Giessen, 15 October 1982, ibid., 206; letter from Donald and Gretel Strauss to Jonathan Friedman, 20 December 1993.

144. Alice Oppenheimer, "A Few Days of My Life," 7, 21-22, Leo Baeck Institute ME 482; Levy, "Mein Leben," 40-44; interviews with Harth, Freimuth, and Neumann; interview with Leo and Settie Sonnenborn, in Friedman, *Amcha*, 43-44.

145. In two 1937 suits prosecuted by the Hessian Chamber of the German Labor Front (Deutsche Arbeitsfront), the Nazi-directed trade union, Gentiles were punished for *judenfreundliches Verhalten* (DAF Ehrengerichtsurteil, Gau Hessen-Nassau, 4 August, 15 November 1937, Hessisches Hauptstaatsarchiv Wiesbaden, Abteilung 483, Nrs. 7172, 7171).

146. Ausschluss des SA Obersturmführer Karl Brinkwerth (Frankfurt) wegen persönlicher Verwendung für Juden (1937), Abteilung 483/3307b; Ausschluss des SA Oberscharführers Karl Raab (Frankfurt) wegen Konsultierung eines jüdischen Arztes (1937), Abteilung 483/3321; Entlassung des SA Obertruppenführers Rosch (Immenhausen) wegen der Annahme von Geschenken von Juden und wegen Geschäftsverbindungen mit diesem (1937), Abteilung 483/3322a; Verweis für den SA Scharführer und Senator Paul Rott (Frankfurt) wegen Geschäftsverbindungen mit Juden (1936), Abteilung 483/3322b; Entlassung des SA Sturmführers Georg Seiboldt (Niedereschbach) wegen Geschäftsverbindungen mit Juden (1937), Abteilung 483/3326a. Added to that sample, however, were two cases involving SA extortion of Jews, and two of maltreatment of them: Abteilung 483/3308a, 3308b, 3319a. From Kreis Eschwege: Ermittlung gegen Dr. Hans Mengel (Netra) wegen verwandschaftlicher Beziehungen zu Juden und Kontakten zu dem früheren Vorwaerts Redakteur Stampfer (1938), Abteilung 483/4947; Parteigerichtsverfahren gegen den Bauern Heinrich Simon (Luderbach) wegen fortgesetzten Handels mit Juden (1934), Abteilung 483/4959. From Kreis Frankenberg: Parteiausschluss des Landwirt Konrad Christ (Herbelshausen) wegen Viehandels mit einem Juden (1935), Abteilung 483/4984; Parteiausschluss des NS Ortsgruppenleiters Heinrich Faber (Gemünden) wegen Kontakte zu Juden (1935), Abteilung 483/4986a; Forderung nach nach Abberufung des Waisenrats Hartmann Mette (Huttenrode) wegen fortgesetzten Handels mit Juden (1936), Abteilung 483/4989b; Parteiausschluss des Wilhelm Kessler (Allendorf) wegen Ankaufs von Butter im Sperrbezirk Ellershausen und denen Beforderung durch den Juden Isidor Katzenstein (1935), Abteilung 483/4992b; Parteigerichtsverfahren gegen Wiegand Koch (Frohnhausen) wegen Verkaufs eines Kalbes an einen Juden (1936), Abteilung 483/4994; Amtsenthebung des Wilhelm Moescheid (Rosenthal) als Gemeindegruppenführer des Reichsluftsschutzbundes wegen angeblichen Handels mit Juden (1938), Abteilung 483/4999a. Kreis Hanau: Parteiausschlussverfahren gegen Hans Hermann (Hanau) wegen Heirat mit einer Judin (1935), Abteilung 483/4685a; Parteigerichtsverfahren gegen den Schuhhandler Alfred Mussig (Grossauheim) wegen geschäftlicher Beziehungen zu Juden (1938), Abteilung 483/4707c; Parteiausschluss des Reichsbahnaspiranten und NSDAP Blockleiters Georg Narbe (Hersfeld) wegen dessen Vorgehen gegen Juden (1939), Abteilung 483/4708a;

Gnadengesuch des wegen geschäftlicher Beziehung zu Juden aus der NSDAP ausgeschlossenen Karl Stiehl (Windecken, 1937), Abteilung 483/4728. All are in Hessisches Hauptstaatsarchiv, Wiesbaden.

147. Sarah Gordon's sample contained 177 cases of *Rassenschande* from 1933 to 1944 and 275 cases of *Judenfreundliches Verhalten*. Her table on page 239, compiled from data in the *Statistik des deutschen Reiches*, Vol. 577 (1942), and Hans Robinsohn's *Justiz als politische Verfolgung: Die Rechtsprechung in Rassenschandefallen beim Landgericht Hamburg, 1936-1943* (Stuttgart, 1977), had a *Rassenschande* sample of 838, spanning the years 1935 to 1943 (Gordon, *Hitler, Germans, and the Jewish Question*, 216, 239; Deutschland Bericht der Sopade, 3 January, 3 August, 1936, A II: Der Terror, in *Sopade*, 40-41, 988-91; Deutschland Bericht der Sopade, 3 December 1936, A III: Der Terror, in *Sopade*, 1660-64).

148. The Nazis developed a hierarchy in their prison system. The harshest prisons were the concentration camps, and by 1939 there were six in Germany, some of which had numerous subsidiaries. They were overseen by Himmler's SS, and the inmates were classified as *Schutzhäftlinge*, prisoners in protective custody. The next level of incarceration was the *Strafanstalt*, which meant either a *Zuchthaus* (penitentiary) or a *Gefängnis* (prison). These came under the authority of the Ministry of Justice, and, unlike concentration camps, inmates in these institutions were actually tried and convicted by courts. The vast majority of *Rassenschänder* served terms of one year or more, and most non-Jewish convicts did their time in *Gefängnisse*, not *Zuchthäuser*. (Gordon, *Hitler, Germans, and the Jewish Question*, 238).

149. Strafsache gegen den Händler [Konrad Rosenthal], geboren 1879, verwitwet, vorbestraft, wegen dieser Sache seit dem 24 Dezember 1935 in Untersuchungshaft wegen Rassenschande, 12 February 1936; Strafsache gegen den Packer Albert P., geboren 1909, geschieden, vorbestraft, seit dem 3 April 1936 in der vorliegenden Sache in Untersuchungshaft wegen Rassenschande, 29 May 1936; Strafsache gegen den Schriftleiter [Julius Schwarz], geboren 1897, wegen Rassenschande, 22 December 1936; Strafsache gegen den kaufmännischen Angestellten [Alfred Rapp] und die Schneiderin [Margarete Lehmann], wegen Rassenschande, 28 January 1937; Strafsache gegen den Buchdrücker [Konrad Meyer], wegen Rassenschande, 14 October 1937; Strafsache gegen den berufslosen [Ernst Schloss], wegen Rassenschande, 26 March 1938; Strafsache gegen den Kaufmann [Max Reichenberger], wegen Rassenschande, 28 May 1938; Strafsache gegen den Kaufmann Sally K., wegen Rassenschande mit einer Prostituierten, 11 June 1938, in Ernst Noam and Wolf-Arno Kropat, *Juden vor Gericht, 1933-1945: Dokumente aus hessischen Justizakten mit einem Vorwort von Johannes Strelitz* (Wiesbaden, 1975), 118-69; See also the collection of *Rassenschande* trials in the Staatsanwaltschaft beim Landgericht Frankfurt am Main, Abteilung 461, Hessisches Hauptstaatsarchiv, Wiesbaden.

150. Interview with Martin Scheuer, in Friedman, *Amcha*, 33.

151. Schreiben der Zellenobmann an Personalamtsleiter, Frankfurt, 8 August 1935, Schreiben der Limpert an den Bürgermeister, Frankfurt, 17 August 1935, Schreiben des Personalamts an den Bürgermeister, Personalakten, Richard Limpert, Akten 74/373, Stadtarchiv Frankfurt, 193-94, 199-200, 201, 215.

152. In addition to V-persons, there were A-persons, or nonparty agents, Z-persons, *Zubringer*, H-persons, assistants, and U-persons, unreliables. See Walter Otto Weyrauch, *Gestapo V-Leute: Tatsachen und Theorie des Geheimdienstes—Untersuchungen zur Geheimen Staatspolizei während der nationalsozialistischen Herrschaft* (Frankfurt, 1992). See also Adolf Diamant, *Gestapo Frankfurt am Main: Zur Geschichte einer verbrecherischen Organisation in den Jahren 1933-1945* (Frankfurt, 1988), 22; Diamant, *Das zweite Buch Ruth: Der Leidensweg einer Frankfurter jüdischen Familie bis in die Vernichtungslager* (Frankfurt, 1986).

153. Heinrich Baab, "Erinnerungen," 5, Leo Baeck Institute, ME 746. Robert Gellately further argues that the Gestapo had a rather small number of officials. In 1937, there were at most seven thousand Gestapo officials in all of Germany. See Reinhard Mann, *Protest und Kontrolle im Dritten Reich: Nationalsozialistische Herrschaft im Alltag einer rheinischen Grossstadt* (Frankfurt, 1987); Gellately, *Gestapo*, 62-63.

154. A variation on this theme was provided by cases in which Jews became the victims of "sexual vendettas." In Frankfurt, a wife reported her husband for helping Jews who had gone into hiding, after discovering his liaison with a girl. See Meldung des Parteigenossen Friedrich Schneiders, 23 April 1935, in Personalakten Richard Jakobs, 17/141, Stadtarchiv Frankfurt; Aktennotiz betrifft des Juden Westheimers, Frankfurt, 16 August 1937, in Diamant, *Gestapo*, 383; Denunzierung eines Polizei Oberwachtmeisters, weil seine Frau als Putzfrau im jüdischen Gemeindehaus und in der Synagoge arbeitet, 1936, Personalakten 110/298, Stadtarchiv Frankfurt; Eyewitness Account File P III d/192, Wiener Library; and for additional material on the latter, Richard Grunberger, *The Twelve-Year Reich: A Social History of Nazi Germany* (rpt. New York, 1995), 113; interview with Schnabel.

155. Denunziation einer Familie in Eschwege an die Zeitung Der Stürmer wegen angeblicher geschäftlicher Beziehung zu Juden (1938), Johann Stephan (Absender) an die Zeitung Der Stürmer, 8 November 1938, Der Stürmer an Ortsgruppe Eschwege, 14 November 1938, Abteilung 483/4960; Denunzierung eines SA Mannes (Limburg) wegen Einkaufs bei einer jüdischen Firma (1933), Abteilung 483/4530e; Denunziation des Pfarrers Noll (Battenfeld) wegen Stellungsnahme zugunsten der Juden in einer Predigt (1936), Schneider von Ortsgruppe Berghofen an die Kreisleitung der NSDAP in Frankenberg, 12 September 1936, Abteilung 483/5006, all in Hessisches Hauptstaatsarchiv Wiesbaden; Denunziation eines Opernsängers, weil er angeblich Jude ist, durch einen Pfarrer (1933), Personalakten 10/175; Denunziation einer jüdischen Arztin (Hospitanten an der Universitäts-

Augenklinik) durch eine Krankenschwester (1935), Personalakten 52/576, both in Stadtarchiv Frankfurt.

156. Gellately, *Gestapo*, 171; Robinsohn, *Justiz als politische Verfolgung: Rechtsprechung in "Rassenschandefällen" beim Landgericht Hamburg* (Stuttgart, 1977), 78. Diamant, *Gestapo*, 27; Grunberger, *Twelve-Year Reich*, 108.

157. Some Gentiles endorsed antisemitism but occasionally criticized its application as suggested by Gestapo reports from Cologne, Koblenz, Königsberg, and Kösslin, analyzed by Bankier. See Gestapo Köln, Report May 1935, R 58/480, and RP Koblenz, Report August–September 1935, R 18/1565, Bundesarchiv, Koblenz; Gestapo Koenigsberg, Report July 1935, REP/ 90 P, and Gestapo Kösslin, Report August 1935, REP/ 90 P, Geheimes Staatsarchiv, Berlin; Bankier, *Germans and the Final Solution*, 74-75. See also Gordon, *Hitler, Germans, and the Jewish Question*, 206-7.

Chapter 7

1. Schreiben des Kreisleiters der NSDAP an den Oberbürgermeister Frankfurt am Main, 27 July 1938; Burleigh and Wippermann, *Racial State*, 83, 326.

2. Niederschrift des Sportamtes über die Besprechung beim Oberbürgermeister, Frankfurt, 2 November 1938, Document VII 34, in *DGF*, 368.

3. Charged with the task of facilitating migration from Austria was a little-known *Untersturmführer*, Adolf Eichmann. Eichmann forced more than fifty thousand Jews to leave within six months. See Leni Yahil, *The Holocaust: The Fate of European Jewry* (New York, 1990), 109.

4. For an understanding of how various nations declined to admit more than a minimal number of Jews, see Arthur Morse, *While Six Million Died: A Chronicle of American Apathy* (New York, 1967); Henry Feingold, *The Politics of Rescue* (New Brunswick, N.J., 1971); David Wyman, *Paper Walls* (Amherst, Mass., 1968); Wyman, *The Abandonment of the Jews* (New York, 1984); Saul Friedman, *No Haven for the Oppressed* (Detroit, 1973); Monty Penkower, *The Jews Were Expendable* (Urbana, 1983); Bernard Wasserstein, *Britain and the Jews of Europe, 1935-1945* (London, 1979).

5. Schleunes, *Twisted Road*, 229-40.

6. Hitler regarded Munich as a disappointment, believing Chamberlain to have stolen the limelight and imposed his solutions (D.C. Watt, *How War Came* [New York, 1989], 30-40).

7. Sybil Milton, "The Expulsion of Polish Jews from Germany, October 1938 to July 1939," *Leo Baeck Institute Yearbook* 29 (1984): 169-200; Rita Thälmann and Emmanuel Feinermann, *Crystal Night, 9-10 November 1938* (New York, 1972), 56-89; Herbert Schultheis, *Die Reichskristallnacht in Deutschland* (Bad Neustadt, 1985); 32; Schleunes, *Twisted Road*, 236-42. See also Uwe Dietrich Adam, "How Spontaneous Was the Pogrom?" in Walter Pehle, *November 1938: From Kristallnacht to Genocide* (Oxford, 1991), 73-94.

8. Some of the Hessian towns in which pogroms occurred on the

night of 7/8 November were Felsberg, Grebenstein, Wiztenhausen, Rotenberg a.d. Fulda, Guxhagen, Hoof, Borken, Melsungen, and Hersfeld, and Mittelhessen, Kirchhain, Neustadt, and Wachenbuchen near Hanau. That some of the first pogroms occurred in Kassel was significant because several influential Nazi administrative offices were located there, among them the *Ober* and *Regierungspräsident* of Hessen-Nassau, the *Gauleitung* of Kurhessen, the SS-Division XXX, and an SD-Division. More salient was the fact that nearly all of the documents of Hessian *Ortsgruppenleiter*, mayors, and SA and SS commandos asserted that ordinary citizens were responsible for the pogroms. The exception to this half-truth was a communique from the mayor of Bad Schwalbach which implicated an SA-Rollkommando in the destruction of the Jewish synagogue. See "Der Chef der Sicherheitspolizei Heydrich an Reichsminister Lammers: Bericht über die Ausschreitungen in Kassel am 7. und 8. November 1938," and Hessisches Hauptstaatsarchiv Wiesbaden, Abteilung 418, Nr. 1564, all in Wolf-Arno Kropat, *Kristallnacht in Hessen: Der Judenpogrom vom November 1938; Eine Dokumentation* (Wiesbaden, 1988), 24, 26, 27, 31, 71, 197-201, 271.

9. In the case of the Fulda synagogue, SS *Sturmbannführer* Grüner maintained that the order to set the synagogue ablaze had come from the SS-*Standarte* in Giessen (Aus dem Urteil des Landgerichts Marburg vom 16 September 1952, Abteilung 274 Acc. 1984/19 Marburg Nr. 26 and 125, Staatsarchiv Marburg).

10. Abteilung 274, Acc. 1983/86, Nr. 111, 194, Aus dem Urteil des Landgerichts Hanau vom 20 November 1948, and Schreiben des SA Brigade-führer Solbrig an alle Kreisleiter, Kassel, 9 November 1938, Staatsarchiv Marburg.

11. In January 1938, Frankfurt University became the first German institution of higher learning to annul all professorships to Jews (Bericht der Sopade, [A] III: Der Terror gegen die Juden, 5 February 1938, in *Sopade*, 187).

12. Heuberger, *Hinaus aus dem Ghetto*, 178.

13. Aus dem Urteil des Landgerichts Frankfurt am Main, 23 April 1953, and Verlautbarung des Nationalsozialistischen Gaudienstes Hessen-Nassau, 10 November 1938, *Frankfurter Zeitung*, 11 November 1938, all in Kropat, *Kristallnacht*, 86-88, 272; Anthony Read and David Fisher, *Kristallnacht: The Nazi Night of Terror* (New York, 1989), 93-94; *Die Synagogen brennen . . .* (Frankfurt, 1988); Thomas Hoffmann, *Pogrommnacht und Holocaust: Frankfurt am Main, Weimar, und Buchenwald* (Weimar, 1994), 47.

14. Deutschland-Berichte der Sopade, AII: Der Terror gegen die Juden, November 1938, in *Sopade*, 1190. The caretaker of the West End synagogue tried in vain to protect it from a group of SA men by refusing to open its main gates. Of the twenty-three synagogues and chapels in Frankfurt destroyed on Kristallnacht, however, the West End synagogue was the only one to be rebuilt after the war (Paul Arnsberg, *Bilder aus dem jüdischen Leben im alten Frankfurt* [Frankfurt, 1970], 260).

15. Even "Aryanized" businesses were not exempt from attack. A perfumery that had been "Aryanized" only the night before and that was 75 percent American-owned was demolished.

16. Heuberger, *Hinaus aus dem Ghetto*, 180.

17. According to records from the Giessen City Archives, the IG had over forty thousand marks worth of property insured by two agencies, but it was never reimbursed (Akten Nrs. 197, 198, 1239, Stadtarchiv Giessen; Heyne, "Judenverfolgung," 92).

18. Interview with Erich Deeg, 2 September 1979, Akten bei Dr. Erwin Knauss, Dieter Trautwein, "Als die Kirche der Väter brannte," all ibid., 91.

19. A discrepancy exists in the description of the Steinstrasse synagogue fire. The *Giessener Anzeiger* maintained that the blaze began at ten o'clock, while the *Oberhessische Tageszeitung* listed the time as eleven (*Giessener Anzeiger*, 11 November 1938; *Oberhessische Tageszeitung*, 11 November 1938; Heyne, "Judenverfolgung," 91).

20. In Rüdesheim, SA men and mob onlookers were particularly violent, and the synagogue was burned to the ground ("Zuschauer begafften endgültige Zerstörung der Synagoge: Rüdesheimer löschten Feuer im Jüdischen Betthaus/Polizei erstattet Anzeige gegen Brandstifter der "Reichskristallnacht," *Wiesbadener Kurier*, 9 November 1988, 4).

21. Interviews with Horst Dickel, Elisabeth Will, and Bernharde Wilhelmy; "Gejohle der Menge: Aktion gegen Geisenheimer Juden," *Wiesbadener Kurier* 9 November 1988, 4; Kropat, *Kristallnacht*, 68, 272; Abteilung 468, Nr. 264, Hessisches Hauptstaatsarchiv, Wiesbaden.

22. Kershaw, *Popular Opinion*, 231-38; 242-46; 258-59; Gordon, *Hitler, Germans, and the Jewish Question*, 207, 216; Bankier, *Germans and the Final Solution*, 85-88.

23. Otto Dov Kulka and Aron Rodrigue, "The German Population and the Jews in the Third Reich: Recent Publication and Trends in Research on German Society and the 'Jewish Question,'" *Yad Vashem Studies* 16 (1984): 428.

24. Jahresbericht des Sicherheitsdienstes, 1938, 63, 64, R58/1094, Bundesarchiv, Koblenz.

25. Hilfrich, as cited by Klaus Schatz, *Geschichte des Bistums Limburg* (Mainz, 1983), 278; and in Wippermann, *Widerstand*, 71.

26. Georg Salzberger, "Erlebnischbericht," 10, Jüdisches Museum Frankfurt, Oppenheimer, "A Few Days of My Life," 20, Oppenheimer, "Erinnerungen an den Novemberpogrom in Frankfurt am Main," in Kropat, *Kristallnacht*, 221-22.

27. Elizabeth Bamberger, "Die Geschichte und Erlebnis," 40; Levy, "Mein Leben," 43; Artur Lauinger, "Erinnerungen," S1/48/Rep. 573/Nr. 18, 5, Stadtarchiv Frankfurt; interview with Leo and Settie S., in Friedman, *Amcha*, 46-47.

28. Valentin Senger provided one of the few kinder evaluations, main-

taining that the people of Frankfurt adopted a wait-and-see attitude toward the pogrom rather than one of frenzied support. But he took a more critical stance against city authorities (Valentin Senger, *Kaiserhofstrasse* 12 [Darmstadt, 1978], 111-16; "Kaiserhofstrasse: Synagogen wurden zerstört. Feuerwehr griff nicht ein," *Frankfurter Rundschau,* 9 November 1978). For additional assessments, see Max Oppenheimer, "Die Generalprobe: Die organisierte Spontaneität," *Diskussionsbeiträge: Aus dem jüdischen Lehrhaus in Frankfurt* (Frankfurt, 1986), 76-87; Wilfried Ehrlich, "Wir dachten, der Spuk könne nicht lange dauern," *Frankfurter Allgemeine Zeitung,* 5 November 1988; Henry Jaeger, "Die Nacht des befohlenen Terrors: Vor 25 Jahren brannten die Synagogen," *Frankfurter Rundschau,* 9 November 1963; Claudia Michels, "Und dennoch war die gesamte Grausamkeit nicht zu erfassen," *Frankfurter Rundschau,* 8 November 1988; Heinrich Wassernmenn, "Vor vierzig Jahren brannten die Synagogen," *Frankfurter Allgemeine Zeitung,* 4 November 1978; Andreas Werner, "Sie hiessen Blumenthal, Levy, und Lippmann," *Frankfurter Rundschau,* 1 November 1988.

29. Nachlass Kurt Blaum, S1/38/Nr. 9, 1, Stadtarchiv Frankfurt, Sydney Baumann, "Eyewitness Under God," 3-4, Leo Baeck Institute, ME 709; Georg Salzberger, *Leben und Lehre* (Frankfurt, 1982), 115; Lauinger, "Erinnerungen," 1-2; Josef Berolzheimer, "KZ-Experiences," Leo Baeck Institute, ME 54; Hans Berger, "Remembrances of Kristallnacht and My Experiences in the Concentration Camp Buchenwald, " in Richarz, *Jewish Life in Germany,* 389. See also "Israel and Sarah," in Friedman, *Amcha,* 63; Diamant, *Gestapo,* 130.

30. Accounts of events in Bad Nauheim also suggest that the popularity of Kristallnacht was low. Reports for Friedberg, by contrast, point to extensive popular involvement in the violence. See Siegfried Oppenheim, "Meine Erlebnisse am 10. November 1938, und mein Aufenthalt in Buchenwald bis zu meiner Rückkehr am 14. Dezember 1938 nach Bad Nauheim," and Bericht Maenni Seligmann, Stadtarchiv Giessen. See also Heyne, "Judenverfolgung," 94.

31. Protokoll des Gespräches mit Auguste Wagner, 20 October 1982, in Heyne, "Judenverfolgung," 181; interview with Frau Dora Scheuer, 15 October 1982, ibid., 196; interview mit Erich Deeg zur "Reichskristallnacht" in Giessen, Document M2b, in *Faschismus in der Provinz,* 19.

32. That did not mean that no Jew received help. It meant only that there was no record of an arrest of anyone for aiding Jews. In addition, the passage cited here referred only to assistance of Jewish families. See Klaus Mortiz and Ernst Noam, *NS-Verbrechen vor Gericht, 1945-1955: Dokumente aus hessischen Justizakten* (Wiesbaden, 1978), 6; Heyne, "Judenverfolgung," 91; interview with Harth. Betty and Jenny Student also suffered harassment and arrest (Betty and Jenny Student, 2, Wiener Library Testimony, O2-683).

33. This information comes admittedly secondhand, from letter from Alfredo Strauss to Jonathan Friedman, São Paulo, 22 December 1993.

34. This sentiment was held by Killian, Wilhelmy, and Freimuth.

35. Thälmann and Feinermann, *Crystal Night*, 89-117; Schleunes, *Twisted Road*, 248-51.

36. Alf Krüger, *Die Lösung der Judenfrage in der deutschen Wirtschaft: Kommentare zur Judengesetzgebung* (Berlin, 1940), 44; Schleunes, *Twisted Road*, 221.

37. Nora Levin, *The Holocaust: The Destruction of European Jewry, 1933-1945* (New York, 1968), 185. Otto Dov Kulka and Esriel Hildesheimer, "The Central Organization of German Jews in the Third Reich and Its Archives." *Leo Baeck Institute Yearbook* 34 (1989): 194-95.

38. Bekanntmachung zur Durchführung des Gesetzes über Mietverhältnisse mit Juden, Frankfurt, 30 January 1939, Document V20B, in *DGF,* 236.

39. Bericht der Sopade, 5 February 1938, [A] III: Der Terror gegen die Juden, in *Sopade*, 178.

40. Vorlage des Oberbürgermeisters an die Gemeinderäte, 30 March 1939, Entwurf des Bauamtes, Liegenschaftsverwaltung, Document VI 8, in *DGF,* 258-62; Vertrag der Stadt Frankfurt am Main mit der Jüdischen Gemeinde, 3 April 1939, Document VI 9, in *DGF,* 262-75. The Gestapo forced the merger of the IG and IRG on 1 April 1939. Additional contracts with Frankfurt's Jewish community were drawn up on 30 November 1942 and 6 April 1943.

41. Interview with Leo and Settie S., in Friedman, *Amcha*, 47. Documentary information regarding the problem of the Jewish cemeteries can be found in *DGF,* 281-92.

42. Frankfurt Zuzug und Abwanderung der Juden von Januar 1936 bis September 1939, Zusammengestellt nach den Monatsberichten des Polizeipräsidenten an den Oberbürgermeister, Document IX 20, in *DGF,* 418-19.

43. Interview with Leo and Settie S., in Friedman, *Amcha*, 48-49.

44. "Verzeichnis der Liegenschaften, die in jüdischem Eigentum standen, 1946/49, Rückerstattung jüdischen Vermögens," Schreiben des Office of Military Government for Giessen 10 November 1945 an den Oberbürgermeister, Akten Nr. 3045, Stadtarchiv Giessen; Documents 35 and 36, in Heyne, "Judenverfolgung," 99-103, 254-58.

45. *75 Jahre Rheingaukreis*, 196.

46. "Geisenheim: Rassische Verfolgung und Euthanasie," in *Studienkreis zur Erforschung und Vermittlung der Geschichte des Widerstandes, 1933-1945, Heimatgeschichtlicher Wegweiser zur Statten des Widerstandes und der Verfolgung* (Cologne, 1984), 98.

47. Lucy Dawidowicz maintained that Hitler never really considered Madagascar a viable option. Richard Breitman has argued, however, that until the planning for the invasion of Russia, the Madagascar proposal had backers in Hitler, Himmler, and officials in the foreign ministry. Raul Hilberg and Nora Levin have suggested that the plan remained a serious option until 1941-42. See Lucy Dawidowicz, *The War Against the Jews, 1933-1945* (New York, 1975),

118-19; Raul Hilberg, *The Destruction of the European Jews* (1961; reprint, New York, 1985), 160-61, Levin, *Holocaust*, 200-203, and her citation of H. Picker, ed., *Hitlers Tischgespräche* (Bonn, 1951), 311; Richard Breitman, *The Architect of Genocide: Himmler and the Final Solution* (New York, 1991), 95-140.

48. Unlike the second period of deportation, which began in October 1941, Jews were sent neither to closed ghettos nor to extermination camps. The Nazis simply assigned deportees to Poland a residence in existing Jewish communities in the region between the Vistula and Bug Rivers, a move unpopular with both local officials charged with absorbing the deportees and with the Reichsvereinigung, which brought foreign pressure to bear. The deportations were halted in response to mounting domestic and foreign criticism. See Yahil, *Holocaust*, 234; Gerald Reitlinger, *The Final Solution: The Attempt to Exterminate the Jews of Europe* (New York, 1961), 40.

49. Unemployed Jews were put to work on construction and reclamation projects, while destitute Jews, ineligible for public relief, were pushed into hard labor. By November 1940, more than fifty thousand German and Austrian Jews (as well as two hundred thousand shipped to Germany from the occupied territories) had been drafted into the German labor service where they worked at bridge building, hewing wood, and laboring in vital industries. When Germany declared war against Russia on 22 June 1941, the demand for labor became more acute. As the Einsatzgruppen began their killing sweep of Soviet Jews, a decree in Germany ordered the closing of Jewish schools for boys over age twelve and conscripted them for work in munitions factories. Until the fall of 1941, the Nazis continued to rely on Jewish slave labor as a means of manpower. See Levin, *Holocaust*, 185-88.

50. Of course, this too is a subject of debate. Lucy Dawidowicz, Gerald Fleming, and Eberhard Jäckel—the so-called Intentionalists—believe that Hitler wanted to kill the Jews from the very beginning of the war. Jäckel even traces Hitler's desire to exterminate European Jewry back to *Mein Kampf.* Helmut Krausnick argues that the decision to liquidate Jews came during the planning of Operation Barbarossa, Germany's code name for the Russian attack. Raul Hilberg and Christopher Browning see that decision coming in July 1941, whereas Uwe Dietrich Adam, Martin Broszat, and Arno Mayer insist that the Final Solution was a product of the realization that the war against Russia was lost. By their account, after conceding the military struggle against the Soviet Union, the Nazis concentrated on winning the "race" war against Jews. Richard Breitman points to correspondence from Himmler's office to an obscure SS officer named Künsberg in January and February 1941, which discussed the Einsatzgruppen, as evidence of an early date for the Nazis' decision to pursue a policy of genocide. See Dawidowicz, *War Against the Jews;* Gerald Fleming, *Hitler and the Final Solution* (Berkeley, 1984); Jäckel, *Hitler's Weltanschauung;* Helmut Krausnick and Martin Broszat, *Anatomy of the SS State* (London, 1968); Hilberg, *Destruction of the European Jews;* Breitman, *Architect of Genocide,* 148; Künsberg Aufzeichnungen, 4 February 1941 and 10 February

1941, RG 238. T-1139/R 52/1100-101, Picot to Künsberg, 10 February 1941, RG 238, M-946/R 1/113, National Archives, College Park, Md.; Christopher Browning, *The Final Solution and the German Foreign Office: A Study of Referat DIII of Abteilung Deutschland* (New York, 1978); Adam, *Judenpolitik im Dritten Reich;* Martin Broszat, "Hitler and the Genesis of the Final Solution: An Assessment of David Irving's Thesis," *Yad Vashem Studies* 13 (1979): 73-125; Arno Mayer, *Why Did the Heavens Not Darken?* (Princeton, 1989).

51. Arrests for "Jewish-friendly behavior" between 1940 and 1944 were down from their peak in 1938-39, but they remained higher than *Rassenschande* incarcerations. In Sarah Gordon's sample of Düsseldorf police cases, she found that the proportion of *Judenfreunde* fell from 41.1 percent in 1938 to 30.2 percent between 1940 and 1944. The percentage of *Rassenschänder,* meanwhile, fell from 35 percent in 1938 to 25.4 percent between 1940 and 1944 (Gordon, *Hitler, Germans, and the Jewish Question,* 216).

52. Salzberger, "Autobiographische Skizze," 8, Leo Baeck Institute, ME 542.

53. The Institute for Research into the Jewish Question also opened in Frankfurt during this period. See Referat Deutschland—Inland II A/B, Fach 79, Paket 43, Az. 83-21, Sdh., VII, Bd. 1, 1941, Bs. 2, 1941-44, Politisches Archiv des Auswärtigen Amtes, Bonn; Staatspolizeistelle Frankfurt am Main, an die Landräte des Bezirks, 21 September 1939, Document XII 3, in *DGF,* 433; Die Geheime Staatspolizei, Staatspolizeistelle Frankfurt am Main an den Oberbürgermeister, 8 January 1940, Document XII 11C, in *DGF,* 444.

54. Bamberger, "Die Geschichte und Erlebnis," 57-62.

55. The "unbelievable situation" to which this memo refers is not the plight of the Jews but rather their thievery. See Schreiben des Kreisleiters (Maintaunus-Obertaunus) an den Landrat in Frankfurt-Höchst, 8 October 1941, Document XII 14, in *DGF,* 449.

56. Frankfurt Zuzug und Abwanderung der Juden von 1 Oktober 1939 bis 30 September 1944, Zusammengestellt nach den Halbjahresberichten des Polizeipräsidenten an den Oberbürgermeister, Document IX 21, in *DGF,* 420.

57. *Statistik des Deutschen Reiches: Die Bevölkerung des Deutschen Reiches nach den Ergebnissen der Volkszählung 1939,* 4:32.

58. Heyne, "Judenverfolgung," 112, 120.

59. An example of Gentiles who secretly bought groceries for Jewish friends were the Christs. Only they, however, could confirm that they actually helped Jews (interview with Mr. and Mrs. Christ, 29 December 1982, ibid., 120-21).

60. See interview with Gusti Wagner, Giessen, 20 January 1983, ibid., 119; Schreiben der Frau Rudolph an das Amtsgericht Giessen, 6 November 1940, Frau A.S. an den Oberbürgermeister, Giessen, 26 November 1940, Beschluss des Amtsgerichts, 19 March 1941, Schreiben der Gestapo Frankfurt am Main an den Oberbürgermeister, Giessen, 21 January 1942, all in Akten 1526, Stadarchiv Giessen; Heyne, "Judenverfolgung," 133-34.

61. The story is recounted in Heyne, "Judenverfolgung," 119.

62. *International Military Tribunal* (Nuremberg, 1947) 26, PS 710: 266.

63. In total, the *Einsatzgruppen* numbered twenty-seven hundred men, many of whom came from disparate occupations and social classes (Breitman, *Architect of Genocide*, 67).

64. Paragraph 3 of the provision said that Jews living in mixed marriages that produced no children and Jewish women in childless marriages did not need to wear the yellow star and could leave their homes without prior permission. See SD Bericht: Verwaltung und Recht: Zur Auswirkung der Polizeiverordnung über die Kennzeichnung der Juden 1 September 1941, Report Nr. 256, February 1942, in Heinz Boberach, *Meldungen aus dem Reich: Auswahl aus den geheimen Lageberichten, 1939-1944* (Berlin, 1965), 221.

65. According to Michael Phayer, the response of the Catholic church to the badge was disappointing. Even worse was the sentiment of Cardinal Adolf Bertram of Breslau, who said in a letter to a group of bishops that Jewish concerns would have to sacrificed to the other, more pressing interests of the NSDAP. See SD Bericht: Versuche der Kirchen, die judengegnerische Haltung der Bevölkerung durch die konfessionelle Gegenarbeit zu untergraben, Report Nr. 240, 24 November 1941, in Boberach, *Meldungen*, 195-96, Bertram to German bishops, Breslau, 17 September 1941, as cited in Michael Phayer, *Protestant and Catholic Women in Nazi Germany* (Detroit, 1990), 210-11, 271.

66. Landgericht Frankfurt 1950, in *Justiz und NS-Verbrechen: Sammlung deutscher Strafurteile wegen nationalsozialistischer Tötungsverbrechen* (Amsterdam, 1968), 407-8; Henry Friedländer, "The Deportation of the Ger-man Jews: Postwar German Trials of Nazi Criminals," *Leo Baeck Institute Year-book* 29 (1984): 224.

67. A less tragic end befell Helene Hammerschlag, even though she too was denounced for not wearing a yellow star. Toni Rudolph endured harassment from Gentile neighbors as well, until she moved out of her apartment. See interview with Gusti Wagner, Giessen, 20 January 1983, in Heyne, "Judenverfolgung," 119; Schreiben der Frau Rudolph an das Amtsgericht Giessen, 6 November 1940, Frau A.S. an den Oberbürgermeister, Giessen, 26 November 1940, Beschluss des Amtsgerichts, 19 March 1941, Schreiben der Gestapo Frankfurt am Main an den Oberbürgermeister, Giessen, 21 January 1942, all in Akten 1526, Stadtarchiv Giessen; Heyne, "Judenverfolgung," 133-34.

68. K. Scheurenberg, *Ich will Leben: Ein autobiographischer Bericht* (Berlin, 1982), 78-81; E. Bukofzer, *Laws for Jews and Persecution of Jews Under the Nazis* (Berlin, 1946), 11; "Recollections of Leo Baeck," in Erich Boehm, *We Survived: The Stories of Fourteen of the Hidden and Hunted of Nazi Germany* (New Haven, 1949); 288; "Memoirs of Jacob Jacobsen," in Richarz, *Jüdisches Leben*, 402; Inge Deutschkron, *Ich trug den gelben Stern* (Cologne, 1978), 85-88; Bankier, *Germans and the Final Solution*, 124-25, 182.

69. *Irgun Olej Merkaz Europa: Die letzten Tage der deutschen Judentums*

(Tel Aviv, 1943), 33, as cited in Bankier, *Germans and the Final Solution*, 182.

70. This was the second deportation of Jews from Vienna in 1941, following a roundup in February. In addition, there was a transport of about five hundred Jews from Luxembourg and five thousand Gypsies. Friedrich Übelhör, the governor of Lodz, opposed a large influx of Jews, and the initial number of planned deportees was reduced from sixty thousand to twenty thousand.

71. Brubaker, *Citizenship and Nationhood*, 167.

72. Landgericht Frankfurt 1950 in *Justiz und NS-Verbrechen*, 431, 397; Friedländer, "Deportation of German Jews," 225.

73. Lina Katz, "Deportationen 1941 und 1942: Geschrieben 1961," Document XIV 1, in *Spuren des Faschismus in Frankfurt: Das Alltagsleben in Frankfurt am Main, 1933-1945* (Frankfurt, 1988), 91. See also Adolf Diamant, "Stummes Spalier am Strassenrand: Deportation vor 50 Jahren," *Allgemeine Jüdische Wochenzeitung*, 24 October 1991.

74. Der Führer des Sturmbannes IV/63 an die SA-Standarte 63, 21 October 1941, Document XIV 2, in *Spuren*, 94.

75. Dr. Antonius Hilfrich, Bischof von Limburg, an Bischof Wienken, Berlin, 27 October 1941, Document XIV 4, ibid., 91.

76. In Berlin as well, all evacuees under the age of sixty made their way from the synagogue to the railway station on foot. See Bankier, *Germans and the Final Solution*, 131; Katz, in *Spuren*, 91; Akten 3042 and 3094; Stadtarchiv Giessen; Bericht von Dr. Scheuer und Frau, in Knauss, *Die jüdische Bevölkerung Giessens*, 82; Bericht von Walter Deeg, Document M9, in *Faschismus in der Provinz*, 45; Heyne, "Judenverfolgung," 143.

77. British Embassy in Washington to Foreign Office, 24 July 1942, Public Record Office, FO 371/30400, as cited in Bankier, *Germans and the Final Solution*, 108, 178.

78. Many Germans simply discounted Hitler's 30 January 1939 speech to parliament, which prophesied the annihilation of European Jewry. To date it is not known whether the general German public had knowledge of Hitler's telegram to Italian monarch Victor Emmanuel and Mussolini, dated 30 January 1942, and his proclamation read in absentia at a Nazi Party anniversary celebration in Munich on 24 February 1943, both of which made reference to the extermination of Jews. Himmler mentioned the killing of Jews on 4 October 1943, but his audience was limited to the SS. See Hitler Telegram of 30 January 1942, in Max Domarus, *Hitler: Reden und Proklamationen, 1932-1945* (Wiesbaden, 1973), 1828-29; Proclamation written by Hitler, delivered at the Parteigründungsfeier in Munich, 24 February 1943, ibid., 1990-93; and Document PS-1919, *International Military Tribunal*, 29, (Nuremberg, 1947): pp., 110-73.

79. Osthofen closed in November 1933. Other early camps in Hessen included Breitenau in Guxhagen, operational from April 1933 to March 1934. Whether there was press coverage of this camp, I do not know. See *Giessener Anzeiger*, 6 May 1933; Document M13, in *Faschismus in der Provinz*, 57;

International Tracing Service, *Verzeichnis der Haftstätten unter Reichsführer SS, 1933-1945* (Arolsen, 1979).

80. It is unclear whether the handful of town residents who knew of the camp also knew that its female inmates were KZ prisoners. Charges against the Krupp works for exploitation of slave labor were dropped once internees testified that they had not been maltreated. See *International Military Tribunal* 9 (1950): 4422; Schriftsatz der Verteidigung über Einsatz und Behandlung von Arbeitskräften in Geisenheim, June 1948, Document I, and Historisches Archiv, Fa.Krupp GmbH Essen, WA 40/681, both in *Hessen hinter Stacheldraht: Verdrängt und Vergessen: KZs, Lager, Aussenkommandos* (Frankfurt, 1984), 37, 50-55, 60; Hungarian letter from 1945, Yad Vashem, O15-2627; interview with Killian.

81. Howard Smith, *The Last Train from Berlin* (New York, 1943), 202; Bankier, *Germans and the Final Solution*, 137. See also Konrad Kwiet, "The Ultimate Refuge—Suicide in the Jewish Community Under the Nazis," *Leo Baeck Institute Yearbook* 29 (1984): 135-68.

82. Übersicht über die Transporte, die von Frankfurt am Main aus abgingen, 1941-1944, Nach den Listen der Gestapo Frankfurt am Main, ergänzt aus den Akten des Polizeipräsidenten, in *Spuren*, 95.

83. Schreiben des Bischofs von Limburg, Hilfrich, an den Reichsminister der Justiz, 13 August 1941, in Johann Neuhausler, *Kreuz und Hakenkreuz: Der Kampf des Nationalsozialismus gegen die katholische Kirche und der katholische Widerstand* (Munich, 1946,) 363. See also Robert Jay Lifton, *The Nazi Doctors: Medical Killing and the Psychology of Genocide* (New York, 1986).

84. Hearing of the gassing of Jews and actually believing that it could occur were two very different things, however, according to Hans Mommsen in "What Did Germans Know of the Genocide of the Jews," in Pehle, *November 1938*, 187-221.

85. Public Record Office, FO 371/30400; Bankier, *Germans and the Final Solution*, 111, 179. *Life* magazine's publication of photos of the Warsaw ghetto in February 1942 leaves little doubt that most Americans must have known something of Nazi atrocities (*Life*, 23 February 1942, 26-27).

86. British Legation, Bern, to Foreign Office, 17 September 1941, Public Record Office, 371/26513; Bankier, *Germans and the Final Solution*, 111, 179.

87. Lili Hahn, . . . *bis alles in Scherben fällt. Tagebuchblätter* (Cologne, 1979), entry for 30 November 1941; Bankier, *Germans and the Final Solution*, 111. These were in fact not tunnels but long gas vans.

88. Lisbon Legation to PID London, 1 April 1942, Public Record Office, FO 371/34429; Lisbon Legation to PID London, 16 June 1943, Public Record Office, FO 371/34431; Bankier, *Germans and the Final Solution*, 111-12, 180.

89. Records show that only 1,016 Jewish residents of the city were

deported to the East that month (Übersicht über die Transporte, die von Frankfurt am Main aus abgingen, 1941-1944, Nach den Listen der Geheimen Staatspolizei Frankfurt, ergänzt aus den Akten des Polizeipräsidenten, Document XIV15, in *Spuren*, 95).

90. Two additional transports, affecting nearly two thousand Jews, followed later that month and in June. All three transports were sent to Lublin with Sobibor as the final destination. Police Battalion 306, which originated in Frankfurt and would have been responsible for executions in Lublin, ended its stay in the city on 18 February 1942, three months before the incoming transport of Jews from Frankfurt. To my knowledge, there were no other Order Police killing units that originated in Frankfurt, thus eliminating the possibility of finding an incident when a victim recognized his or her would-be executioner and received a reprieve. See case 589, "Andere Massenvernichtungsverbrechen: Biala-Podlaska und Umgebung—Distrikt Lublin/Polen," *Justiz und NS-Verbrechen*, 20:822.

91. In all, nearly ten thousand Frankfurt Jews were deported to their deaths between 1941 and 1945 (Document XIV15, in *Spuren*, 95).

92. Arnsberg, *Die Geschichte der Frankfurter Juden*, 3:453.

93. H.G. Adler, *Der verwaltete Mensch* (Tübingen, 1974), 337.

94. Robert Kirschner, trans., *Rabbinic Responsa of the Holocaust Era* (New York, 1985), 54-65; Heuberger, *Hinaus aus dem Ghetto*, 191.

95. Frankfurter Historische Kommission, *Frankfurt am Main*, 487; Arnsberg, *Geschichte der Frankfurter Juden*, 27, 430-31. Landmann died on 5 March 1945 and Sinzheimer on 16 September.

96. Liste der Juden, die deportiert wurden, in Knauss, *Die jüdische Bevölkerung*, 152; Akten 3042, 3094, Stadtarchiv Giessen; Heyne, "Judenverfolgung," 143.

97. *Hedwig Burgheim, oder die Reise nach Giessen: Bericht über das Leben einer Lehrerin* (Giessen, 1981), 28-29.

98. Interview with Dr. Horst Dickel, Geisenheim, 3 October 1993.

99. Interview with Killian.

100. David Luebke, "Nazi Sterilizations: Blacks, Asocials, Sinti, and the 'Genetically Defective,'" (unpublished research brief), 13 August 1990, United States Holocuast Memorial Museum, Washington, D.C.; Case XI, NG 2586-I, and NO 2419 of the Trials of War Criminals before the Nuremberg Military Tribunal, as cited in Reitlinger, *Final Solution*, 174, 558.

101. Interestingly, Cardinal Bertram of Breslau, who had waffled on the issue of the yellow badge, dispatched a strong protest to top Nazi brass against the roundup and efforts to force divorces of intermarried couples. See Bertram to Lammers, Mühs, and Goebbels, Breslau, 3 March 1943; Bertram to Frick, Mühs, Thierack, Lammers, and the RSHA, Breslau, 2 March 1943, as cited in Phayer, *Protestant and Catholic Women*, 212, 271; Kurt Jakob Ball-Kaduri, "Berlin wird Judenfrei: Die Juden in Berlin in den Jahren 1942/43," *Jahrbuch*

für die Geschichte Mittel und Ostdeutschlands 22 (1973): 196-241; Sybil Milton, "The Camera as Weapon: Documentary Photography and the Holocaust," *Simon Wiesenthal Center Annual* 1 (1984): 45-68; Hilberg, *Perpetrators, Victims, Bystanders*, 132.

102. Der Vertrauensmann der Reichsvertretung der Juden in Deutschland, 8 February 1945, Document XIV 13, in *DGF,* 531.

103. Gespräch mit Dora Scheuer, in Heyne, "Judenverfolgung," 151.

104. Bericht vom Ernst Holland, 16 April 1943, as cited by Wippermann, *Judenverfolgung*, 145.

105. One of Mrs. Fraenkel's friends, Eduard Stern, a hairdresser, whose job it had been to cut the hair of the deportees at the collecting center, was on the list to be deported. See Johanna Fraenkel, "Experiences of a 'Mischling' in Franfkurt am Main," 2-4, Wiener Library Testimony, O2-177, Yad Vashem, Jerusalem.

106. Oberbürgermeister Ritter an die Gestapo, Giessen, 16 February 1940, Akten 1301, Akten der Bürgermeisterei Giessen, Stadtarchiv Giessen.

107. Interview with Kurt and Alfred St., 10 December 1982, in Heyne, "Judenverfolgung," 148.

108. Jeremy Noakes, "The Development of Nazi Policy Towards the German-Jewish 'Mischlinge' 1933-1945," *Leo Baeck Institute Yearbook* 34 (1989): 353-54; Ursula Buettner, "The Persecution of Christian-Jewish Families in the Third Reich," *Leo Baeck Institute Yearbook* 34 (1989): 267-90.

109. According to David Gushee, many friendships between Jews and Gentiles were put to the test during the Holocaust. The great majority of those relationships had not, before the war, reached a level of intensity and commitment that would make either party consider risking their lives for the other an obvious moral obligation. The preexisting friendships in these cases provided the initial open hand or open door for limited help. Over time, in those relationships that survived the test, relief evolved into long-term rescue. Other factors that were important for rescue included resource capabilities, opportunity, and personality traits such as adventurousness, social marginality, and social responsibility. According to the Oliners, while 67 percent of rescuers reported having been asked by either a Jew or an intermediary for help, only 25 percent of nonrescuers did. Sarah Gordon discovered that *Judenfreunde* tended to be older, between the ages of forty and fifty-nine. She suggested that the disproportionate representation of older Germans was rooted in the lack of financial and other rescue resources among the younger generation and perhaps in higher levels of antisemitism among the impressionable young. Eva Fogelman discovered a significant group of child rescuers (12 percent under the age of twenty) in her sample. Gordon and Manfred Wolfson found more men than women in their samples, but Frances Henry reported that the opposite was true of her sample, surmising that gender differences occurred because most of the aid given in Sonderburg involved women's work such as the procurement of food. The Oliners concluded that even though occupations and economic status

favored a few rescuers, they were not critical factors influencing the decision to rescue. Finally, Fogelman classified only 12 percent of her sample as people who acted out of an explicit sense of religious duty. See Samuel Oliner, *The Altruistic Personality* (New York, 1988), 93, 125, 129, 134-35, 137, 275, Table 5.1; Gordon, *Hitler, Germans, and the Jewish Question*, 220, 222; Henry, *Victims and Neighbors*, 104; Manfred Wolfson, "Zum Widerstand gegen Hitler: Umriss eines Gruppenportrats deutscher Retter von Juden," *Tradition und Neubeginn: Internationale Forschungen Deutscher Geschichte im 20. Jahrhundert* 26 (1975): 396; Eva Fogelman, "The Rescuers: A Sociopsychological Study of Altruistic Behavior During the Nazi Era" (Ph.D. diss., City University of New York, 1987), 80-81, 132; David Gushee, "Many Paths to Righteousness: An Assessment of Research on Why Righteous Gentiles Helped Jews," *Holocaust and Genocide Studies* 7 (Winter 1993): 372-401.

110. Wippermann, *Widerstand*, 56.

111. Heinrich Baab, "Erinnerungen," 8, Leo Baeck Institute, ME 746.

112. Bericht Franz Neuland, in Barbara Mausbach-Bromberger, *Arbeiterwiderstand in Frankfurt am Main gegen den Faschismus, 1933-1945* (Frankfurt am Main, 1976), 170.

113. Baab, "Erinnerungen," 6-7.

114. Gespräch mit August Wagner, in Heyne, "Judenverfolgung," 181; Meldungen wichtiger staatspolizeilicher Ereignisse, Berlin, 20 February 1942, Document 160, in Heinz Boberach, *Berichte des SD und der Gestapo über Kirchen und Kirchenvolk in Deutschland, 1934-1944* (Mainz, 1971), 620.

115. Bericht von Maria Deeg über den Widerstand in Giessen, Document M11, in *Faschismus in der Provinz*, 55.

116. Gespräch mit August Wagner, 20 October 1982, Interview with Herrn and Frau Otto Christ, Giessen, 29 December 1982, Gesprach mit Frau Dora Scheuer, Giessen, 15 October 1982, in Heyne, "Judenverfolgung," 183, 189, 199, 150.

117. None of the following documents mention anything other than minor difficulties or "frictionless cooperation" (*reibungslose Zusammenarbeit*): Der Führer des Sturmbannes IV 63, in *Spuren*, 94; Schreiben der Gestapo Darmstadt an den Oberbürgermeister Giessen, 8 October 1942, Akten 198, Stadtarchiv Giessen. For additional material on resistance in Frankfurt, see Wiener Library Collection of Testimonies, O-2/293, Central Historical Commission at the Central Committee of Liberated Jews in the U.S. Zone—Munich, M-1/DN-21/1311-89.

118. Dora Scheuer also endured verbal abuse from an official dispensing ration cards who yelled, "Jews remain Jews," and she was eventually sent on the February 1945 transport to Frankfurt and Theresienstadt. See Gespräch mit Dora Scheuer, 15 October 1982, Gespräch mit Walter Deeg, Gespräch mit Alfred und Kurt S., 10 December 1982, and Gespräch mit Heinz Sommerkorn, 27 April 1982, in Heyne, "Judenverfolgung," 138.

119. Georg Edward, "Tagebuch," Document 65, ibid., 289.

120. Facsimile in R.W. Kempner, *Eichmann und Komplizen* (Vienna, 1961), 118-19; and Bankier, *Germans and the Final Solution*, 135, 184.

121. The few church leaders who spoke up against antisemitism, apart from Martin Niemöller and Dietrich Bonhöffer, included Provost Bernard Lichtenberg of St. Hedwig's Cathedral in Berlin and Clemens August Count von Galen. A Protestant resistance group that helped Jews emigrate was Büro Grüber, established by Pastor Heinrich Grüber of Berlin-Kaulsdorf. Gerhard Kittel, professor of New Testament at Tübingen, presents the interesting case of a theologian who held Jews and Judaism in a negative light during the 1920s, supported the Nazis early on, and then went on to oppose the direction of Hitler's Jewish policy. The opposition of Cardinal Bertram of Breslau and Cardinal Faulhaber of Munich was also complex, if not downright inconsistent. Bankier cites isolated incidents of church-sponsored protest in Bremen, Bielefeld, and Minden in 1941. See Edwin Robertson, *The Shame and the Sacrifice: The Life and Martyrdom of Dietrich Bonhoeffer* (New York, 1988); James Bentley, *Martin Niemoeller, 1892-1984* (New York, 1984); Gerhard Kittel, "Judentum und Christentum," in *Religion in Geschichte und Gegenwart* (Tübingen, 1929), 3:491-94; Robert Ericksen, *Theologians Under Hitler: Gerhard Kittel, Paul Althaus, and Emanuel Hirsch* (New Haven, 1985), 36-37; Report of 3 December 1941, from Bremen, SD Hauptaussenstelle Bielefeld, 16 December 1941, SD Aussenstelle Minden, 6 and 12 December 1941, National Archives, Washington, T 175 R 577 F 675; Bankier, *Germans and the Final Solution*, 184. For general resistance see Peter Hoffmann, *German Resistance to Hitler* (Cambridge, Mass., 1988), originally published in German in 1979; Herbert Mason, *To Kill the Devil: The Attempts on the Life of Adolf Hitler* (London, 1979); Michael Balfour, *Withstanding Hitler in Germany, 1933-1945* (London, 1988); Ian Kershaw, "German Popular Opinion and the 'Jewish Question,' 1939-1943: Some Further Reflections," in *The Nazi Holocaust*, Vol. 5, *Public Opinion and Relations to the Jews in Nazi Europe*, ed. Michael Marrus (London, 1989), 182-203; Christof Dipper, "The German Resistance and the Jews," ibid., 204-48; and Michael Geyer and John Boyer, eds., *Resistance Against the Third Reich, 1933-1990* (Chicago, 1994). For church-related resistance, see Phayer, *Protestant and Catholic Women;* Donald Dietrich, *Catholic Citizens in the Third Reich: Psycho-Social Principles and Moral Reasoning* (New Brunswick, N.J., 1988); Shelley Baranowski, *The Confessing Church, Conservative Elites, and the Nazi State* (Lewiston, N.Y., 1986); Saul Friedlander, *Pius XII and the Third Reich: A Documentation* (New York, 1980); Richard Gutteridge, *Open Thy Mouth for the Dumb! The German Evangelical Church and the Jews, 1879-1950* (Oxford, 1976); Ernst Christian Helmreich, *The German Churches Under Hitler: Background, Struggle, and Epilogue* (Detroit, 1979); Peter Matheson, ed., *The Third Reich and the Christian Churches* (Grand Rapids, Mich., 1981); and Klaus Scholder, *The Churches and the Third Reich*, trans. John Bowden (Philadelphia, 1989).

122. Gemeinsamer Hirtenbrief der katholischen Bischöfe, 19 August 1943, in Wippermann, *Widerstand*, 72.

123. See Kershaw, *Popular Opinion*, and his "Normality and Genocide: The Problem of Historicization," in *Reevaluating the Third Reich*, ed. Thomas Childers and Jane Coplan (New York, 1993), 35.

124. Robert Jay Lifton and Eric Markusen, *The Genocidal Mentality: Nazi Holocaust and Nuclear Threat* (New York, 1990), 242.

125. See the conclusion of Goldhagen, *Hitler's Willing Executioners*.

126. Christopher Browning has focused on the incremental path to mass murder and the co-opting of groups in German state and society in the Final Solution and the German Foreign Office, in *Ordinary Men*, and "Bureacracy and Mass Murder," in *The Path to Genocide: Essays on Launching the Final Solution*, ed. Browning (Cambridge, 1992). See also Gordon, *Hitler, Germans, and the Jewish Question*, 48-49.

Epilogue

1. James Neuman, an American school superintendent, served as military governor, and Karl Geiler, a professor of law at Heidelberg University who had been dismissed by the Nazis in 1939, became the unified state's first minister president. Franz Schramm, a former *Oberstudiensekretär* in Geisenheim, went on to become Hessen's minister of education, following the short tenure of Franz Böhm. See James Tent, *Mission on the Rhine: Re-Education and Denazification in American Occupied Germany* (Chicago, 1982), 167-71. See also Franklin Davis, *Come as a Conquerer: The U.S. Army's Occupation of Germany* (New York, 1967); John Gimbel, *The American Occupation of Germany: Politics and the Military, 1945-1949* (Stanford, 1968); Jean E. Smith, ed., *The Papers of General Lucius Clay* (Bloomington, 1974), 103.

2. Office of the Military Government United States, Fragebogen, Frankfurt, RG 260, Dossier 783, National Archives, College Park, Md.

3. Heinrich Müller, overall head of the Gestapo, also disappeared at the end of the war and escaped prosecution. See Vernehmung des Regierungsrats a.D. Reinhard Breder, durch den Oberstaatsanwalt beim Landgericht Frankfurt am Main, 14 October 1968, Document 32 A, and Einstellung des Ermittlungsverfahrens durch Verfügung des Obertstaatsanwalts beim Landgericht Frankfurt am Main, 6 January 1969, in Moritz and Noam, *NS-Verbrechen vor Gericht*, 261, 266; Diamant, *Gestapo*, 299-301.

4. Popular opposition ultimately forced Krebs's resignation from the city council. Meanwhile, Social Democrat and concentration camp internee Walter Kolb became Frankfurt's mayor in 1946 (Frankfurter Historische Kommission, *Frankfurt am Main*, 502).

5. Between 1945 and 1946 340 survivors from concentration camps, mostly Jews, returned to Frankfurt (Rodney Livingstone, "Germans and Jews Since 1945," *Patterns of Prejudice* 29 [1995]: 45).

6. Valentin Senger, *Kurzer Frühling* (Zurich, 1984), 59-60. For other accounts of Frankfurt Jews in the postwar era, some very critical, see Lea Fleischmann, *Dies ist nicht mein Land: Eine Jüdin verlässt die Bundesrepublik* (Hamburg, 1980), and Susann Heenen-Wolf, *Im Haus des Henkers: Gespräche in Deutschland* (Frankfurt, 1992).

7. John Houston Hill to United States Holocaust Memorial Council, 21 February 1981, in the 1981 International Liberators Conference Collection of Liberator Tesitmonies, RG 09.005, United States Holocaust Memorial Museum, Washington, D.C.

8. Office of the Military Government United States, Fragebogen, Giessen, RG 260, Box 138, National Archives.

9. Arnsberg, *Die jüdischen Gemeinden*, 1:260-61. See also *In memoriam Dr. Lucie Jacobi, Oberstudienratin an der Ricarda-Huch-Schule in Giessen, 1947-1952* (Bad Nauheim, 1984).

10. *75 Jahre Rheingaukreis*, 196.

11. Susan Stern, "Jews in Germany," *German Life*, March 1995, 29; Wolf-Arno Kropat, "Die Jüdischen Gemeinden in Hessen nach 1945," in *Neunhundertjahren*, 460-61; Heuberger, *Hinaus aus dem Ghetto*, 195-96; Harry Maor, "Über den Wiederaufbau der jüdischen Gemeinden in Deutschland seit 1945" (Ph.D. diss., University of Mainz, 1961), 16.

12. The right-wing Republican Party, headed by former SS official Franz Schönhüber, won seats on the Frankfurt city council in 1989. See Erwin Scheuch and Ute Scheuch, "The Federal Republic of Germany—Endangered by Right-Wing Extremism? An Assessment of Opinion Polls and Federal Elections" (unpublished paper for Inter-Nationes, 1995), 3; Stern, "Jews in Germany," 26.

13. See Robin Ostow, *Jüdisches Leben in der DDR* (Frankfurt, 1988); H. Eschwege, "Die jüdische Bevölkerung der Jahre nach der Kapitulation Hitlerdeutschlands auf dem Gebiet der DDR bis zum Jahre 1953," in *Juden in der DDR*, ed. Julius Schoeps (Duisburg, 1988); Peter Honigmann, "Über den Umgang mit Juden und jüdischer Geschichte in der DDR," ibid.; and Traverso, *Jews and Germany*, 182.

14. Friedrich Meinecke, *Die deutsche Katastrophe: Betrachtungen und Erinnerungen* (Wiesbaden, 1946). For commentary on Germany's "return to normality" in the 1950s, see Arthur Koestler, *The Trail of the Dinosaurs and Other Essays* (New York, 1955), 218.

15. This was the heyday of the Bielefeld schools, which promoted the now infamous theory of Germany's peculiar modernization, or *Sonderweg*. This trend away from ideology and toward social history, however, gave rise to the so-called functionalists, who have been criticized for minimizing the importance of Hitler and Nazi antisemitism. See Hans Ulrich Wehler, *Entsorgung der deutschen Vergangenheit? Ein polemischer Essay zum 'Historikerstreit'* (Munich, 1988), and Jürgen Kocka, "German History Before Hitler: The Debate about the German Sonderweg," *Journal of Contemporary History* 23 (1988).

16. Ernst Nolte, "The Past That Will Not Pass Away," *Frankfurter Allgemeine Zeitung*, June 1986; Nolte, *Der europäische Bürgerkrieg, 1917-1945: Nationalsozialismus und Bolschiwismus* (Frankfurt, 1987); Michael Wolffsohn, *Ewige Schuld? 40 Jahre deutsch-jüdisch-israelitisch Beziehungen* (Munich, 1988); Andreas Hillgrüber, *Zweierlei Untergang: Die Zerschläge des deutschen Reiches und das Ende des europäischen Judentums* (Berlin, 1986); Jürgen Habermas, "A Kind of Settlement of Damages: The Apologetic Tendencies in German History Writing," Klaus Hildebrand, "The Age of Tyrants: History and Politics: The Administrators of the Enlightenment, the Risk of Scholarship, and the Preservation of a Worldview, a Reply to Jürgen Habermas," and Joachim Fest, "Encumbered Remembrance," in James Knowlton et al., *Forever in the Shadow of Hitler?* (Atlantic Highlands, N.J., 1993).

17. Some important prereunification controversies over the Third Reich and antisemitism included the Jenninger affair and the debate over Rainer Fassbinder's play *Der Müll, die Stadt, und der Tod*. In the former, Philip Jenninger, the president of the Bundestag, was forced to resign after delivering what many considered an apologia for Nazi Germany during a ceremony commemorating the fiftieth anniversary of Kristallnacht in November 1988. Fassibinder's play generated controversy in 1985 because it featured a property speculator referred to only as the "rich Jew." See Michael Schneider, *Die abgetriebene Revolution: Von der Staatsfirma in die DM-Kolonie* (Berlin, 1990), 128; Livingstone, "Germans and Jews Since 1945," 58; Traverso, *Jews and Germany*, 184.

18. For a consideration of Gentile-Jewish relations in textbooks, see Wolfgang Marienfeld, "Die deutsch-jüdische Beziehungsgeschichte von der Aufklärung bis zum zweiten Weltkrieg in der Darstellung, gegenwärtiger Schulgeschichtsbücher der Bundesrepublik Deutschland," *Internationale Schulbuchforschung* 7 (1985): 327-39.

19. Michael Wolfssohn, a conservative historian who regards himself as a "German-Jewish patriot," has also called for the dismantling of the negative image of the Germans in the Jewish community. See Wolffsohn, as cited in Livingstone, "Germans and Jews Since 1945," 59; Hans Mommsen, "The New Historical Consciousness and the Relativizing of National Socialism," in Knowlton et al., *Forever in the Shadow*; Jane Kramer, "The Politics of Memory," *New Yorker*, 15 August 1995, 48-65; Otto Dov Kulka, "Singularity and Its Relativization: Changing Views in German Historiography on National Socialism and the Final Solution," *Yad Vashem Studies* 19 (1988): 151-86; Konrad Jarausch, "Removing the Nazi Stain: The Quarrel of German Historians," *German Studies Review* 9 (1988): 285-302; Richard Evans, In *Hitler's Shadow: West German Historians and the Attempt to Escape from the Nazi Past* (New York, 1989); Charles Maier, *The Unmasterable Past: History, Holocaust, and German National Identity* (Cambridge, Mass., 1988).

20. The Allensbach Opinion Research Institute carried out this poll. Interestingly, its figures did not differ much from estimates made by the occupying forces of the United States after the war and were down from around

33 percent in the 1950s. Office of the Military Government United States Fragebogen, Report 122, pp. 7, 10, Report 49, p. 3, RG 260 350/3-5, National Archives. See also Jack Zipes, "The Vicissitudes of Being Jewish in West Germany," in Anson Rabinbach et al., *Germans and Jews Since the Holocaust: The Changing Situation in West Germany* (New York, 1986); Rabinbach and Zipes, "The Jewish Question and the German Question," *New German Critique* 44 (1988); Gordon, *Hitler, Germans, and the Jewish Question*, 202; Stern, "Jews in Germany," 28.

Conclusion

1. Peukert, *Weimar Republic*, 160-61.
2. Gordon, *Hitler, Germans, and the Jewish Question*, 48.
3. Similar sentiment is echoed in Fein, *Persisting Question*, 84-85.

Bibliography

Archival Material

Berlin Document Center Schumacher Archiv, Folder 240 I
Bundesarchiv, Koblenz
    Gestapo Frankfurt, R 58/1151
    Jahresbericht des Sicherheitsdients, R 58/1094
    NS Akten 26/528-26/533
    Reich Chancellery, R 431/2193L-382281-84
Catholic Parish Office (Katholisches Pfarramt), Geisenheim
    Civilistandsregister der Proclamierten und Copulierten, 1918-33
Central Archives of the Evangelical Church in Hessen (Zentralarchiv der
    evangelischen Kirche Hessen), Darmstadt
    Kirchlich-Statistische Haupttabelle: Tabelle II des
        Kirchenbundesamtes Pfarrerei Giessen—Dekanat
        Giessen, 1930-1932, 17/500
    Konfessionswechsel: Tabellen über Austritte und
        Übertritte zu der evangelischen Landeskirche, 1909-1928,
        Stadtkreis Giessen, 17-470
Evangelical Community Center (Evangelisches Gemeindehaus),
    Geisenheim
        Verzeichnis der Getrauten
Frankfurt Cathedral Archives (Dompfarramt)
    Matrikel—Übertritte und Austritte, Eheschliessungen 1918-1935
Frankfurt City Archives (Stadtarchiv Frankfurt)
    Magistratsakten, R 1376
    Nachlass Kurt Blaum, S1/38 Nr. 9
    Nachlass Johanna Harris, S1/18/20/1960
    Nachlass Artur Lauinger, S1/48/Rep. 573/Nr. 18
    Personalakten Josef Hoffmann, 6/119
    Personalakten Richard Jakobs, 17/141
    Personalakten, Richard Limpert, 74/373
    Personalakten, 10/175, 110/298, 52/576
    Tagebuch Oberbürgermeister Friedrich Krebs, S1/50
Friedrich Ebert Foundation (Friedrich Ebert Stiftung), Bonn
    Emigration Sopade, 63-6
Geisenheim City Archives (Stadtarchiv Geisenheim)
    Einwohnerliste, 123-03

Verzeichnis der abgemeldete Personen, May 1928–April 1942,123-03
Giessen City Archives (Stadtarchiv Giessen)
   Akten der Bürgermeisterei, 82/163, 82/206, 1141, 1151, 1301, 1526,
      2138, 3042, 3094
   Handakten der Stadt Giessen, 2108/03/2 Akten 1426
   Schülerbestand der Oberrealschule, 1914-42, 2602/1 Akten 1569
Hessian Main State Archives (Hessisches Hauptstaatsarchiv),
   Wiesbaden
      Abteilungen 405, 418/1564, 461, 468/264, 483/2630a/P86,
         2630b, 2632, 3307b, 3308a, 3308b, 3319a, 3321, 3322a,
         3322b, 3326a, 4530e, 4685a, 4707c, 4708a, 4728, 4947,
         4959, 4960, 4984, 4986a, 4989a, 4992b, 4994, 499a, 5006
Hessian State Archives (Hessisches Staatsarchiv), Darmstadt
   Abteilung 612/Konv. 23
Hessian State Archives (Hessisches Staatsarchiv), Marburg
   Abteilung 274/Acc. 1984/19, Acc. 1983/86
   Akten 327/2b
Jewish Museum (Jüdisches Museum), Frankfurt am Main
   Georg Salzberger, "Erlebnisbericht"
Leo Baeck Institute, New York
   Erich Ahrens Collection, AR4389 A11/5
   Erich Ahrens, "Franz Rosenzweig," ME 705
   Martin Buber Collection, AR 3866
   Franz Rosenzweig Collection, AR C-1935.5043

Memoirs

Salomon Andorn, ME 8/9
Heinrich Baab, ME 746
Elizabeth Bamberger, ME 387
Sydney Baumann, ME 709
"Before the Storm," ME 37
Josef Berolzheimer, ME 54
Margarete Sallis Freudenthal, ME 550
Heide Hermanns Holde, ME 864
Bertha Katz
Joseph Levy
Friedel Rothschild Lichtenberg, ME 521
Ernst Noam, ME 477
Alice Oppenheimer, ME 482
Nora Rosenthal, ME 532
Hans Salfeld, ME 578
Georg Salzberger, ME 542
Caesar Seligmann, ME 595

Selmar Spier, ME 611
Salomon Spiro, ME 614
National Archives, College Park, Maryland
RG 260, OMGUS Fragebogen
Political Archives of the German Foreign Office, Bonn (Politisches Archiv
des Auswärtigen Amtes)
Referat Deutschland, Inland II A/B, Fach 79, Packet 43
Staatsarchiv Leipzig Collection Polizeipräsident Leipzig V, Folders 4537
and 4538.
United States Holocaust Memorial Museum, Washington, D.C.
RG 09.005, Liberator testimonies
Yad Vashem, Jerusalem
Wiener Library, Eyewitness testimonies, O2/683, O2/177, O2/293

Unpublished Memoir

Erich Neumann, "To Life"

Interviews

Horst Dickel, Geisenheim, 3 October 1993
Margot Freimuth, Geisenheim, 12 September 1993
Fritz Hallgarten, by Horst Dickel, Geisenheim, 1988
Martin Harth, New York City, 10 July 1993
Martin Killian, Geisenheim, 24 September 1993
Florence Newman, New York City, 20 July 1993
Annelise Schnabel, Geisenheim, 9 October 1993
Friedrich Schwank, Geisenheim, 11 October 1993
Bernharde Wilhelmy, Geisenheim, 10 October 1993
Elisabeth and Wilhelm Will, Geisenheim, 15 September 1993

Letters

Mayor's Office to Martin Killian, 1 June 1933
Alfredo Strauss to Jonathan Friedman, São Paulo, 22 December 1993
Gretel Strauss to Jonathan Friedman, San Francisco, 20 December 1993

Newspapers

Akademischer Beobachter
Central-Verein Zeitung
Evangelisches Sonntagsblatt
Frankfurt Israelitisches Gemeindeblatt

Frankfurter Nachrichten
Frankfurter Zeitung
Geisenheim Lokal Anzeiger
Giessener Anzeiger
Der Israelit
Israelitisches Familienblatt
Der Jude
Jüdische Liberale Zeitung
Jüdische Rundschau
Kartel-Convent Blätter
Mitteilungen aus dem Verein zur Abwehr des Antisemitismus
Der Morgen
Oberhessiche Tageszeitung
Rhein-Mainische Volkszeitung
Der Schild
Völkischer Beobachter

Statistical Sources

Beiträgen zur Statistik der Stadt Frankfurt a.m: Tabellarische Übersichten Betreffend den Zivilstand der Stadt. Frankfurt, 1931-37.
Mitteilungen des hessischen Landesstatistischen Amtes. Darmstadt, 1924-33.
Silbergleit, Heinrich. "Die jüdische Wohnbevölkerung am 16. Juni 1925 nach Wirtscahftsabteilungen, -gruppen, und-zweigen sowie nach der Stellung im Beruf." in *Die Bevölkerungs- und Berufsverhältnisse der Juden im deutschen Reich: Freistaat Preussen.* Berlin, 1930.
Statistik des deutschen Reiches. (1925, 1933, 1939 censuses).
Statistische Jahresübersichten der Stadt Frankfurt am Main 1931/32. Frankfurt, 1933.
Statistisches Handbuch der Stadt Frankfurt: Zweite Ausgabe Enthaltend die Statistik der Jahre 1906/07 bis 1926/27. Frankfurt, 1928.
Statistisches Handbuch für Volkstaat Hessen: Dritte Ausgabe. Darmstadt, 1924.
Statistisches Jahrbuch für das deutsche Reich. Berlin, 1919-45.
Troschke, Paul. *Evangelisches Kirchentstatistik Deutschlands: Hefte 2 u. 3.* Berlin, 1929.
Verwaltungsbericht des Oberbürgermeisters der Provinzialhauptstadt Giessen für das Rechnungsjahr 1912. Giessen, 1913.
Verwaltungsblatt des preussischen Landesverbands jüdischer Gemeinden. 9 (1931).
Zeitschrift für Demographie und Statistik der Juden.

Published Primary Sources

Anne aus Frankfurt: Leben und Lebenswelt Anne Frank. Frankfurt, 1990.
Arnsberg, Paul. *Bilder aus dem jüdischen Leben im alten Frankfurt.* Frankfurt, 1970.

————. *Die Geschichte der Frankfurter Juden seit der französischen Revolution*. 3 vols. Darmstadt, 1983.

————. *Die jüdischen Gemeinden in Hessen*. Frankfurt, 1971.

Bembenek, Lothar, et al., eds. *Materialen Zum Unterricht: Sekundärstufe 1, Heft 34: Nationalsozialismus, Unterrichtsvorschläge und Materialen*. Wiesbaden, 1985.

Berger, Trudi. *A Daughter's Gift of Love: A Holocaust Memoir*. Philadelphia, 1992.

Berichte gegen Vergessen und Verdrängen: von 100 Überlebenden jüdischen Schülerinnen und Schülern. Über die NS Zeit in Frankfurt Bonn, 1995.

Boberach, Heinz. *Berichte des SD und der Gestapo Über Kirche und Kirchenvolk in Deutschland, 1934-1944*. Mainz, 1971.

————. *Meldungen aus dem Reich: Auswahl aus den geheimen Lageberichten, 1939-1944*. Berlin, 1965.

Breitbach, Michael, et al., eds. *Beamte im Nationalsozialismus: Dokumente und Erläuterungen zur Giessener Ausstellung Oktober 1988*. Giessen, 1988.

Buber, Martin. *Der Jude und sein Judentum: Gesammelte Aufsätze und Reden*. Cologne, 1963.

Deutschland Berichte der Sopade. Paris and Prague, 1934-40.

Dokumentation zum Kirchenkampf in Hessen-Nassau. Darmstadt, 1979.

Dokumente zur Geschichte der Frankfurter Juden, 1933-1945. Frankfurt, 1963.

Faschismus in der Provinz: Lokalgeschichtlicher Unterricht am Beispiel von Giessen. Kassel, 1985.

Festschrift zum 75jährigen Bestehen der Realschule mit Lyzeum der israelitischen Religionsgesellschaft. Frankfurt, 1928.

Freudenthal, Margarete Sallis. *Ich habe mein Land gefunden*. Frankfurt, 1977.

Friedman, Saul S. *Amcha: An Oral Testament of the Holocaust*. Lanham, Md., 1979.

Glatzer, Nahum, and Mendes-Flohr, Paul. *The Letters of Martin Buber: A Life of Dialogue*. New York, 1991.

Goldman, Nahum. *Mein Leben als deutscher Jude*. Munich, 1980.

Hahn, Lili. *. . . bis alles in Scherben fällt. Tagebuchblätter* Cologne, 1979.

————. *White Flags of Surrender*. Washington, D.C., 1974.

Heimatgeschichtlicher Wegweiser zur Statten des Widerstandes und der Verfolgung. Cologne, 1984.

Heyne, Kurt. "Judenverfolgung in Giessen und Umgebung, 1933-1945." *Mitteilungen der oberhessischen Geschichtsvereins Giessen 69* (1984), 1-287.

Jenny Apolant zum Gedächtnis. Frankfurt, 1926.

Jüdisches Jahrbuch für Hessen-Nassau. Frankfurt, 1932-33.

Jugend im nationalsozialistischen Frankfurt. Frankfurt, 1987.

Klein, Thomas, ed. *Die Lageberichte der Gestapo über die Provinz Hessen-Nassau, 1933-1936*. Cologne, 1986.

Knauss, Erwin. *Die jüdische Bevölkerung Giessens, 1933-1945:* Eine Dokumentation. Wiesbaden, 1976.

Lacqueur, Naomi. *A Memoir, 1920-1995.* Frankfurt, 1996.

Moritz, Klaus, and Ernst Noam. *NS-Verbrechen vor Gericht, 1945-1955: Dokumente aus hessischen Justizakten.* Wiesbaden, 1978.

Noakes, Jeremy, and Geoffrey Pridham. *Nazism, 1919-1945: A History in Documents and Eyewitness Accounts.* 2 vols. New York, 1983.

Noam, Ernst, and Wolf-Arno Kropat. *Juden vor Gericht, 1933-1945: Dokumente aus hessischen Justizakten mit einem Vorwort von Johannes Strelitz.* Wiesbaden, 1975.

Das Philanthropin zu Frankfurt am Main: Dokumente und Erinnerungen. Frankfurt, 1964.

The Proceedings of the International Military Tribunal. Nuremberg, 1947-49.

Reimann, Bruno, et al., eds. *Antisemitismus und Nationalsozialismus in der Giessener Region.* Giessen, 1991.

Der Rheingaukreis in den Jahren 1869-1890. Ansgabe, 1893.

Richarz, Monika. *Jewish Life in Germany.* Bloomington, 1991.

———. *Jüdisches Leben in Deutschland: Selbstzeugnisse zur Sozialgeschichte, 1918-1945.* New York, 1982.

Rosenheim, Jakob. *Erinnerungen, 1870-1920.* Frankfurt, 1950.

Rosenstock-Huessy, Eugen. *Judaism Despite Chistianity: The Letters on Christianity and Judaism Between Eugen Rosenstock-Huessy and Franz Rosenzweig.* Tuscaloosa, Ala., 1969.

Rosenzweig, Franz. *Briefe.* Berlin, 1935.

Salzberger, Georg. *Leben und Lehre.* Frankfurt, 1982.

Seligmann, Caesar. *Erinnerungen.* Frankfurt, 1975.

Sender, Toni. *Autobiographie einer deutschen Rebellin.* Frankfurt, 1981, reprint from the English, 1939.

Senger, Valentin. *Kaiserhofstrasse 12.* Darmstadt, 1978.

Spuren des Faschismus in Frankfurt: Das Alltagsleben in Frankfurt am Main, 1933-1945. Frankfurt, 1988.

Stern, Josef. *Stark wie ein Spiegel.* Giessen, 1989.

Die Synagogen brennen. . . . Frankfurt, 1988.

Walk, Joseph, ed. *Das Sonderrecht für die Juden im NS-Staat.* Heidelberg, 1981.

Wassermann, Jakob. *Mein Weg als Deutscher und Jude.* Berlin, 1921.

Westheimer, Ruth. *All in a Lifetime.* New York, 1987.

Zernik, Charlotte E. *Im Sturm der Zeit: Ein persönliches Dokument.* Düsseldorf, 1977.

Secondary Sources

Adam, Uwe Dietrich. *Judenpolitik im Dritten Reich.* Düsseldorf, 1979.

Adler, H.G. *Die Juden in Deutschland von der Aufklärung bis zum Nationalsozialismus.* Munich, 1960.

Adler-Rudel, Salomon. *Ostjuden in Deutschland, 1880-1940.* Tübingen, 1959.
Allen, William Sheridan. *The Nazi Seizure of Power: The Experience of a Single German Town, 1930-1935.* Chicago, 1965.
Allport, Gordon. *The Nature of Prejudice.* 25th ed. Reading, Mass., 1979.
Arendt, Hannah. *The Origins of Totalitarianism.* Rev. ed. New York, 1966.
Arndt, Ino. "Die Judenfrage im Lichte der evangelischen Sonntagsblätter, 1918-1938." Ph.D. Diss., Tübingen, 1960.
Aschheim, Steven. *Brothers and Strangers: The East European Jew in German and German-Jewish Consciousness, 1800-1933.* New York, 1982.
Bankier, David. *The Germans and the Final Solution: Public Opinion Under the Nazis.* Oxford, 1992.
Bergmann, Werner, ed. *Error on Trial: Psychological Research on Antisemitism.* Berlin, 1988.
Bering, Dietz. *The Stigma of Names: Antisemitism in German Daily Life, 1812-1933.* Translated by Neville Plaice. Ann Arbor, Mich., 1992.
Bessel, Richard, ed. *Life in the the Third Reich.* Oxford, 1987.
Bibiliographie zur Geschichte der Juden in Hessen. Wiesbaden, 1992.
Blau, Bruno. *Die Entwicklung der jüdischen Bevölkerung in Deutschland.* New York, 1950.
Bolkosky, S.M. *The Distorted Image: German-Jewish Perceptions of Germans and Germany, 1918-1936.* New York, 1975.
Bracher, Karl Dietrich. *The German Dictatorship: The Origins, Structure and Effects of National Socialism.* New York, 1970.
Die braune Machtergreifung: Universität Frankfurt, 1930-1945. Frankfurt, 1989.
von Braun, Christina, et al., eds. *Der ewige Judenhass: Christlicher Antijudaismus, Deutschnationale Judenfeindlichkeit, und Rassistischer Antisemitismus.* Stuttgart, 1990.
Breitman, Richard. *The Architect of Genocide: Heinrich Himmler and the Final Solution.* New York, 1991.
Broszat, Martin. *Hitler and the Collapse of Weimar Germany.* Leamington Spa, 1987.
———. *Der Staat Hitlers: Grundlegung und Verfassung seiner inneren Entwicklung.* Munich, 1969.
Browning, Christopher. *Ordinary Men: Reserve Police Battalion 101 and the Final Solution in Poland.* New York, 1992.
Brubaker, Rogers. *Citizenship and Nationhood in France and Germany.* Cambridge, Mass., 1992.
Buettner, Ursula. "The Persecution of Christian-Jewish Families in the Third Reich." Leo Baeck Institute Yearbook 34 (1989), 267-90.
Burleigh, Michael and Wolfgang Wippermann. *The Racial State: Germany, 1933-1945.* Cambridge, 1990.
Cahnman, Werner. "Village and Small-Town Jews in Germany." In *German Jewry: Its History and Sociology,* Joseph Maier et al., New Brunswick, N.J., 1989.

Childers, Thomas. *The Nazi Voter: The Social Foundations of Fascism in Nazi Germany, 1918-1933.* Chapel Hill, 1984.

Childers, Thomas, and Jane Caplan, eds. *Reevaluating the Third Reich.* New York, 1993.

Dawidowicz, Lucy. *The War Against the Jews, 1933-1945.* New York, 1975.

Demandt, Karl. *Die Geschichte des Landes Hessen.* Kassel, 1972.

Demeter, Karl. *Die Frankfurt Loge zur Einigkeit.* Frankfurt, 1967.

Diamant, Adolf. *Gestapo Frankfurt am Main: Zur Geschichte einer verbrecherischen Organisation in Jahren 1933-1945.* Frankfurt, 1988.

———. *Das zweite Buch Ruth: Der Leidensweg einer Frankfurter jüdischen Familie bis in die Vernichtungslager.* Frankfurt, 1986.

Drexler, Sigmund, et al. *Ärztliches Schicksal unter der Verfolgung, 1933-1945, in Frankfurt am Main und Offenbach.* Frankfurt, 1990.

Fein, Helen. *The Persisting Question: Sociological Perspectives and Social Contexts of Modern Antisemitism.* New York, 1987.

Flannery, Edward. *The Anguish of the Jews: Twenty-three Centuries of Antisemitism.* New York, 1985.

Frankel, Jonathan, and Steven Zipperstein. *Assimilation and Community: The Jews in Nineteenth Century Europe.* Cambridge, England, 1992.

Frankfurter Historische Kommission. *Frankfurt am Main: Geschichte der Stadt.* Sigmaringen, 1991.

Friedländer, Henry, "The Deportation of the German Jews: The Postwar German Trials of Nazi Criminals," *Leo Baeck Institute Yearbook* 29 (1984), 201-28.

Fritzsche, Peter. *Rehearsals for Fascism: Populism and Political Mobilization in Weimar Germany.* New York, 1990.

Furet, François. *Unanswered Questions: Nazi Germany and the Genocide of the Jews.* New York, 1989.

Gellately, Robert. *The Gestapo and German Society.* Oxford, 1990.

Gilman, Sander. *The Jew's Body.* New York, 1991.

Gilman, Sander, et al., eds. *Antisemitism in Times of Crisis.* New York, 1991.

Goldhagen, Daniel. *Hitler's Willing Executioners: Ordinary Germans and the Holocaust.* New York, 1996.

Gordon, Milton. *Assimilation in American Life: The Role of Race, Religion, and National Origins.* New York, 1964.

Gordon, Sarah. *Hitler, Germans, and the Jewish Question.* Princeton, 1984.

Gramsci, Antonio. *Selections from the Prison Notebooks of Antonio Gramsci.* Translated by Quinton Hoare. New York, 1977.

Grunberger, Richard. *The Twelve-Year Reich: A Social History of Nazi Germany.* Reprint. New York, 1995.

Gushee, David. "Many Paths to Righteousness: An Assessment of Research on Why Righteous Gentiles Helped Jews." *Holocaust and Genocide Studies* 3 (1993): 372-401.

Hamilton, Richard. *Who Voted for Hitler?* Princeton, 1982.

Hammerstein, Notker. *Die Johann Wolfgang von Goethe Universität: Von der Stiftungsuniversität zur staatlichen Hochschule: Band I, 1914-1950.* Frankfurt, 1989.

Hannot, Walter. *Die Judenfrage in der katholischen Tagespressen Deutschland und Österreichs, 1918-1933.* Mainz, 1990.

Harris, James. *The People Speak! Antisemitism and Emancipation in Nineteenth Century Bavaria.* Ann Arbor, 1994.

Heilbronner, Oded. "The Role of Nazi Antisemitism in the Nazi Party's Activity and Propaganda: A Regional Historiographical Study." *Leo Baeck Institute Yearbook* 35 (1990), 397-442.

Henry, Frances. *Victims and Neighbors: A Small Town in Nazi Germany Remembered.* South Hadley, Mass., 1984.

Hessen hinter Stacheldraht: Verdrängt und Vergessen, KZs, Lager, Aussenkommandos. Frankfurt, 1984.

Hessen unterm Hakenkreuz: Studien zur Durchsetzung der NSDAP in Hessen. Frankfurt, 1983.

Heuberger, Rachel. *Hinaus aus dem Ghetto: Juden in Frankfurt am Main, 1800-1950.* Frankfurt, 1988.

Hilberg, Raul. *Perpetrators, Victims, Bystanders: The Jewish Catastrophe, 1933-1945.* New York, 1992.

Jäckel, Eberhard. *Hitlers Weltanschauung: Blueprint for Power.* Cambridge, Mass., 1971.

Jarausch, Konrad. "Removing the Nazi Stain: The Quarrel of German Historian." *German Studies Review* 11 (1988), 285-302.

Jatho, Jorg-Peter. *Wenn es hoffentlich bald nach Blut und Eisen riecht: Ein NS Bericht aus der Kampfzeit in Giessen, 1927-1933.* Giessen, 1986.

Jüdische Stiftungen in Frankfurt am Main: Stiftungen, Schenkungen, Organisation, und Vereine mit Kurzbiographien jüdischer Bürger. Frankfurt, 1988.

Kaplan, Marion. "Tradition and Transition: The Acculturation, Assimilation, and Integration of Jews in Imperial Germany: A Gender Analysis." *Leo Baeck Institute Yearbook* 27 (1982), 3-36

Kater, Michael. "Everyday Antisemitism in Prewar Nazi Germany: The Popular Bases." *Yad Vashem Studies* 16 (1984).

———. *Studentenschaft und Rechtradikalismus in Deutschland, 1918-1933.* Berlin, 1974.

Katz, Jacob. *From Prejudice to Destruction: Antisemitism 1700-1933.* Cambridge, Mass., 1980.

———. *Out of the Ghetto: The Social Background of Jewish Emancipation.* New York, 1973.

Kershaw, Ian. *Popular Opinion and Political Dissent in the Third Reich: Bavaria, 1933-1945.* Oxford, 1983.

Kirchholtes, Hans-Dieter. *Jüdische Privatbanken in Frankfurt am Main.* Frankfurt, 1969.

Kluke, Paul. *Die Stiftungsuniversität Frankfurt am Main, 1914-1932.* Frankfurt, 1972.

Knauss, Erwin. "Kurzgefasste Geschichte der Juden in Giessen: 13es Jahrhundert bis 1945." In *Zur Statistik Giessens und seines Umlandes: Aufsatz und Reden*. Giessen, 1987.

König, Fritz, et al., eds. *Gewerkschaften, Sozialdemokraten, und Friedensfreunden in Frankfurt, 1900-1935*. Frankfurt, 1985.

Koshar, Rudy. *Social Life, Local Politics, and Nazism: Marburg, 1880-1935*. Chapel Hill, 1986.

Kralovitz, Brigitte. *Hedwig Burgheim oder die Reise nach Giessen: Bericht über das Leben einer Lehrerin*. Giessen, 1981.

———. *Kristallnacht in Hessen: Der Judenpogrom vom November 1938, Eine Dokumentation*. Wiesbaden, 1988.

Kulka, Otto Dov. "Public Opinion in Nazi Germany and the Jewish Question." *Jerusalem Quarterly* 25 (1982): 121-44.

Levin, Nora. *The Holocaust: The Destruction of European Jewry, 1933-1945*. New York, 1968.

Levy, Richard. *The Downfall of the Antisemitic Parties in Imperial Germany*. New Haven, 1975.

Liberles, Robert. "Emancipation and the Structure of Jewish Community in the Nineteenth Century." *Leo Baeck Institute Yearbook* 37 (1986), 51-70.

———. *Religious Conflict in Social Context: The Resurgence of Orthodox Judaism in Frankfurt, 1838-1877*. Westport, Conn., 1985.

Lieberman, Ben. "Testing Peukert's Paradigm: The Crisis of Classical Modernity in the 'New' Frankfurt, 1925-1930." *German Studies Review* 17 (1994), 287-304.

Lifton, Robert Jay, and Eric Markusen. *The Genocidal Mentality: Nazi Holocaust and Nuclear Threat*. New York, 1990.

Livingstone, Rodney. "Germans and Jews Since 1945." *Patterns of Prejudice* 29 (1995), 45-59.

Lowenstein, Steven. "The Pace of Modernization of German Jewry in the Nineteenth Century." *Leo Baeck Institute Yearbook* 21 (1976), 41-56.

Lüdtke, Alf. "Formierung der Massen oder mitmachen und hinnehmen: Alltagsgeschichte und Faschismusanalyse." In *Alltagsgeschichte: Zur Rekonstruktion historischer Erfahrungen und Lebensweisen*. Frankfurt, 1988.

Mann, Reinhard. *Protest und Kontrolle im Dritten Reich: Nationalsozialistische Herrschaft im Alltag einer rheinischen Grosstadt*. Frankfurt, 1987.

Marrus, Michael. *Les juifs de France a l'epoque de l'affaire Dreyfus*. Paris, 1972.

———. "Theory and Practice of Antisemitism." *Commentary*, August 1982, 38-42.

Maurer, Trude. *Ostjuden in Deutschland, 1918-1933*. Hamburg, 1986.

Mausbach-Bromberger, Barbara. *Arbeiterwiderstand in Frankfurt am Main gegen den Faschismus, 1933-1945*. Frankfurt, 1976.

Merkl, Peter. *Political Violence Under the Swastika*. Princeton, 1975.

Mommsen, Hans. "The Realization of the Unthinkable: The Final Solution of the Jewish Question in the Third Reich." In *The Politics of Genocide: Jews and Soviet Prisoners of War in Nazi Germany*, edited by Gerhard Hirschfeld. London, 1986.

Mosse, George. *The Crisis of German Ideology: The Intellectual Origins of the Third Reich*. New York, 1964.

Mosse, Werner. *Entscheidungsjahr 1932: Zur Judenfrage in der Endphase der Weimar Republik*. Tübingen, 1965.

———. *The Jews in the German Economy: The German-Jewish Economic Elite, 1820-1935*. Oxford, 1987.

Mosse, Werner, Arnold Paucker, and Reinhard Rürup, eds. *Revolution and Evolution: 1848 in German-Jewish History*. Tübingen, 1981.

Neunhundert Jahre Geschichte der Juden in Hessen: Beiträge zur politischen, wirtschaftlichen, und kulturellen Leben. Wiesbaden, 1983.

Niewyk, Donald. "The Impact of Inflation and Depression on German Jews." *Leo Baeck Institute Yearbook* 28 (1983): 19-36.

———. *The Jews in Weimar Germany*. Baton Rouge, 1980.

———. *Socialist, Antisemite, and Jew: German Social Democracy Confronts the Problem of Antisemitism, 1918-1933*. Baton Rouge, 1971.

Noakes, Jeremy. "The Development of Nazi Policy Towards the German-Jewish Mischlinge, 1933-1945." *Leo Baeck Institute Yearbook* 34 (1989), 291-356.

———. *The Nazi Party in Lower Saxony, 1921-1933*. Oxford, 1977.

Owings, Alison. *Frauen: German Women Recall the Third Reich*. New Brunswick, N.J., 1993.

Pehle, Walter. *November 1938: From Kristallnacht to Genocide*. Oxford, 1991.

Petuchowski, Jakob. "Frankfurt Jewry: A Model of Transition to Modernity." *Leo Baeck Institute Yearbook* 29 (1984), 405-18.

Peukert, Detlev. *Inside Nazi Germany*. New Haven, 1987.

———. *The Weimar Republic: Crisis of Classical Modernity*. New York, 1992.

Poppel, Stephen. *Zionism in Germany, 1897-1933: The Shaping of a Jewish Identity*. Philadelphia, 1977.

Proctor, Robert. *Racial Hygiene: Medicine Under the Nazis*. Cambridge, Mass., 1988.

Pulzer, Peter. *The Jews and the German State: The Political History of a Minority, 1848-1933*. Oxford, 1992.

———. *The Rise of Antisemitism in Germany and Austria*. New York, 1964.

Rausch, David. *Legacy of Hatred: Why Christians Must Not Forget the Holocaust*. Grand Rapids, Mich., 1990.

Rebentisch, Dieter. *Ludwig Landmann: Frankfurts Oberbürgermeister in der Weimar Republik*. Wiesbaden, 1975.

Reichmann, Eva. *Hostages of Civilization: The Social Sources of National Socialist Antisemitism*. London, 1950.

Reinharz, Jehuda. *Fatherland or Promised Land? The Dilemma of the German Jew, 1893-1914.* Ann Arbor, 1975.

Reinharz, Jehuda, and Walter Schatzberg, eds. *The Jewish Response to German Culture: From the Enlightenment to the Second World War.* Hanover, 1985.

Reitlinger, Gerald. *The Final Solution: The Attempt to Exterminate the Jews of Europe.* New York, 1961.

Rodrigue, Aron. "German Popular Opinion and the Jews under the Nazi Dictatorship." B.A. Thesis, University of Manchester, 1978.

Röhm, Eberhard, and Jorg Thierfelder, *Juden-Christen-Deutsche, 1933-1945.* Stuttgart, 1990.

Rose, Paul Lawrence. *Revolutionary Antisemitism in Germany from Kant to Wagner.* Princeton, 1990.

Rozenblit, Marsha. *The Jews of Vienna, 1867-1914: Assimilation and Identity.* Albany, 1983.

Ruppin, Arthur. *The Jewish Fate and Future.* London, 1940.

Rürup, Reinhard. *Emanzipation und Antisemitismus: Studien zur "Judenfrage" der bürgerlichen Gesellschaft.* Göttingen, 1975.

———. "The Tortuous and Thorny Path to Legal Equality—'Jew Laws' and Emancipatory Legislation in Germany from the Late Eighteenth Century." *Leo Baeck Institute Yearbook* 31 (1986): 3-34.

Schembs, H.O. *Bibliographie zur Geschichte der Frankfurter Juden, 1781-1945.* Frankfurt, 1978.

Schivelbusch, Wolfgang. *Intellektuellendämmerung; Zur Lage der Frankfurt Intelligenz in den zwangziger Jahren.* Frankfurt, 1982.

Schleunes, Karl. *The Twisted Road to Auschwitz: Nazi Policy Toward German Jews, 1933-1939.* Urbana, 1970.

Schoeps, Hans Joachim. *Unbewältigte Geschichte: Stationen deutschen Schicksals seit 1763.* Berlin, 1964.

Scholem, Gerschom. "On the Social Psychology of Germans and Jews." In *The Problematic Symbiosis: Germans and Jews, 1880-1933,* edited by David Bronsen. New York, 1981.

Schön, Eberhard. *Die Entstehung des Nationalsozialismus in Hessen.* Meisenheim, 1972.

Schorsch, Ismar. *Jewish Reactions to German Antisemitism, 1870-1914.* New York, 1972.

Schuler, Gideon, ed. *Zwischen Unruhe und Ordnung: Ein deutsches Lesebuch für die Zeit von 1925-1960 zum Beispiel einer Region:* Mittelhessen. Giessen, 1989.

75 Jahre Rheingaukreis: Herausgegeben vom Landrat Bausinger im Auftrag des Kreistages und des Kreisausschußes. Rüdesheim, 1962.

Shirer, William. *The Rise and Fall of the Third Reich: A History of Nazi Germany.* New York, 1969.

Sorkin, David. *The Transformation of German Jewry, 1780-1870.* Oxford, 1987.

Steinert, Marlis. *Hitler's War and the Germans: Public Mood and Attitude During the Second World War,* edited and translated by Thomas de Witt. Athens, Ohio, 1977.

Stern, Susan. "Jews in Germany." *German Life,* March 1995, 29.

Stokes, Lawrence. "The German People and the Destruction of the European Jews." *Central European History* 6 (1973), 167-91.

Strauss, Herbert, ed. *Hostages of Modernization: Studies on Modern Antisemitism, 1870-1939, Germany, Great Britain, France.* Berlin, 1993.

————, "Jewish Emigration from Germany: Nazi Policies and Jewish Responses," *Leo Baeck Institute Yearbook* 25 (1980): 313-62.

Struck, Wolf Heino. *Geschichte der Stadt Geisenheims.* Frankfurt, 1972.

Tal, Uriel. *Christians and Jews in Germany: Religion, Politics, and Ideology in the Second Reich, 1870-1914.* Ithaca, 1975.

Toury, Jacob. "Types of Municipal Rights in German Townships: The Problem of Local Emancipation." *Leo Baeck Institute Yearbook* 22 (1977), 55-80.

Traverso, Enzo. *The Jews and Germany: From the Judeo-German Symbiosis to the Memory of Auschwitz.* Lincoln, Neb., 1995.

Volkov, Shulamit. *The Rise of Popular Antimodernism in Germany: Urban Master Artisans, 1873-1896.* Princeton, 1978.

————. "Judenverfolgung und nichtjüdische Bevölkerung," In *Bayern in der NS-Zeit,* edited by Martin Broszat et al. Munich, 1977.

Weiss, John. *Ideology of Death: Why the Holocaust Happened in Germany.* Chicago, 1996.

Wertheimer, Jack. *Unwelcome Strangers: Eastern European Jews in Imperial Germany.* New York, 1987.

Weyrauch, Walter Otto. *Gestapo V-Leute: Tatsache und Theorie des Geheimdienstes—Untersuchungen zur Gestapo während der NS Herrschaft.* Frankfurt, 1992.

Wippermann, Wolfgang. *Das Leben in Frankfurt zur NS-Zeit: Band 1, Die nationalsozialistische Judenverfolgung—Darstellung, Dokumente, und didaktische Hinweise.* Frankfurt, 1986.

————. *Das Leben in Frankfurt zur NS-Zeit: Band 5, Der Widerstand—Darstellung, Dokumente, und didaktische Hinweise.* Frankfurt, 1986.

Yahil, Leni. *The Holocaust: The Fate of European Jewry.* New York, 1990.

Index

acculturation, 7, 8, 62
actors, 84, 171
Adickes, Franz, 64, 65
Adler, H.G., 6, 189, 263
Adler, Salo, 21
Adorno, Theodor, 9, 64
agriculture, 37, 39, 40, 82-84
Agudas Israel, 52
Allen, William Sheridan, 12, 103, 225, 231
Allies, 181
Allport, Gordon, 10, 190-91
Alltagsgeschichte, 187
Alltagshistoriker, 1
antidefamation, 21, 56
anti-Jewish decrees, 129-37, 153, 154
antisemitism, 6, 11-13, 16, 19-23, 29, 30, 37, 45, 62, 63, 67-72, 77-82, 103, 106-79, 185, 186, 195, 219, 228, 236
Apolant, Hugo, 21
Apolant, Jenny, 43, 66, 68, 89, 221
Arendt, Hannah, 7, 11, 190, 192
aristocracy, 115
Arnsberg, Paul, 141, 188, 189, 193, 199, 200, 203, 207, 210, 211, 223, 254, 263, 268
artisans, 115, 240
artists, 84
"Aryanization," 163, 164
Asch, Bruno, 43, 66, 68, 108, 117, 141, 174, 209, 231
assimilation, 7-9, 19, 90
Association to Resist Antisemitism (Verein zur Abwehr des Antisemitismus), 21, 70
Auerbach, Ernst, 21
Aufklärung, 6, 8, 17, 21, 23
Auschwitz, 173

Baab, Heinrich, 150, 181, 252, 265
Baden, 133
Bad Nauheim, 256
Baeck, Leo, 19, 139, 168, 185, 194
Bahr, Hermann, 7
Bamberger, Elizabeth, 81, 89, 129, 147, 160, 166, 213, 219, 221, 237, 249, 255, 259
Bankier, David, 12, 159, 187, 246, 261
banks, 42, 83, 220
Barth, Karl, 142
Bavaria, 92
Berger, Trudi, 82, 219
Berlin, 9, 23, 88, 92, 94, 135, 175, 266
Best, Werner, 126
Bieber, Margarete, 79, 239
Bildung, 17, 47
Blau, Julius, 48
Blaum, Kurt, 161
Bock, Alfred, 44, 84
Böckel, Otto, 20, 83, 219
Bolkosky, S.M., 6, 185, 189
Bonhöffer, Dietrich, 248, 266
boycott, 128-30, 132, 237
Bracher, Karl Dietrich, 11
Braun, Otto, 120
Breuer, Salomon, 51
Brixuis, Martha, 129
Broszat, Martin, 12, 103, 184, 187, 192, 225, 235, 258
Browning, Christopher, 192, 258, 267
Brüning, Heinrich, 116, 120
Buber, Martin, 43, 51, 63, 64, 71, 139, 141, 143, 207, 215, 248
Burgheim, Hedwig, 44, 80, 131, 151, 174, 175, 263

Cahnman, Werner, 63, 82, 211, 219
Carlebach, Emil, 56, 142, 248

Carolium, 64
Catholic Center Party (Zentrum), 47,
    65, 66, 106-11, 117-22, 144
Catholics, 20, 27, 30, 66, 67, 70, 71,
    76, 93, 95-97, 106-11, 116-22,
    129, 144, 145, 168, 178, 200,
    201, 203, 214, 216, 222, 235,
    260, 263, 266
Central Association of German
    Citizens of the Jewish Faith
    (Centralverein), 21, 22, 49, 56,
    59, 221, 230, 241
Central-Verein Zeitung, 116, 139, 195,
    206, 216, 217, 230, 241, 244, 246
Chamberlain, Houston Stewart, 20·
Chamberlain, Neville, 155
Childers, Thomas, 103, 225 229, 231
children, 27, 29, 72-76, 78, 80, 81, 84,
    86, 87, 89-91, 130, 131, 146
Christianity, 11, 21, 27-31, 70, 71,
    89-98, 124, 142, 143, 159, 168,
    195, 200, 219, 224, 266
citizenship, 7, 15, 137
civil rights, 16-19, 21, 56, 65-68,
    70-72, 138, 139
civil servants, 115
Cohen, Hermann, 48
Cologne, 151, 183
commercial activity, 6-8, 16-19, 30,
    36-40, 42, 45
Communist Party (of Germany, KPD),
    65, 105, 118-24, 127, 142, 229,
    231, 248
concentration camps, 171, 173, 251,
    261
Concordat, 144
Confessing Church, 142, 143, 168
Conservative Judaism, 18, 48, 100, 194
conservatives, 115
conversion, 21, 29, 31, 45, 57, 95-99,
    200, 223, 224
cultural activity, 44, 50, 134, 205, 220,
    247
cultural relations, 85, 86, 220

Daluege, Kurt, 169

Darmstadt, 92
Decker, Erich, 147, 249
Deeg, Erich, 161, 255
demography, 25-36, 44, 197, 198, 263
department stores, 38, 81
deportations, 169, 171-76, 261, 263
depression, 1, 6, 29, 30, 38, 45, 68,
    100, 106, 116, 117
Düsseldorf, 183

Ebert, Friedrich, 104, 105
Eckert, Alois, 144
economic activity, 6-8, 16-19, 30, 36-
    39, 45, 81-84, 132-34, 241, 242
economic relations, 81-84
education, 72-81
Eichmann, Adolf, 172, 175, 249
Einsatzgruppen, 168, 171
Einstein, Albert, 23
elections, 106-24, 186, 226, 231, 233, 234
emancipation, 6, 15-17, 37, 198
emigration, 30, 45, 140, 153, 165, 247
Enabling Act, 123, 126
Erzberger, Matthias, 115
Evangelicals, 27, 30, 93, 95-99, 200,
    201, 203
Evangelisches Sonntagsblatt, 116

Fein, Helen, 9, 190, 229, 270
Feldman, Gerald, 113
fertility, 27, 28, 98
Feuchtwanger, Lion, 22
Fink, Elias, 21
forced labor, 258
Fraenkel, Johanna, 176, 264
Frank, Otto, 81, 84, 141, 173
Frankel, David, 18
Frankfurt a. M., 1-5, 8-10, 15-23, 25,
    27-33, 37, 38, 40, 41, 43, 47-57,
    61, 62-68, 72-74, 78, 84-89, 92-
    99, 106-8, 111-13, 117-24, 127,
    128, 130-32, 134-41, 144, 146,
    147, 149, 150, 154, 156, 157, 159-
    61, 163, 164, 166, 168-71, 173,
    175-78, 181, 183, 186, 194, 198,
    200, 201, 203, 204, 206-21, 224-

34, 237-39, 241-45, 248-50, 252, 255, 256, 259, 260, 262, 264
Frankfurt Israelitisches Gemeindelbatt, 48, 49, 116, 199, 210, 216, 246
fraternities, 77, 80, 217
Free Jewish House of Learning (Lehrhaus), 50, 51, 56, 71, 139, 207
Freimuth, Margot, 67, 87, 220-23, 234, 237, 248, 256
Freudenthal, Margarete Sallis, 78, 86, 89, 128, 129, 213, 218, 220, 237
Frick, Wilhelm, 137
Friedberg, 61, 233
Friedman, Earl, 182
Fritsch, Theodor, 20
Fritzsche, Peter, 103, 225
Fromm, Erich, 43, 51, 64
Fulda, 124
functionalists, 11, 258
Fürth, Henriette, 43, 66, 68, 209

gassing, 172, 262
gas vans, 172
Geiger, Abraham, 18
Geiger, Rudolf, 21
Geis, Sali, 22
Geisenheim, 1-5, 10, 15, 16, 18-20, 22, 23, 25-29, 32, 35-38, 40-44, 47, 62, 67, 71, 81-88, 91-99, 106, 110, 112, 113, 122, 127, 129, 131, 133, 140, 141, 145-47, 150, 158-62, 171, 175, 178, 182, 186, 187, 194, 201, 204, 211, 218-21, 225, 231, 233, 235-37, 248, 249, 255, 262, 263
Gellately, Robert, 126, 151, 235, 252
Gemeinde, 15
Gemeindeorthodox, 18, 22, 33, 48, 56
Gemeinschaft, 63
General German Student Council (AStA), 77, 80, 111
German Christian Movement, 142
German Democratic Party (DDP), 47, 65-67, 105-11, 117-22, 232
German National People's Party (DNVP), 105-11, 117-22

German People's Party (DVP), 106-11, 117-22
Germany, East, 183, 268, 269
Germany, West, 183, 268, 269
Gesellschaft, 63
Gestapo, 2, 12, 132, 133, 147, 156, 157, 168-70, 175-77, 181, 235, 246, 248, 252, 253, 260, 265
Giessen, 1-5, 10, 15, 16, 18-20, 22, 23, 26-31, 33, 36, 37-44, 47, 57-62, 67, 71, 72, 78-80, 84, 86-88, 91-99, 106, 108, 110-12, 121, 122, 127, 129, 131, 133, 134, 140-42, 146, 147, 158-62, 166, 168, 170, 171, 174-78, 181, 182, 186, 187, 194, 200, 201, 204, 211-15, 217-21, 224, 225, 228, 233, 234, 237, 239, 240, 245, 247-49, 250, 255, 256, 259, 260, 264
Glusman, Bernhard, 59
Goebbels, Joseph, 111, 132, 156, 263
Goerderler, Carl Friedrich, 192
Goitein, Jakob, 22
Goldhagen, Daniel, 12, 179, 192, 267
Goldmann, Nahum, 22
Goldmann, Salomon Hirsch, 22
Gordon, Milton, 7, 190
Gordon, Sarah, 159, 179, 187, 225, 251, 255, 264, 270
Göring, Hermann, 127, 153, 155, 162
Grünberg, Carl, 43
Grynszpan, Herschel, 156, 157
Gutsmuth, Alfred, 146

Haavara Transfer Agreement, 140
Habimah Theater Troupe, 85
Hadamar, 172
Hahn, Lili, 146, 173, 235, 262
Hamburg, 92, 127, 151, 169, 183
Hanukkah, 86, 140
Harris, Leopold, 65, 69, 213
Harth, Martin, 58, 61, 63, 80, 86-88, 91, 129, 135, 141, 147, 158, 162, 211, 213, 218, 220, 222, 223, 233, 237, 250, 256
Harth, Meyer, 81

Haskalah, 17
health care, 64
Heller, Hermann, 65, 66
Henry, Frances, 8, 87, 92, 95, 190, 205,
    221-23, 264
Henry and Emma Budge Foundation,
    64
Hesse, Wilhelm, 145
Hessen, 1-4, 16, 18, 20, 22, 27, 28, 83,
    103-5, 125, 127, 133, 150, 156,
    181, 197, 202, 203, 225, 226-34,
    248-54
Hessen-Darmstadt, 2-5, 28, 44, 104,
    105, 123, 197, 202
Hessen-Kassell, 2-5, 16, 17, 146, 254
Hessen-Nassau, 2-5, 17, 27, 28, 33, 39,
    44, 103-5, 123, 197, 202, 254
Heydrich, Reinhard, 155, 156, 175
Hilfrich, Bishop Antonius, 159, 170,
    173, 261, 262
Himmler, Heinrich, 153, 155, 156, 261
Hindenburg, Paul von, 105, 120, 130
Hirsch, Samson Raphael, 18, 51, 52, 65
Hirschfeld, Leo, 58, 140
Historikerstreit, 184, 269
historiography, 1, 11
Hitler, Adolf, 1, 87, 122-30, 137, 138,
    144, 162, 218, 261, 265, 269
Hoffmann, Jakob, 48, 156
Hofjuden, 16
Holde, Heide Hermanns, 9, 89, 190,
    221
Holland, Ernst, 175
Holocaust, 1, 13, 165-79, 185, 186,
    262, 264, 269
Horkheimer, Max, 64
Horovitz, Jakob, 48, 156
Horovitz, Joseph Jona, 52
Horovitz, Markus, 22, 48, 52

Imperial Union of Jewish Front
    Soldiers (Reichsbund jüdischer
    Frontsoldaten), 23, 67, 135, 136
industry, 37, 38, 39, 42
inflation, 105, 107, 226, 227
integration, 5, 7-10, 23, 62, 72, 100, 106

intentionalists, 11, 258
intercommunal relations, 63, 68, 70, 72
intermarriage, 10, 23, 27, 30-32, 45,
    57, 91-99, 137, 199, 200, 222-24,
    245
Israelit, Der 51, 52
Israelitische Gemeinde (IG), 15, 16, 22,
    25, 30, 33, 48, 51-54, 57-59, 68,
    76, 96, 138, 181, 224
Israelitische Religionsgesellschaft
    (IRG), 18, 25, 30, 35, 51-54, 58,
    59, 76, 140, 156, 207, 216, 224
Israelitischer Kulturbund, 139, 140

Jäckel, Eberhard, 11, 258
"Jew Badge," 168
Jewish Agency, 50, 117
Jewish-Christian dialogue, 70, 71,
    143, 215
Jewish identity, 8, 9, 57
Jewish nationalism, 21, 50, 52
Jewish patriotism, 57
Jewish People's Party (JVP), 50
"Jewish Problem," 7, 13, 184
"Jewish Question," 7, 13, 159, 167,
    168, 179
Jews (*see either specific locations or
    individuals*)
Johann Wolfgang von Goethe
    University, 43, 51, 64, 77, 111,
    130, 228, 239
Jost, Isaac Marcus, 18
Judenfreundliches Verhalten ("Jew-
    friendly behavior"), 148, 149
Judenzählung, 22
Justus Liebig University (*see also*
    Ludwigs University), 5

Kaffeeklatsch, 88
Kantorowicz, Ernst, 130, 139, 239
Kaplan, Marion, 94, 190, 222, 223
Kater, Michael, 128, 187, 192
Katterfield, Anna, 143
Katz, Bertha, 78, 90, 219, 221
Katz, Jacob, 7, 15, 190-94
Katz, Lina, 170, 261

Keller, Karl, 108, 121, 123, 127, 215
Kershaw, Ian, 12, 159, 187, 267
Killian, Martin, 88, 127, 142, 145,
    146, 175, 221, 222, 229, 233,
    234, 247-49, 256, 263
Kittel, Gerhard, 143
Kölner Hof, 87
Koshar, Rudy, 83, 103, 187, 217, 219,
    225, 226, 234
Krebs, Friedrich, 127, 130, 132, 153,
    181, 238, 244, 267
Kristallnacht, 140, 155-62, 164, 183,
    253-56
Kropat, Wolf Arno, 149, 193
Kühne, Wolfgang, 134
Kulka, Otto Dov, 12, 159, 192, 255, 257
Küntzel, Georg, 77, 111

Lacqueur, Naomi, 86
Landmann, Ludwig, 8, 66, 68, 108,
    117-21, 123, 127, 174, 212,
    235, 263
Langmuir, Gavin, 114, 229
Laqueur, Richard, 79
Lasker, Edward, 65
Lazarus, Arnold, 48
League of Defense and Defiance
    (Schutz und Trutz Bund), 106,
    115, 231
Leibzoll, 16
Levi, Benedict Samuel, 57
Levi, Paul, 65
Levy, Joseph, 147, 148, 160, 223, 229
Lewandowski, Lewis, 84
"liberal Jewish model," 19, 65
Lifton, Robert Jay, 178
Limpert, Richard, 149
Lodz, 171-74
Lohmeyer, Ernst, 143
Ludwigs University (see also Justus
    Liebig University), 79, 111, 132,
    239
Lueger, Karl, 20
Luxemburg, Rosa, 65

Madagascar Plan, 258

Main-Rhein Clerical Front, 144
Mainz, 92, 137
Makkabi Sport Club, 135, 221
Mann, Reinhard, 150
Marburg, 20, 83, 124, 129, 226, 234
Marcuse, Herbert, 63
Marr, Wilhelm, 20
marriage, 10, 23, 27, 30, 31, 90-99,
    201, 222, 245
Marrus, Michael, 11, 13, 97, 190,
    192
Maurer, Trude, 90, 221, 223, 224
May, Ernst, 66, 108
Mayer, Eugen, 50
Mayer, Helene, 135
Meiser, Hans, 143
memory, 183
Merton, Richard, 65, 88, 117
Merzbach, Richard, 57
Meyer, Elisabeth, 182
Michel, Max, 66
Minsk, 171-74
Mischlinge, 11, 132, 137, 145, 146,
    166, 168, 175, 176, 222, 234,
    245, 264
Mizrachi Zionists, 52
modernization theory, 6
Mommsen, Hans, 12
mortality rates, 31, 99
Mosse, George, 195
Mosse, Werner, 84, 220
Müller, Heinrich, 171, 267
Müller, Ludwig, 142
Munich, 183, 266
Munich Conference, 155, 253
musicians, 84

Nathan, Dr. Siegfried, 44, 62, 131,
    141, 146, 239
National Socialists, 1, 2, 12, 13, 30,
    31, 64, 68, 77, 79, 83, 87, 91, 103,
    105, 106, 110-24, 127-36, 144,
    145, 153-79, 181, 184-86, 214,
    215, 225, 228-35, 239, 241, 247,
    251, 261, 269
Neo-Nazism, 183, 184

Neo-Orthodoxy (*see* Israelitische Religions-gesellschaft; Orthodox Jews)
Neues Theater, 43, 85
Neumann, Erich, 59, 140, 211
Neumann, Florence, 90, 250
Niemöller, Martin, 142, 248, 266
Niewyk, Donald, 6, 76, 95, 189, 190, 193, 197, 203, 204, 207, 209, 214, 216-18, 224, 227, 230
Noakes, Jeremy, 12, 103, 225, 263
Noam, Ernst, 78, 90, 149, 218, 221, 256, 267
Nobel, Nehemiah, 48, 49, 52
Nolte, Ernst, 184, 269
nondenominationalism, 29, 57, 95, 199
Nuremberg Laws, 136-38

occupational structure (of Jews), 39, 40
Oliner, Samuel and Pearl, 177, 264
Olympics, 135, 138, 244
Oppenheim, Moritz, 85
Oppenheimer, Alice, 148, 159, 160, 250, 255
Oppenheimer, Franz, 6, 22, 64, 197
Orthodox Jews, 8, 10, 18, 19, 21, 30, 33, 35, 38, 45-60, 76, 78, 89, 91, 100, 156, 194, 204, 206-9, 216
Ostjuden, 7-10, 19, 22, 30, 31, 48, 52, 53, 57, 60, 61, 68, 69, 70, 79, 90, 94, 96, 100, 106, 112, 139, 155, 157, 200, 207, 208, 216, 221, 223, 240
Östrich-Winkel, 5, 147, 211, 220, 223
Ostrovsky, Bruno, 52, 209
Owings, Alison, 88, 221

Pappenheim, Bertha, 43, 66, 139
peasants, 21, 82, 83, 103, 114, 121, 219
Peukert, Detlev, 185, 187, 197, 201, 224, 233, 270
Philanthropin, 33, 48-50, 68, 139, 206, 216
philanthropy, 63, 64, 76
Plant, Richard, 87
Poland, 155

political affiliation (of Jews), 43, 64-66, 212
population, 25-33, 44
Prague, 169
professions, 38-40, 43, 130-32, 238
professors, 43, 44, 77, 79, 111, 112, 217, 238
Protestants, 27, 30, 32, 70, 71, 76, 93-99, 116, 129, 142, 143, 168, 199, 200, 214, 216, 222, 248, 266
public opinion, 1, 12, 125-33, 152, 153, 159-68, 170, 175, 177-79, 246, 249, 260, 265, 266
publishers, 84
Pulzer, Peter, 7, 189, 190, 195, 196, 232

racism, 20, 218, 226
Rassenschande, 148, 149, 251
Rathenau, Walther, 105, 106
Reform Judaism, 10, 18, 21, 33, 35, 45, 48-55, 58-60, 90, 91, 96, 100, 194, 207, 209
refugees, 153, 165
Reichmann, Eva, 11, 114, 229
Reichsbanner, 67
Reichsvereinigung, 162, 177
Reichsvertretung, 139
Reinharz, Jehuda, 50, 207
relations, 1, 10, 63, 100, 101, 124, 125, 152, 153, 159-62, 166, 179, 185, 186, 189, 264, 269
rescue, 177, 178, 264-66
resistance, 142, 144, 145, 159, 160
Rheingau, 22, 182
Rhein-Mainische Volkszeitung, 116, 117, 144, 214, 248
Richarz, Monika, 6, 27, 197-201, 204, 205, 207
Riga, 170-74
Ritter, Heinrich, 123, 127, 133, 134, 264
Robinsohn, Hans, 151
Rodrigue, Aron, 12, 159, 255
Rosenheim, Jakob, 51, 52
Rosenthal, Nora, 107

Rosenzweig, Franz, 50, 51, 63, 71, 86, 215
Rothschild Lichtenberg, Friedel, 90, 222
Rothschilds, 81, 84
Rozenblit, Marsha, 94, 97, 223
Rüdesheim, 5, 62, 211, 227, 233, 255
Ruppin, Arthur, 98, 99

SA (see Sturmabteilung)
Salfeld, Hans, 78, 89, 218, 221
Salzberger, Georg, 48, 50, 67, 138, 159, 160, 166, 213, 256, 259
Sander, David, 58
Schacht, Hjalmar, 132, 138, 153
Scheidemann, Philip, 104
Scheuer, Dora, 96, 147, 161, 178, 224, 249, 265
Scheuer, Martin, 87, 107, 146, 149, 249
Scheuneviertel Riots, 69
Schild, 135, 221
Schleunes, Karl, 132, 187, 237, 240, 253
Schnabel, Annelise, 82, 147, 150, 221, 234, 242, 248
Schneider, Paul, 145
Schnitzler, Georg von, 88
Schoeps, Hans Joachim, 7
Scholem, Gershom, 6, 18, 51, 88-90, 94, 99, 185, 189, 223, 224
Schönerer, Georg von, 20
Schreiber, Eduard, 130
Schutzstaffel (SS), 12, 126, 127, 129, 136, 138, 156, 158, 178, 236, 254, 258, 266
SD (see Sicherheitsdienst)
secularization, 8, 19, 56, 57, 95
Seligman, Caesar, 48, 49, 57, 139, 207, 209, 210
Sender, Toni, 65, 209, 213
sexual relations, 136, 137
Sicherheitsdienst (Security Service or SD), 2, 12, 153, 156, 168, 178, 254, 260, 265
Simon, Julius, 50
Sinzheimer, Hugo, 65, 68, 141, 174,

209, 213, 261
Sklare, Marshall, 94, 223
Social Darwinism, 20
Social Democratic Party (SPD), 2, 47, 65-70, 105-11, 113-21, 125, 127, 128, 142, 208, 213, 230, 232, 233, 248, 249, 254, 267
social relations, 86-100, 137, 146, 153
socioeconomic structure (of Jews), 36-45, 201, 202
Sondheimer, Fritz, 22
Sonnemann, Leopold, 65, 76
Sonnenborn, Leo and Settie, 128, 129, 141, 160, 164, 237, 250, 255, 257
Sopade, 2, 12, 147, 148, 157, 241
Sorkin, David, 8, 190, 193
Spartacists, 104
Speyer, Georg, 64, 210
Spier, Selmar, 56, 57, 213
sport clubs, 9, 86, 87, 135, 210, 243, 244
Sprenger, Jakob, 103, 111, 127, 133, 135, 155, 175, 228
SS (see Schutzstaffel)
Stahl, Franz, 110, 122, 123, 127
Stammtisch, 87, 88
Steinert, Marlis, 12
Steinreich, Eva, 87, 146
sterilization, 234, 263
Sterling, Eleanore, 20
Stern, Josef, 59-61, 82, 91, 141, 175, 211, 220, 222
Stöcker, Adolf, 20
Stokes, Lawrence, 12
Strauss, Alex, 87, 91, 135, 141, 147
Strauss, Alfredo, 91, 162, 165, 256
Strauss, Auguste, 91, 142, 165
Strauss, Emma, 82, 91
Strauss, Georg, 82, 91, 129, 134, 147, 158, 175
Strauss, Karoline, 142, 158, 175
Strauss, Liebmann, 129, 141, 158, 175
Strauss, Max, 81, 91, 129, 142, 158
Strauss family, 32, 35, 42, 82
Streicher, Julius, 133
Stresemann, Gustav, 67

students, 72-81, 115, 122, 127, 131, 215-17
Sturmabteilung (storm troopers or SA), 110, 125-28, 136, 145, 156, 158, 170, 178, 236
suicides, 171, 203
survivors, 267

Tal, Uriel, 7, 8, 190, 195
Talmon, Jakob, 11
Talmud, 60
taxes, 38
theater, 85, 134
Theresienstadt, 170-76
Third Reich, 1, 11, 12, 125-79, 186
Tietz, Erna, 83
Tietz department store, 38, 81
Tönnies, Ferdinand, 211
trade, 37
Traverso, Enzo, 6, 188, 197, 229, 239, 269
Treitschke, Heinrich von, 20
Tschammer und Osten, Hans von, 135, 221

unemployment, 38, 113, 117
urbanization, 32, 33, 45, 201
U.S. occupation, 181-82, 267, 268

Valfer, Ernst, 146
Veidt, Karl, 144
Vereine, 67, 220
Versailles Treaty, 77, 107
Vienna, 97, 169
Vom Rath, Ernst, 156, 157

Wagner, Auguste, 161
Wassermann, Jakob, 23

Weil, Felix, 43
Weimar Constitution, 104
Weimar Republic, 1, 6, 8-11, 19, 21, 23, 25, 40, 44, 45, 47, 48, 56, 63-66, 76, 95, 100, 104, 129, 202
Weiss, John, 12, 114, 192, 229
welfare organizations (for Jews), 53, 57, 66, 139, 140
Werfel, Franz, 23
Werner, Ferdinand, 103, 127, 233
Wertheimer, Max, 43
Westheimer, Ruth, 89, 101, 221
Weyrauch, Walter Otto, 150
Wiesbaden, 150
women, 29, 42, 48, 49, 53, 66, 93, 94, 116, 219, 222
workers, 42, 113, 115
World War I, 11, 19, 22, 23, 25, 50, 68, 88, 103, 114, 228, 233
World War II, 164-79, 183, 228, 233
writers, 84
Wronker department store, 38, 81
Wurm, Theophil, 71, 143
Württemberg, 127, 133

Yeshiva, 47, 48, 50, 158, 206
Yiddish, 8, 52

Zernik, Charlotte Elke, 82, 219, 220
Zettler, Annelise, 83
Zionist Association of Germany (Zionistische Vereinigung für Deutschland), 21, 22, 54
Zionists, 8, 47-50, 53-56, 60, 195, 206-9, 221, 237
Zweig, Stefan, 23
Zunz, Leopold, 18